The Assessment of L2 Written English across the MENA Region

Lee McCallum · Christine Coombe
Editors

The Assessment of L2 Written English across the MENA Region

A Synthesis of Practice

palgrave
macmillan

Editors
Lee McCallum
Social Sciences and International Studies
University of Exeter
Exeter, UK

Christine Coombe
Dubai Men's College
Higher Colleges of Technology
Dubai, United Arab Emirates

ISBN 978-3-030-53253-6   ISBN 978-3-030-53254-3 (eBook)
https://doi.org/10.1007/978-3-030-53254-3

© The Editor(s) (if applicable) and The Author(s), under exclusive licence to Springer Nature Switzerland AG 2020
This work is subject to copyright. All rights are solely and exclusively licensed by the Publisher, whether the whole or part of the material is concerned, specifically the rights of translation, reprinting, reuse of illustrations, recitation, broadcasting, reproduction on microfilms or in any other physical way, and transmission or information storage and retrieval, electronic adaptation, computer software, or by similar or dissimilar methodology now known or hereafter developed.
The use of general descriptive names, registered names, trademarks, service marks, etc. in this publication does not imply, even in the absence of a specific statement, that such names are exempt from the relevant protective laws and regulations and therefore free for general use.
The publisher, the authors and the editors are safe to assume that the advice and information in this book are believed to be true and accurate at the date of publication. Neither the publisher nor the authors or the editors give a warranty, expressed or implied, with respect to the material contained herein or for any errors or omissions that may have been made. The publisher remains neutral with regard to jurisdictional claims in published maps and institutional affiliations.

Cover illustration: Maram_shutterstock.com

This Palgrave Macmillan imprint is published by the registered company Springer Nature Switzerland AG
The registered company address is: Gewerbestrasse 11, 6330 Cham, Switzerland

…To our parents…

Acknowledgments

We would like to thank all contributors for their hard work in producing this volume. Their dedication and timely response to feedback and guidance helped ensure the volume contained high quality engaging research that writing assessment stakeholders can benefit from. We would also like to thank the team at Palgrave Macmillan especially Cathy Scott, Alice Green, Preetha Kuttiappan and Hemapriya Eswanth and the two reviewers who provided helpful feedback on our original book proposal.

Contents

Test Design and Administration: Connections to Curriculum and Teacher Understandings of Assessment

Introduction 3
Lee McCallum and Christine Coombe

Language Assessment Literacy: Task Analysis in Saudi Universities 13
Mubina Rauf and Lee McCallum

Creational Reverse Engineering: A Project to Enhance English Placement Test Security, Validity, and Reliability 43
Hadeel El Rahal and Huda Dimashkie

Rebuilding the Tower of Babel? Promises and Problems of World Englishes for Writing Assessment 69
Esmat Babaii

Grading and Feedback Connections: Exploring Grading Criteria, Practices and the Provision of Feedback

CAF Profiles of Iranian Writers: What We Learn from Them and Their Limitations — 93
Niloufar Shahmirzadi

Exploring the Essay Rating Judgements of English Instructors in the Middle East — 113
Analynn P. Bustamante and Selahattin Yilmaz

How Writing Teachers' Beliefs Influence Grading Practices — 143
Najoua Ben Hedia

Designing Scoring Rubrics for Different Writing Tasks: The Case of Resume Writing in Iran — 171
Mojtaba Mohammadi and Jaber Kamali

Primary Trait Rubric: The Case of MENA Countries — 195
Reza Vahdani-Sanavi

Teaching and Assessment Connections: Exploring Learner Performance and the Impact of Instruction

Assessing L2 Argumentation in the UAE Context — 225
Jingjing Qin

Integrated Summarizing Read-to-Write Tasks: Patterns of Textual Borrowing and the Role of the Written Genre — 241
Katayoun Rezaei and Elaheh Sotoudehnama

Changing Practices to Overcome Writing Difficulties in EFL Courses at University: A Lebanese Case Study — 269
Tamara Al Khalili

Integrating Computer- and Teacher-Provided Feedback
in an EFL Academic Writing Context 297
Mojtaba Heydari and Fahimeh Marefat

Research on Feedback in EFL Classes in the MENA
Region: State of the Art 325
Moez Athimni, Safa Yaakoubi, and Hanin Bouzaiene

Using Research Methods to Capture the Nature of Writing
Proficiency and its Assessment

Spelling Errors in the Preliminary English B1 Exam:
Corpus-Informed Evaluation of Examination Criteria
for MENA Contexts 359
Niall Curry and Tony Clark

Learning What Works in Improving Writing:
A Meta-Analysis of Technology—Oriented Studies Across
Saudi Universities 393
Lee McCallum and Mubina Rauf

Index 429

Notes on Contributors

Tamara Al Khalili is a Ph.D. candidate at the University of Exeter and a part-time English instructor. Tamara has been teaching English as a foreign language for several years in the MENA region. Her research interests include writing instruction and assessment, foreign language challenges at the tertiary level in Lebanon, equality in education and blended learning in higher education.

Moez Athimni is an Assistant Professor of English language and linguistics at the Higher Institute of Languages of Tunis (ISLT). He is also the coordinator of the Applied Research Center for Language Teaching and Evaluation and the local chair of Language Testing Research Colloquium (LTRC) 2021. He has participated in several national and international conferences and has published two book chapters on assessment literacy and feedback practices in Tunisia. His research interests include the areas of language teaching, testing, and evaluation.

Esmat Babaii is Professor of applied linguistics at Kharazmi University, Iran, where she teaches research methods, language assessment and discourse analysis to graduate students. She has published articles and book chapters dealing with issues in Systemic Functional Linguistics, Appraisal theory, language assessment, test-taking processes, discursive analysis of textbooks, and critical approaches to the study of culture and language. Her assessment-oriented works have appeared in *Language Testing*, *System*, and *Studies in Educational Evaluation*. She also writes fiction in her first language, Persian. She finds her experience of academic and literary writing quite fulfilling and curiously complementary.

Hanin Bouzaiene holds an M.A. in English Applied Linguistics from the Higher Institute of Languages of Tunis (ISLT). She is also a part-time researcher at the Applied Research Center for Language Teaching and Evaluation, ISLT. Her fields of interest include literacy studies and employability, ESP, and language planning and policy.

Analynn P. Bustamante is a Ph.D. student and doctoral fellow at Georgia State University in Applied Linguistics, focusing on language testing and her M.A. is in ESL. She has taught English in South Korea, China, the U.S. and Iraq.

Tony Clark is a Senior Research Manager at Cambridge Assessment English, managing research on the IELTS exam. One of his principal research interests is education in the MENA region, following an extended posting at the British Council in Morocco. His Ph.D. focused on how L2 English users learn to write in academic English, and how test preparation in their country of origin relates to their subsequent UK university experience. His ESRC-funded Ph.D. thesis (supervised by Dr. Guoxing Yu and Dr. Talia Isaacs) received a British Council Research Assessment Award in 2014. In 2015/2016 Tony was a recipient of the Newton Fund Scholarship (a grant to promote researcher mobility and encourage British–Chinese academic relations), and also received funding from the Worldwide Universities Network (WUN) and the ESRC to support overseas research trips. In 2016 he spent two months at the British Council in Tokyo and six months at Zhejiang University in China. Tony has contributed to research projects on language and admissions testing, language acquisition and test development, collaborating with Bristol University, Swansea University, Assessment Europe and the British Council throughout the MENA region and beyond.

Christine Coombe has a Ph.D. in Foreign/Second Language Education from The Ohio State University. She is currently an Associate Professor of General Studies at Dubai Men's College. She is the former Testing and Measurements Supervisor at UAE University and Assessment Coordinator of Zayed University. Christine is co-editor of *Assessment Practices* (2003, TESOL Publications); co-author, *A Practical Guide to Assessing English Language Learners* (2007, University of Michigan Press); co-editor, *Evaluating Teacher Effectiveness in EF/SL Contexts* (2007, UMP); co-editor, *Language Teacher Research in the Middle East* (2007, TESOL Publications), *Leadership in English Language Teaching and Learning* (2008, UMP) *Applications of Task-based Learning in TESOL* (2010, TESOL Publications), *The Cambridge Guide to Second Language Assessment* (2012, Cambridge University Press), *Reigniting, Retooling and Retiring in English Language Teaching* (2012, University of Michigan Press) and *The Cambridge Guide to Research in Language Teaching and Learning* (Cambridge University Press, 2015), Volume 8 of the TESOL Encyclopedia of ELT (Wiley Blackwell, 2018) and *The Role of Language Teacher Associations in Professional Development* (2018, Springer).

Niall Curry is a Lecturer in Academic Writing at the University of Coventry and conducts research on language and language pedagogy to inform materials development. Previously, Niall has worked as a lecturer and teacher trainer in language teaching, academic writing, linguistics, and translation in universities in Ireland and France. Niall has given international talks and plenaries on research-informed strategies for exam preparation and has published on contrastive studies of academic writing, and language learning. Niall regularly gives workshops on learner corpus research, working with the University of Cambridge, Cardiff University, the University of Murcia and University of Warsaw among others and collaborates on research projects on language, linguistics, and writing nationally and internationally with various universities, including the University of Cambridge, Leeds University, the University of Limerick in Ireland, and METU and Mugla universities in Turkey.

Huda Dimashkie is an Instructor in the Department of Writing Studies at the American University of Sharjah. She graduated with her Master of Arts-M.A. Degree in English Literature in 2010 from the American

University of Beirut. She is an experienced instructor with a demonstrated history of working in the higher education industry. She is skilled in academic writing, professional email communication, and creative writing. Her research interests are in L2 Evaluation and L2 plagiarism.

Najoua Ben Hedia is a Lecturer at the Institut Supérieur des Sciences Humaines de Tunis, University of Tunis El Manar. She has been teaching at the university since 1994. She obtained an M.A in Applied Linguistics from the University of Reading, England and a Ph.D. in Applied Linguistics from the Faculty of letters, University of Manouba, Tunisia. Najwa has co-authored textbooks and presented papers at national and international conferences.

Mojtaba Heydari is a Ph.D. candidate of Applied Linguistics at Allameh Tabataba'i University and a visiting researcher at the University of Ottawa. His research interests include second language assessment in general and assessing writing in particular. His publications have appeared as an article in *Assessing Writing* journal and as a book chapter published by Routledge.

Jaber Kamali is a University Lecturer at Farhangian and Allameh Tabataba'i University and a Ph.D. candidate of TEFL at Allameh Tabataba'i University. He is a British council teacher trainer, a DELTA holder from Cambridge University and has passed all TKT exams with the highest scores. He has also been a trained agent of Cambridge University since 2017. He has published a number of articles and presented in different conferences worldwide. His fields of interest include teacher education, classroom discourse, strategy training, and interactional competence.

Fahimeh Marefat is an Associate Professor of Applied Linguistics at Allameh Tabataba'i University, Iran. Her research program focuses on writing, assessment, CALL, and recently she is working on English for research publication purposes. Her publications have appeared in international journals including *Assessing Writing* and *RELC*.

Lee McCallum is a Postdoctoral Research Fellow at the University of Exeter. She has extensive teaching experience in EAP from the Middle

East, Europe and China. Her research interests include language assessment and writing instruction with a focus on how corpus-based methods can enhance these areas. Her most recent work, forthcoming in 2021, is a co-authored book titled: *Understanding Development and Proficiency in Writing: Quantitative Corpus Linguistics Approaches,* which will be published by Cambridge University Press.

Mojtaba Mohammadi is an Assistant Professor in the ELT Department of the Islamic Azad University, Roudehen Branch in Tehran, Iran. He has been teaching English for more than 20 years in English language centers and universities. He has published in scholarly international journals. He has recently co-authored an entry on listening assessment in *TESOL Encyclopedia of English Language Teaching* (Liontas, 2018) published by Wiley. He has attended and presented at a number of national and international conferences. His areas of interest include testing and assessment, teacher education, CALL/CALT, and culture.

Jingjing Qin (Ph.D.) is an Associate Professor in the English Department at College of Education at Zayed University, Abu Dhabi, UAE. Her research interests include second language writing, written discourse, second language pedagogy. Her publications have appeared in *Language Teaching Research, System, TESL Canada,* and *TESOL Publications.* She has been teaching argumentative writing in the UAE for the past five years. Prior to this, she taught undergraduate and graduate students in the U.S., China, and Turkey.

Hadeel El Rahal has been working at the American University of Sharjah since 2003. Before joining AUS, she has worked as a computer literacy teacher at Sharjah Private School for two years. She has a bachelor degree in Computer Science from the University of Sharjah, and an M.A. TESOL degree from the American University of Sharjah. Hadeel's research interest is in L2 assessment and evaluation and her graduate thesis was related to the aforementioned area of research.

Mubina Rauf is a Lecturer at Imam Abdurrahman bin Faisal University in Dammam, Saudi Arabia and an Ed.D. candidate at the University of Exeter, UK. She has degrees in English literature, ELT and a Cambridge DELTA with many years teaching experience in Saudi

Arabia. Her research interests include academic reading and writing, language assessment and non-native teachers' professional development.

Katayoun Rezaei is a Ph.D. candidate in TEFL at Alzahra University and a Lecturer of general and specific English courses at Shahid Beheshti University of Medical Sciences. She has been actively working in different language testing projects as the head of the language assessment group in the department of English, Alzahra University, since 2016. Her main areas of interest include Language test design and validation, Language assessment, CALL, and academic writing skill.

Reza Vahdani-Sanavi is currently working as an Assistant Professor in the Professional Development Unit (PDU) of Social Sciences University of Ankara (SSUA), School of Foreign Languages. His research interests include error correction, attitudinal studies, and teaching and assessing writing and listening.

Niloufar Shahmirzadi has a Ph.D. in Applied Linguistics from the Islamic Azad University, Central Tehran Branch, Iran. She is a part-time Lecturer, and has published some articles and books. She has also attended some national and international conferences. She is a member of the Young Researchers and Elite Club. Her major area of research lies in language testing and assessment. She published work in the ILTA Newsletter in 2019.

Elaheh Sotoudehnama holds a Ph.D. in TEFL and has been teaching for 29 years in the Department of English Language at Alzahra University in Iran being a full professor. Her areas of interest include psycholinguistics, culture, skills, morality, and writing.

Safa Yaakoubi is enrolled in the M.A. program in Applied Linguistics at the Higher Institute of Languages of Tunis. She is also a part-time researcher at the Applied Research Center for Language Teaching and Evaluation, ISLT. Her fields of interest include language testing and curriculum design. Her M.A. dissertation investigates the degree of alignment between assessment and instruction in the Tunisian primary school standardized tests.

Selahattin Yilmaz is a doctoral candidate in Applied Linguistics, and a graduate research and teaching assistant at Georgia State University, Atlanta. His research focuses on English for Specific/Academic Purposes, English as a Lingua Franca, and corpus-based analysis of linguistic patterns in academic texts.

List of Figures

Language Assessment Literacy: Task Analysis in Saudi Universities

Fig. 1	Test item 1 instructions 'University 2'	35
Fig. 2	Test item 1 instructions for 'University 3'	37

Creational Reverse Engineering: A Project to Enhance English Placement Test Security, Validity, and Reliability

Fig. 1	Sample of an old EPT prompt	55
Fig. 2	Sample of a new EPT prompt	56
Fig. 3	New EPT rubric	58
Fig. 4	EPT new rubric [no direct placement in level 102]	59
Fig. 5	Sample of new EPT prompt instructions paragraph	64

Rebuilding the Tower of Babel? Promises and Problems of World Englishes for Writing Assessment

Fig. 1	Samples of writing prompts	76

CAF Profiles of Iranian Writers: What We Learn from Them and Their Limitations

Fig. 1	L2 writing assessment	96
Fig. 2	Example of Q-matrix	103

Integrating Computer- and Teacher-Provided Feedback in an EFL Academic Writing Context

Fig. 1	Feedback provided by the Write & Improve platform	305
Fig. 2	A screenshot of one of the prompts assigned to the students	306
Fig. 3	The range of the scores gained by each student through the 8 writing tasks	311
Fig. 4	Example sentence highlighted by Write & Improve that needs improvement	312
Fig. 5	Feedback provided by Write & Improve to help writers understand the meaning of each color	312
Fig. 6	Explanations for each type of icon to suggest a type of revision required	314

Spelling Errors in the Preliminary English B1 Exam: Corpus-Informed Evaluation of Examination Criteria for MENA Contexts

Fig. 1	Years of exam scripts per subcorpus in percentage	366
Fig. 2	Ages of exam takers per subcorpus in percentage	366
Fig. 3	Type of writing per subcorpus in percentage	367
Fig. 4	Task type per subcorpus in percentage	367
Fig. 5	95% confidence interval for spelling errors across subcorpora	372
Fig. 6	Boxplot of spelling error distribution across subcorpora	373
Fig. 7	Countries represented in PAOB1	387
Fig. 8	Countries represented in PAB1	387
Fig. 9	First languages represented in PNAB1	388

Learning What Works in Improving Writing: A Meta-Analysis of Technology—Oriented Studies Across Saudi Universities

Fig. 1	Study breakdown per year	404
Fig. 2	Funnel plot of weighted effect size ($d = 2.35$; $k = 22$)	419

List of Tables

Language Assessment Literacy: Task Analysis in Saudi Universities

Table 1	Scoring table to determine the alignment of assessment with learning outcomes	22
Table 2	Scale with descriptors (adapted from Webb [1997])	24
Table 3	Scoring according to the alignment of assessment with learning outcomes	30
Table 4	Test item details for 'University 1'	35

Rebuilding the Tower of Babel? Promises and Problems of World Englishes for Writing Assessment

Table 1	Main assessment criteria of some widely used writing scales	78

CAF Profiles of Iranian Writers: What We Learn from Them and Their Limitations

Table 1	Complexity	99
Table 2	Accuracy	99

| Table 3 | Fluency | 99 |
| Table 4 | CAF learner profiles | 101 |

Exploring the Essay Rating Judgements of English Instructors in the Middle East

| Table 1 | Summary of TAP findings | 136 |

How Writing Teachers' Beliefs Influence Grading Practices

Table 1	Participants' teaching experience	148
Table 2	Lesson focus	151
Table 3	Grades awarded to essay 1	153
Table 4	Types of corrective feedback	154
Table 5	Changes in teaching practices	158
Table 6	Essays grading practices	159
Table 7	Feedback focus	160

Designing Scoring Rubrics for Different Writing Tasks: The Case of Resume Writing in Iran

| Table 1 | Resume rubric | 187 |

Primary Trait Rubric: The Case of MENA Countries

Table 1	Holistic rubric used for an integrated writing task (Reprinted with permission from the School of Foreign Languages, the Social Sciences University of Ankara)	205
Table 2	Critical Thinking Value Rubric (VALUE Rubric, 2020)	208
Table 3	Primary Trait scoring for expressive discourse (Adapted from Lloyd-Jones, 1977, pp. 60–63)	212
Table 4	Draft Version of Primary Trait Rubric (Adapted from Lloyd-Jones, 1977, pp. 47–50)	212

Assessing L2 Argumentation in the UAE Context

Table 1	Description of the use of argumentative elements	231
Table 2	Description of the quality of argumentative writing	233
Table 3	Analytical scoring rubric	236

Integrated Summarizing Read-to-Write Tasks: Patterns of Textual Borrowing and the Role of the Written Genre

Table 1	Features of the source reading texts	249
Table 2	Sample extracts of textual borrowing patterns	252
Table 3	Descriptive statistics of textual borrowing patterns	253
Table 4	Multivariate tests for the patterns of textual borrowing	256

Changing Practices to Overcome Writing Difficulties in EFL Courses at University: A Lebanese Case Study

Table 1	Pre-post-test diagnostic results	278
Table 2	Analytical rating scale	289

Integrating Computer- and Teacher-Provided Feedback in an EFL Academic Writing Context

Table 1	Examples for the categories of uptake used in the coding	307
Table 2	Frequency and percentage of comments and corrections made by the computer and teacher	309
Table 3	Frequency and percentage of successful, unsuccessful, and unattended feedback	310

Research on Feedback in EFL Classes in the MENA Region: State of the Art

Table 1	Distribution of feedback research articles in the MENA region	333
Table 2	Research focus	333
Table 3	Research on feedback types	336

Spelling Errors in the Preliminary English B1 Exam: Corpus-Informed Evaluation of Examination Criteria for MENA Contexts

Table 1	Size of subcorpora of B1 preliminary for libyan Arabic, UAE Arabic, remaining Arabic speakers, all Arabic speakers and non-Arabic speakers	368
Table 2	Top 5 errors in each subcorpus	370
Table 3	Spelling errors per corpus per 10,000 words	371

Table 4	Top 5 parts of speech in which spelling errors occur in each subcorpus per 10,000 words	374
Table 5	Top 10 most commonly misspelled words in each Arabic subcorpus per 10,000 words	375
Table 6	Top 10 most commonly misspelled verbs in each Arabic subcorpus per 10,000 words	375
Table 7	Top 10 misspelled words in PNAB1 per 10,000 words	389

Learning What Works in Improving Writing: A Meta-Analysis of Technology—Oriented Studies Across Saudi Universities

Table 1	Coding variables for study descriptors (# = number)	403
Table 2	Samples size in the meta-analysis ($k = 27$)	405
Table 3	Study overview ($k = 27$)	406
Table 4	Context overview	408
Table 5	Journal information ($k = 22$)	409
Table 6	Design features associated with quality in experimental research ($k = 27$)	410
Table 7	Statistical analyses used ($k = 27$)	411
Table 8	An overview of reporting practices (Descriptive statistics) ($k = 27$)	411
Table 9	An overview of reporting practices (Inferential statistics) ($k = 27$)	411
Table 10	An overview of other reporting practices ($k = 27$)	412
Table 11	Features of proficient writing	416

Test Design and Administration: Connections to Curriculum and Teacher Understandings of Assessment

Introduction

Lee McCallum and Christine Coombe

Research into second language writing has developed in depth and scope over the past few decades and researchers have shown a growing interest in new approaches to the teaching and assessing of writing. In the past two decades, there has been a healthy surge of research studies that have tackled issues relating to the process of L2 writing and writing assessment as well as important related elements such as the use of rubrics, written corrective feedback and rater reliability in general (e.g., Knoch, 2009a, b; Knoch, Rouhshad, & Storch, 2014; Rakedzon & Baram-Tsabari, 2017; Wang, Engelhard, Raczynski, Song, & Wolfe, 2017) and in the MENA context in particular (e.g., Aryadoust & Fox, 2016; Assalahi, 2013; Coombe, 2010; Coombe, Jendli, & Davidson, 2008; Ezza, 2017;

L. McCallum (✉)
University of Exeter, Exeter, UK
e-mail: lm489@exeter.ac.uk

C. Coombe
Dubai Men's College, Higher Colleges of Technology, Dubai, UAE
e-mail: ccoombe@hct.ac.ae

Ghalib & Al-Hattami, 2015; Hamouda, 2011; Hidri, 2019; Mohammad & Hazarika, 2016; Obaid, 2017; Reynolds, 2018).

At the heart of such a surge in the MENA context lies the ever-increasing need to communicate in English. The status, demand and use of English across the region have continued to grow and takes on an increasingly important role in professional contexts. In light of this increase, there has been a subsequent need to ensure that citizens in the MENA region have a recognisable and often professionally accredited level of English language proficiency. In line with this need, there has also been an increasing need for citizens to have a level of written English proficiency that allows them to communicate in writing at local, regional and international levels. This need for written proficiency in English is also being considered through a more critical lens as the ability to write well in English impacts on the academic and professional success of MENA region citizens. The assessment of written English proficiency therefore has a considerable role to play in determining current and future levels of success in education and the opportunities it brings to citizens both regionally and internationally.

The assessment of written English proficiency across the MENA region on the surface may appear homogenous as the countries that make up the region by and large share a common first language in Arabic and have historically similar backgrounds. However, there remain several nuanced differences between the countries in the region in terms of populations, wealth and resource distribution, and cultural beliefs, all of which impact the practices we see being taken in the teaching and assessing of English writing. Indeed, the primary motivation for this book was to uncover the why and how of these practices. It is our belief that this book uncovers and critiques a number of observations about how writing is currently assessed and most importantly provides a platform where the assessment of writing across the region can be established theoretically and empirically. In providing such a platform, it is hoped that the book will add weight to the understandings of writing assessment already presented in other book-length works (e.g., Ahmed & Abouabdelkader, 2018; Ahmed, Troudi, & Riley, 2020; Hidri, 2019). We also believe this contribution is a timely one given the interest in writing at the present time in the region.

Arguably, at the time of bringing this synthesis together, interest in Language Assessment Literacy (e.g., see Davidson & Coombe, 2019) and the complete assessment cycle (e.g., see Coombe, 2010) has never been greater with our synthesis also joining initiatives in assessment that characterise the region. Examples of these initiatives include teaching and testing organisations and committees (e.g., TESOL Arabia, 2020) and scholarly journals which provide a platform for the discussion of assessment throughout the MENA region (e.g., *Arab Journal of Applied Linguistics* (*AJAL*, 2020) as well as collaborations with international testing committees (e.g., the hosting of the Language Testing Research Colloqium (LTRC) via the International Language Testing Association (ILTA) in Tunisia, planned for 2021).

The fifteen chapters in this volume have investigated several important issues in the assessment of second language writing skills and have discussed the implications of their findings for teaching and assessment. The studies attempt to shed light on long-held lingering questions in the field and offer suggestions for future research. Chapter authors based in seven MENA countries have situated their research on writing assessment in varied contexts while drawing on theories of language, assessment literacy and psychometrics as well as other interpretive traditions and paradigms. It is the intention of this book to highlight areas in which research into writing in a second language in MENA contexts can and does inform classroom practice. Chapter authors have focused on the complexity of the writing assessment process and the interplay between the various issues that must be addressed by teachers and students who engage in writing and writing assessment activities in second language classrooms.

Part 1, *Test Design and Administration: Connections to Curriculum and Teacher Understandings of Assessment*, brings together issues of test design and administration with a focus on how teachers understand the assessment process, and how it relates to their wider ELT curriculum and notions of writing proficiency. In Chapter 2, Rauf and McCallum look at the importance of language assessment literacy and carry out an analysis of how teacher-designed assessment tasks match the goals of the course learning outcomes in three Saudi universities. They find that teachers' task design needs to be sharpened to better meet course outcomes. In

Chapter 3, El Rahal and Dimashkie describe how they redesigned a local placement test in a UAE university and how they sought to better police their department's testing policy/procedures by creating test banks of appropriate essay prompts and improving the rubric scoring process. In the last chapter of Part I, Babaii takes a broad view of these traditional assessment issues by reminding us of the need to consider and implement an understanding of World Englishes into the assessment process. In this chapter, Babaii sets out the key considerations and challenges that those involved in writing assessment in the MENA need to be constantly aware of.

Part II, *Grading and Feedback Connections: Exploring Grading Criteria, Practices and the Provision of Feedback*, explores grading criteria, grading practices and the provision of feedback across different tasks and writing instructional techniques. In a move towards considering the construct of writing proficiency and how teachers understand and describe it, Shahmirzadi's chapter revisits the key constructs of Complexity, Accuracy and Fluency (CAF) in judging learners' writing proficiency in an Iranian university. She notes the need for this linguistic description to also take into account contextual and task factors via the use of Cognitive Diagnostic Assessment (CDA). She advocates that this combination of CAF considerations of language and the use of CDA can help us understand how learner performance is judged and acted upon. In Chapter 6, Bustamante and Yilmaz, compare and contrast the grading practices of EAP teachers in Turkey and Kurdistan. They find that writing/learning context and teacher experience have a notable influence on grading practices. In another study of grading practices, Ben Hedia looks at how Tunisian EFL instructors at a university held similar and different beliefs about grading writing that did not always match their actual evidenced grading practices. The last two chapters of Part II consider how rubrics are best designed for different assessment stakeholders. In covering rubric design, Mohammadi and Kamali's chapter reports on the issue of tailoring different scoring rubrics to different tasks. They report on the design and implementation of a rubric that assessed resume writing on a language course in Iran. Among their key findings was the need to consider making the rubric comprehensive in terms of construct coverage but also accessible to learners. Sanavi's chapter provides an overview of the theoretical considerations of rubric types and how this theory relates to using and implementing rubrics in the MENA region.

Part III, *Teaching and Assessment Connections: Exploring Learner Performance and the Impact of Instruction*, looks at the connections made between teaching and assessment and aspects of learner performance. In her chapter, Qin explores how argumentative writing is assessed in a UAE university. Crucially, Qin's chapter describes how the learners' cultural environment and beliefs about argumentation shape their practices and concludes by noting how critical thinking can be incorporated into argumentative writing and how it may be assessed.

Rezaei and Sotoudehnama focus on learners' completion of integrated writing tasks and summarise how learners display different patterns of source use. In addition to their qualitative examination of these patterns of source use, they also note that the increased practice of referring to sources appears to have a positive relationship with writing quality grades. In her chapter, Al-Khalili makes a connection between methods of teaching writing and how writing proficiency scores increase. In a Lebanese university course, Al-Khalili carries out a mixed-methods study that looks at how using the process writing approach helps learners improve their essay writing skills. The learners themselves report how their confidence and writing skills developed through the processes taught to them. Heydari and Marefat describe the provision of feedback and the differences between computer and teacher feedback. Computer feedback is provided by Cambridge's *Write & Improve* software and is compared to teacher feedback in terms of focus and learner uptake. In the last chapter of Part III, Athimni, Yakoubi and Bouzaiene carry out a scoping review of feedback provision across the MENA region with a focus on how it relates to assessment practices and claims about writing improvement and development. Their systematic review covered 37 studies across the region with a number of research gaps and initiatives presented to guide future research.

As the final part of the book, Part IV, *Using Research Methods to Capture the Nature of Writing Proficiency and its Assessment*, looks at how different research methods can illuminate different aspects of the construct of writing proficiency. In Chapter 15, Curry and Clark use corpus linguistics methods to evaluate spelling errors as a key writing proficiency criterion across the CEFR levels in the Cambridge Learner Corpus. In the last chapter of the book, McCallum and Rauf carry out a meta-analysis of 27 studies from Saudi universities to show how technology improves writing proficiency scores. Across the 27 studies, they detail a number of flaws in the reporting of these primary studies, suggest how intervention studies like these should be reported and conducted in the future and ultimately report that the use of technology has a large positive effect on writing proficiency scores.

Bringing these chapters together, there are a number of observations that readers may be drawn to; and which we would like to comment on. Taken together as a synthesis, this book helps highlight how the state of writing assessment is influenced by the blending of internationally recognised assessments, assessment tools and approaches to test design, feedback and grading with local adaptations and applications. Readers are encouraged to actively engage with the authentic materials provided in chapter appendices so as to appreciate how these have been influenced by established international practice and locally adapted to meet contextual needs. With this in mind, the synthesis makes a case for future research to uncover the underlying rationale for the use of such assessment materials and adaptations; and ultimately pushes the MENA assessment community to continue to explore the decision-making processes and contextual constraints that underpin much of these decisions, choices and practices.

It is also worth pointing out an interrelated observation from these practices. The chapters in the synthesis overwhelmingly follow two broad patterns. First, the majority of chapters focus explicitly on the role teachers and students have in the assessment process. That is to say, chapters shed light on how teachers assess and to a lesser extent how students approach or are expected to approach these assessments. In this manner, it is perhaps an unexpected observation that much of this focus on the practices of assessment does not make an overly explicit reference to the role of technology. In this regard, chapter contributions point to a 'back-to-basics' approach to understanding assessment, whereby focus, at least on the face of it, appears to remain on the fundamentals of the whole assessment cycle. With the exception of later chapters that do make explicit reference to technology (e.g., Chapters 13 and 16), the contributions still point to researchers and their contexts being grounded in looking at the basics of task and test design, rubric design and uncovering grading criteria, practices and aspects of learner performance. This focus may be an unexpected one given the number of technology-informed teaching and assessment initiatives that are known to exist across the region (e.g., See Weber & Hamlaoui, 2018 for an overview).

A second related observation focuses on the research methodologies and methods used by chapter authors. This synthesis helps bring to light the continuing use of interpretivist research paradigms with many studies using qualitative research methods on small numbers of teachers and students. This again points to the local nature of their enquiry but also leads us to question why some studies did not also supplement these detailed understandings with quantitative test data and/or larger-scale empirical enquiry in their contexts. This indicates a possible area of future research for not only our chapter authors to undertake but also readers and assessment stakeholders in these contexts.

A further observation this synthesis brings to light is understanding how the construct of writing proficiency has been defined and unpacked in individual studies. A striking feature of this unpacking is that assessment seems to closely adhere to principles and beliefs that writing is assessed under a 'Standard English' model where adherence to accurate native speaker English is a theme throughout. This adherence is seen in the task analysis work of Rauf and McCallum's chapter where accuracy plays a key role in university learning outcomes, in the grading practice chapters by Bustamante and Yilmaz, and Ben Hedia, as well as in chapters that explicitly focus on spelling errors (in the work of Curry and Clark), and overall linguistic accuracy (in the work of Shahmirzadi). We believe that the clear influence of a native speaker model needs further critical discussion, not only in the institutions where these studies took place, but at a much more macro level. This discussion should take place across the region to challenge and fundamentally put forward viable alternatives and discussions to be had as Babaii's chapter here and others have recommended elsewhere (e.g., Brown, 2014; Canagarajah, 2006; Davies, 2013; McCallum, 2019).

This introductory chapter concludes by putting forward some recommendations for future areas of development that the synthesis has helped illuminate and question. In many of the individual contexts our synthesis focuses on, there is an underlying disparity in what teachers report as their beliefs and what their practices actually show. This is perhaps evident when we look at Chapter 2 on task analysis and language assessment literacy (LAL) whereby learning outcomes and writing tasks show degrees of mismatch. It is again apparent in the studies on uncovering grading practices in Chapters 6 and 7 that teachers report employing different approaches to grading depending on their individual contexts, and their own belief systems. These studies help highlight disparities across and within individual raters and contexts.

These types of observations raise important questions about the role LAL has in these contexts. Although the synthesis does not support generalisation across the whole MENA region; or indeed across any broad spectrum of its institutions, the synthesis does indicate that further language assessment training is of immense importance to the region as a whole. It is hoped that this synthesis encourages readers, chapter authors, participants in the studies and the wider assessment community to consider the level of literacy in their contexts and work on improving it.

Overall, the take-home message that this synthesis hopes to deliver is that the assessment practices across the region appear to be diverse, grounded in the traditional fundamentals of good assessment, clearly context-informed and in a constant state of development.

References

Ahmed, A., & Abouabdelkader, H. (2018). *Assessing EFL writing in the 21st century Arab world: Revealing the unknown.* Cham, Switzerland: Palgrave Macmillan.

Ahmed, A., Troudi, S., & Riley, S. (2020). *Feedback in L2 English writing in the Arab world: Inside the black box.* London: Palgrave Macmillan.

Arab Journal of Applied Linguistics. (2020). Retrieved June 4, 2020, from http://www.arjals.com/index.php/Arjals/index.

Aryadoust, V., & Fox, J. (Eds.). (2016). *Trends in language assessment research and practice: The view from the Middle East and the Pacific Rim.* Newcastle: Cambridge Scholars.

Assalahi, H. M. (2013). Why is the grammar-translation method still alive in the Arab world? Teachers, beliefs and its implications for EFL teacher education. *Theory and Practice in Language Studies, 3*(4), 589–599. https://doi.org/10.4304/tpls.3.4.589-599.

Brown, J. D. (2014). The future of world Englishes in language testing. *Language Assessment Quarterly, 11*(1), 5–26.

Canagarajah, S. (2006). The place of world Englishes in composition: Pluralization continued. *College Composition and Communication, 57*(4), 586–619.

Coombe, C. (2010). Assessing foreign/second language writing ability. *Education, Business and Society: Contemporary Middle Eastern Issues, 3*(3), 178–187.

Coombe, C., Jendli, A., & Davidson, P. (2008). *Teaching writing skills in EFL: Theory, research and pedagogy.* Dubai: TESOL Arabia Publications.

Davies, A. (2013). *Native speakers and native users: Loss and gain.* Cambridge: Cambridge University Press.

Davidson, P., & Coombe, C. (2019). Language assessment literacy in the Middle East and North Africa (MENA) region. *Arab Journal of Applied Linguistics, 4*(2), 1–23.

Ezza, E.-S. Y. (2017). Criteria for assessing EFL writing at Majma'ah University. In S. Hidri, & C. Coombe (Eds.), *Evaluation in foreign language education in the Middle East and North Africa* (pp. 185–200). Cham: Springer. https://doi.org/10.1007/978-3-319-43234-2_11.

Ghalib, T. K., & Al-Hattami, A. A. (2015). Holistic versus analytic evaluation of EFL writing: A case study. *English Language Teaching, 8*(7), 225–236. https://doi.org/10.5539/elt.v8n7p225.

Hamouda, A. (2011). A study of students and teachers' preferences and attitudes towards correction of classroom written errors in Saudi EFL context. *English Language Teaching, 4*(3), 128–141. https://doi.org/10.5539/elt.v4n3p128.

Hidri, S. (2019). *English language teaching research in the Middle East and North Africa: Multiple perspectives.* London: Palgrave Macmillan.

Knoch, U. (2009a). Diagnostic assessment of writing: A comparison of two rating scales. *Language Testing, 26*(2), 275–304. https://doi.org/10.1177/0265532208101008.

Knoch, U. (2009b). *Diagnostic writing assessment: The development and validation of a rating scale.* Frankfurt: Peter Lang.

Knoch, U., Rouhshad, A., & Storch, N. (2014). Does the writing of undergraduate ESL students develop after one year of study in an English-medium university? *Assessing Writing, 21,* 1–17. https://doi.org/10.1016/j.asw.2014.01.001.

Language Testing Research Colloquium (LTRC) in Tunisia. (2021). Retrieved June 4, 2020, from: https://www.iltaonline.com/page/LTRC2021.

McCallum, L. (2019). Assessing second language proficiency under 'unequal' perspectives: A call for research in the MENA region. In S. Hidri (Ed.), *English language teaching research in the Middle East and North Africa* (pp. 3–28). New York: Palgrave Macmillan.

Mohammad, T., & Hazarika, Z. (2016). Difficulties of learning EFL in KSA: Writing skills in context. *International Journal of English Linguistics, 6*(3), 105–117. https://doi.org/10.5539/ijel.v6n3p105.

Obaid, R. (2017). Second language writing and assessment voices from within the Saudi EFL context. *English Language Teaching, 10*(6), 174–181.

Rakedzon, T., & Baram-Tsabari, A. (2017). To make a long story short: A rubric for assessing graduate students' academic and popular science writing skills. *Assessing Writing, 32,* 28–42. https://doi.org/10.1016/j.asw.2016.12.004.

Reynolds, D. (2018). Writing assessment. In Coombe, C. (Ed.), *The TESOL encyclopaedia of English language teaching* (Vol VIII, p. 5323-5329). *Assessment and Evaluation.* Hoboken, NJ: Wiley Blackwell.

TESOL Arabia. (2020). Retrieved June 4, 2020, from https://www.tesol-arabia.org/.

Wang, J., Engelhard, G., Jr., Raczynski, K., Song, T., & Wolfe, E. W. (2017). Evaluating rater accuracy and perception for integrated writing assessments using a mixed-methods approach. *Assessing Writing, 33,* 36–47. https://doi.org/10.1016/j.asw.2017.03.003.

Weber, A. S., & Hamlaoui, S. (Eds.). (2018). *E-learning in the MENA region.* London: Springer.

Language Assessment Literacy: Task Analysis in Saudi Universities

Mubina Rauf and Lee McCallum

1 Introduction

Assessing student performance is a crucial part of a teacher's responsibilities. According to Biggs (2003) assessment fulfils two aims: it keeps a check on the quality of learning, and it identifies what needs to be learned. Therefore, it is important to improve assessment procedures in order to enhance learning (Coombe, Troudi, & Al-Hamly, 2012).

Teachers are expected to use various methods of assessment to measure student learning and adjust their instructional approaches accordingly (Deluca & Klinger, 2010). However, many teachers do not feel confident about their own assessment abilities (Mertler, 2003). Suitable assessment methods and practices are the key to maximizing student learning and a

---

M. Rauf (✉)
Imam Abdulrahman Bin Faisal University, Dammam, Saudi Arabia
e-mail: mrauf@iau.edu.sa

L. McCallum
University of Exeter, Exeter, UK

teacher equipped with a sound understanding of these assessment practices is a pre-requisite to an effective learning system (Popham, 2013; Stiggins, 1991). In order to make these methods meaningful, teachers should work on developing a basic understanding of assessment practices, that is, they should be 'assessment literate' (Stiggins, 1995, p. 241).

Regarding English language assessment, according to Fulcher (2012, pp. 114–115), if language teachers want to know how their institutions and teaching practices are influenced by certain forces and 'to have a measure of control over the effects that these have, it is important for them to develop assessment literacy'. Assessment literacy particularly entails teachers' ability to construct and implement high-quality assessment instruments to check student progress (Plake, 2015). Keeping in mind the link between teachers' assessment literacy and student progress, this study aims to find out the level of Saudi EFL teachers' assessment literacy and its relationship to student learning outcomes. The research is significant as findings could lead to suitable training sessions and professional development courses for teachers and an improvement in their assessment literacy in particular and student achievement in general.

In the context of higher education in Saudi Arabia, the last decade has witnessed an enormous drive in Saudi universities to equip students with the necessary language skills in order to prepare them for advanced university studies. English Language Skills departments in Preparatory Year Programs (PYP) have been set up to prepare students for this purpose. These departments have assessment units that prepare assessment tools with the help of teachers who are in some cases trained and in some cases not trained for test item writing.

Recent research in this context has indicated major gaps in EFL teachers' assessment literacy despite suitable qualifications (Ezza, 2017; Hakim, 2015). This study will investigate Saudi EFL teachers' development of assessment tasks and the extent to which these tasks are aligned with student learning outcomes. These tasks are limited to writing skills. The study will examine the gaps in teachers' knowledge of assessment practices in classrooms and incongruity, if any, between the tasks and learning outcomes. Suggestions will be made as to how teachers' language assessment literacy can be improved in future in-service professional development courses.

2 Literature Review

2.1 Assessment Literacy

Assessment literacy is a term first coined by Stiggins (1991, p. 535) which indicates the knowledge and skills teachers should have about assessment. He noted that assessment literate teachers are aware of what, why and how they assess. They are familiar with the problems, solutions to the specified problems and preventive measures so that these problems do not recur. They know the repercussions of inaccurate assessment tools and find new methods that are more effective and beneficial for students.

Popham (2009) stated that assessment literacy entails knowledge of reliability and the threats associated with it, content validity, fairness, design of test items, use of alternative assessment such as formative assessment, portfolios, student test preparation and other assessment procedures. According to Popham (2009), assessment literacy is significant for teachers so that they are aware of the power of tests in the field of education. However, even though they assess students regularly, teachers do not have an acceptable understanding of the basics of assessment, e.g. reliability, validity and fairness. Brookhart (2011) did not completely agree with Popham (2009) and questioned if the assessment standards set by him are comprehensive enough for teachers. She argued that assessment literacy involves how students learn in a specific subject; connections between assessment, curriculum and instruction; designing clear marking schemes, administering tests designed externally and using feedback to improve learning. Other areas included in assessment literacy are statistics for measurement, multiple methods of assessment, use of technology in assessment and student motivation (Popham, 2011; White, 2009).

Garies and Grant (2015, p. 14) define assessment literacy as 'the ability to create and use valid and reliable assessments as a classroom teacher to facilitate and communicate student learning'. They believe that each teacher should possess a basic set of knowledge and skills related to assessment. They acknowledge that there are other assessment-related competencies but the ones presented in their list are specially meant for classroom teachers. A teacher should have a clear understanding of learning outcomes, the aim of different forms of classroom assessment and its alignment with the content and learning outcomes. The teacher should also be able to use formative assessment and feedback to ascertain student progress, create level-appropriate test items and communicate student performance efficiently that lead to sound decisions at the instructional and curricular level (Garies & Grant, 2015).

However, research has indicated that teachers' assessment practices are not aligned with the recommended best practices which impacts student learning outcomes negatively (Galluzo, 2005; Mertler, 2003). Stiggins (2006) claimed that a significantly low level of assessment literacy has been observed among teachers of schools and universities. This has resulted in inaccurate results and means that students do not reach their full potential. Mertler (2003) observed that the majority of teachers receive inadequate pre- and in-service training. This leaves them unprepared to assess students' development. Whatever skills they acquire later are gained through experience while on the job. Research shows that a typical teacher spends 30–50% of their professional time in assessment-related activities (Giraldo, 2018; Stiggins & Conklin, 1992). According to Stiggins (2007), almost all of them do so without any formal training in assessment. Unsurprisingly, research indicates that teachers are generally unable to interpret assessment theories and align them with classroom assessment practices (Deluca & Klinger, 2010; MacLellan, 2004).

2.2 Measuring Teachers' Assessment Literacy

The most significant point in developing teacher assessment literacy is to establish a strong knowledge base. The America Federation of Teachers, the National Council on Measurement in Education and the National Education Association (1990) set up *The Standards for Teacher Competence in Educational Assessment of Students*. These standards are based on seven areas of competencies that make the teacher's assessment literate. The *Standards* state that teachers should be able to choose and develop suitable assessment methods; administer, score and interpret assessment results; use the results while making important educational decisions, develop valid grading processes; communicate results to stakeholders; and identify unethical practices in assessment.

Many surveys on teacher assessment literacy have subsequently been conducted based on various competencies included in these standards. Most of this research has been conducted at the school level. The strengths and weaknesses varied in different competencies but overall the teachers' assessment knowledge was not adequate according to the standards. The results of these surveys have many common points. They generally show that the number of correct answers for both in-service and pre-service teachers is from low to medium and the scores regarding assessment knowledge and test development are higher among pre-service teachers (Deluca & Klinger, 2010; Elshawa, Abdullah, & Rashid, 2017; Mertler, 2003; Plake, Impara, & Fager, 1993; Volante & Fazio, 2007). Plake and Impara (1996, p. 67) identified the 'woefully low level of assessment competency' among teachers. Volante and Fazio (2007, p. 762) indicated that teacher candidates are 'graduating with sizable knowledge gaps' in asssessment and evaluation. This suggests that teachers' knowledge about what, when and how to assess should be developed through continuous professional development courses in order to make the assessment frameworks efficient.

2.3 Language Assessment Literacy

Recent times have witnessed a phenomenal increase in the role of teachers in language testing and assessment (Fulcher, 2012). They are involved in assessing students and evaluating the assessment data to improve student learning and their own instructional strategies (Malone, 2013). This highlights the significance of ESL teachers' assessment literacy in relation to their ability to construct and implement high-quality assessment instruments and performance in achieving the specified learning outcomes necessary for student success (Stiggins, 2002). However, research consistently shows inadequate levels of assessment literacy among teachers in designing efficient assessment tools to achieve the desired learning outcomes (Mertler, 2003; Plake, 1993).

Fulcher (2012) defined language assessment literacy (LAL henceforth) as 'the knowledge, skills and abilities required to design, develop, maintain or evaluate, large-scale standardized and/or classroom-based tests, familiarity with test processes and awareness of principles and concepts that guide and underpin practice, including ethics and codes of practice'. It 'refers to the language instructor's familiarity with testing definitions and the application of this knowledge to classroom practices in general and specifically to issues related to assessing language' (Malone, 2013, p. 329). Inbar-Lourie (2013, p. 304) described LAL as 'a multi-layered entity and… defining it is a major challenge'. An agreed-upon definition, according to Inbar-Lourie (2013) is difficult to reach because of the lack of consensus among experts as to what entails assessment knowledge in language teaching. Giraldo (2018, pp. 180/182) argued that LAL is a 'competency' that involves various people, from teachers to school administrators'. Moreover, LAL is 'a construct of its own' which means 'different things to different people'. Davies (2008) argued that LAL is set within three constructs: knowledge, skills and principles of language assessment. He stated that skills provide training in methodology: item writing, statistics, test analysis and software programmes for test delivery and reportage. Knowledge relates to background in measurement and language description, context familiarity and various models of language learning, teaching and testing such as communicative language teaching. According to Giraldo (2018, p. 183) skills and knowledge are 'directly related to assessing language'. The skills needed for test design, such as test item writing, interpreting statistics and test evaluation are used to assess language ability particularly. Principles entail proper use of tests, their fairness and impact, ethics and professionalism, responsibilities of language testers and impact of their work in this field. The three constructs are equally important in that ignoring any one of them negatively affects the entire teaching and learning system. For instance, selecting low-quality assessment methods has an adverse impact on student learning (e.g. See Umer, Javid, & Farooq, 2015).

2.4 Tests and Learning Outcomes

Previous research has shown there is a significant link between testing practices and student learning, also known as the washback effect (Shohamy, 1993). The way tests are designed affects the way students learn and teachers teach. Students work on learning and developing only those cognitive skills that they are required to demonstrate for assessment purposes.

According to Scouller (1998, p. 454), assessment shapes 'how much, how (their approach), and what (the content) students learn'. For example, Ferman (2004) investigated how a high stakes oral test impacted classroom activities in that teachers spent more time preparing students in oral skills as compared to other skills. They stopped teaching speaking after the test was over.

Stecher, Barron, Chun, and Ross (2004) investigated the impact of test-driven reforms of writing on school and classroom practices which include both instruction and learning. In addition to a major influence of revised test specifications on student learning, the results also indicated that teachers spent more time on test preparation according to the test samples than working on the standards or learning outcomes set according to the curriculum. In a study related to student preferences for learning approaches at university-level teacher training program, Gijbels, Segers, and Struyf (2008) found that students preferred surface learning to deep learning as the assessment tasks involved lower level cognitive abilities.

The above-cited examples manifest that aligning each test item with student learning outcomes is central to education (Webb, 1997). Tests aligned to student learning outcomes lead to students' improved performance in analysis, synthesis, evaluation and other higher order skills.

Although much work has been done on the alignment between learning outcomes and assessment practices, most of it has been at the school level as the examples discussed above. There is a paucity in research on the relationship between assessment and student learning outcomes in higher education, specifically in the MENA region.

2.5 The Saudi Context

Despite the signifcant role of assessment literacy among teachers and its relation to student learning, studies on this subject are rare in Saudi Arabia. The few research studies done on this topic have indicated major gaps in EFL teachers' assessment literacy despite suitable qualifications (Ezza, 2017; Hakim, 2015; Umer, Farooq, & Gulzar, 2016). Hakim (2015) investigated the assessment literacy levels of English teachers in the language centre of a Saudi university and found that despite being aware of assessment rules and techniques in general, the actual assessment practice in the classroom was not adequate. Ezza (2017, p. 194) noted that despite the writing curriculum and a variety of rubrics for writing tasks, most of the students 'suffer from acute lexical deficiency and production of grammatically ill-formed sentences'. The teachers spend a substantial amount of time teaching basic sentence structure and writing mechanics and it is hard for such students to complete longer written assignments. Ezza (2017) pointed out that teachers are usually not aware of the theories of writing instruction and assessment. They are 'maybe susceptible to basing their evaluations of NNS writing more on sentence level concerns than on content or rhtorical concerns' (Sweedler-Brown, 1993, as cited in Weigle, 2007, p. 201). They probably take written work as a means to assess accuracy and form only and not as evidence of transformative learning (Bereiter & Scardamalia, 1989; MacLellan, 2004). Ezza (2017) has proposed more training and courses for teachers to enhance their knowledge of assessment and how it should be practiced. Another factor is the pressure on teachers to prepare such assessment tasks so that the majority of students pass because failing students is considered detrimental (Obeid, 2017). In this context, it is necessary to investigate teachers' assessment literacy with a focus on writing and determine the overall effect of writing tasks on student learning outcomes in PYP at Saudi universities. The anticipated findings might help teachers prepare writing tasks that encourage transformative learning and develop higher order skills among students.

The study will therefore be guided by the following questions:

RQ 1: To what extent are the writing assessment tasks designed by teachers aligned with student learning outcomes?

RQ 2: To what extent are the teachers' writing assessment practices congruent with standard language assessment principles?

3 Methodology

Six test items, designed by six teachers working in the PYP of 3 different Saudi universities, were selected to investigate if they were congruent with the learning outcomes and recommended assessment principles. The data was collected from level 2 and 3 teachers. These levels, according to the CEFR, are A2 (elementary) and B1 (intermediate) levels, respectively. The first step was getting familiar with the data, both the assessment tasks and learning outcome documents. Then the tasks and learning outcomes by teachers of all three universities were separated and each test item (the writing question) was studied and mapped against learning outcomes using a set of criteria and scoring system adapted from Webb (1997). The tasks were examined through content analysis procedures.

The assessment tasks were examined through content analysis to determine the extent of alignment with the learning outcomes of writing skills. In this context, content analysis is defined as 'a research technique for making valid inferences from texts (or other meaningful matter) to the contexts of their use' (Krippendorff, 2004, p. 403). The test items created by the teachers were analysed to study their alignment with the learning outcomes and recommended assessment principles.

Webb's (1997) framework for alignment between the tasks and outcomes was adapted for this purpose. The tasks were scored according to the criteria given in Table 1.

Table 1 shows the common features of language learning from the learning outcomes that the students will practice in the classroom and then should be tested upon. The major points included in all the learning outcomes, e.g. word count, skills, knowledge of lexis and paragraphing are included in the scoring table. However, according to Webb (1997), judging the alignment between assessment and outcomes is difficult. In

Table 1 Scoring table to determine the alignment of assessment with learning outcomes

Task#	Word count	Skills			Knowledge			Structure		Balance of representation
		Tenses	Connectors	Sentence structure	Lexis	Spelling	Cohesion and Coherence	Genre	Paragraphing	
UNI 1										
1										
2										
UNI 2										
1										
2										
UNI 3										
1										
2										

the case of academic writing, the assessment is of various types and is done at different times during the academic year. The learning outcomes, on the other hand, are finalized and fixed at the beginning of the academic year. It is difficult to bring out a complete picture in this situation. For example, one of the significant goals of ESL learners at level 1 is being able to use appropriate words and phrases in simple sentences. The aim is for students to have knowledge of a range of vocabulary appropriate to their level. This can be measured by giving students a familiar topic and asking them to write a few sentences on it. But when students get all the prompts, key words and other factual information, their competence on vocabulary cannot be measured fully.

The scoring system used a three-point scale, with a description of the score for each criterion to help improve the reliability of scoring. Each assessment task was scored using the scale in Table 2.

Table 2 shows the major content categories for writing as the criterion. These include word count, skills, knowledge and structure. The balance of representation criterion identifies the degree to which one learning outcome is given more emphasis on assessment tasks than another (Webb, 2002). The criteria above were used to judge whether a comparable span of the assessment task content is similar to or corresponds to the learning outcomes. According to Webb (2002), the number of test items representing different learning outcomes should be balanced. This increases the chance that students will have to demonstrate knowledge on more outcomes to achieve the minimum passing score.

There are three scales of agreement: insufficient, acceptable and full. The first one is 'insufficient' wherein students' performance is acceptable without emphasis on learning outcomes. 'Acceptable' means the students' performance depicts some knowledge of nearly all learning outcomes. 'Full' is exceptional performance which means there are enough examples in students' work that show complete correspondence between the test items and learning outcomes.

Table 2 Scale with descriptors (adapted from Webb [1997])

Criteria	Scales of agreement		
	Insufficient (1)	Acceptable (2)	Full (3)
1. Length (Word count/no. of paragraphs)	Students can perform at an acceptable level on the test without having to follow a suitable word count/no. of paragraphs according to the given genre as mentioned in specific learning outcomes	The test item covers the word count/no. of paragraphs specifically so the student tested to have to follow it strictly	The test item corresponds with the LOs in covering either the number of paragraphs or the word count
2. Range of writing skills tested 1. Subject-verb agreement 2. Appropriate use of tenses 3. Use of connectors 4. Use simple, compound and complex sentences suitably	Important writing skills are excluded to the extent students can perform acceptably and still lack understanding of LOs	The test item covers a number of skills so the student tested to have acceptable knowledge would demonstrate some knowledge on nearly all LOs	A one-to-one correspondence between writing skills covered in LOs and in the test item
3. Range of knowledge tested 1. Use of a range of lexical items 2. High frequency words spelled correctly 3. Awareness of common spelling patterns 4. Use of a range of cohesive devices 5. Write texts on a range of familiar topics	Students can perform at an acceptable level on the test without having to demonstrate for any topic the attainment of cognitively demanding LOs	Some of the cognitively challenging LOs can be compared with the test item	The most cognitively challenging LOs can be compared with the test item

Criteria	Scales of agreement		
	Insufficient (1)	Acceptable (2)	Full (3)
4. Structure 1. Awareness of task development according to genre 2. Awareness of parts of texts, e.g. introduction, body and conclusion 3. Awareness of a range of written genres in academic writing, e.g. narrative, descriptive, opinion essay, explaining a process, etc.	Students can perform at an acceptable level on the test without having to demonstrate the knowledge of basic/advanced writing structures, e.g. introduction, body, conclusion, topic sentence, supporting details according to the genre	The test item covers a number of writing structures so the student tested to have acceptable knowledge would demonstrate some knowhow of structures on nearly all LOs	A one-to-one correspondence between writing structures covered in LOs and in the test item
5. Balance of representation	The weightage given to different writing skills in LOs is different from that in the test such that a student could perform acceptably without knowledge of emphasized skills	Test item elicits information according to general patterns how students' writing skills develop over time and how students use these skills	Test item elicits information compatible with how students' knowledge of a range of writing skills develops over time and how students use these skills

4 Results and Discussion

4.1 University 1 (Course: ENG 102)

Looking into the learning outcomes and the assessment task of this level, one can see a clear mismatch between the two (see Appendix 1). Most of the learning outcomes require the student to write simple emails, and simple sentences about habits and routines. Students should be able to use basic grammar features like articles and cohesive devices such as *so* and *because* to express reason and result. Also, the students need to generate ideas through free writing, use suitable connectors to show reason and result and write cohesive, analytical paragraphs. The assessment task, however, requires students to write a comparison between two places using the given detailed information. It should be noted that in the given task, writing can be cohesive but not analytical as the task does not involve analysis. Analytical paragraphs are written when students have to think on their own for which they are not prepared at this level. The task is easy in the sense that all details have been provided to students and they have to use the given information to arrange a logical piece of writing. Comparison, however, is a complex process and involves minute details of the things or events being compared. There is no given learning outcome that goes with it. Admittedly, this makes the task more complicated for students.

4.2 University 1 (Course: ENG 103)

The learning outcomes at this level need students to master writing longer narrative texts of multiple paragraphs describing events sequentially using time expressions and time clauses. They should also be able to make outlines at both paragraph and essay level (see Appendix 1). The assessment task designed for this level, however, is writing a narrative paragraph only with the outline already provided. The length of the task does not match the learning outcomes which clearly state writing longer narratives. There is no scope of using time expressions as a sequence of dates is already present in the given prompts. The prompts make a useful outline so students do not need to demonstrate the skill of making an outline either for a paragraph or essay. No original ideas are needed as students have to write according to the given prompts only. Providing students detailed prompts of the topic to be written makes them used to spoonfeeding. They will spend time on writing something that was not their intended goal. They will not be prepared and be confused about what they should learn and what they should not learn.

4.3 University 2 (Course: REAP 1)

The learning outcomes at the beginners' level require students to be able to write their personal information in simple phrases and sentences using basic linear connectors. They should also be familiar with appropriate word order and basic punctuation marks. However, the level seems to jump significantly in the last two outcomes. According to the outcomes, the students should be able to write longer well-structured essays including simple, compound and complex sentences (see Appendix 1). Although designing level-appropriate learning outcomes is out of the scope of this study, it can be seen that the last two outcomes do not align with the first six outcomes. Students will not be able to write complex sentences after learning to use basic linear connectors. Nor will they be able to write a 5-paragraph essay before learning to structure a paragraph.

If we look into the task designed for this level, it requires students to write four sentences only. A vocabulary list of four words is also provided and students need to write at least four sentences. The learning outcomes refer to writing about people, names, nationality and date of birth, etc., but the task is about a room. Having said that, if the beginner/pre-intermediate-level students have enough practice of numbers 3–6, they will be able to do the task easily.

4.4 University 2 (Course: REAP 2)

The student learning outcomes are only three in number for REAP 2. According to these learning outcomes, the students should be able to write 3 cohesive and coherent paragraphs or an academically structured

4 paragraph essay of any kind of expository writing. They should also be able to use a range of lexis, grammatical structures and cohesive devices. The task given does not align with the learning outcomes as the students have to write at least four sentences using the four words given in the task. As compared to be able to write a variety of long academic texts, they have been asked to write at least 4 sentences only. They are not required to achieve proficiency in using a range of grammatical structures and vocabulary mentioned in the learning outcomes. There is no balance in representation (Table 1) as the learning outcomes are quite exhaustive as compared to the task wherein students have to write only four sentences using the words provided.

4.5 University 3 (Course: Pre-Intermediate)

The 7 learning outcomes for pre-intermediate level in this institution are written in detail with specific points, e.g. proper nouns, correct word order, subject-verb agreement, simple connectors, simple adjectives, simple grammar structures and writing simple texts for different genres. They cover almost all features a student at this level should be familiar with. The task aligns with the outcomes in that there is a question with three prompts, with examples that give information about how to use the prompts to write with logical flow of ideas. There are no word lists or other details given about the question. An imaginary situation is provided along with a few prompts to structure the writing. This gives the students opportunity to use lexis and grammatical structures that they have learned in the classroom.

4.6 University 3 (Course: Intermediate Plus)

The fourteen student learning outcomes are detailed identifying specific writing subskills that students will learn. These include a wide range of vocabulary, grammatical structures, punctuation, planning, editing, paraphrasing, a variety of registers. Each learning outcome elaborates on various points which clarifies the learning goals and makes the outcomes more measurable. There are separate outcomes for a variety of writing genres at this level. This gives the test designers options while writing test items.

The task aligns with the learning outcomes in that it requires the student writers to express their opinions. Although the prompts provide them with hints, they get enough space to express their own ideas in a coherent manner.

4.7 Scores

After the collection of tasks, they were throughly checked and marked through content analysis. Before discussing the scores, it should be highlighted that the process of matching the outcomes with the tasks and scoring is based on the researcher's subjective judgement. As the data for this study was from three universities that compete at equal level, it helped in comparing the data and allocating scores instead of allocating scores based on guesses (Bruce & Lack, 2009; David, 1963).

Table 3 shows the scores according to the alignment of learning outcomes with the assessment tasks. University 1 scores, except for the word count, show that assessment tasks can be acceptable even if they fail to cover all learning outcomes. University 2 scores are quite similar to University 1 except for the word count which is not mentioned in the task. University 3 fared better than the other two for all the criteria. The scores highlight teachers' understanding of the process of writing test tasks and what they understand by assessment literacy.

This study looked into one aspect of LAL which was designing assessment tasks. The aim was to find out the extent to which the writing assessment tasks designed by teachers aligned with the learning outcomes and were congruent with standard language assessment principles. In this section, each of the research questions is discussed according to the findings presented above.

The first question looked at how tests designed by teachers aligned with the student outcomes. The content of the assessment tasks must be consistent with what is to be measured (Brookhart, 2011). This requires agreement between learning outcomes and the content of the

Table 3 Scoring according to the alignment of assessment with learning outcomes

Task#	Length/word count	Skills				Knowledge				Structure	
		Tenses	Connectors	Sentence structure	Lexis	Spelling patterns	Cohesion and Coherence			Genre	Paragraphing

UNI 1											
1	3	1	1	2	1	1	1			1	1
2	3	1	1	2	1	1	2			1	1
UNI2											
1	1	1	1	1	2	2	2			1	1
2	1	1	1	1	1	1	1			1	1
UNI3											
1	3	2	2	3	3	2	3			3	2
2	3	2	2	3	3	2	3			3	3

test. The findings of this study, except for a few exceptions, indicate a serious concern about this aspect of assessment literacy. Firstly, it can be seen that the tasks designed by teachers do not cover all the learning outcomes. Not aligning the outcomes with an assessment task demotivates students. If, for example, according to the outcomes, students come prepared to write an analytical paragraph or essay and they have to write a description with all details provided, it will be frustrating for them that the task does not measure what they were prepared for. On the other hand, it might be that the teacher has practiced the same kind of writing exercises in the classroom and that is the reason she has designed the task the way it is and students would find it easy to do. Research elsewhere shows that teachers tailor their test items according to what students expect from them (Saville & Hawkey, 2004). Whatever might be the case, this is an example of lack of teacher's 'pedagogical content knowledge' (Guerriero, 2017, p. 5), wherein she might have the content knowledge but not the pedagogical knowledge to teach and assess the content following the outcomes.

Another significant point worth mentioning is the length of the task, specifically for University 1 and University 2. It raises the question if one paragraph can cover the content of a specific writing course. Is the assessment in this case valid (Coombe & Evans, 2005)? This kind of testing allows false inferences from the results, students graduating with high grades but severely lacking the relevant skills and knowledge. With reference to this study, they might achieve good results without learning some of the key academic writing skills (Green, 2007).

The results also show that learning outcomes at a higher cognitive level have not been assessed and the tasks are constructed on easier, lower level learning outcomes that entail surface-level learning. This also supports Alderson and Wall's (1993) hypothesis that assessment has significant influence on the depth of students' learning. This practice leads to producing graduates who do not have adequate cognitive skills to satisfy job market requirements which goes against the country's 2030 vision for skilled human capital (Umer, Zakaria, & Alshara, 2018). Research shows that ESL students believe good writing is writing that meets the instructor's marking criteria (El-Ebyary, 2009). As observed in this study, the criteria is focused on simple sentences, basic connectors and provided prompts. It is suggested in this context to incorporate in the test items learning outcomes that include higher order skills like longer analytical writing at intermediate level at least. This will facilitate the process when students enter the work environment in real life (Bachman, 2002; Beneditti, 2006).

The second research question is related to teachers' testing practices and recommended assessment principles. The results of this study show that teachers are not fully aware of these principles. Most of the test items analysed are not valid, specifically with reference to the course content and learning outcomes. The test items do not include all the constructs included in the courses. Most of the assessment is based on writing subskills that belong to lower order learning and students' performance is acceptable even if they have not mastered all the skills and knowledge identified in the course specifications. This is because the teachers do not have knowledge about creating suitable writing tasks that align with the learning outcomes. It is usually after the results of the assessment that the teachers realize the gaps between learning outcomes, the test and what they actually do in classrooms to prepare their students for assessment. The need is to make teachers aware of this weakness beforehand and support them to gain the fundamental LAL competencies.

Research indicates many factors such as effective teacher education programs and professional development opportunities (Beziat & Coleman, 2015), professional teachers (Yan & Cheng, 2015), teachers' content knowledge (Herman, Osmundson, Yunyun, Ringstaff, & Timms, 2015) that influence teachers' assessment literacy. Teachers equipped with LAL have the control of assessing their students. Their knowledge and skills of developing assessment tasks according to the learning outcomes would help them work on their own instruction and learners' weaknesses and eventually strengthen the assessment system. Alderson and Wall (1993) have stated that teachers' awareness of formats, skills and content to be tested is the most important factor in shaping teachers' approach towards teaching and assessment. Their awareness levels determine the impact. Hidri (2016) has suggested that test item writers and designers should be familiar with a variety of testing methods, test specifications, ethics in testing, testing outcomes, professional assessment standards, item analysis and classroom testing procedures. He further recommended that assessment courses should be a part of university-level courses.

5 Implications for the Context and Conclusion

Rea-Dickens (2004) considers language teachers as agents in the assessment process. According to her, the teacher plays a decisive and important role in the intelligent use of assessment techniques as a learning tool. This can happen only when the teachers are assessment literate. Assessment practices that are aligned with the learning outcomes and are suitable to students' needs improve the learning and teaching processes. They influence student learning positively. It is essential for teachers to implement appropriate assessment techniques and create suitable tasks efficiently in their classrooms.

The findings of this study show the gap between assessment principles and teachers' assessment practices. The overlap between the assessment principles, learning outcomes, and actual assessment tools is minimal which results in surface-level learning among students. The findings also illustrate the fact that in order to develop their assessment literacy, university teachers, like school teachers, need formal training in designing and creating assessment tasks (Ezza, 2017). It should be highlighted that LAL is a specific field in the language assessment discipline without which testing, teaching and learning cannot achieve their desired goals. It should also be noted that our understanding of LAL is restricted to a limited number of writing tasks in a limited number of PYPs in Saudi universities. Therefore, the results cannot be generalized to the level of LAL across other PYPs.

Appendix 1: Learning Outcomes and Selected Course and Test Items

University 1 (Course: ENG 102)
Writing SLOs

1. Can write short simple emails providing and asking for personal information (e.g. about family, people, possessions and local environment) incorporating correct spelling and punctuation.
2. Can write a series of simple sentences providing information about their own and others' habits, routines and preferences.
3. Can produce drafts and a revised final draft of a cohesive analytical paragraph describing the essential features of a job.
4. Can write sentences using so and because to show reason and result, with correct punctuation.
5. Can use a/an, the or no article appropriately with familiar countable and uncountable nouns.
6. Can begin the process of planning writing by generating ideas on a familiar topic through free writing.
7. Can revise writing by understanding and implementing peer and instructor feedback and by checking own writing for simple mechanical and grammatical mistakes.

Test item 1
Write a comparison of two malls. Your paragraph should:
Have a topic sentence, supporting ideas and a concluding sentence.
Compare location, age, size, hours, and number of floors, shops and car park spaces.
Use comparative adjectives. Write 90–120 words (Table 4).

University 2 (Course: REAP 1)
Writing SLOs

1. Write simple phrases and sentences about themselves and imaginary people, where they live and what they do.

Table 4 Test item details for 'University 1'

Name	360 Mall	The Avenues Mall
Location	Al Zahra, Kuwait City	Al Rai, Kuwait City
Opened in	July 2009	April 2007
Size	82,000 square metres	117,000 square metres
Hours	10:00 am–10:00 pm every day	10:00 am–10:00 pm every day
Number of floors	5	3
Number of shops	Over 150	Over 800
Number of spaces in the car park	Over 2440	Over 10,000

2. Write numbers and dates, own name, nationality, address, age, date of birth or arrival in the country, etc.
3. Write correct simple phrases and sentences.
4. Use very basic linear connectors such as **and** or **then** correctly to link words or groups of words.
5. Employ basic punctuation such as full stops, commas and capital letters correctly.
6. Use appropriate word order in subject-verb, subject-verb-object, subject-verb-adjective and subject-verb-adverb sentence structures.
7. Write a 4 to 5 paragraph essay including an introduction, body and conclusion.
8. Use simple, compound and complex sentences in writings (Fig. 1).

Test item 1
University 3 (Course: Pre-intermediate)
Pre-Int (SLOs/Writing)

Write a paragraph about <u>your favorite room. Why do you like it?</u> (4 marks)
- Write at least **four** sentences
- Use the appropriate verb tenses, linking words and punctuation marks.
- The following key words / phrases/questions may help you:
  a. relax   b. good-sized   c. enjoy   d. rest

Fig. 1 Test item 1 instructions 'University 2'

Pre/W1 demonstrate some fluency in cursive writing in sentences and paragraphs

a. legible form

Pre/W2 use appropriate punctuation symbols in sentences

a. full stops
b. capital letters
c. proper nouns
d. question marks

Pre/W3 write simple and compound sentences on familiar topics

a. correct word order
b. appropriate use of tense
c. subject-verb agreements
d. simple grammatical structures
e. use simple connectors to construct clauses

Pre/W4 spell familiar words with reasonable phonetic accuracy

a. identify simple letter patterns

Pre/W5 complete a simple questionnaire or standardized form using words, phrases and short sentences

Pre/W6 write simple descriptions using simple and compound sentences on familiar topics

a. use simple grammatical structures accurately
b. use simple adjectives

Pre/W7 write simple texts for different genres identifying appropriate format (Fig. 2)

Test item 1

> If you have a chance to travel to any country in the world, where would you travel to? Mention:
> - Why would you choose this country?
> - What is their traditional food?
> - What are they known for in the world? (Ex: coffee, pizza, tall buildings, clothes etc.)

Fig. 2 Test item 1 instructions for 'University 3'

References

Alderson, J. C., & Wall, D. (1993). Does washback exist? *Applied Linguistics, 14*(2), 115–129.

American Federation of Teachers, National Council on Measurement in Education & National Education Association. (1990). Standards for teacher competence in educational assessment of students. *Educational Measurement: Issues and Practice, 9*(4), 30–32.

Bachman, L. (2002). Some reflections on task-based language performance assessment. *Language Testing, 19,* 453–476.

Beneditti, K. D. (2006). Language testing: Some problems and solutions. *MEXTESOL Journal, 30*(1), 25–40.

Bereiter, C., & Scardamalia, M. (1989). Intentional learning as a goal of instruction. In L. Resnick (Ed.), *Knowledge, learning and instruction* (pp. 361–392). Hillsdale, NJ: Lawrence Erlbaum Associates.

Beziat, T. L., & Coleman, B. K. (2015). Classroom assessment literacy: Evaluating pre-service teachers. *The Researcher, 27*(1), 25–30.

Biggs, J. (2003). *Aligning teaching and learning to course objectives.* Paper presented at the International conference on Teaching and learning in higher education: New trends and innovations. University of Aveiro.

Brookhart, S. (2011). Educational assessment knowledge and skills for teachers. *Educational Measurement: Issues and Practice, 30*(1), 3–11.

Bruce, J. C., & Lack, M. L. (2009). Using subjective judgement to determine the validity of a tutorial performance-evaluation instrument. *Health SA Gesondheid, 14*(1), 1–6.

Coombe, C., & Evans, J. (2005). Writing assessment scales: Making the right choice. In D. Lloyd, P. Davidson, & C. Coombe (Eds.), *Fundamentals of language assessment: A practical guide for teachers* (pp. 99–104). Dubai: TESOL Arabia Publications.

Coombe, C., Troudi, S., & Al-Hamly, M. (2012). Foreign and second language teacher assessment literacy: Issues, challenges, recommendations. In C.

Coombe, P. Davidson, B. O'Sullivan, & S. Stoynoff (Eds.), *The Cambridge guide to second language assessment* (pp. 20–29). Cambridge, UK: Cambridge University Press.

David, H. A. (1963). *The method of paired comparison.* London: Charles Griffin.

Davies, A. (2008). Textbook trends in teaching language testing. *Language Testing, 25*(3), 327–347.

Deluca, C., & Klinger, D. A. (2010). Assessment literacy development: Identifying gaps in teacher candidates' learning. *Assessment in Education: Principles, Policy & Practice, 17*(4), 419–438.

El-Ebyary, K. (2009). Deconstructing the complexity of washback relation to formative assessment in Egypt. *Cambridge ESOL: Research Notes, 35,* 2–5.

Elshawa, N., Abdullah, A. N., & Rashid, S. M. (2017). Malaysian instructor's assessment beliefs in tertiary ESL classrooms. *International Journal of Education & Literacy Studies, 5*(2), 29–46.

Ezza, E. S. (2017). Criteria for assessing writing at Majmah University. In S. Hidri, & C. Coombe (Eds.), *Evaluation in foreign language education in the Middle East and North Africa, second language learning and teaching* (pp. 185–200). Switzerland: Springer International Publishing.

Ferman, I. (2004). The washback of an EFL national oral matriculation test to teaching and learning. In L. Cheng, Y. Watanabe, & A. Curtis (Eds.), *Washback in language testing: Research context and methods* (pp. 191–210). London: Lawrence Erlbaum Associates.

Fulcher, G. (2012). Assessment literacy for language classroom. *Language Assessment Quarterly, 9*(2), 113–132.

Galluzo, G. R. (2005). Performance assessment and renewing teacher education. *Clearing House: A Journal of Educational Strategies, Issues and Ideas, 78*(4), 142–145.

Garies, C. R., & Grant, L. W. (2015). *Teacher-made assessments: How to connect curriculum, instruction, and student learning.* New York, NY: Routledge.

Gijbels, D., Segers, M., & Struyf, E. (2008). Constructivist learning environments and the (im)possibility to change students' perceptions of assessment demands and approaches to learning. *Instructional Science, 36*(5), 431–443.

Giraldo, F. (2018). Language assessment literacy: Implications for language teachers. *Profile: Issues in Teachers' Professional Development, 20*(1), 179–195.

Green, A. (2007). Washback to learning outcomes: A comparative study of IELTS preparation and university pre-sessional language courses. *Assessment in Education, 14*(1), 75–97.

Guerriero, S. (2017). *Teachers' pedagogical knowledge and the teaching profession: Background report and project objectives*. OECD.

Hakim, B. (2015). English language teachers' ideology of ELT assessment literacy. *International Journal of Education and Literacy Studies, 14*(1), 75–97.

Herman, J., Osmundson, E., Yunyun, D., Ringstaff, C., & Timms, M. (2015). Investigating the dynamics of formative assessment: Relationship between teacher knowledge, assessment practice and learning. *Assessment in Education: Principles, Policy & Practice, 22,* 1–24. https://doi.org/10.1080/0969594X.2015.1006521.

Hidri, S. (2016). Conceptions of assessment: Investigating what assessment means to secondary and university teachers. *Arab Journal of Applied Linguistics, 1*(1), 19–43.

Inbar-Lourie, O. (2013). Guest editorial to the special issue on language assessment literacy. *Language Testing, 30*(3), 301–307.

Krippendorff, K. (2004). *Content analysis: An introduction to its methodology*. London: Sage.

MacLellan, E. (2004). Initial knowledge states about assessment: Novice teachers' conceptualizations. *Teaching and Teacher Education, 20,* 523–535.

Malone, M. E. (2013). The essentials of assessment literacy: Contrasts between testers and users. *Language Testing, 30*(3), 329–344.

Mertler, C. A. (2003). *Preservice versus inservice teachers' assessment literacy: Does classroom experience make a difference?* Paper presented at the annual meeting of the Mid-Western Educational Research Association, Columbus, OH.

Obeid, R. (2017). Second language writing and assessment: Voices from within the Saudi EFL context. *English Language Teaching, 10*(6), 174–181.

Plake, B. S. (1993). Teacher assessment literacy: Teachers' competencies in the educational assessment of students. *Mid-Western Educational Researcher, 6*(1), 21–27.

Plake, B. S. (2015). *Assessment in the service of learning*. Paper presented in the Second International Conference for assessment and evaluation: Learning outcome assessment.

Plake, B., & Impara, J. C. (1996). Teacher assessment literacy: What do teachers know about assessment? In G. D. Phye (Ed.), *Handbook of Classroom Assessment: Learning, Achievement and Adjustment* (pp. 53–68). New York, NY: Academic Press.

Plake, B. S., Impara, J., & Fager, J. (1993). Assessment competencies of teachers: A national survey. *Educational Measurement: Issues and Practices, 12*(4), 10–39.

Popham, W. J. (2009). Assessment literacy for teachers: Faddish or fundamental? *Theory into Practice, 48*(1), 4–11.
Popham, W. J. (2011). Assessment literacy overlooked: A teacher educator's confession. *The Teacher Educator, 46*(4), 265–273.
Popham, W. J. (2013). *Classroom assessment: What teachers need to know.* Boston, MA: Pearson.
Rea-Dickens, P. (2004). Understanding teachers as agents of assessment. *Language Testing, 21*(3), 249–258.
Saville, N., & Hawkey, R. (2004). The IELTS impact study: Investigating washback on teaching mater. In L. Cheng, A. Watanabe, & A. Curtis (Eds.), *Washback in language testing: Research context and methods* (pp. 73–96). London, UK: Lawrence Erlbaum Associates.
Scouller, K. (1998). The influence of assessment method on students' learning approaches: Multiple choice question examination versus assignment essay. *Higher Education, 35,* 453–472.
Shohamy, E. (1993). *The power of tests: The impact of language tests on teaching and learning.* Washington: National Foreign Language Center.
Stecher, B., Barron, S., Chun, T., & Ross, K. (2004). The effects of assessment-driven reform on the teaching of writing in Washington state. In L. Cheng, Y. Watanabe, & A. Curtis (Eds.), *Washback in language testing: Research context and measures* (pp. 53–71). London: Lawrence Erlbaum Associated.
Stiggins, R. J. (1991). Assessment literacy. *The Phi Delta Kappan, 72*(7), 534–539.
Stiggins, R. J. (1995). Assessment literacy for the 21st century. *Phi Delta Kappan, 77*(3), 238–245.
Stiggins, R. J. (2002). Assessment crisis: The absence of assessment for learning. *Phi Delta Kappan, 83,* 758–765.
Stiggins, R. J. (2006). Assessment for learning: A key to student motivation and learning. *Phi Delta Kappa Edge, 2*(2), 1–19.
Stiggins, R. J. (2007). Conquering the formative assessment frontier. In J. McMillan (Ed.), *Formative classroom assessment: Theory into practice* (pp. 8–28). New York, NY: Columbia University Teachers College Press.
Stiggins, R. J., & Conklin, N. (1992). *In teachers' hands: Investigating the practice of classroom assessment.* Albany, NY: SUNY Press.
Sweedler-Brown, C. O. (1993). ESL essay evaluation: The influence of sentence-level and rhetorical features. *Journal of Second Language Writing, 2*(1), 3–17.

Umer, M., Farooq, M. U., & Gulzar, M. A. (2016). Formative assessment has to be made formative: It does not work itself. *Journal of Education and Research, 12*(2), 1–18.

Umer, M., Javid, C. Z., & Farooq, M. U. (2015). *Formative assessment and consequential validity: A practice yet to be effectively implemented in Saudi higher education.* Paper presented in the Second International Conference for assessment and evaluation: Learning outcomes assessment.

Umer, M., Zakaria, M. H., & Alshara, M. A. (2018). Investigating Saudi University EFL teachers' assessment literacy: Theory and practice. *International Journal of English Linguistics, 8*(3), 345–356.

Volante, L., & Fazio, X. (2007). Exploring teacher candidates' assessment literacy: Implications for teacher reform and professional development. *Canadian Journal of Education, 30*(3), 749–770.

Webb, N. L. (1997). *Criteria for alignment of expectations and assessment in mathematics and science education (Research Monograph No. 6).* Washington: National Institute for Science Education Publications.

Webb, N. L. (2002). *An analysis of the alignment between language arts standards and assessments for four states.* Wisconsin: Wisconsin Centre of Educational Research, University of Wisconson-Madison.

Weigle, S. C. (2007). Teaching writing teachers about assessment. *Journal of Second Language Writing, 16,* 194–209.

White, E. (2009). Are you assessment literate? Some fundamental questions regarding effective classroom-based assessment. *OnCue Journal, 3*(1), 3–25.

Yan, Z., & Cheng, E. K. (2015). Primary teachers' attitude, intentions, and practices regarding formative assessment. *Teaching and Teacher Education, 45,* 128–136.

Creational Reverse Engineering: A Project to Enhance English Placement Test Security, Validity, and Reliability

Hadeel El Rahal and Huda Dimashkie

1 Introduction

Language testing, as asserted by Fulcher and Davidson (2007, p. xix), is all about "building better tests, researching how to build better tests and, in so doing, understanding better the things that we test". Language placement tests, as a strand of language testing, are a common and valuable evaluation tool used in colleges and universities to provide information relevant to the proficiency levels of test takers (Delaney, 2008). As a result, these tests facilitate making placement decisions such as registering test takers in the subject or course level that best corresponds to the knowledge or skills they demonstrated in the placement test (Bachman & Palmer, 1996).

In this chapter, the processes of updating a customized local English Placement Test (EPT) used at an American University in the Middle

---

H. E. Rahal (✉) · H. Dimashkie
American University of Sharjah, Sharjah, United Arab Emirates
e-mail: helbakhour@aus.edu; halrahal@aus.edu

East to enhance its administration—mainly its security and ultimately its validity and reliability—are discussed.

The EPT has been administered since the founding of the university. For test improvement purposes, several features in the test had changed over the years including its purpose, content, format, discourse, specifications, and evaluation criteria. The changes occurred for different reasons and at different times. The test's discourse mode, for example, changed from being a narrative (an expository prompt-based academic writing test) to an integrative read-to-write source-based academic essay (argumentative/persuasive) writing test. According to Delaney (2008), the integrative skill read-to-write has its roots in theories of language assessment. The assessed language ability (reading-to-write argumentative essay) in the EPT, as well as its evaluation criteria (coherence, unity, support, mechanics, and critical thinking), are based on integrated skills language assessment theory.

Despite the several changes implemented to the test, the test never had an official written specification document as a test development reference which resulted in inconsistency in its item development and evaluation, and ultimately affected its validity and reliability. Following the Reverse Engineering concept defined by Davidson and Lynch (2001), we coined a new Reverse Engineering variant named *Creational Reverse Engineering* (CRE) to develop the EPT Specification Document. The newly developed (written) test specification document aimed at defining the test's overall goals and construct, streamlining the process of item development, enlarging the test item bank, streamlining its scoring criteria, and eventually improving the test validity (security) and reliability.

This chapter is divided into six main sections starting with the literature review section and ending with a conclusion and further research discussion. The theoretical framework highlights topics relevant to reverse engineering, test security, test bank, and more. The main issues identified with the EPT are discussed in the project problem and hypothesis section. The methodology section introduces the newly adopted CRE model, the steps followed to create the new Test Specification Document as well as the enlargement of the test's bank. Before closing with the conclusion and further research discussion, the project's findings and discussion as well as its limitations and implications are presented.

2 Literature Review

In the academic context, tests and exams are generally used as a measurement tool of students' skills, concept acquisition, and their proficiency demonstration. Placement tests are likewise used to assess students' capabilities for placement purposes. Bachman and Palmer (1996, p. 97) define placement as a decision which "[involves] determining in which of several different levels of instruction it would be most appropriate to place the test taker". Hence, with placement tests, there is another dimension added to the test development stage because of the test's significance in determining the students' corresponding placement.

Most, if not all, test developers agree that test development involves different phases and considerations (Bachman & Palmer, 1996; Coombe, 2009; Davidson & Lloyd, 2009; Douglas, 2010; McNamara, 2000; Weigle, 2002). While several researchers present test development as a "linear" process that involves reiterative stages (Bachman & Palmer, 1996; Douglas, 2010; McNamara, 2000; Weigle, 2002), Bachman and Palmer (1996) argue that the test development process is not only reiterative but also "conceptual". Thus, while Bachman and Palmer (1996) agree that the process of test development is divided into three stages: test design, test operationalization, and test administration (Bachman & Palmer, 1996; Douglas, 2010; McNamara, 2000; Weigle, 2002), they believe that tests may be revisited during different stages of the test development process.

2.1 Test Development Process

The test design stage involves mainly two major steps: needs analysis and construct definition (Weigle, 2002). The needs analysis process is the one in which test developers decide on what to test and how (Douglas, 2010). Defining the construct in assessment is "the trait or traits that a test is intended to measure. A construct can be defined as an ability or set of abilities that will reflect a performance, and about which inferences can be made on the basis of test scores" (McNamara, 2000, p. 31). According to Weigle (2002, p. 79), defining the construct of a language test could be based on either a "course syllabus" or "a theoretical definition of language ability more generally, or writing ability in particular". Weigle (2002) explains the importance of theory-based construct definitions for exams like placement tests that do not depend on an explicit curriculum.

2.2 Test Operationalization Stage

In the test operationalization stage, the rationale behind the test and its questions must be documented in a document referred to as the test specifications document. This document includes detailed instructions on how to design test items and the steps of turning them into a complete test. As for designing effective test items, several conditions, such as clarity of the language (Weigle, 2002) and its simplicity (Bachman & Palmer, 1996), should be considered. The language should be clear to ensure students understand what is required, and it should be simple and straightforward, so students do not waste time decoding the test item requirements.

Essay prompts, as a test item, "initiate and direct the act of writing that produces the sample for evaluation" (Ruth & Murphy, 1984, p. 410). Hence, effective essay prompts, according to Ruth and Murphy (1988), are neutral ones that instruct the students to write about topics they have adequate knowledge about and not content-specific ones. They also emphasize the importance of training ESL students on how to write academically in different styles instead of only writing based on information retrieved from memory. Such writing tasks enable the writers to make decisions about how to organize their written products and what information to include in support of their arguments and what information to exclude.

Moreover, writing prompts could come in the form of a question (such as "Would you rather eat processed food or organic food?") or in the form of a statement (such as "Write an essay expressing the advantages and disadvantages of eating processed food, and explain your point of view"). Weigle (2002) elaborates that prompts should provide clear instructions, indicate the purpose of the writing, and dictate how long the targeted response should be.

Davidson and Lloyd (2009) list the characteristics of a good writing prompt as: clarity, audience, context, and rhetorical situation awareness. Prompts designed to elicit essay writing in language assessment, according to Weigle (2004), are divided into two types: prompt-based and source-based. Prompt-based essay questions, known as timed impromptu essay prompts in the language assessment literature, target a single language criterion (writing) similar to the prompts used in the Test of Written English (TWE). Source-based essay prompts, on the other hand, target multiple language skills such as reading and writing or listening and writing and are used in integrative language tests. According to Davies et al. (1999, p. 83), integrative skills tests are "[tests] in which learners are required to combine various skills in answering test items". Weigle (2002) confirms that integrated skills language tests are becoming increasingly popular in college and university settings.

Weigle (2002) explains that integrative writing tests aim to assess the skill of writing in a specific genre (e.g. narrative, persuasive, descriptive, etc.) based on another language skill, which could be either reading or listening. Therefore, integrative writing assessment requires an agreement or disagreement with the expressed point of view (Weigle, 2002). Such prompt types (e.g. compare/contrast, agree/disagree, cause/effect) are usually associated with argumentative/persuasive writing, and they help elicit the test takers' ideas in relation to those expressed by the author of the selected text. In integrative tests, according to Weigle (2002), using a reading text, as a source of input for writing, provides all test takers equal access to the same source of information about the targeted topic. As a result, all test takers will be referring to the same source for information to support their positions in writing, and therefore, will not be delayed by limitations of access to information in the process of trying to find what to say about the topic. An extended production response is longer than one sentence or utterance to a form of free oral or written composition (Bachman & Palmer, 1996).

Test items could be gathered in a database which in the language assessment literature is referred to as a test bank, test pool, or item collection and defined as a "relatively large collection of easily accessible test questions" (Millman & Arter, 1984, p. 315). Test banks come in different formats such as paper-based (test folders) or electronic-based (computer databases). The ease of accessibility of test items could be accomplished by using indexing or unique labelling information for each test item.

Millman and Arter (1984) acknowledge test banks' ability to offer a wider and more inclusive assessment setting; as a result, they are easily adjusted for the setting they might be used in. From a socio-political point of view, a test bank grants "ownership and control of the questions" (Millman & Arter, 1984, p. 317) by the test developers, and thus, full access and control for future adjustments if needed. An item bank could also allow easy retrieval of tasks and important information about test items. Finally, and most importantly, archiving facilitates and maximizes test security (Bachman & Palmer, 1996). The more items in the test bank, the better it is for the effectiveness of the process. A great deal of research on test banks development recommends a large pool of items to avoid cheating and memorization incidents that usually happen in the long run due to repetitive use of a limited number of items. In addition to the large number of items added to a test bank, developers should also try to achieve quality, content validity, and suitable statistical characteristics when developing test items (Millman & Arter, 1984).

2.3 Test Administration

The last stage in the test development process is test administration. Bachman and Palmer (1996) define two administrative stages: a try-out equivalent to a pilot, and operational test use equivalent to the actual administration. Language test developers, however, are involved in a continuous evaluation of the usefulness of the developed test at every stage of the development process (design, operationalization, and administration) (Bachman & Palmer, 1996). The evidence collected from each production stage, which facilitates the validation process at that particular stage, should never be treated in separation, explain Bachman and Palmer (1996). They add that the production stages as well as the evidence related to them are "interrelated and iterative" (Bachman & Palmer, 1996, p. 13).

The validation process could therefore be applied as needed at any point in the production stages: at the beginning during the design stage, halfway through at the operationalization stage, or towards the end after the administration of the test (McNamara, 2000; Weir, 2005). McNamara (2000) asserts that validation is an ongoing process that should be revisited as long as the test is administered. Weir (2005) adds that no single evidence of validity is more important than the others at any implementation stage, and that shortage in any one raises questions about the accuracy of interpretations made at a particular implementation stage using that deficit evidence.

The evidence related to the design stage, according to Weir (2005, p. 14), includes the theory-based evidence of validity and context-related evidence of validity, in which construct validity is a function of the "interaction between these two aspects of validity and not just a matter of ability within the individual in isolation".

During the operationalization stage, however, the data generated from the try-out administration stage is valuable evidence for validation of the operationalization stage. Additionally, statistical analysis could be done with the test data, which could reveal information about the accuracy of the obtained scores in a test and how much we can depend on its scores in making inferences about learning or placement, for instance. In the language assessment literature, such evidence of validity is called scoring validity (Weir, 2005).

Finally, the data collected at the stage after the test design and administration are mostly important and valuable to the end users, as such data provide inferences about test takers' performance and capabilities (Weir, 2005). The forms of evidence of validity associated with this last stage are known in the language assessment literature as criterion-related evidence of validity and consequential-related evidence of validity.

2.4   Test Reverse Engineering

Though Bachman and Palmer (1996) identified and advised the test development stages mentioned above, they suggested that the test creation process is recursive. This means that certain test development stages might need to be revisited for further improvement at different times, even after the test implementation process to reassure the test's ongoing validation.

Davidson and Lynch (2001) build on Bachman and Palmer's notion of conceptual test development procedure by introducing the concept of *reverse engineering* (RE) to the language assessment literature. Reverse engineering is the process of building or modifying an existing test using the test itself or another existing test (Davidson & Lynch, 2001). Davidson and Lynch (2001, p. 41) acknowledge that not "all testing is spec-driven. 'Spec-driven' tests are those that have been created from a specification [...]. However, tests can exist without this overt, active role for specifications".

The term "reverse engineering" was first coined by Davidson and Lynch, and different scholars had built up on their term by identifying different types or variants within RE. Fulcher and Davidson (2007) identify five different types of reverse engineering: straight RE, historical RE, critical RE, test deconstruction RE, and parallel RE. In 2010, W. F. Scott introduced a 6th RE variant which is standards RE. Each of the aforementioned variants is "Spec-driven" (Davidson & Lynch, 2001) using different ideas and perspectives to modify an existing exam and specification document to update and suit different test administration purposes. It is significant to note that all of these different existing variants rely on the existence of a previously developed test specification document. These RE variants update the existing specification document to match the test's context requirements.

2.5 Reverse Engineering for the EPT

As all the existing variants mentioned above are spec-driven, our EPT did not have an existing specifications document. Therefore, using the concept of reverse engineering to update the test and ensure more accurate placement decisions, we coined a new RE variant named "Creational RE". Creational RE is the creation of a new specifications document from an existing test that had no existing specifications document. While the concept of Creational RE is not new, the name, nonetheless, is new.

We found it important to coin this new RE variant as Davidson and Lynch, and other scholars, did not specify a name when RE is used to create a test specification document from scratch.

3 Project Problem and Hypothesis

The English Placement Test is an integrated skills academic writing placement test designed to examine the level of academic writing skills of newly admitted students to an American University in the Middle East. Two main issues were detected with the test:

1. Test security is highly jeopardized due to administering the test weekly using dated and limited test items from a test bank including repetitive reading texts and prompts.
2. The absence of a well-defined test construct in a well-defined test specification document.

Improving the test's security was a pressing need. According to Millman and Arter (1984, p. 317), "large [test] item collections decrease the concern about item security as remembering the answers to all the questions without having the knowledge or skill becomes more difficult". Therefore, developing an updated and larger test bank for the EPT is a very important step towards enhancing the EPT administration circumstances (particularly security) and thus increasing its reliability validity, which would consequently lead to more accurate test evaluations and, as a result, more accurate placements.

Millman and Arter (1984) also point out that customized and tailor-made test banks have a socio-political advantage, which allows full ownership and control of the test. As a result, the final product of this project (EPT test specifications and test bank) will be tailored to more effectively address the targeted university English academic writing skills evaluated in its EPT.

Although the test's construct (writing an argumentative essay based on a reading text) is always present in the minds of the raters when evaluating an EPT essay, this aspect of the EPT construct has never been clearly defined in a test specification document. Specifically, there was no mention of what types of writing prompts are appropriate for the EPT and can effectively elicit an argumentative essay which demonstrates the academic writing characteristics of coherence, unity, support, mechanics, and critical thinking, nor was there indication of desired characteristics for the reading texts. The lack of an official test specifications document for years has resulted in an unclear item development procedure and criteria, which made the item development procedure a daunting job for the test developers. Moreover, the unclear item development criteria resulted in some discrepancy in the quality of the selected readings as well as the written prompts. According to Davidson and Lynch (2001, p. 15), "a well-written specification is to result in a document that, if given to a group of similarly trained teachers ... will produce a set of test tasks that are similar in content and measurement characteristics". Therefore, the newly produced EPT specifications document, as one of the end products of this project, can clarify the test development criteria and EPT construct and, at the same time, work as a generative blueprint for the EPT developers to refer to whenever they need to develop new EPT items.

4 Methodology

Prior to the implementation of the main stages of this project, written official approval was sought from the official developers of the EPT. Abiding by the written agreement obtained from the administration office before the start of the implementation of this project, neither the general instructions of the current EPT, nor its administration time (90 minutes), its grading rubric or procedure were changed. The following sections discuss the two main stages of this project's methodology (1) Construct Development and (2) Drafting Test Specification Document.

The design of the test specifications document, as well as the new EPT items, was based on the current EPT administered in the university Testing Centre. The process of building or modifying an existing test using the test itself or another existing test is known in the language assessment literature as RE (Davidson & Lynch, 2001). The fact that the

EPT never had a test specification document, a new variant of RE was invented to cater to that project's special case of RE and was named the Creational RE variant. Creational RE, therefore, is the process of writing a test specification document for the first time using an existing test to build or modify the same test or another existing test.

4.1 EPT Construct

Identifying the EPT construct was essential as it worked as a cornerstone when drafting the test specification document. This EPT construct is a theoretical construct based on integrated skills language assessment theory. It is designed to assess test takers' academic English proficiency level by writing an argumentative essay based on reading an academic text and supporting their argument with information retrieved from the provided text. The EPT has characteristics of both low stakes and high stakes exams. It is a placement test to students (high stakes exam) to determine which academic writing course offered by the university they need to take; yet, the results may be overruled at the discretion of the faculty member, teaching the academic writing courses. This is done by offering the students a diagnostic test during the first week of the semester to evaluate the students' academic writing skills outside the test administration context to verify the results obtained from the EPT. Students accordingly are either kept in the assigned writing course or moved to a higher one should their in-class writing reveal better capabilities.

4.2 EPT Test Specification Document and EPT Prompts

As mentioned earlier, the EPT has experienced different changes and updates over the years of its use in the university. However, such additions or modifications were implemented without being subjected to any approved test criteria or specifications, which resulted in conflict with the test's main purpose and consequently negatively influenced the clarity as well as content validity of the test. Therefore, writing the EPT specifications document was a necessity because it would then serve as the "generative blueprint from which test items or tasks can be produced" (Davidson & Lynch, 2001, p. 4) by the developers of the test.

The process of designing this EPT followed the reverse engineering model in which existing tests are modified (Davidson & Lynch, 2001). The EPT had been a non-specification-driven placement test, and, in this project, its test specifications document (see Appendix 1) was drafted based on the EPTs that were in use. The EPT test specifications document, generated from the currently used EPTs, could serve as the preliminary and starting point EPT specifications document which would evolve to a more finalized and official one in the future with continuous improvements and modifications implemented by the test and test specifications developer(s) (Coombe, 2009; Davidson & Lynch, 2001). Writing a test specification document for the EPT exams was very important to help facilitate updating/modifying the tests in the future as needed. This was also needed to help test creators and raters abide by the test's criteria and specifications which will result in meeting the content and rating validity of the test.

The development of the test specifications document depended heavily on carefully examining a sample of six currently administered EPTs. Only the prompt statements and readings were reviewed in the selected EPT sample. Administered EPTs were also reviewed to learn more about the reading genres, level, and length, and finally learn the overall academic writing expectations from the test takers in the EPT. The idea of developing new items was to enlarge and diversify the EPT item bank, which would consequently enhance test administration reliability by improving test security.

Based on the Flesch-Kincaid feature in Microsoft Word-© and an online vocabulary profiler resource (http://www.lextutor.ca/vp/), it was concluded that the reading difficulty of the text used in the EPT should be at the level of educational texts used in grades 9–12 at a reading ease of 45% or above. This reading level (difficulty) reflects what newly admitted students are either familiar with from high school or expected to demonstrate during their first year of university. This measure matches the placement decision at the level of academic writing (level 101/middle level) when evaluating the produced essays in the EPT exams. The genre, length, and reading levels were examined. The reading topics selected are authentic, controversial, and relatable to students to minimize the factor of surprise during EPT. The readings were selected from previous intermediate academic writing course textbooks and local newspapers. The classification of the selected reading texts under one or more of the five prompt type categories based on their content was completed by an Ad hoc Committee (see Ad hoc Committee section below) formed to rate, assess, and help in the completion of this project.

As for the prompts, five academic writing prompts (agree/disagree, advantages/disadvantages, compare/contrast, cause/effect, and problem/solution), which were demonstrated to be comparable in terms of difficulty (Golub-Smith, Reese, & Steinhaus, 1993), were selected to be used in the new EPTs. The prompts were rewritten to ensure they were clearer and more flexible to accommodate test takers with low academic writing proficiency levels, yet sufficiently challenging for test takers with intermediate and advanced academic writing proficiency levels. Unlike the old prompts, the new prompts directly ask the test takers to use ideas from the source text to support their ideas and use examples from their personal life, if applicable. These instructions were placed in the EPT instructions paragraph instead of placing it alone above the instructions prompt paragraph (as it was done previously). Figures 1 and 2, respectively, show samples of the old and new EPT prompt.

Instructions

Carefully read the article on the next page by Geeta Pandey titled "The Disappearing Tribe of India's Letter Writers." Pandey discusses how technological development has affected letter writers in India.

Write a well-developed essay (4-6 paragraphs) in which you discuss 2-3 possible advantages and/or disadvantages associated with technological advancements of the recent decades.

Fig. 1 Sample of an old EPT prompt

> **Answer the question below in the form of a well-developed essay. You may use information from the article to justify your point of view.**
>
> In the article, "X," the author discusses why the issue YZ exists. Read the article to learn more about the author's point of view, and then write a fully developed essay which discusses your opinion of the advantages and disadvantages of having YZ. Make sure to use specific reasons and examples from your personal life and / or the article to support your argument.

Fig. 2 Sample of a new EPT prompt

4.3 The Ad hoc Committee

An Ad hoc committee was formed, and it included only two EPT raters from the test's development department as the formation of the committee and participation were voluntary. The Ad hoc committee was formed specifically to help with the development of the new EPT bank and was responsible for verifying the appropriateness of the selected reading texts and their reading difficulty level as well as approving the classification of the modified reading texts into their correct corresponding test prompt categories. A priori *evidence* (Bachman & Palmer, 1996) was utilized to validate the newly developed test items, including the prompt instructions and reading selection, as well as the readings classification. Thus, in addition to the aforementioned duties of the Ad hoc committee related to the development of the new EPTs, they were also responsible for carefully reviewing the newly developed items (prompts and readings), and particularly examining the language and effectiveness of each composed prompt under each prompt type category. They were also requested to suggest corrections and rephrasing of word choice, when necessary, to make the developed prompts clearer and as effective as possible in eliciting the desired argumentative essay from the EPT future test takers (Breland, Lee, Najarian, & Muraki, 2004; Golub-Smith et al., 1993; Hale, 1992; Spaan, 1993).

5 Results and Discussion

Despite the absence of a designed pilot stage, and due to the pressing need to improve the test security conditions, the new test bank was used immediately upon its completion. The completion of the new EPT bank introduced a new stage in test administration and test validation overall.

A major finding was that the old scoring method did not suit the revamped EPTs. Before designing the new EPT prompts, the old EPTs were evaluated holistically based on the evaluators' judgement on whether the produced academic writing piece demonstrates few, some, or adequate knowledge of the goals and objectives of the first three offered academic writing courses by the university (001, 101, and 102). The old EPT rubric merely jotted down raters' expectations for each writing level without offering a proper scale and criteria for each placement level. The modified rubric, conversely, had defined the scoring criteria to include five distinct categories: response to prompt, development, essay form, and grammar and language (see new rubric in Fig. 3).

The old scoring method involved raters' discrepancy and, sometimes, miss-placement. This gap in the test grading between the old EPTs and the new ones identified the need to design a new rubric; a rubric that caters to the new changes particularly the upgrade in the quality of the selected reading pieces and the expected level of academic writing produced. The new rubric was more oriented as it included more defined academic writing criteria in line with the goals and objectives (construct valid) of the first three academic writing courses (001,101, and 102) offered by the university. The evaluation criteria were clearly defined as well as the levels' grading scale. One academic year after implementing the aforementioned changes, faculty reflected positively on the enhancement in the placement process and the frequency of change-of-placement requests dropped.

The scoring section in the newly drafted test specification document (see Appendix 1) was modified accordingly to reflect the new scoring criteria used when grading the new EPTs. The change was highly needed to bridge the gap between the old scoring method and the scoring needs in the new EPTs.

Rubric

	Student ID #	Rater Name	Score

Name: EPT Rubric Final
Description: 4–7 = Level 001, 8–10 = Level 101, 11–12 = Level 102
Rubric Detail

Levels of Achievement

Criteria	Level 1	Level 2	Level 3
Response To Prompt	**1 Points** — Generally answers prompt question or is off topic.	**2 Points** — Answers some aspects of prompt.	**3 Points** — Directly answers all facets of prompt.
Development	**1 Points** — Minimal or no ideas are connected in logical sequence; minimal or no support from prompt; little or no correct use of transitions.	**2 Points** — Most ideas are connected in a logical sequence; partially supported with evidence from prompt; mostly correct use of transitions.	**3 Points** — Ideas are connected in a logical sequence; supported with evidence from prompt; correct use of transitions.
Essay Form	**1 Points** — Does not demonstrate an awareness of components of an essay.	**2 Points** — Contains most components of an essay.	**3 Points** — Contains all components of an essay (introduction with thesis statement; body paragraphs with topic sentences; concluding paragraph).
Grammar and Language	**1 Points** — Inaccurate word choice; basic syntax; incorrect grammar and spelling; minimal or no use of standard English.	**2 Points** — Mostly accurate word choice; mostly complex syntax; few grammar and spelling mistakes; mostly correct use of standard English.	**3 Points** — Accurate word choice; complex syntax; no grammar or spelling mistakes; consistent use of standard English.

Fig. 3 New EPT rubric

One year after the design of the new rubric and as an attempt to further improve placement decision reliability, the direct placement in level three (102) was eliminated (see Fig. 4) and in replacement a new

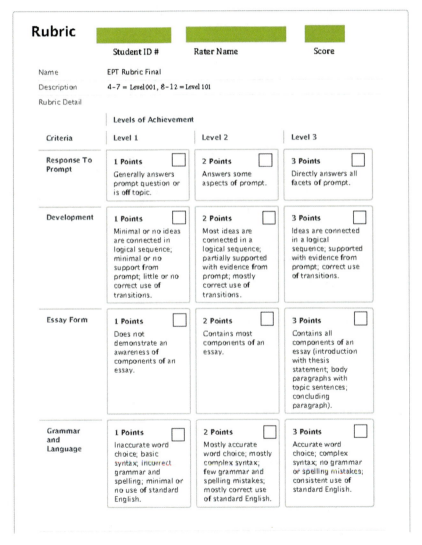

Fig. 4 EPT new rubric [no direct placement in level 102]

admissions feature was introduced. Newly admitted students (test takers) who earn 580 in TOEFL or 7.5 in IELTS can be exempted from sitting for the placement test and be directly placed in level two (101). The new feature was helpful for students and raters alike. As for the students, it motivated them to perform better in their language proficiency tests to earn the exemption from the EPT and be directly placed at a higher level. On the raters' side, it improved the placement decision making and lessened the pressure put on them to make a quick placement decision during peak periods (beginning of the fall and spring semesters) to help enrol a large number of newly admitted students. The exemption decision in addition to the EPT testing schedule (weekly every Monday) helped distribute the big numbers of test takers across different test sessions during the academic year. The test takers distribution together with the new test bank, on the other hand, contributed significantly in enhancing the test security validity while at the same time enhancing the test scoring and administration conditions overall.

6 Implications for the Context and Conclusion

Improving the test security conditions as well as building a larger test item bank significantly improved placement testing conditions. For the raters, it improved the raters' reliability as the changes in the grading rubric, which was as well preceded with norming sessions, helped lower the grading discrepancy and improve placement decision making. Designing the new tests based on a theory-based construct and, at the same time, meeting the goals and objectives of the middle-level course offered by the university (101) makes the test construct valid. This can help newly admitted students in their academic writing journey and pre-empt them about what academic writing skill is expected from them to demonstrate and improve while completing their writing courses at the university. With the enlargement of the test item bank, the test security—which was the main concern—was addressed in our research. Our new suggestions improved test security as it offered an enlargement of the test item bank, making it less likely to repeat the same test. Thus, the testing conditions improved.

Despite the absence of a pilot stage of the newly designed test, putting the tests into practice introduced a new start of a much more organized and oriented EPT testing environment at the hosting university and, ultimately, a more secure testing environment. The new expanded test bank will facilitate the work of the testing centre staff as they can increase the number of test sessions to cater for more students during the academic year. The larger database also provides them with more resources which minimizes the probability of repetitive tests. As for the students, the modified EPTs set their expectations, prepare them for future academic courses, and expose them to the minimum academic writing skills they are expected to acquire.

As for the test developers, they now have a clearer framework and skeleton to follow when they would like to update the EPT. With the new specifications document created, there is a clear purpose of the test requirements and goals. This will ensure a consistency of exam development in the future as test developers will have a clear idea of the test purpose and test development over time. Altogether, this will minimize marginal error in test development in the future.

During the implementation of the project, some limitations were encountered. Due to the absence of a pilot stage, as mentioned earlier, and the fact that this project's main goal was to enhance the test's security, exposing the designed tests for examination, experimentation, and review prior to actually using them was quite challenging. According to the assessment and evaluation literature, it is recommended to have some *posteriori evidence* claimed from the designed tests before putting them into actual use. At least some wider reflection from more than two raters in the Ad hoc Committee would have been beneficial for obtaining *posteriori evidence* during the design stage. This suggestion should not take away from the excellent validation and verification the two members have provided during the readings' selection as well as reading classification under suitable prompt type. However, had more than two rater members joined the Ad hoc Committee, it would have allowed additional and more diversified feedback to be obtained from the test developers/raters resulting in enhancing the a priori *evidence* validation (construct and content validity) process of the new EPT items (prompts and readings).

This study sought at first to rectify the issue of test security associated with the EPT administration conditions (over exposure of test items, multiple use of a limited number of items, and the additional test administration sessions between the semesters) and lack of test specifications for the EPT. Hence, the idea of developing a test bank with newly developed test items (new prompt types and new readings) was implemented.

Despite not going ahead with a proper pilot stage, the newly developed EPT test item bank, after being used at the university testing centre and validated, guaranteed the department full ownership and access to a local EPT item bank which they can refer to and use alternatively across the academic year.

In addition to the new EPT bank, the implementation of this project has produced the first EPT test specifications document, which faculty could refer to as a generative item blueprint to develop new EPT items, amend problematic ones, or discard and replace items, if needed.

In conclusion, a few suggestions for future research could be made involving the development of more items to be added to the newly developed test bank. Due to the new weekly EPT administration sessions, it is recommended to increase the test items up to 150 total items instead of the 28 items currently in use to guarantee item and test security for at least five academic years, which is the equivalent to 30 EPTs per one academic year. Additionally, it is highly recommended to automate (computerize) the currently used EPT test items which hopefully could enhance the test's rater and administration reliability, validity (content and construct), authenticity, and effectiveness compared to the currently implemented ones. This is possible should there be a second phase for this project which would allow full execution of a pilot stage for the automated tests rather than a partial one. The full pilot stage will help run a posteriori evidence check on the test's effectiveness overall and particularly on the accuracy of placement between the computerized and human raters.

Appendix 1: English Placement Test (EPT) Specifications Document

General Description of the EPT

The English Placement Test (EPT) was designed in 1997 and has since been used as the official English Academic Writing placement test at the American University. The EPT examines the academic writing proficiency level of newly admitted students who score 6 points or above in the International English Language Testing System (IELTS) exam or score 530 or above in the paper-based TOEFL or its equivalent score in the Internet-Based TOEFL. Based on the obtained EPT results, the students are placed in three academic writing courses (001, 101, and 102) offered by the Academic Writing Department.

The EPT is administered at the university Testing Centre (TC), and it takes place before the start of each academic semester—fall, spring, and summer. Extra EPT administration sessions are also offered by the TC to accommodate the applicants who are admitted in between the semesters. The extra EPT sessions are scheduled weekly every Monday at the TC. For example, applicants who apply to join in the spring semester, which usually starts in February, after being admitted can register and sit for one of the EPT extra sessions scheduled in October, November, or December.

Newly admitted students are asked to compose an essay in response to the provided reading. The TC employees are responsible for scheduling and selecting EPT versions for a specific exam session, as well as printing, assembling, and invigilating EPTs. The EPT development and grading, however, is completed in the Academic Writing Department by its faculty members.

The Design of EPT Items
EPT Prompt Attributes

The EPT is administered in pen and paper format, and no other materials are allowed in the test administration session, such as e-dictionaries or paper dictionaries.

In order for the test takers to successfully demonstrate the integrated skill of reading-to-write in the EPT, each EPT test version consists of one unique prompt designed in response to the genre of the reading text selected to be used in a particular EPT version. For example, if the reading text discusses a controversial issue such as racial profiling, then the corresponding prompt type might require the test takers to write an argumentative essay to express their position about racial profiling and support their argument by referring to the information from the reading text and/or personal knowledge. Therefore, the newly developed prompts will be in the form of short sentences and should "not contain difficult vocabulary, require specialized knowledge, involve highly controversial or emotional subjects, or encourage students to identify their institutions in their essays" (Weigle, 2004, p. 31). In order to guarantee effectiveness in eliciting the desired argumentative essays from the test takers in response to the prompt type used in a particular EPT version, the prompts should also brief the test takers about the main idea of the text and should be precise in their purpose by clearly instructing the test takers on how to address the topic and from which perspective (see Fig. 5).

EPT prompt type categories include compare/contrast, cause/effect, advantages/disadvantages, agree/disagree, and problem/solution. For examples of test items using these five prompt types, see the electronic version of the EPT Project Test Item Data Base.

The font type of the EPT prompt paragraph should be Times New Roman and the font size should be 12 with line spacing 1.5. The prompt paragraph should also be aligned as Justify Text. Justify Text alignment could be found under paragraph format options in Microsoft Office Word-©.

The topics of the EPT reading texts, which follow the prompt sentence in any EPT, should be authentic and reflect issues related to the test takers' daily lives such as texting and driving or Facebook and social

---

Answer the question below in the form of a well-developed essay. You may use information from the article to justify your point of view.

In the article, "X," the author discusses why the issue YZ exists. Read the article to learn more about the author's point of view, and then write a fully developed essay which discusses your opinion of the advantages and disadvantages of having YZ. Make sure to use specific reasons and examples from your personal life and / or the article to support your argument.

Fig. 5 Sample of new EPT prompt instructions paragraph

life. Authentic and relevant readings could be found in previously used academic writing course level (101) textbooks and local newspapers.

The length of the reading texts should be one-and-a-half pages, and their reading difficulty should be at that of academic writing course level (101), which was identified to be at the reading level of grades 9–12 and at a reading ease of 45% or above. The identified (101) reading difficulty level was obtained by selecting reading texts from previously used (101) textbooks and entering them in a Microsoft Word-© document to identify their reading difficulty by using the Flesch-Kincaid feature in Microsoft Word-©. An online vocabulary profiler resource (http://www.lextutor.ca/vp/) should be used to check the breakdown of words' frequency in any potential reading text, including how many words fall in the first and second thousand levels and how many academic words there are in a selected text. Before approving using a reading text in the EPT, its reading difficulty level should be verified first using the Flesch-Kincaid feature in Microsoft Word-© and the online vocabulary profiler resource.

The reading passage should follow the prompt paragraph in the test paper. The reading text should begin with the title and the author (bold font) in the first line followed in the second line by the source (not bold and italic), and publication date if available (not bold), and all should be aligned in the middle.

The font of the reading passage should be Times New Roman, and its size should be 12 with line spacing 1.5. The beginning of the reading passage paragraphs should be indented at 1.27 cm and there should be no spacing between the paragraphs. The adopted reading text should also be proofread by the test developers to have its spelling unified for American spelling.

Once the reading difficulty decisions are finalized, then the readings should be classified based on their content under one or more of the five prompt categories. The classification of the readings should be verified and approved by the test development department members.

Response Attributes

In response to the EPT prompt, the test takers are expected to write an argumentative essay demonstrating coherence, unity, support, mechanics, and critical thinking. In their argumentative essays, the test takers need to take a position on the discussed topic in the reading text and support their argument with information retrieved from the text.

In order for the produced essay to meet the EPT essay response requirements, it should also be of several paragraphs, including an introduction, a thesis statement, supporting paragraphs, and a conclusion. Finally, test takers should provide an appropriate title for their argumentative essay.

EPT Scoring

As mentioned above in the general description section, the completed EPTs are sent to Academic Writing Department for grading. Informal measures are taken to assure that the rating of the EPT is reliable. The grading rubric as well as its grading procedure are a result of different norming sessions between the test developers in the department. The norming sessions were held to agree on one scoring criteria to be applied by all raters when rating the EPT, and the unified scoring criteria was translated into the EPT scoring rubric currently used by the raters. The norming sessions, according to the raters, are important as they enhance rater reliability and minimize rating discrepancy.

Thus, two faculty members read each test paper and separately give it a grade. Based on the obtained test result, which is generated from adding the grades of reader 1 and reader 2, the test taker is placed in the appropriate academic writing courses (001, 101, or 102). If the test result is between four and seven, then the test taker is placed in 001. If the test result is between eight and twelve, then the test taker is placed in 101. If there is a discrepancy between the grades of raters one and two, then the EPT paper is read by a third rater. The new total grade will then be the sum of the third grade plus the adjacent grade to it, of either rater one or two.

References

Bachman, L. F., & Palmer, A. S. (1996). *Language testing in practice: Designing and developing useful language tests.* Oxford: Oxford University Press.

Breland, H., Lee, Y., Najarian, M., & Muraki, E. (2004). *An analysis of TOEFL CBT writing prompt difficulty and comparability for different gender groups.* Princeton, NJ: Educational Testing Service.

Coombe, C. (2009). Developing test specification. In D. Lloyd, P. Davidson, & C. Coombe (Eds.), *The fundamentals of language assessment: A practical guide for teachers* (pp. 24–30). Dubai: TESOL Arabia.

Davidson, P., & Lloyd, D. (2009). Principles of language assessment. In D. Lloyd, P. Davidson, & C. Coombe (Eds.), *The fundamentals of language assessment: A practical guide for teachers* (pp. 94–105). Dubai: TESOL Arabia.

Davidson, F., & Lynch, B. K. (2001). *Testcraft: A teacher's guide to writing and using language test specifications.* New Haven, CT: Yale University Press.

Davies, A., Brown, A., Elder, C., Hill, K., Lumley, T., & McNamara, T. (1999). *Studies in language testing: Dictionary of language testing.* Cambridge: Cambridge University Press, NY.

Delaney, A. Y. (2008). Investigating the reading-to-write construct. *Journal of English for Academic Purposes, 7*(3), 140–150.

Douglas, D. (2010). *Understanding language testing.* London, UK: Hodder Education.

Fulcher, G., & Davidson, F. (2007). *Language testing and assessment: An advanced resource book.* Oxon, UK: Routledge.

Golub-Smith, M., Reese, C. M., & Steinhaus, K. (1993). *Topic and topic type comparability on the Test of Written English.* Princeton, NJ: Educational Testing Service.

Hale, G. A. (1992). *Effects of amount of time allowed on the Test of Written English.* Princeton, NJ: Educational Testing Service.

McNamara, T. F. (2000). *Language testing.* Oxford: Oxford University Press.

Millman, J., & Arter, J. A. (1984). Issues in item banking. *Journal of Educational Measurement, 21*(4), 315–330.

Ruth, L., & Murphy, S. (1984). Designing topics for writing assessment: Problems of meaning. *College Composition and Communication, 35*(4), 410–422.

Ruth, L., & Murphy, S. (1988). *Designing writing tasks for the assessment of writing* (4th ed.). Norwood, NJ: Greenwood Publishing Group.

Scott, W. F. (2010). Cultivating assessment literacy: Standards evaluation through language-test specification reverse engineering. *Language Assessment Quarterly, 7*(4), 317–342.

Spaan, M. (1993). The effect of prompt in essay examinations. In D. Douglas & C. Chapelle (Eds.), *A new decade of language testing research: Selected papers from the twelfth annual Language Testing Research Colloquium* (pp. 98–122). Washington, DC: Teachers of English to Speakers of Other Languages.

Weigle, S. C. (2002). *Assessing writing*. Cambridge: Cambridge University Press.

Weigle, S. C. (2004). Integrating reading and writing in a competency test for non-native speakers of English. *Assessing Writing, 9*(1), 27–55.

Weir, C. J. (2005). *Language testing and validation*. Houndmills, Basingstoke: Palgrave Macmillan.

Rebuilding the Tower of Babel? Promises and Problems of World Englishes for Writing Assessment

Esmat Babaii

1   Introduction

Writing in a second/foreign language has proved to be an intricate phenomenon to deal with. As early as the 1960s, language educators, most notably Kaplan (1966), recognized that writing proficiency goes beyond the mastery of formal properties of language, and that writing assessment could not be limited to checking grammatical accuracy and appropriate lexical choice (cf. Huot, 1990; Weigle, 2002). Analyzing rhetorical organization of the paragraphs written by a number of ESL students with diverse cultural and L1 backgrounds, Kaplan (1966, 1976) found recurring patterns alien to the English style and was quick to ascribe the differences to different culturally induced thought patterns. He depicted the English paragraph as a linear progression from topic sentence to supporting statements ending in conclusion, and other languages somehow 'deviating' from the line: zigzag (Semitic languages),

---

E. Babaii (✉)
Kharazmi University, Tehran, Iran

circular (Oriental Languages)or digressive (Romance Languages). Influenced by the Sapir–Whorf hypothesis, which assumes speakers of different languages have different world views and thought patterns (Werner, 1997), Kaplan (1976) set forth the concept of 'contrastive rhetoric'(CR) predicating upon the assumption that 'the rhetorical patterns of a language are unique, culturally coded phenomena which in intercultural communication situations can cause *blockages*' (p. 12). Describing non-English native language, and native culture for that matter, as 'blockage', 'interference' and a source of 'negative transfer' was, in fact, in line with an essentialist, normative view dominant in that era when post-structuralism had no place in ELT scholarship.

Following the trail of Kaplan's CR model, several studies documented notable rhetorical differences among diverse languages (see Silva, 1993, for a detailed review). At the same time, Kaplan's study was widely criticized, not so much for its methodology and findings but for its implications which could lead to marginalization of non-Anglo-American cultures and rhetorical traditions (e.g., Kubota, 1999, 2001; Leki, 1991; Severino, 1993; see Connor, 1996, 2002 for defense and clarification). To be more precise, many critics of CR were (and are) concerned about what might be called the treatment of 'difference' as 'deficit', or 'diversity-as-problem' orientation in Jenkins' (2014, p. 76) words, that does not tolerate any rhetorical deviation from the English rhetoric—which enjoys the privilege of being the international standard of (written) communication. According to this mindset, the writers coming from other cultural backgrounds are expected to follow Anglophone rhetoric if they want their works to be understood and appreciated on a large scale.

Consistent with this mentality, Heard (2016) believes that modern science owes its advancement to the linear, clear and non-digressive rhetorical organization advocated by seventeenth-century English scholars like Thomas Sprat who explained the philosophy behind this style of writing as:

> … a constant resolution, to reject all the *amplifications, digressions*, and *swellings* of style . . . a close, naked, *natural* way of speaking; positive expressions, *clear sense, a native easiness*: bringing all things as near *the*

mathematical plainness, as they can: and preferring the language of artisans, countrymen, and merchants, before that of wits, or scholars. (Sprat, 1667, p. 113, cited in Heard, 2016, p. 5; emphasis mine).

Note that the positive and negative adjectives used in this quotation resonate with the descriptors used by many contemporary academic gatekeepers for describing English and non-English discourse, respectively. While most educators nowadays may not openly subscribe to this ardent defence of the English rhetoric, the (academic) written works of non-natives are still negatively evaluated with certain descriptors reminiscent of Sprat's criteria of writing unacceptability: 'discontinuity in the argumentative process', 'lack of consistency', 'failure to convincingly introduce, link or conclude various key elements in several parts of the demonstration' (see Sionis, 1995, p. 101). In fact, as Flowerdew (1999, p. 127) mentions, in evaluating non-native (scholarly) writings, global problems such as 'textual organization', 'structuring of argument' and 'interference of different cultural views' receive more serious penalties than local grammatical problems. Discussing culture-based rhetorical differences between English and Finnish academic writing, Mauranen (1993) reminds us that Finnish writers tend to appear 'less convincing', 'illogical' and 'incoherent' to their foreign, especially Anglo-American colleagues. As a result, she maintains, Finnish scholars' control over their communicative output can be reduced and 'their rhetorical intentions may fall short of the target despite their best efforts' (p. 171). Along the same line, Melliti (2019) describes how challenging it is for the researchers in the Middle East and North Africa (MENA) region to publish in English-speaking academic journals. Fifty-two per cent of MENA researchers participating in his study revealed they had received comments from the editors noting 'organizational problems' in their writings.

Similar unfortunate results may plague other non-native professionals who are somehow involved with writing in English. Kasztalska (2019), for instance, observes that non-native International Teaching Assistants (ITAs) struggle with linguistic insecurity in English composition classes. Many ITAs, as non-native composition teachers, worry about their 'accented writing' and despite years of education, feel their writing is not good enough, especially for teaching writing to English native students and they are afraid of being challenged and rejected by their students. Addressing non-native student writing, Stambouli and Belmekki (2019) refer to overall dissatisfaction with students' incoherent essay writing in the Algerian context. With no postulates about the possible sources of incoherence, they suggest the explicit teaching of metacognitive strategies to rectify the problem.

On the other hand, citing Lisle and Mano (1997), Y. Kachru (2001) mentions several cultural norms where adhering to English linear organizational patterns is not considered an advantage. For example, Chinese students are expected to devote their opening paragraph to a general fact, not to topic development or that Arabic writers value verbal art and emotional impact more than factual evidence when examining persuasive power of one's writing. In a similar vein, Asante (1987, p. 51) considers indirection as a dominant African writing strategy: '[in African rhetoric] the person who gets directly to the issue is said to have little imagination and even less flair for rhetorical style'.

The above-mentioned observations imply that non-native English writing is rarely treated favourably when the yardstick is the English linear organizational pattern but they say little about the unfortunate consequences of assessment of non-native writings in the Anglo-American context, be it failing high-stakes writing examinations, or rejection of one's submission to an Anglophone academic journal. In fact, as Y. Kachru (2001, p. 59) observes:

> There are numerous references to the conventions of writing in Arabic, Chinese, Japanese, Persian and other languages, and accounts of African American and Native American oral traditions of discourse, but the recommendation is the same: the ELT profession has to uphold the ideal of direct, linear progression of ideas in academic writing.

As discussed by Canagarajah (2006), there seems to be a tacit agreement to keep WE for speaking and local transactions, and not for writing and international communication. A non-native's rhetorical heritage is mostly seen as something embarrassing and discreditable to be exposed only in one's own cultural circles. Even the cases of WE divergences

Canagarajah (2006) encourages, like 'can be able to' used by (East)Asian-English users, include micro-level WE codes which can hardly affect the readers/raters' judgement, especially if highlighted in a footnote or through a parenthetical explanation. Rhetorical deviations, however, tend to be treated by English natives as 'incoherence', 'lack of focus', etc., which happens to be more detrimental to the overall evaluation of non-native writings and can hardly be remedied through footnoting or other authorial techniques.

In what follows, I shall try to examine the necessity as well as feasibility of accommodating WE in writing assessment. To do this, I will first problematize current writing assessment scales for remaining obscure about the criteria used for evaluating text generation ability of non-native English users and, in doing so, letting subjectivity creep into the assessment procedure. I will also attempt to demonstrate that through presupposing an idealized native speaker/writer as the perfect norm of performance, the rating schemes leave no room for other non-English rhetorical traditions to survive as legitimate non-standard varieties. I will end the chapter by further inspection of possible outcomes of conservative and radical positions towards the treatment of WE in writing assessment.

2 Literature Review

Writing assessment in what is commonly referred to as 'open-ended essay tests' or 'direct tests of writing' (Huot, 1990; Weir, 2005) requires careful advance planning regarding two major issues: (a) writing prompt(s), to which the test takers are expected to provide an essay- or paragraph-long response; and (b) rating criteria that specify how the test takers' written production is to be assessed. Due to the determining role of human agency in dealing with the above-mentioned issues, assessing writing is prone to the exercise of constructor/rater's subjective power and preferences. As such, writing assessment is interwoven with certain degrees of subjectivity the nature of which will be explained in what follows.

2.1 Subjectivity in Selecting Writing Prompts

It appears that subjectivity in choosing writing prompts is not conceived of as a serious issue in language testing. Weir (2005), for instance, considers providing the 'input' or the 'stimulus' a relatively easy task since 'the topics tend to be *very general* and rely heavily on the candidate providing the context, either through *background* or *cultural knowledge*, or *imagination*' (p. 164, emphasis mine). In fact, prompt selection does seem to be a straightforward task for the test constructor but it may not be so easy for the test taker to handle the presented topic. As Weir (2005) rightly reminds us, test takers tend to approach the writing task differently. Let us ponder over the nature of this differential performance. Adopting a culturally informed perspective, I assume that there may be a notable difference between the candidates who, perhaps due to sharing similar worldviews and life experiences with the test constructor(s), can make active use of their storage of *cultural background knowledge* and those who are deprived from this asset and need to resort to their *imagination* and creativity. In line with this concern, Jennings, Fox, Graves and Shohamy (1999, p. 426) speak of 'topic effect' in topic-based tests of language proficiency including the writing module of high-stakes standardized test batteries and consider it a threat to validity through introducing construct-irrelevant variance.

To further examine the issue, we may also ask how 'general' a general topic can be. For example, certain topics, such as 'paternity leave', 'genetically modified food ingredients', 'ethical questions in cloning' or 'access to abortion as a constitutional right' which can be mundane social issues of general interest in many industrialized countries, and thus, tend to be part of the background knowledge of an average European citizen, might seem quite far-fetched and an infrequently discussed theme to think (and write) about for a sizeable population in Asia and Africa. Although providing a 'choice' among a number of writing prompts seems to reduce the resulting bias and discrimination, it may also make comparison of written performance more difficult for the raters (Weir, 2005) especially if adopting a different choice would require further choices regarding the text type, register and style. In short, the subjectivity inherent in the selection of writing prompts is not a trivial issue as it can potentially influence validity in an undesirable way. Nevertheless, in comparison to the next stage, writing prompt subjectivity can be rectified fairly well. Subjectivity in rating procedure is of a different nature and appears more complicated to deal with. It is also more pertinent to the main concern of this paper, i.e. the treatment of WE in language assessment.

2.2 Subjectivity in Rating Writing Samples

Weigle (2002, p. 110) discusses three types of rating scales in the writing assessment literature: *primary trait*, *holistic* and *analytic* scales. As she mentions, the *primary trait* scale is principally used in the American educational system to 'understand how well students can write within a narrowly defined range of discourse' such as a congratulatory letter or a persuasive essay. This scale which requires detailed specifications of several expected achievement goals for each type of writing is rarely used in second language writing assessment.

In *holistic* scoring, a single score is assigned to the test taker's written text 'based on the overall impression' the text may leave on the rater. As Weigle (2002, p. 112) states:

> In a typical holistic scoring session, each script [or text] is read quickly and then judged against a rating scale, or scoring rubric, that outlines the scoring criteria.

She believes that the mere 'existence of a scoring rubric' makes this type of rating more reliable than 'general impression marking'. However, it is difficult to imagine how 'overall impression' and 'explicit criteria' team up in the mind of the rater, especially in a quick reading. Holistic rating is praised for its practicality but criticized for its little diagnostic value as well as its being influenced by construct-irrelevant factors such as length and handwriting (cf. Weigle, 2002).

Here, I would add the 'rater's worldview' and 'cultural preferences' to the list of the factors (unduly) affecting the rating process. To clarify this point, let us consider these two writing prompts I encountered on a TOEFL preparation website: TOEFL Resources shown in Fig. 1.

> **Prompt (A)**
>
> Do you agree or disagree with the following statement? "When people succeed, it is entirely because of hard work. Luck has nothing to do with their success." Use specific reasons and examples to explain your position.
>
> **Prompt (B)**
>
> Neighbors are the people who live near us. In your opinion, what type of neighbor is the best to have?
>
> -someone who is quiet
> -someone who we are similar to
> -someone who is supportive

Fig. 1 Samples of writing prompts

The prompts look quite 'general' and they do not appear to sensitize any particular religious, ethnic or national community. However, some possible test takers' responses to these innocuous topics may trigger communication misfire. Let us imagine a hypothetical situation where an English native speaker is rating an essay written by a non-native Middle-Eastern test taker with religious beliefs forming his/her cultural schema. Regarding prompt (A), if the test taker adheres to common Islamic notions of 'God's willing' and 'kismet' (and not luck, of course), he/she may not give the lion's share to 'hard work' and would condition one's success to the will of God. The rater, say, with a secular mentality, may see the argument in favor of fatalism and may resent the whole line of reasoning. As a result, the negative emotional reaction might cloud the rater's rational decision making, ending in an unfair evaluation. That is, the mismatch between writer's and rater's attitude/position, as an instance of construct-irrelevant factor, may impede impartial scoring. Some testing experts would dismiss this situation as highly improbable, especially in the case of trained raters, but I have already challenged the myth of impersonality in other types of academic evaluations (cf. Babaii, 2011). There is no reason to assume writing assessment is an exception.

In the case of prompt (B), most Eastern cultures, unlike Western cultures, have a traditional tendency towards 'collectivism' (Hofstede, 2001) which values an individual's contribution and/or conformity to the society more than his/her independence. As such, an Eastern test taker, especially one supporting the traditions, would prefer a 'supportive' neighbour and someone with 'similar' characteristics to a 'quiet' one. At first, it may seem a matter of personal preference, but when the test taker starts elaborating on the reasons behind the choice, cultural disparities surface and the essay may end up criticizing individualist culture and people. Then, it would be too much to expect the individualist native speaker to stick to cold reason and be indifferent to the negative tone of the passage. I used these two (a bit exaggerated) examples to demonstrate that the nature of rater–writer interaction seems a somehow neglected part of writing assessment in the literature and that we need to be cognizant of possible areas of miscommunication and their potential effects on the fairness of the assessment procedure.

Unfortunately, the *analytic* scale, the third type of rating, is not immune to the above-mentioned complications, either. Analytic scoring, which is described as the procedure through which texts are rated 'on several aspects of writing, [...] such as content, organization, cohesion, register, vocabulary, grammar or mechanics' (Weigle, 2002, p. 114), employs more systematic and detailed specifications of assessment criteria and is much more favored than *holistic* scale among testing scholars. However, a brief comparison of available rating schemes reveals that defining the construct of L2 writing proficiency has been a controversial issue and scale developers have mostly relied on their intuition (Fulcher, 2003) which can seriously undermine the construct validity of writing assessment. In fact, the most notable commonality among all the scales is devoting a fraction of the score to the accurate use of surface-level formal features like grammar, vocabulary and mechanics of writing, to which objective measurement can be fairly applied. Interestingly, this is the area of little contribution to the overall score (Knoch, 2011; Weigle, 2002; Weir, 2005). The scales usually assign bigger shares to other features like content, organization, coherence and the like. Table 1 provides a brief account of a number of scales proposed by some testing specialists and/or

Table 1 Main assessment criteria of some widely used writing scales

Jacobs et al. (1981)	Content
	Organization
	Vocabulary
	Language use
	Mechanics
Weir (1988)	Relevance and adequacy of content
Test in English for Educational Purposes (TEEP)	Compositional organization
	Cohesion
	Adequacy of vocabulary for purpose
	Grammar
	Mechanical accuracy I (punctuation)
	Mechanical accuracy II (spelling)
Hamp-Lyons (1990)	Ideas and arguments
Michigan Writing Assessment Scoring Guide	Rhetorical features
	Language control
International English Language Testing System (IELTS) (cited in Hawkey & Barker, 2004)	Format and register
	Organization
	Cohesion
	Structure and vocabulary range
	Accuracy
	Task fulfillment
	Effect on reader
	Communicative quality
Hawkey & Barker (2004)	Sophistication of language
	Organization and cohesion
	Accuracy
Knoch (2011)	Accuracy
	Fluency
	Complexity
	Mechanics
	Cohesion
	Coherence
	Reader/writer interaction
	Content

used by well-known testing organizations. Note that I have not included the descriptors of the criteria due to space constraints.

As it can be observed, each scheme considers 'what' (the content) and 'how' (the organization) of the writing task. Of course, Knoch (2011) seems somehow ambivalent about the inclusion of 'content' as one of the criteria, reasoning that:

It can, of course, be argued that content is not part of language ability, but rather a cognitive aspect which is unrelated to language. However, it seems that raters see content as an important aspect of writing assessment. (p. 91)

I believe this ambivalence is quite understandable: on the one hand, 'content' of a message carries its pragmatic force and communicative value. It is, in fact, the reason why we read a written piece. On the other hand, although it involves the use of language exponents, it goes beyond the language. It is the ingredient of a message to which we 'respond' cognitively and emotionally. As I discussed earlier, it may not be easy for a reader/rater to appreciate the 'content' of an essay if he/she finds it challenging and attacking one's viewpoints. And sharp cultural differences between rater and writer may sometimes lead to such a situation. The reality of rater–writer interaction is explicitly acknowledged by IELTS and Cambridge ESOL rating schemes as 'effect on reader', though the nature of which is kept obscure and subjective (cf. Hawkey & Barker, 2004). Most likely, the scheme developers only thought about a 'desirable effect on reader', and not an undesirable one. At any rate, the problem can be partially handled by avoiding culturally loaded and sensitive topics. However, the issues related to the 'how' of presenting ideas are here to stay.

In the introduction of this chapter, I talked about the early days of contrastive rhetoric and the way other languages and their rhetorical organizations were compared to English and that there was a tacit treatment of the observed 'differences' as 'deficits'. Writing assessment is the domain where this treatment is not just a matter of opinion. Assessment, like it or not, involves the exercise of the assessor's power in determining who passes and who fails. Adopting what I may call a 'difference as deficit' frame of thought (cf. Jenkins, 2014), English native raters would probably underrate the writing tasks produced by non-natives—who do not conform to English rhetorical organization—using labels, such as: 'lacking rhetorical control', 'hard to recognize the overall shape of the essay' (Michigan Writing Assessment, Level 2; Weigle, 2002, p. 119), 'inadequate control of organizational skills' (TEEP, Level 2; Weigle, 2002, p. 117) or 'lacking logical sequencing and development' (Jacobs, et al.'s scheme, grade 10–13; Weigle, 2002, p. 116). Unfortunately, I do not have access to the writing module database of international standardized test batteries to systematically examine my conjecture. However, in a brief account of notable writing problems of EFL students in several Arab countries, Ahmed (2019) mentions qualities such as 'lack of cohesion', 'lack of coherence and organization', and 'ineffective composing strategies' (p. 13) which sound similar to the descriptors of low-level 'organizational skills' in the writing assessment schemes in Table 1.

The 'difference as deficit' approach undervalues the non-native writing pieces that would be considered quite acceptable in their domestic setting. As an example, in many traditional Persian written texts, it was a common practice to entertain narrative, in the form of a fable or anecdote, into expository texts including argumentative and didactic essays. The narrative was used as a point of reference to buttress the main argument. I suppose this technique, which is still used by some Iranian contemporary non-fiction writers and journalists, may seem as 'digression', 'beating around the bush' or a 'lack of rhetorical control' to Anglophone readers/raters. As such, it would be wise for me, as an Iranian English user, to avoid 'sounding' Persian in my English writings! In the same vein, it is not surprising to find that in most Iranian language centers, where the majority of learners aim at getting an international English proficiency certificate, both learners and teachers are strongly discouraged from practicing Iranian identity through using Persianate forms and discourse conventions (Elahi Shirvan, Karahan, & Taherian, 2015). Weber (2019) provides another relevant example from an Arabic context, i.e. Qatar, where Arab students, raised in a 'high context' cultural setting in which 'unsaid and unwritten norms are communicated in subtle ways such as the social situation, dress, age, etc.' (p. 140), tend to skip needed background information and further explications of ideas because they take them as shared knowledge. As such, their writings may not seem sufficiently informative and persuasive to English native raters.

The fact is that international standardized tests of English proficiency explicitly or implicitly consider native-like proficiency as the highest level of achievement (cf. Jenkins & Leung, 2013). This is incongruent with the criterion of 'intelligibility' (Jenkins, 2008) which is obviously more tolerant towards deviations from the native speaker standard. As noted by Jenkins and Leung (2013), these tests are:

> 'international' in the sense of being *used* (marketed and administered) internationally rather than in the sense of reflecting international *use* (the diverse ways in which English is used internationally (p. 97, emphasis in the original)

These 'international' examinations adopt an 'idealized' educated native speaker's competence (Davies, 2013) as a gold standard of ultimate attainment in English language proficiency, a norm that does not reflect the reality of current use of English as an international language. The reality pictures diverse groups of non-native speakers' everyday communication through English without expecting native-speaker perfection on the part of their interlocutors. Nevertheless, native-speaker-oriented international test constructors, as gatekeepers in the ELT enterprise, set unattainable targets for huge numbers of non-native users of English who need an English proficiency certificate for educational and occupational purposes or for immigration and citizenship application. Although Brown (2014) wishes to downplay the detrimental impact of native speakerism in international testing by highlighting the existence of other measures of proficiency like portfolios, dynamic assessment and the like, we should not forget that none of these reasonably valid measures go beyond classroom or institutional utility. That is, more often than not, the fate of the test takers depends on their performance on a one-shot administration of the internationally recognized examination like IELTS, TOEFL or Cambridge ESOL test batteries. The sad fact in many EFL contexts is that very few test takers get the passing score through reaching native-like proficiency. A large majority of test takers approach the task through trial and error or bypass the tests objectives with the help of test-wiseness and test-taking techniques taught in preparation courses. For these EFL users, an international test is just a hurdle to clear, not an incentive to learn the English language.

3 Native Speakerism in Writing Assessment: Good, Bad, Ugly

Designating native speaker performance as the standard of writing proficiency, or native speakerism, so to say, is the major obstacle for accommodating WE in writing assessment. Practicing this doctrine, nevertheless, is not simply an irrational whim of a select few native speakerist authorities enjoying veto power in testing organizations. Available research documents non-native teachers' and learners' reluctance to adopt their own localized version of English for pedagogical purposes. Reference can be made to Taylor (2006), reporting on German EFL learners' preferences for native-like variety, and Wang (2015) demonstrating the unpopularity of China English for formal use among Chinese EFL learners and teachers (to cite but a few). As Canagarajah (2006) has reminded us, even those TESOL scholars (e.g., Barbour, 2002; Widdowson, 1993) who support diverse varieties of English, recommend keeping local varieties for informal, intra-community transactions and employing standard, native variety for formal, international communication. In a word, an overnight introduction of WE to language tests tends to induce overwhelming adverse reactions on the part of potentially all stakeholders, which, by itself, can threaten the (face) validity of the assessment procedure. Therefore, it is not difficult to understand why language testing has adhered to conservatism when it comes to introducing WE to test design (see Brown, 2014; Elder & Harding, 2008). Consistent with Elder and Harding's (2008) concerns, Brown (2014) mentions several constraints for WE inclusion such as stakeholder's preference for Standard English along with the problem of sampling appropriate tasks, general and inclusive enough to measure English proficiency of heterogeneous groups of non-standard variety users in a valid and unbiased way.

To get to the root of stakeholders' negative attitudes towards the use of WE for pedagogy and assessment, we need to go beyond the realm of testing scholarship and search the history of English promotion at the expense of local languages during the colonial period (Phillipson, 2011, 2016). The process, as Phillipson (2011) points out, tended to be 'subtractive', eliminating the role of local languages in education and other prestigious social institutions and leading to 'unequal rights' for speakers of different languages (p. 443). Allocating the inferior position to non-Anglophone languages has been a longitudinal course of action aiming at depicting English dominance as natural to the dominated groups. The deep, long-lasting effects of experiencing centuries of dominance cannot be easily undone. As Kumaravadivelu (2016, p. 79) puts it:

> Coloniality has survived colonialism not only in the economic, social, and cultural arena but also in academia—in books, in the criteria for academic performance, and in the self-image of subaltern intellectuals.

This is not to say that the fate of WE testing is sealed. On the contrary, in our teacher education and testing programs, we need to raise students' and would-be teachers' awareness regarding the philosophy and mission of WE and encourage them to think about possible ways to teach and test through WE. Hopefully, the prospects for WE tests will be brighter than its present status and it will be able to gain stakeholders' support.

The sampling issue of WE tests, however, needs extensive research to provide empirical evidence in support of their validity as well as fairness. The first step, as McCallum (2019) recommends, can be collecting diverse WE spoken and written corpora, such as those used in the MENA region, and compare different varieties with one another. Without reliable corpus-based information, we cannot make sure if some particular non-standard varieties such as Black English Vernacular or Indian English are used as input in, say, listening or reading tasks, this selection will not lead to the disadvantage of those who are not practicing these varieties like MENA region language learners. Decades ago, Davidson and Lowenberg (1996, cited in Brown, 2014, p. 6) warned about the sampling dilemma for WE testing:

> The general problem can be put thus: how can English tests be best designed to accommodate varietal differences of Englishes around the world? That is, if an English test developed and normed in Variety X is subsequently used in a country which speaks Variety Y, is the X-test therefore inappropriate in the country where Variety Y is spoken? (p. 1)

Regrettably, we seem to witness little progress in tackling this issue. Therefore, to do justice to native-speaker-oriented assessment, we can consider trouble-free sampling as its merit; the *Good* aspect of using the native model. Indeed, looking through an optimistic lens, establishing Standard English as a common norm has its own benefits: As the saying goes, a rule isn't unfair if it applies to everyone. Native-speakerism, just like an equal-opportunity tyrant, prevents rebuilding a postmodern Tower of Babel. So, WE test advocates should think about fair replacements of the old, familiar norm to avoid the chaos resulting from competition among non-standard varieties.

It is fortunate, however, that assessing writing while catering for WE varieties, is not entangled with the sampling issue because the WE variety is provided by the test takers, not the test constructors. That is, the 'response' to the 'writing prompt'—in the form of a paragraph or an essay—can be described as a variant of WE. As such, I suspect accommodating WE in writing assessment does not require a drastic shift in test design but needs more understanding and acceptance of WE on the part of the raters. Basically, if the raters agree to recognize non-English rhetorical traditions as legitimate ways of expressing one's ideas and writing craft, the *Bad* and the *Ugly* consequences of practicing the native model in writing might be minimized to a great extent.

I think the *Bad* side of sticking to the native speaker norm comes into view when non-native test takers fail to or are unwilling to conform to the norm and its rhetoric. Subsequently, they receive punishment in the form of failing or a low score. The undesirable feedback forces them to think about the solution that most writing instructors provide: Think in English! Doing so, takes more than learning English rhetorical patterns. That is to say, the successful non-natives by the end of the day are those who learn self-censorship in expressing their culture-bound ideas and values since native speakerism in not just about the dominance of the English language but also about the supremacy of Anglo-American cultural values. Drudging along their bumpy road of progress in English writing, the non-native learners learn to dismiss their L1 background as an extra load. And at this time, the *Ugly* shows up.

The *Ugly* side of native-oriented writing assessment, in fact, concerns its washback for non-English rhetorical diversity. Elsewhere, in a co-authored paper (Babaii & Ramazani, 2017), I have talked about the reverse transfer of English rhetorical organization to L1 writing of Iranian TEFL graduates where we found a considerable degree of 'Englishness' in the Persian essays of those who had been studying English for a number of years as compared to those who were majoring in Persian literature. This finding, in line with Hirose (2003), who documented the transfer of English rhetoric to L1 writing of Japanese EFL students, warns about the early signs of the disappearance of rhetorical diversity. In fact, such studies demonstrate the palpability of the discursive threat of the global spread of English. Swales (1997) cautioned against this phenomenon by using 'English as Tyrannosaurus Rex' metaphor for the title of his article in *World Englishes*. Here, I earnestly invite EFL teachers, testers and students to consider this issue in the context of consequential validity of writing modules in international standardized tests. We are all responsible to prevent this great loss before it is too late.

4 Implications for the Context and Conclusion

In this chapter, I tried to discuss the feasibility as well as necessity of incorporating WE into the design of writing tests from different perspectives. All said, deciding to include WE in the test design is not an easy, once-for-all decision. Far from being a simple ideological choice on the part of test constructors, it requires solid data obtained through the description of Target Language Use (TLU) domain of the test along with the investigation of the stakeholders' perceptions and needs. A systematic description of the TLU which is defined as the 'situation or context in which the test taker will be using the language outside of the test itself' (Bachman & Palmer, 1996, p. 18) would involve detailed accounts of the genres and text types a given population of English users will be expected to produce as well as the discourse community in which the described written productions will be used and judged on. Without sufficient research-based evidence of the communication potentials of certain

WE varieties chosen to be used in receptive tests, we cannot justify the fairness and validity of our measurement, especially for users of a different variety. As for productive tests, we should develop standards to differentiate between deviations due to adopting a given non-English rhetorical pattern and those due to insufficient command of English. We also need to investigate the characteristics of the people who will be potentially involved with the process of text production and reception. The criteria of appropriateness we set for test task A which is expected to be used under X circumstances might be different from those used for task B under Y purposes and with different stakeholders. Any ad hoc attempt to replace Standard English by a local variety, without these serious considerations, tends to have undesirable consequences within and beyond the language testing community.

As discussed before, WE inclusion is not just a testing issue. To find its place in testing, WE needs to be introduced and justified in ELT circles, that is, ELT practitioners and students may need to examine essentialist doctrines that have presided over the field since its inauguration. As demonstrated by Kasztalska (2019), ELT non-native teachers' self-esteem increased once they were introduced to the tenets of WE. This implies that resistance against the inclusion of WE in assessment may be reduced through awareness-raising and systematic training of teachers, testers and students.

This chapter, with its heavy focus on examining the feasibility of accommodating WE in international English tests, has not offered any solution and/or recommendation with regard to WE for classroom assessment. This, by no means, implies the insignificance of the latter. Vigorous research should address different dimensions of WE for classroom assessment, ranging from the washback effects of high-stakes tests on teaching and assessing WE writing samples in classroom settings to teachers' and students' readiness for, as well as their concerns and preferences regarding WE-based writing tests. Needless to say, perhaps, all stakeholders should have their voice in the WE testing scholarship.

References

Ahmed, A. (2019). Assessment of EFL writing in some Arab world university contexts: Issues and challenges. In A. Ahmed & H. Abouabdelkader (Eds.), *Assessing EFL writing in the 21st century Arab world: Revealing the unknown*, (pp. 1–20). New York: Palgrave Macmillan.

Asante, M. (1987). *The Afrocentric idea*. Philadelphia, PA: Temple University Press.

Babaii, E. (2011). Hard science, hard talk? The study of negative comments in physics book reviews. In F. Salager-Meyer & B. Lewin (Eds.), *Crossed words: Criticism in scholarly writing* (pp. 55–78). Frankfurt: Peter Lang Publishers.

Babaii, E., & Ramazani, K. (2017). Reverse transfer: Exploring the effects of foreign language rhetorical patterns on L1 writing performance of Iranian EFL learners. *RELC Journal, 48*(3), 341–356.

Bachman, L., & Palmer, A. (1996). *Language testing in practice*. Oxford: Oxford University Press.

Barbour, S. (2002). Language, nationalism, and globalism: Educational consequences of changing patterns of language use. In P. Gubbins & M. Holt (Eds.), *Beyond boundaries: Language and identity in contemporary Europe* (pp. 11–18). Clevedon, UK: Multilingual Matters.

Brown, J. D. (2014). The future of world Englishes in language testing. *Language Assessment Quarterly, 11*(1), 5–26.

Canagarajah, S. (2006). The place of world Englishes in composition: Pluralization continued. *College Composition and Communication, 57*(4), 586–619.

Connor, U. (1996). *Contrastive rhetoric: Interdisciplinary approaches in cross-cultural writing*. Cambridge: Cambridge University Press.

Connor, U. (2002). New directions in contrastive rhetoric. *TESOL Quarterly, 36*(4), 493–510.

Davidson, F., & Lowenberg, P. (1996, December). *Language testing and World Englishes: A proposed research agenda*. Paper presented at the 3rd Conference of the International Association of World Englishes, Honolulu, HI.

Davies, A. (2013). *Native speakers and native users: Loss and gain*. Cambridge: Cambridge University Press.

Elahi Shirvan, M., Karahan, P., & Taherian, T. (2015, May). *Intelligibility, comprehensibility, and interpretability overshadowed by linguistic insecurity: A case of Persian English*. Paper presented at the 21st Conference of the International Association for World Englishes (IAWE). Istanbul, Turkey.

Elder, C., & Harding, L. (2008). Language testing and English as an international language: Constraints and contributions. *Australian Review of Applied Linguistics, 31,* 34.1–34.11.

Flowerdew, J. (1999). Writing for scholarly publication in English: The case of Hong Kong. *Journal of Second Language Writing, 8,* 123–145.

Fulcher, G. (2003). *Testing second language speaking.* London: Pearson Longman.

Hamp-Lyons, L. (1990). Second language writing: Assessment issues. In B. Kroll (Ed.), *Second language writing: Research insights for the classroom* (pp. 69–87). Cambridge: Cambridge University Press.

Hawkey, R., & Barker, F. (2004). Developing a common scale for the assessment of writing. *Assessing Writing, 9*(2), 122–159.

Heard, S. (2016). *The scientist's guide to writing.* Princeton & Oxford: Princeton University Press.

Hirose, K. (2003). Comparing L1 and L2 organizational patterns in the argumentative writing of Japanese EFL students. *Journal of Second Language Writing, 12,* 181–209.

Hofstede, G. (2001). *Culture's consequences: Comparing values, behaviors, institutions and organizations across nations* (2nd ed.). London: Sage Publications.

Huot, B. (1990). The literature of direct writing assessment: Major concerns and prevailing trends. *Review of Educational Research, 60,* 237–263.

Jacobs, H., Zingraf, S., Wormuth, D., Hartfiel, V., & Hughey, J. (1981). *Testing ESL composition: A practical approach.* Rowley, MA: Newbury House.

Jenkins, J. (2008). *English as a lingua franca.* Retrieved July 20, 2019, from http://www.jacet.org/2008convention/JACET2008_keynote_jenkins.pdf.

Jenkins, J. (2014). *English as a lingua franca in the international university: The politics of academic English language policy.* New York, NY: Routledge.

Jenkins, J., & Leung, C. (2013). English as a lingua franca. In A. Kunnan (Ed.), *The companion in language assessment (Vol. IV): Assessment around the world* (pp. 95–104). New York, NY: Wiley.

Jenkins, J., & Leung, C. (2019). From mythical 'standard' to standard reality: The need for alternatives to standardized English language tests. *Language Teaching, 52*(1), 86–110.

Jennings, M., Fox, J., Graves, B., & Shohamy, E. (1999). The test-takers' choice: An investigation of the effect of topic on language-test performance. *Language Testing, 16,* 426–456.

Kachru, Y. (2001). World Englishes and rhetoric across cultures. *Asian Englishes, 4,* 54–71.

Kaplan, R. (1966). Cultural thought patterns in intercultural education. *Language Learning, 16,* 1–20.

Kaplan, R. (1976). A further note on contrastive rhetoric. *Communication Quarterly, 24*(2), 12–19.

Kasztalska, A. (2019). International teaching assistants in the composition classroom: From world Englishes to translingualism and beyond. *Journal of Language, Identity & Education, 18,* 161–175.

Knoch, U. (2011). Rating scales for diagnostic assessment of writing: What should they look like and where should the criteria come from? *Assessing Writing, 16,* 81–96.

Kubota, R. (1999). Japanese culture constructed by discourses: Implications for applied linguistics research and English language teaching. *TESOL Quarterly, 33,* 9–35.

Kubota, R. (2001). Discursive construction of the images of U.S. classrooms. *TESOL Quarterly, 35,* 9–38.

Kumaravadivelu, B. (2016). The decolonial option in English teaching: Can the subaltern act? *TESOL Quarterly, 50,* 66–85.

Leki, I. (1991). Twenty-five years of contrastive rhetoric: Text analysis and writing pedagogies. *TESOL Quarterly, 25,* 123–143.

Lisle, B., &Mano, S. (1997). Embracing the multicultural rhetoric. In C. Severino., J. C. Guerra., & J. E. Butler (Eds.), Writing in multicultural settings (pp. 12–26). New York: The Modern Language Association of America.

Mauranen, A. (1993). Cultural differences in academic discourse: Problems of a linguistic and cultural minority. In L. Lofman., L. Kurki-Suonio., S. Pellinen., & J. Lehtonen (Eds.), *The competent intercultural communicator* (pp. 157–174). Helsinki: AFinLa Yearbook.

McCallum, L. (2019). Assessing second language proficiency under 'unequal' perspectives: A call for research in the MENA region. In S. Hidri (Ed.), *English language teaching research in the Middle East and North Africa* (pp. 3–28). New York: Palgrave Macmillan.

Melliti, M. (2019). Publish or perish: The research letter genre and non-anglophone scientists' struggle for academic visibility. In S. Hidri (Ed.), *English language teaching research in the Middle East and North Africa* (pp. 225–254). New York, NY: Palgrave Macmillan.

Phillipson, R. (2011). English: From British empire to corporate empire. *Sociolinguistic Studies, 5*(3), 441–464.

Phillipson, R. (2016). Promoting English: Hydras old and new. In P. Bunce., R. Phillipson., V. Rapatahana, & R. Tupas (Eds.), *Why English? Confronting the*

Hydra (pp. 35–46), *Linguistic diversity and language rights, Vol. 13.* Bristol: Multilingual Matters.

Severino, C. (1993). The doodles in context. *The Writing Center Journal, 14*(1), 44–62.

Silva, T. (1993). Toward an understanding of the distinct nature of L2 writing: The ESL research and its implications. *TESOL Quarterly, 27*(4), 657–677.

Sionis, C. (1995). Communication strategies in the writing of scientific research articles by non-native users of English. *English for Specific Purposes, 14,* 99–113.

Sprat, T. (1667). *The history of the royal society of London.* London: J. Martyn.

Stambouli, M., & Belmekki, A. (2019). A proposed metacognitive-based approach to promoting EFL cohesion and coherence in essay writing of Algerian master students. In S. Hidri (Ed.), *English language teaching research in the Middle East and North Africa* (pp. 95–112). New York: Palgrave Macmillan.

Swales, J. (1997). English as Tyrannosaurus Rex. *World Englishes, 16,* 373–382.

Taylor, L. (2006). The changing landscape of English: Implications for language assessment. *ELT Journal, 60,* 51–60.

Wang, W. (2015). Teaching English as an international language in China: Investigating university teachers' and students' attitudes towards China English. *System, 53,* 60–72.

Weber, A. (2019). English writing assessment and the Arabic speaker: A qualitative longitudinal retrospective on Arabic-speaking medical students in Qatar. In A. Ahmed., & H. Abouabdelkader (Eds.), *Assessing EFL writing in the 21st century Arab world: Revealing the unknown* (pp. 137–162). New York, NY: Palgrave Macmillan.

Weigle, S. C. (2002). *Assessing writing.* Cambridge: Cambridge University Press.

Weir, C. (1988). Construct validity. In A. Hughes., D. Porter., & C. Weir (Eds.), *ELT validation project: Proceeding of a conference held to consider the ELTS validation project report.* The British Council and the University of Cambridge Local Examination Syndicate.

Weir, C. (2005). *Language testing and validation: An evidence-based approach.* Hampshire: Palgrave Macmillan.

Werner, O. (1997). Sapir-Whorf hypothesis. In P. Lamarque (Ed.), *Concise encyclopedia of philosophy of language* (pp. 76–83). Oxford: Pergamon Press.

Widdowson, H. (1993). Proper words in proper places. *ELT Journal, 47*(4), 317–329.

Grading and Feedback Connections: Exploring Grading Criteria, Practices and the Provision of Feedback

CAF Profiles of Iranian Writers: What We Learn from Them and Their Limitations

Niloufar Shahmirzadi

1 Introduction

To understand second language writing proficiency, it is important to consider the linguistic development of students (e.g. Crossley, Salsbury, & McNamara, 2012; Ferris, 1994; Frase, Faletti, Ginther, & Grant, 1999; Jarvis, Grant, Bikowski, & Ferris, 2003; Lu, 2011). In practice, the results of research have shown that lexical complexity and grammatical complexity are two main problematic features in students' writing (Crossley et al., 2012; Lu, 2011, 2012). According to scholars (e.g. Crossley & McNamara, 2009; Lu, 2011, 2012; Ortega, 2003; Wolfe-Quintero, Inagaki, & Kim, 1998), these two features are indicators of students' second language writing proficiency, as they may use complex grammar and lexicon differently depending on their levels of proficiency. However, Ferris (1994), Grant and Ginther (2000), Jarvis et al. (2003), and Lu (2011) point out the flaws with CAF measures. Elsewhere, some scholars propose that some factors including genre, topic, planning time,

N. Shahmirzadi (✉)
Islamic Azad University, Tehran, Iran

and instructional topics play crucial roles in second language writing development (Ellis & Yuan, 2004; Lu, 2011; Ortega, 2003; Sotillo, 2000; Way, Joiner, & Seaman, 2000; Yang, Lu, & Weigle, 2015).

First Language (L1) differences can also considerably influence second language writing performance. For example, Persian as the first language of students in the current study includes a writing system which is totally different from the English language. In addition, there are also cognitive processing differences, where the mind mapping processes for idea generation are different in Persian compared to English. In this case, there is a growing body of research on L1 to show differences (Carson & Kuehn, 1992; Edelsky, 1982; Jarvis & Crossley, 2012; Lally, 2000; Lefrançois, 2001; Liu, 2008; Paquot, 2013; Rankin, 2012; Uysal, 2008; van Vuuren, 2013; van Weijen, van den Bergh, Rijlaarsdam, & Sanders, 2009) in terms of idea generation (Lally, 2000), information structure (van Vuuren, 2013), rhetoric patterns (Liu, 2008; Uysal, 2008), syntactic structures (Rankin, 2012), lexical bundles (Paquot, 2013), and most importantly lexical and grammatical complexity (Lefrançois, 2001). As a result, these studies may contribute to the identification of students' first language in their second language writing development (Jarvis & Crossley, 2012; Tetreault, Blanchard, & Cahill, 2013). Despite these intervening variables, the present study has the basic aim of simply using CAF indices to measure vocabulary and grammar, accuracy, and fluency to report the writing performance of students studying Translation at a university in Iran.

2 Literature Review

Over the past decades, there has been a growing number of studies on CAF measurement. Despite providing various definitions and studies for CAF constructs, there is still evidence that various studies with different measures and results coexist (Housen & Kuiken, 2009). These studies involve second language writing development with regard to different CAF measurement scales. However, it remains unclear which measure is appropriate in which context in terms of CAF constructs.

Generally, writing has been analysed by measuring complexity, accuracy, and fluency as a powerful analysis. With regard to extant literature, Ellis and Barkhuizen (2005, p. 139) note that complexity refers to "…elaborated language; relative to proficiency, as language that is at the upper limit of the student's inter-language system connecting with a wider repertoire, which is not fully internalised or automatized by the learner". The manifestation of complexity improves the proficiency of language learners. According to Jarvis (2017), Lexical Diversity (LD) is useful in measuring students' complexity in general and overall ability in particular.

Many scholars report that lexical complexity includes different aspects of use (Read, 2000). This may consist of lexical sophistication and lexical diversity. Elsewhere, Bulte and Housen (2012) believe that LD measures the breadth of L2 lexical items and collocations. LD reveals learners' ability to form complex words and use inflexions which might be lost in the process of lemmatization. Johnson (1944) also notes that types and tokens are two important features in determining lexical diversity. According to Housen and Kuiken (2009), lexical diversity as the subcomponent of linguistic complexity manifests the L2 system. In this regard, Storch and Tapper (2009) have examined L2 writing development in different contexts. They found that following 10 to 14 weeks of instruction the results of students' achievements showed a trade-off in the case of measuring accuracy, and lexical complexity constructs. However, measures of syntactic complexity and fluency revealed no significant change. For the present study, LD and syntactic complexity as important attributes of L2 writing proficiency are reported (Crossley et al., 2012; Lu, 2011, 2012). Syntactic complexity consists of C-units which include "verbal elements with additional elements such as an adverbial clause or an object" (Foster, Tonkyn, & Wigglesworth, 2000, p. 366).

As for accuracy, Schachter and Celce-Murcia (1977, p. 59) define accuracy as being "… about the difficulty in classifying an identified error. Often, an ungrammatical sentence can be corrected in more than one way because the coder does not definitively know what the intention would be". Ellis and Barkhuizen (2005, p. 151) also believe that accuracy is "the learner's suppliance of the specific form in obligatory context, suited for the focused task".

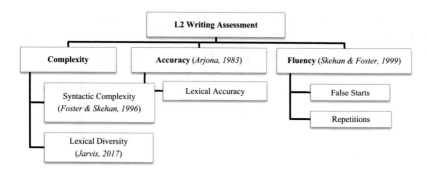

Fig. 1 L2 writing assessment

Fluency is also characterised as writing at a normal rate without any noticeable interruption. According to Chambers (1997), Freed (2000), Guillot (1999), Hilton (2008), Koponen and Riggenbach (2000), and Lennon (1990), fluency determines the eloquence and smoothness without any further interruption in writing. Skehan (1998a) believes that fluency in writing denotes having linear performance. Housen and Kuiken (2009, p. 6) believe that linear performance is "due to the differential development of knowledge analysis and knowledge automatization in L2 acquisition and the ways in which different forms of implicit and explicit knowledge influence the acquisition process". As for the process of producing accurate and complex structures, there is not a linear path unless learners have reached automatization. From the literature reviewed, it is clear that CAF measures focus only on linguistics rather than measuring cognitive factors as well. Figure 1 brings together an overview of CAF constructs that are the focus of the present study.

3 Research Problem

Theoretically, according to Skehan (1998b), utterances are mainly analysed in terms of the Complexity, Accuracy, and Fluency of the target language, of which it is suggested that the writers need to operate much like native speakers. Yet, in Iran little work has been done in the field of assessing written performance objectively through CAF measurement scales, because raters do not have enough writing assessment literacy. Hence, it is often scored in terms of personal taste rather than in terms of concrete criteria in practice. Alderson (2007) and Hulstijn (2007) criticise practitioners since they lack sufficient objective knowledge of validation of data based on the CEFR. To rectify this, appropriate training requires increasing the knowledge of practitioners.

In addition, a few theoretical studies (e.g. Crookes, 1989; Ellis, 1987; Foster & Skehan, 1996; Underwood, 1990) have examined the effects of three aspects on performance analysis (Fangyuan & Ellis, 2003; Ortega, 1999); namely, complexity, accuracy, and fluency on each other. The majority of studies have reviewed lexical richness, syntactic complexity, and accuracy (Ai & Lu, 2013; Biber, Gray, & Staples, 2016; Bulte & Housen, 2014; Chen & Baker, 2016; Jarvis, 2017; Lu & Ai, 2015). It has been proposed that due to their limited processing capacity, test takers may prioritise one aspect of performance over certain other aspects (Anderson, 1995; Fangyuan & Ellis, 2003; Skehan, 1998a; Van Patten, 1990). As for measuring CAF to provide skill diagnostic information in fine-grained detail, Norris and Ortega (2009); Ortega and Iberri-Shea (2005); Verspoor, Lowie and Van Dijk (2008) assert that there is a need in the literature to collect longitudinal information on the writing skill development of test takers. To do so, some research has been conducted to meet the requirements of CAF in the writing skill. For instance, some studies have attempted to reveal the written performance quality (Larsen-Freeman, 2009; Larsen-Freeman & Long, 1991). Vercellotti (2012) calls for revealing different details with respect to tasks applied in the process of writing development. Daller and Xue (2007) conclude that choosing a measurement model in L2 production requires attention in the case of adopting specific tasks. In an Iranian context, Dahmardeh and Shahmirzadi (2016) observe a trade-off in the written performance quality of students in an academic year. Results of these studies in terms of valuing complexity, accuracy, and fluency reveal repetitive changes in the writing of test takers. That is to say, they may obtain different pictures of CAF constructs.

However, care needs to be taken, because there is still not enough literature to report the details of L2 production development objectively. Knoch, Rouhshad, and Storch (2014, p. 13) in a longitudinal study conclude that "institutions could focus on 'training' content lecturers to provide some corrective feedback or to identify students needing support and guide them to develop language courses on campus". As a result, longitudinal performance assessment through CAF does not guarantee consistency of intention to measure the construct thoroughly. The current study is also an attempt to provide a profile of Iranian written performance to report the current status of students' language ability. Few attempts have been made to describe CAF profiles of freshman students in the writing skills of Iranian learners as it is not cost effective to invest in and maintain a rater training programme.

To measure the written performance of students, the following research question is posited:

RQ 1: What different CAF profiles exist across the written exam scripts of Iranian university students?

4 Methodology

4.1 Participants

The participants of the study were freshman students who were studying English Translation at university. All participants had passed the University Entrance Examination, which is a national proficiency test in Iran, and in doing so had entered the university. The test assumed that students had a high enough language level to cope with the demands of undergraduate study. In this research, participants were randomly selected to include 12 female and 10 male students ($N = 22$) with an age range of 18–25.

4.2 Data Collection

The course included peer review that is to say, students were supposed to peer review each other's writing, vocabulary, and grammar during the semester. To analyse participants' final writing production, some elements consisted of grammatical complexity (Foster & Skehan, 1996),

Table 1 Complexity

Syntactic complexity Foster and Skehan (1996)	The proportion of subordination and calculated through separate clauses on C-units Separate Clauses\C – units = X\100
Lexical diversity Jarvis (2017)	Average type–token ratio Average Type and Token\Text Length = X\100

Table 2 Accuracy

Lexical accuracy Arjona (1983)	The inappropriate word choice *Inappropriate equivalents - word types = appropriate equivalents* Appropriate Equivalents\Word Types = X\100

Table 3 Fluency

False starts Skehan and Foster (1999)	The ratio of false started sentences or utterances on T-units False Starts\T -units = X\100
Repetitions Skehan and Foster (1999)	The ratio of repeated words, phrases or clauses without any modification on T-units Repetitions\T -units = X\100

lexical diversity (Jarvis, 2017), lexical accuracy (Arjona, 1983), false starts (Skehan & Foster, 1999), and repetitions (Skehan & Foster, 1999). These CAF measures are shown in Tables 1, 2, and 3. Examples of coding a student's text using these measures is shown in Appendix 1.

5 Results and Discussion

Foster and Skehan's (1996) framework, and Jarvis (2017) were adapted to measure syntactic complexity and lexical diversity, as shown in Table 1. To measure syntactic complexity, C-units first defined as "utterances, for example, words, phrases and sentences, grammatical and ungrammatical, which provide referential or pragmatic meaning" (Pica, Holliday, Lewis, & Morgenthaler, 1989, p. 72) were used. In lexical diversity, the total number of types and tokens was counted, and then types were divided by tokens. At last the result was divided by the text length and estimated in percentage.

To analyse accuracy, the researcher analysed students' writing passages by using Arjona's (1983) lexical accuracy framework as shown in Table 2. Inappropriate word choice refers to those words which are similar to the intended meaning; however, they are still difficult to understand.

Table 3 shows that fluency was measured using Skehan and Foster's measures (1999). In Iran, one of the prominent problems that students suffer from is a lack of sufficient vocabulary. This problem was addressed in repetitions and lack of lexical diversity. Any repetition of a word, phrase or clause in a T-unit was counted as a repetition (hesitation phenomenon) since the equivalent was not used appropriately and test takers resorted to repetitions. To count an average length of a T-unit the definition from Hunt (1965, p. 20) was adopted. According to Hunt (1965, p. 20), a T-unit includes "a main clause with all subordinate clauses attached to it".

Table 4 shows the CAF profiles (in percentages) of Iranian students majoring in English translation.

The findings presented a low level of lexical accuracy, and a number of false starts and repetitions compared to the benchmark of 100 calculated in percentage. As for complexity, students scored high lexical diversity; however, their syntactic complexity was not so rich. To compare this research with Dahmardeh and Shahmirzadi (2016) who longitudinally conducted a study in Iran, the result of the cross-sectional study in L2 writing showed the same outcomes in terms of the writing skill. That is to say, the majority of students were not advanced enough in L2 writing, because many of them have limited experience in academic English writing tests.

Similarly, low scores for lexical accuracy were also reported. The next step was to estimate the fluency of students including false starts and repetitions. The findings revealed a low level of fluency. Regarding syntactic complexity and lexical diversity, students scored higher in lexical diversity than syntactic complexity. As Table 4 shows, those with a high score for lexical diversity scored low in lexical accuracy. Here, CAF constructs of writing were not reported at the same rate. The complex

Table 4 CAF learner profiles

	Lexical accuracy	False starts	Repetitions	Syntactic complexity	Lexical diversity
1	16.66	24	50	5	83.33
2	3.44	48	90	37	44
3	10.81	58	70	28	62.16
4	2.22	74	50	57	80.64
5	23.5	62	68	16	67.85
6	4.54	56	56	48	58
7	10.52	64	44	33.33	60.69
8	17.24	80	20	20	71.42
9	9.83	50	38	54.45	67.97
10	6.08	50	77	9.09	56.71
11	1.09	90	62	16.66	63.1
12	11.04	70	20	30.76	67.47
13	4.31	68	25	66.66	67.30
14	2.15	98	40	25	54.49
15	6.45	56	28	33.33	63.26
16	6.25	44	42	33.36	54.16
17	3.27	20	51	80	65
18	17.30	38	61	0	15
19	15.55	16	49	0	23.21
20	17.14	89	35	100	85.15
21	17.64	67	19	33.33	13.85
22	5.06	73	94	0	26.05

interaction of CAF aspects of writing makes great differences in students' performance.

In sum, the description of test takers' performance showed that they had different CAF profiles suggesting they perceived language structures incompletely. Although this study measured and obtained the different profiles of CAF for each test taker, these profiles are only linguistically informed. The next section of this chapter explores how the implementation of CDA can complement this linguistic information by considering the cognitive aspects of writing performance.

6 Implications for the Context and Conclusion

Cognitive Diagnostic Assessment (CDA) has been used to identify skill mastery or non-mastery profiles of students. These profiles consist of each individual sub-competency which allows for comparing the achievement among different groups of students (George & Robitzsch, 2014). The ultimate goal of CDA is to assess underlying abilities in a real context. In comparison to CAF, which reports the abilities by a single score, CDA reveals the relationship between attributes or traits in a hierarchical manner.

CDA has recently drawn the attention of language testing and measurement scholars in methodological developments (Alderson, 2005; Chen & de la Torre, 2014; Chen, de la Torre, Zhang, 2013; Cui & Leighton, 2009; Hou, la Torre, & Nandakumar, 2014; Jang, 2009; Kunnan & Jang, 2009; Sen & Bradshaw, 2017; Terzi, & Sen, 2019; Wang, Guo, & Bian, 2014). The prominent feature in CDA is its vivid link between learners' competencies in language skills and test characteristics. More specifically, CDA focuses on the mental processes that students engage in when doing the tasks, and then measures the linguistic behaviour of test takers. Bulte and Housen (2014) believe that students' writing development in terms of cognitive complexity may occur due to their mental sophistication in using the knowledge.

CDA can therefore provide cognitive support for the linguistic profiles to better understand writing performance (Jang, 2008). That is to say, CDA informs teachers of the extent to which students develop their writing performance. For example, vocabulary knowledge, structural accuracy, and complexity of sentences could be analysed by CDA both through formative and/or summative assessments. The manifestation of proficiency in these latent behaviours is possible in robust statistical analysis known as the Cognitive Diagnostic Model (CDM). CDM is used to make the findings more objective which contributes to cognitive psychology and statistical analysis (Jang, 2008). As for the present study, the researcher reported students' final exam writing skills. However, through the application of CDA, the strengths and weaknesses of students, and the underlying reasons for these could be estimated.

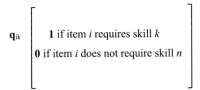

Fig. 2 Example of Q-matrix

To make CDA tangible, it is necessary to construct a Q-matrix to show the latent attributes, skills, or knowledge used while doing the tasks. Through developing a Q-matrix, it is also possible to determine the extent of consistency of expert scoring. De la Torre (2009) emphasises that the Q-matrix explicitly identifies cognitive specification. A rough sketch of a Q-matrix is shown in Fig. 2.

In Q-matrix development 1s and 0s are defined in terms of k and n, where the former presents the number of skills, attributes, or knowledge required, whereas the latter refers to the number of skills not required. In Q-matrix construction, if an individual perceives how to use a word, it means he/she receives 1 for that mastered attribute; otherwise he/she obtains 0. Here, students have been classified by experts based on the attributes mastered.

CDA is used in the investigation of diagnostic assessment, which has long been proposed in a variety of fields such as clinical psychology, and the diagnosis of learning difficulties. However, a few empirical studies have been conducted to provide diagnostic information on perceiving learners' competencies in fine-grained skills (Embretson, 1998; Leighton & Gierl, 2007; Nichols, 1994).

As an innovative approach, CDA investigation could be drawn from the type of diagnostic feedback provided for stakeholders with different levels of proficiency in writing. For instance, lexical accuracy or complexity are two examples of writing attributes which would require more instruction to lower proficiency with regard to students' underlying abilities. CDA yields far more information about why students succeed or fail, and what students understand or do not understand. CDA indicates the attributes were used through the application of robust statistical software like R or R-studio packages. In education and social sciences in general and writing in particular, through the application of robust statistical analysis, collected and classified data show where there is a change in the process of language development.

Overall, in CDA care needs to be taken in converting partial credit scoring into objective scoring, because partial scoring may entail some subjectivity. Practically, in teacher training courses teachers can become familiar with diagnostic test information. This information can aid teachers in that they can learn how to deal with some circumstances either when test takers in different groups do not have equal opportunity to learn the materials being tested, or even when a fair test can be used and interpreted unfairly.

In this study, an attempt was made to show CAF profiles of Iranian freshman university students in writing. Little attention was paid to the kind of feedback that students may receive from the test for improvement in practice. In the present study, writing skills were taught during a semester by the researcher, and then reported on students' final performance as the goal of the study. CAF profiles were enhanced to a small extent which might not be noticeable compared to those at the end of the semester (i.e. final exam).

Finally, it is necessary to conduct more research in the area of assessment to come up with more definitive results. To do so, CDA is recommended for the purpose of using measurement scales objectively. Of course, this would demand spending more time applying appropriate attributes and developing a Q-matrix for the assessment of writing.

Appendix 1: Sample CAF Coding for a Student's Script

Essay Title: Renewing Perspective

One human ability is to get under the influence of other characters and characteristics like happiness, sadness, creativity, independency, and so on. People are able to share all these characteristics with **each other** as long as they are living with **each other (Repetitions)**. When two people are in contact with **each other** for example by working and living in a same place, little by little after they get to know **each other (Repetitions)**, they may want to be like **each other (Lack of lexical diversity, repetition of word type)**. One of the most important characteristics that could be shared in my society, is being logical. I think if any people would be logical or wise, too many **problems** might be gone. Like the **problem (Repetitions)** of economy, finance or other things.

But on the other hand (False starts), intelligence is a kind of characteristics that is being shared between people.

And the third one is happiness, they are always happy. *Even people knows* **(Lack of grammatical accuracy)** *the people of my society* (False start) as welcoming, **happy (Lack of lexical diversity)** and kind **people (Repetitions)** which are all same very good points.

References

Ai, H., & Lu, X. (2013). A corpus-based comparison of syntactic complexity in NNS and NS university students' writing. In A. Díaz-Negrillo, N. Ballier, & P. Thompson (Eds.), *Automatic treatment and analysis of learner corpus data* (pp. 249–264). Amsterdam: John Benjamins.

Alderson, J. C. (2005). *Diagnosing foreign language proficiency: The interface between learning and assessment.* London: Continuum.

Alderson, J. C. (2007). The CEFR and the need for more research. *The Modern Language Journal, 91,* 659–663.

Anderson, J. R. (1995). *Learning and memory: An integrated approach.* New York: Wiley.

Arjona, E. (1983). Language planning in the judicial system: A look at the implementation of the U.S. Court Interpreters Act. *Language Planning Newsletter, 9*(1), 1–6.

Biber, D., Gray, B., & Staples, S. (2016). Predicting patterns of grammatical complexity across language exam task types and proficiency levels. *Applied Linguistics, 37*(5), 639–668.

Bulte, B., & Housen, A. (2012). Defining and operationalizing L2 complexity. In A. Housen, F. Kuiken, & I. Vedder (Eds.), *Dimensions of L2 performance and proficiency—Investigating complexity, accuracy and fluency in SLA* (pp. 21–46). Amsterdam: John Benjamins.

Bulte, B., & Housen, A. (2014). Conceptualizing and measuring short-term changes in L2 writing complexity. *Journal of Second Language Writing, 26,* 42–65.

Carson, J. E., & Kuehn, P. A. (1992). Evidence of transfer and loss in developing second language writers. *Language Learning, 42,* 157–179.

Chambers, F. (1997). What do we mean by fluency? *System, 25*(4), 535–544.

Chen, J. S., & de la Torre, J. (2014). A procedure for diagnostically modeling extant large scale assessment data: The case of the program for international student assessment in reading. *Psychology, 5,* 1967–1978.

Chen, J. S., de la Torre, J., & Zhang, Z. (2013). Relative and absolute fit evaluation in cognitive diagnosis modeling. *Journal of Educational Measurement, 50,* 123–140.

Chen, Y. H., & Baker, P. (2016). Investigating criterial discourse features across second language development: Lexical bundles in rated learner essays, CEFR B1, B2 and C1. *Applied Linguistics, 37*(6), 849–880.

Crookes, G. (1989). Planning and interlanguage variability. *Studies in Second Language Acquisition, 11,* 367–383.

Crossley, S. A., & McNamara, D. S. (2009). Computational assessment of lexical differences in L1 and L2 writing. *Journal of Second Language Writing, 18,* 119–135.

Crossley, S. A., Salsbury, T., & McNamara, D. S. (2012). Predicting the proficiency level of language learners using lexical indices. *Language Testing, 29*(2), 243–263.

Cui, Y., & Leighton, J. P. (2009). The hierarchy consistency index: Evaluating person fit for cognitive diagnostic assessment. *Journal of Educational Measurement, 46,* 429–449.

Dahmardeh, M., & Shahmirzadi, N. (2016). Measuring the written performance quality in terms of (CAF) complexity, accuracy and fluency constructs. *Pertanika Journal of Social Science and Humanities, 24*(2), 639–654.

Daller, H., & Xue, H. (2007). Lexical richness and the oral proficiency of Chinese EFL students. In H. Daller, J. Milton, & J. Treffers-Daller (Eds.), *Modeling and assessing vocabulary knowledge* (pp. 150–164). Cambridge: Cambridge University Press.

De la Torre, J. (2009). DINA model and parameter estimation: A didactic. *Journal of Educational and Behavioral Statistics, 34*(1), 115–130.

Edelsky, C. (1982). Writing in a bilingual program: The relation of L1 and L2 texts. *TESOL Quarterly, 16,* 211–228.

Ellis, R. (1987). Interlanguage variability in narrative discourse: Style in the use of past tense. *Studies in Second Language Acquisition, 18,* 229–323.

Ellis, R., & Barkhuizen, G. (2005). *Analyzing learner language.* New York: Oxford University Press.

Ellis, R., & Yuan, F. (2004). The effects of planning on fluency, complexity, and accuracy in second language narrative writing. *Studies in Second Language Acquisition, 26,* 59–84.

Embretson, S. E. (1998). A cognitive design system approach to generating valid tests: Application to abstract reasoning. *Psychological Methods, 3*(3), 380–396.

Fangyuan, Y., & Ellis, R. (2003). The effect of pre-task planning and on-line planning on fluency, accuracy and complexity in second language oral production. *Applied Linguistics, 2*(1), 1–27.

Ferris, D. R. (1994). Lexical and syntactic features of ESL writing by students at different levels of L2 proficiency. *TESOL Quarterly, 28*(2), 414–420.

Foster, P., & Skehan, P. (1996). The influence of planning and task type on second language performance. *Studies in Second Language Acquisition, 18,* 299–323.

Foster, P., Tonkyn, A., & Wigglesworth, G. (2000). Measuring spoken language: A unit for all reasons. *Applied Linguistics, 21*(3), 354–375.

Frase, L. T., Faletti, J., Ginther, A., & Grant, L. (1999). *Computer analysis of the TOEFL test of written English.* Princeton, NJ: Educational Testing Service.

Freed, B. (2000). Is fluency, like beauty, in the eyes (and ears) of the beholder? In H. Riggenbach (Ed.), *Perspectives on fluency* (pp. 243–265). Ann Arbor, MI: The University of Michigan Press.

George, A. C., & Robitzsch, A. (2014). Multiple group cognitive diagnosis models, with an emphasis on differential item functioning. *Psychological Test and Assessment Modeling, 56*(4), 405–432.

Grant, L., & Ginther, A. (2000). Using computer-tagged linguistic features to describe L2 writing differences. *Journal of Second Language Writing, 9*(2), 123–145.

Guillot, M. N. (1999). *Fluency and its teaching.* Philadelphia: Multilingual Matters.

Hilton, H. (2008). The link between vocabulary knowledge and spoken L2 fluency. *Language Learning Journal, 36*(2), 153–166.

Hou, L., la Torre, J. D., & Nandakumar, R. (2014). Differential item functioning assessment in cognitive diagnostic modeling: Application of the Wald test to investigate DIF in the DINA model. *Journal of Educational Measurement, 51*(1), 98–125.

Housen, A., & Kuiken, F. (2009). Complexity, accuracy and fluency in second language acquisition. *Applied Linguistics, 30*(4), 461–473.

Hulstijn, J. H. (2007). The shaky ground beneath the CEFR: Quantitative and qualitative dimensions of language proficiency. *The Modern Language Journal, 91,* 663–667.

Hunt, K. (1965). *Grammatical structures written at three grade levels.* Champaign, IL: National Council of Teachers of English.

Jang, E. E. (2008). A review of cognitive diagnostic assessment for education: Theory and application. *International Journal of Testing, 8*(3), 290–295.

Jang, E. E. (2009). Cognitive diagnostic assessment of L2 reading comprehension ability: Validity arguments for Fusion Model application to LanguEdge assessment. *Language Testing, 26*(1), 31–73.

Jarvis, S. (2017). Grounding lexical diversity in human judgments. *Language Testing, 34*(4), 537–553.

Jarvis, S., & Crossley, S. A. (Eds.). (2012). *Approaching language transfer through text classification: Explorations in the detection-based approach.* Bristol, UK: Multilingual Matters.

Jarvis, S., Grant, L., Bikowski, D., & Ferris, D. (2003). Exploring multiple profiles of highly rated learner compositions. *Journal of Second Language Writing, 12*(4), 377–403.

Johnson, W. (1944). Studies in language behavior: I. A program of research. *Psychological Monographs, 56,* 1–15.

Knoch, U., Roushad, A., & Storch, N. (2014). Does the writing of undergraduate ESL students develop after one year of study in an English-medium university? *Assessing Writing, 21,* 1–17.

Koponen, M., & Riggenbach, H. (2000). Overview: Varying perspectives on fluency. In H. Riggenbach (Ed.), *Perspectives on fluency* (pp. 5–24). Ann Arbor, MI: University of Michigan Press.

Kunnan, A. J., & Jang, E. E. (2009). Diagnostic feedback in language assessment. In M. Long & C. Doughty (Eds.), *Handbook of second and foreign language teaching* (pp. 610–625). Malden, MA: Wiley-Blackwell.

Lally, C. G. (2000). First language influences in second language composition: The effect of pre-writing. *Foreign Language Annals, 33,* 428–432.

Larsen-Freeman, D. (2009). Adjusting expectations: The study of complexity, accuracy, and fluency in second language acquisition. *Applied Linguistics, 30*(4), 579–589.

Larsen-Freeman, D., & Long, M. H. (1991). *An introduction to second language acquisition research.* Harlow: Longman Group.

Lefrançois, P. (2001). Le Point sur les transferts dans l'ecriture en langue seconde [Transfer in second-language writing]. *Canadian Modern Language Review, 58,* 223–245.

Leighton, J. P., & Gierl, M. J. (2007). Defining and evaluating models of cognition used in educational measurement to make inferences about examinees' thinking processes. *Educational Measurement: Issues and Practice, 26*(2), 3–16.

Lennon, P. (1990). Investigating fluency in EFL: A quantitative approach. *Language Learning, 40*(2), 387–417.

Liu, J. (2008). The generic and rhetorical structures of expositions in English by Chinese ethnic minorities: A perspective from intracultural contrastive rhetoric. *Language and Intercultural Communication, 8,* 2–20.

Lu, X. (2011). A corpus-based evaluation of syntactic complexity measures as indices of college-level ESL writers' language development. *TESOL Quarterly, 45*(1), 36–62.

Lu, X. (2012). The relationship of lexical richness to the quality of ESL learners' oral narratives. *The Modern Language Journal, 96*(2), 190–208.

Lu, X., & Ai, H. (2015). Syntactic complexity in college-level English writing: Differences among writers with diverse L1 backgrounds. *Journal of Second Language Writing, 29,* 16–27.

Nichols, P. D. (1994). A framework for developing cognitively diagnostic assessments. *Review of Educational Research, 64*(4), 575–603.

Norris, J. M., & Ortega, L. (2009). Towards an organic approach to investigating CAF in instructed SLA: The case of complexity. *Applied Linguistics, 30*(4), 555–578.

Ortega, L. (1999). Planning and focus on form in second language oral performance. *Studies in Second Language Acquisition, 21*(2), 109–148.

Ortega, L. (2003). Syntactic complexity measures and their relationship to L2 proficiency: A research synthesis of college-level L2 writing. *Applied Linguistics, 24*(4), 492–518.

Ortega, L., & Iberri-Shea, G. (2005). Longitudinal research in second language acquisition: Recent trends and future directions. *Annual Review of Applied Linguistics, 25,* 26–45.

Paquot, M. (2013). Lexical bundles and L1 transfer effects. *International Journal of Corpus Linguistics, 18,* 391–417.

Pica, T., Holliday, L., Lewis, N., & Morgenthaler, L. (1989). Comprehensible output as an outcome of linguistic demands on the learner. *Studies in Second Language Acquisition, 11,* 63–90.

Rankin, T. (2012). The transfer of V2: Inversion and negation in German and Dutch learners of English. *International Journal of Bilingualism, 16,* 139–158.
Read, J. (2000). *Assessing vocabulary.* Cambridge, UK: Cambridge University Press.
Schachter, J., & Celce-Murcia, M. (1977). Some reservations concerning error analysis. *TESOL Quarterly, 11,* 441–451.
Sen, S., & Bradshaw, L. (2017). Comparison of relative fit indices for diagnostic model selection. *Applied Psychological Measurement, 41,* 422–438.
Skehan, P. (1998a). *A cognitive approach to language learning.* Oxford: Oxford University Press.
Skehan, P. (1998b). Second language acquisition research and task-based instruction. In J. Willis & D. Willis (Eds.), *The challenge and change in language teaching.* Oxford: Heinemann.
Skehan, P., & Foster, P. (1999). The influence of task structure and processing conditions on narrative retellings. *Language Learning, 49,* 93–120.
Sotillo, S. M. (2000). Discourse functions and syntactic complexity in synchronous and asynchronous communication. *Language Learning and Technology, 4,* 82–119.
Storch, N., & Tapper, J. (2009). The impact of an EAP course on postgraduate writing. *Journal of English for Academic Purposes, 8*(3), 207–223.
Terzi, R., & Sen, S. (2019). A nondiagnostic assessment for diagnostic purposes: Q-matrix validation and item-based model fit evaluation for the TIMSS 2011 assessment. *SAGE Open, 9*(1), 1–11.
Tetreault, J., Blanchard, D., & Cahill, A. (2013). A report on the first native language identification shared task. In *Proceedings of the eighth workshop on innovative use of NLP for building educational applications* (pp. 48–57). Atlanta, GA: Association for Computational Linguistics.
Underwood, M. (1990). *Task-related variation in past tense morphology.* Unpublished master's thesis, Institute of Education, University of London.
Uysal, H. H. (2008). Tracing the culture behind writing: Rhetorical patterns and bidirectional transfer in L1 and L2 essays of Turkish writers in relation to educational context. *Journal of Second Language Writing, 17,* 183–207.
Van Patten, B. (1990). Attending to content and form in the input: An experiment in consciousness. *Studies in Second Language Acquisition, 12,* 287–301.
van Vuuren, S. (2013). Information structural transfer in advanced Dutch EFL writing: A cross-linguistic longitudinal study. *Linguistics in the Netherlands, 30,* 173–187.

van Weijen, D., van den Bergh, H., Rijlaarsdam, G., & Sanders, T. (2009). L1 use during L2 writing: An empirical study of a complex phenomenon. *Journal of Second Language Writing, 18,* 235–250.

Vercellotti, M. L. (2012). *Complexity, accuracy, and fluency as properties of language performance: The development of the multiple subsystems over time and in relation to each other* (Doctoral Dissertation). University of Pittsburgh.

Verspoor, M., Lowie, W., & Van Dijk, M. (2008). Variability in second language development from a dynamic systems perspective. *Modern Language Journal, 92*(2), 214–231.

Wang, Z., Guo, L., & Bian, Y. (2014). Comparison of DIF detecting methods in cognitive diagnostic test. *Acta Psychologica Sinica, 46*(12), 1923–1932.

Way, D. P., Joiner, E. G., & Seaman, M. A. (2000). Writing in the secondary foreign language classroom: The effects of prompts and tasks on novice learners of French. *The Modern Language Journal, 84,* 171–184.

Wolfe-Quintero, K., Inagaki, S., & Kim, H.-Y. (1998). *Second language development in writing: Measures of fluency, accuracy, and complexity.* Honolulu: University of Hawaii Press.

Yang, W., Lu, X., & Weigle, S. A. (2015). Different topics, different discourse: Relationships among writing topic, measures of syntactic complexity, and judgments of writing quality. *Journal of Second Language Writing, 28,* 53–67.

Exploring the Essay Rating Judgements of English Instructors in the Middle East

Analynn P. Bustamante and Selahattin Yilmaz

1 Introduction

Variability between raters' decision-making processes has been widely recognized in writing assessment research (e.g. Erdosy, 2004), which leads to challenges for test validity, reliability and fairness. Exploring this issue internationally is becoming more important due to the global spread of English in Higher Education (HE), as English academic writing is a core component of university curricula and language testing in this context (e.g. Jenkins, 2011, 2014). This expansion has led several researchers to highlight the need for renewed understanding of testing outcomes in light of contextual dynamics (Jenkins & Leung, 2019). Additionally, contextual factors influencing assessment practices including rater variability remain underexplored in many settings (e.g.

A. P. Bustamante (✉) · S. Yilmaz
Georgia State University, Atlanta, GA, USA
e-mail: abustamante2@student.gsu.edu

S. Yilmaz
e-mail: syilmaz2@gsu.edu

© The Author(s) 2020
L. McCallum and C. Coombe (eds.), *The Assessment of L2 Written English across the MENA Region*, https://doi.org/10.1007/978-3-030-53254-3_6

Ruecker & Crusan, 2018). Therefore, it is of great importance to investigate essay rater variability in a variety of settings, of which the Middle East (ME) is an example of such an underrepresented context. In studying this underrepresented context, recent work (e.g. Marefat & Heydari, 2018) has helped document the complexity of essay rating given the contextual variation that exists across the region. However, there continues to be a paucity of research concerning rater variability throughout the region (Gebril & Hidri, 2019).

The current study therefore adds further weight to the study of rater variability in the region by focusing on English-medium universities in the Kurdistan Region of Iraq (KRI) and Turkey. These two settings warrant further study for two reasons. First, both KRI and Turkey have experienced increases in English instruction in HE as a move towards globalization (Kırkgöz, 2009a). Second, while there are many similarities, the two contexts also have very distinct dynamics in terms of policies and practices. While Turkey has a long history of government-led language and educational planning (Doğancay-Aktuna, 1998), KRI has a relatively newer system where efforts for improvement have received international support (Ahmed, Puteh-Behak & Sidek, 2015). Due to the diversity of learning contexts throughout the ME, investigating decision-making behaviours involved in rating English learner academic writing can help gain a better understanding of construct validity and rater reliability respective to various teaching contexts. Furthermore, examining which professional experiences influence raters' scoring decisions can help inform rater training programmes and prompt instructors to reflect on their own scoring behaviours.

2 Literature Review

With the proliferation of English-medium universities throughout the ME, researchers have questioned the appropriateness and adequacy of English language testing in the region (Davidson & Coombe, 2019). As we are specifically concerned with rater behaviour, this section will discuss the general state of the rater variability literature. We will also review English writing assessment research in KRI and Turkey to contextualize this study.

2.1 Rater Variability

Assigning scores to students' texts is subject to variability between raters. Raters' personal characteristics, such as professional experience or academic background, have been explored as a source of variability (e.g. Attali, 2016; Erdosy, 2004; Marefat & Heydari, 2016). Cumming, Kantor, and Powers, (2002) noted that raters not only exhibit behaviours related to evaluating elements of the text itself, such as rhetorical devices and language use, but also engage in behaviours that are concerned with issues beyond the text itself. They categorize these behaviours into self-monitoring, rhetorical and language focuses. For example, self-monitoring focuses would be reflecting on the writers' context or evaluating their own biases, rhetorical focuses would be assessing relevance or coherence, and language focuses would be assessing grammar errors or vocabulary use (Cumming et al., 2002). Furthermore, Erdosy (2004) sought to connect raters' professional and academic backgrounds to their rating decision-making processes. In a qualitative case study of 4 participants, Erdosy (2004) concluded that while raters felt their professional experience was influential in their essay scoring, academic background did not seem to emerge as an influential factor. Specifically, regarding essay raters in the ME, Marefat and Heydari (2016) carried out a quantitative study of 12 non-native-English-speaking (NNES) Iranian and 12 native-English-speaking (NES) raters. They found that NES scored essays for organization significantly more severely than their Iranian counterparts, and the reverse held true for grammar. However, there was no significant difference in how each group rated content and vocabulary usage.

2.2 English Writing Pedagogy and Assessment in KRI and Turkey

Both KRI and Turkey have seen increased focus on academic English writing research in recent years.

2.2.1 The Case of KRI

English is increasingly considered a critical component of the education system in KRI (Borg, 2016; Kakabra, 2015). In recent years, there has been an increase in English as the Medium of Instruction (EMI) in universities in KRI (Borg, 2016), which may employ native or near-native English-speaking instructors from abroad, as can be found in other countries in the Gulf region (Diallo, 2014). In a study of professors of undergraduate content courses at 13 EMI universities throughout KRI, Borg (2016) found that 73% of the 416 professors surveyed used English in their classes at least half the time, despite that most participants strongly believed that students did not have the level of English necessary to understand the course's content. Borg (2016) also noted that exams in the EMI context typically required students to write essays in English. Participants mentioned that students may find it challenging to demonstrate their knowledge in English, even if they are familiar with the material (Borg, 2016). Furthermore, Kurdish students feel that many of their issues with English writing stem from the lack of opportunities to practice (Muhammed & Ameen, 2014). Ismael (2013) noted that, at present, traditional testing methods, such as multiple choice or matching tend to be common in KRI; however, no research exists specifically regarding NES instructors in the region.

2.2.2 The Case of Turkey

In the past few decades, EMI in HE has also been on the rise with a great number of public and private Turkish universities offering degree courses that are at least partially in English (Kırkgöz, 2009a). One important theme emerging from the perspectives of both students and faculty in this research is that the English writing pedagogy and assessment does not adequately prepare HE students for their degree studies as both are rather decontextualized and focused primarily on the linguistic and rhetoric structure of essays (Altınmakas & Bayyurt, 2019; Kırkgöz, 2009b). In addition, the language assessment literacy (LAL) research from the Turkish context has shown that teachers have limited assessment knowledge and they consider their pre-service and in-service training to be insufficient and of limited applicability (Ölmezer-Öztürk & Aydın, 2019a, 2019b). Teachers are shown to learn about assessment on the job through exchanges with colleagues and rely on materials from textbooks for assessment purposes (Yastıbaş & Takkaç, 2018). Regarding writing assessment, Ölmezer-Öztürk and Aydın (2019a, 2019b) have also documented that while teachers claimed to be highly competent in writing assessment, their actual knowledge was quite limited in terms of reliable and valid methods of preparing and rating writing tests. Moreover, as for rater variability, Han and Huang's (2017) comparison of the use of holistic and analytic rating scales by Turkish EFL instructors for assessing argumentative essays by Turkish learners of English, showed that rater training led to uniform scoring practices, after which the teachers stated their preference of holistic over analytic rubrics, and content over the others as the most important criterion.

2.3 Present Study

The present chapter serves as an exploratory analysis that presents two profiles of rater behaviour in the ME: NES instructors at a Western-style EMI university in KRI and Turkish instructors of English at major metropolitan universities in Turkey. We chose the multiple-site interview approach to illustrate the diversity of instructors and teaching contexts throughout the region. We addressed the following research questions:

RQ 1: What are raters' articulated behaviours when evaluating NNES student writing?
RQ 2: What are raters' perceptions of how their professional experiences influence their rating behaviours?

We hope to contribute to the rater variability literature in two ways: by adding to the research on rater variability in the ME and to the research that seeks to attribute raters' experiences as influences on their decision-making behaviours.

3 Methodology

A multi-site interview design was chosen for the present study to obtain "thick" description from participants in two separate contexts in order to explore and synthesize the data from each context. While it has been well established that variability exists between individual raters, few studies (e.g. Erdosy, 2004) have taken a qualitative, emic approach to rater variability, in that participants serve as active interpreters of the connections between their background factors and decision-making processes (Barkaoui, 2007).

3.1 Participants

For qualitative research, two to ten participants are sufficient for data collection (Boyd, 2001); therefore, five participants were recruited from each context. Per Holliday (2005), the nature of and access to settings and participants may be opportunistic but can be justified by the researchers. In the case of this study, both researchers had utilized professional networks from their former institutions in the region. Pseudonyms were used for all participants.

The KRI-NES participants were recruited from Western-style EMI universities in KRI and consisted entirely of NES instructors. There were four women, Sara, Molly, Ana and Whitney, and one man, Dan. Their ages ranged from 34 to 39. Ana was South African, while the rest of the participants were American. The female instructors all possessed masters' degrees in a field related to English instruction, while Dan possessed an unrelated master's degree, but held a CELTA. Their years of teaching experience ranged from 7 to 11 years and they all had experience teaching English in multiple countries. The KRI-NES participants all taught non-credit bearing, pre-university EAP courses.

The participants from Turkey consisted of four women, Ceyda, Filiz, Melda, Mercan, and one man, Giray, aged between 28 and 30. They were NNES instructors who spoke Turkish as their native language and learned English in instructed settings in Turkey. They taught English for Academic Purposes (EAP) as instructors in established public and private Turkish universities in large urban areas and had 3–8 years of teaching experience. EMI was at least partially required in many degrees offered by their universities. All the participants held a bachelor's degree and/or a relevant official certification in English Language Teaching (ELT). While Ceyda and Filiz were about to start their doctoral education, Giray and Mercan had been doctoral students for a few years at the time of the study. In the Turkey-NNES group, participants taught two types of courses. Ceyda, Melda and Mercan were teaching non-credit bearing pre-undergraduate EAP courses. Filiz and Giray were teaching degree courses that provided students with continued language support.

3.2 Procedures

The interviews consisted of two parts and were conducted via online video chat programmes such as FaceTime or Zoom. The first part of the interview consisted of a think-aloud-protocol (TAP) where participants articulated any thoughts, they had related to evaluating sample essays (Charters, 2003; McKay, 2009). The second part of the data collection, the post-TAP interview, asked participants to reflect on their rating behaviours and make connections to their personal experiences.

3.2.1 Think-Aloud-Protocol

First, participants engaged in a TAP (viz. Cumming et al., 2002) where they were provided with three sample essays and a rubric. In order to compare rating practices across individual raters, we provided decontextualized essays as TAP stimuli to serve as common ground through which to analyse participants' scoring decisions. Participants rated the essays out loud in a way that reflected their normal scoring practices in order to illuminate their rating decision-making processes. The essays came from an administration of the placement test for incoming NNES students at a large public university in the U.S. The prompt for the essays asked writers to discuss whether globalization was beneficial and to support their assertions with readings given as part of the original test. The essays had been previously rated. Participants were provided with a low-, middle- and high-level essay, per the previous rating. Furthermore, while the original context of the stimulus essays and rubric was explained to the participants, raters did not undergo a rigorous training process as the goal of the study was to elicit individualistic and impressionistic ratings (Charters, 2003). Because the purpose of this study was to explore raters' individualistic impressions of essay components, extensively training raters on the stimulus materials would result in more homogenous rating behaviour. The analytic rubric included four criteria: content, organization, language accuracy and language range/complexity. There were five scoring levels for each criterion, with five being the highest, and one the lowest.

3.2.2 Post-TAP Interviews

After the TAP, participants were asked questions that focused on their previous and current experiences with writing assessment. As suggested by Barkaoui (2011), the post-TAP interviews are essential for the participants to further contextualize their TAP experience, and for the researchers to interpret and report from the data more accurately. By conducting the TAP and an immediate follow-up interview, we were able to observe participants' behaviour during the introspection and verbalization of their decision-making processes, thereby informing our follow-up questions. Furthermore, the essay rating task was fresh in the minds of the participants allowing them to reflect on their decision-making during the post-TAP interview. While the interviews with NES participants were done in English by the NES first author, the Turkish participants preferred to be interviewed in their shared first language with the second author.

3.3 Analysis

All interview data were transcribed. The NES-KRI interviews were originally in English, while the Turkish data were translated into English by the second author by staying faithful to the original content. The TAP data were analysed taking cues from Cumming et al. (2002); however, for the present study, the language and rhetorical focuses were combined into one category, which we refer to as the "in-text" focus. This decision was made because participants articulated focusing on essay features that may not have been explicitly "language" or "rhetoric" but blurred the line between the two. Any behaviours that related to non-text features, such as considering the writer, raters' self-evaluation, considering the rubric, etc., were categorized as "beyond-text" focus. Furthermore, under each category, we then divided the data into more specific subcategories based on which themes emerged for each group.

The Post-TAP interview data were open coded for recurring themes by the interviewer from the respective groups via descriptive coding (Miles, Huberman & Saldaña, 2014). The coding was reviewed by the other interviewer to ensure reliability via intercoder-agreement (Creswell, 2014). Then, consensus was reached by both researchers as to the final themes to be reported in the chapter.

3.4 Researcher Positionality

Addressing one's awareness of their roles and biases as the researcher is crucial for carefully situating the findings of qualitative studies (Bourke, 2014). Hence, we are aware that our positionality as former insiders of both contexts, personal acquaintance with the participants as well as being of similar backgrounds might have influenced how we approached the research process. While coming from similar linguistic, cultural and professional backgrounds with the participants helped us look at the data from an emic (teacher) perspective, we also aimed to have an etic (researcher) perspective. In order to mitigate the influence of our personal biases, several steps were taken. The data collection methods were piloted and revised with an independent group, coding was verified by both researchers, and previous literature was consulted when interpreting the findings. In doing so, we hope to present as objective an analysis as possible.

4 Findings and Discussion

The selected results and discussions presented here are themes that arose during two or more of the interviews in each of the respective groups. For each major section (in-text focus, beyond-text focus, and professional experiences) the results are organized to first discuss themes that were common to both groups. Next, we discuss themes that were specific to the KRI-NES group and then the themes specific to the Turkey-NES group. Finally, we provide a summary and discussion of the findings for each major theme.

4.1 Insights from TAP

Findings from the TAPs were divided into in-text and beyond-text themes, under which commonalities across the contexts were discussed first. Then, the sub-themes that were salient in one context but may be absent from the others followed the common themes.

4.1.1 Beyond-Text Focus: Commonalities Across Contexts

A behaviour that was employed by both sets of participants was to make connections and discuss the relationships between the respective rubric criteria. Five strategies emerged: participants may have considered one criterion more important than the other, considered one criterion less important than the others, considered content and organization to be one category and language accuracy and range/complexity another, considered each rubric criterion separately but of equal importance, or considered all criteria holistically.

With regard to the NES participants from KRI, four of these five strategies were present. Dan's rating elevated language accuracy over the other criteria and it was influenced by his evaluation of the essay as a whole. To illustrate, upon scanning the first essay, Dan remarks that, "it looks fine… but I tend to look for it first as grammar mistakes. I find personally that if there's a lot of grammar mistakes, I tend to find that the writing will only be so good." Conversely, Whitney felt that language accuracy was less important than other criteria. Her articulated priority when rating is to not "focus on grammar," but "to make sure they… can come up with a cohesive idea." On the other hand, Sara makes a distinction between her impressions of the rhetoric- and language-related rubric criteria. Specifically, for the low-level essay, she states that the "ideas are simple, clear. Even though the writing is bad, you can follow it pretty easily," indicating that she evaluates an essay's "writing" and "ideas" separately. Furthermore, during the rating process, Ana methodically checked each rubric criterion and made evaluations separately, respective to the criterion she was focusing on.

As for the NNES participants from Turkey, there were also several divergent perspectives on how to conceptualize the relationships between rubric criteria. Several participants felt that content and organization and language accuracy and range/complexity belonged to two overarching categories. For example, Filiz stated, "I check organization to see if the content has a strong coherence and good transitions." Similarly, Mercan discussed the criteria mostly in two broad categories, but she regarded accuracy and range and complexity as the most critical to "the assessment of general language competence." On the other hand, Ceyda, discussed the criteria independently, and considered content alone to be the most important, while, Mercan, compared the criteria to discuss the opposite, saying, "Content is less important to me because the exam anxiety might lead to misunderstandings, which is fine if the organization and other components are good."

4.1.2 Comparing Stimulus Essays to Own Students' Writing

Participants from both groups tended to compare the decontextualized stimulus essays to the writing of their own students. In the KRI-NES participant group, Ana explicitly states, "I'm almost thinking, 'what can my students produce? Can they produce something like this?'" Additionally, for one essay, Sara remarks that "the thesis is just like my students'." Sara also relied on her overall experiences working with NNES students to evaluate one writer's word choices, "most language learners wouldn't know 'dwell,' 'gobble breakfast cereal,' 'how terrible it is,'" concluding that most NNES students would not know such low-frequency words or native-like collocations. Finally, Whitney uses her program's levels to evaluate the low-level essay writer: upon scanning the essay, she remarked, "is this a level 1 student?"

The Turkish group made similar statements in comparing the stimulus essays to their own students. For instance, Melda noted that the "grammar [of the stimulus essays] was bad. Some of our students do really well in grammar." Upon being asked about how her stimulus essay rating experience was, Ceyda answered, "We also rate the essays the way you do. But it's more about the student level. If a high-level student wrote the first essay, it would mean there was a problem." Ceyda also said about one of the stimulus essays was "more like the type [of essay writing] they do" in her programme which, she added, may have influenced her grading to some extent. This was also the essay to which she assigned the highest score.

4.1.3 Considerations for Severity and Leniency

Another common strategy among participants was considering when to be severe or lenient on the stimulus essays. Several of the NES participants explicitly sought to be more lenient on the low-level essay and more severe on the high-level essay. Molly explains that she "grades a low student a little bit easier than I would grade a high student"; therefore, on the lowest level essay she wanted to "find a place to give this student… an extra point or two." Finally, when evaluating the high-level essay Sara more severely evaluated the writer's word choice but felt that she was "being picky on the best of the three."

Among the Turkish participants, Mercan said she was more lenient about content and organization in order to balance her heightened attention to accuracy, and range and complexity. Commenting on the low-level essay, she said, "It lacks cohesion and is off-topic. But in these cases, I try to balance my rating. If I deduct points from one criterion, I don't deduct as much from another, so the student isn't disadvantaged." Additionally, Melda also admitted that this "institutional pressure" influenced her rating behaviour. When she completed rating the stimulus essays, Melda felt that she was too strict, and explained that her institution is "generally very strict about essay grading."

4.1.4 Beyond-Text Focus: Context-Specific Discussions

KRI-NES raters made assumptions about the writer's intentions and potential abilities. For example, upon reading an awkwardly phrased sentences, Sara predicted the motivation of the writers' word choice. She believed that the writer "didn't want to say 'health' again" and explains that she's "protecting a little bit here, but that's what I would assume." For another essay, Molly states, "based on [the entirety of] this person's writing, they could have done a smoother introduction," showing that she evaluated the introduction more severely when the rest of the essay seemed to be at a higher proficiency level. Similarly, Sara makes a comment on the low-level essay writer's use of the source text, stating the essay is "weak on content, but at least he's using the source text… to the best of his ability." In other words, Sara is evaluating the writer's use of the source text assuming he was a lower proficiency writer. Additionally, Whitney noted that one of the writers, who did not fully follow the prompt, may be the "type of student that just said, 'forget the instructions I'll do what I want to do.'" These examples show that raters' may overlay their own preconceived impressions of EFL writers even in rating decontextualized essays.

For the KRI-NES group, it was clear that several participants made comparisons to a NES model to guide their evaluations of the essays. For example, both Sara and Molly made comments that suggested that they were more lenient on the NNES writers if they believed a task would also be difficult for NES writers. Specifically, Sara gave high marks for accuracy on an essay where the writer made "mistakes... most native speakers wouldn't know how to deal with." Additionally, Ana seemed to perceive that native-like writing was a goal for students, stating that one writer should "refine the writing, so that it's not clearly near-native."

Furthermore, KRI-NES also compared essays to other essays in the stimulus group when assigning scores. Ana gave an essay a high score on language criteria because "it was better than the second one I did." Conversely, Molly took a point off an essay's organization score because "it wasn't as good as the first one."

Several comments by Turkish participants point to limited understanding of certain criteria and lack of familiarity with the context of the rubric. For example, Melda explained that grammar is more important than vocabulary for her due to several reasons:

> I don't pay as much attention to vocabulary because of the vagueness of the rubrics and [institutional] expectations. The [students] use different words either infrequently or incorrectly. That's when I deduct vocabulary points, but recently the coordinator's told us to deduct grammar points instead in such cases.

Similarly, Filiz pointed to the lack of sufficient description in rubrics regarding the expectation of range. Referring to the stimulus essay rating for the study, both Filiz and Ceyda found the descriptors for the organization criterion somewhat underspecified, which influenced their rating. Ceyda in particular stated that she had difficulty rating one of the essays due to the lack of a criterion on "coherence and cohesion" as in her context. She added that she had to deduct from organization only because of the lack of such a criterion. Filiz expected to see details on genre expectations in the organization criterion during TAP. All the participants expressed some concern regarding the accuracy of the TAP rating due to insufficient knowledge of the institutional policies and practices.

The results support Cumming et al.'s (2002) findings that raters engage in behaviours that are not limited to the text. They identified 11 self-monitoring strategies, of which several, such as envisioning writer's situation and revising scoring decision, were observed in our data; however, we also identified behaviours not documented in their study, such as referring to their own teaching context and evaluating their rubric use. With regard to similarities between groups, raters from both contexts critically considered the relationships between rubric criteria, their personal teaching contexts and whether they should be harsh or lenient. The findings regarding the diversity in participants' interpretations of the rubric criteria provides further evidence that the way teachers use rubrics may be influenced by their previous experiences with writing assessment (Crusan, Plakans, & Gebril, 2016). Finally, while it may be natural for teachers to evaluate decontextualized essays based on their own students' writing abilities, this behaviour raises a question about the deviations between raters' experiences and the scores they assign.

There were also behavioural differences exhibited in each group. The data show that the KRI-NES participants were more focused on individual student profiles and compared essays to each other when rating, which are behaviours described in Cumming et al. (2002). However, reliance on a NES model is not mentioned, which further supports a more comprehensive description of rater behaviour. On the other hand, the Turkish participants were often motivated by institutional dynamics. Several Turkish participants referred to their institutional practices when deciding on the score to assign, such as their program's levels or administrative needs, which suggests tangible top-down washback effect (Latif & Haridy, 2018). It is also worth noting differences between the use of first-person pronouns between groups. Specifically, Turkey-NNES participants tended to use "we" when referring to standardized testing, whereas KRI-NES participants generally used "I" potentially because standardized testing is not a factor for their rating decisions.

4.1.5 In-Text Focus: Commonalities Across Contexts

During the TAP, organization was a salient topic of the comments from participants from both groups. For example, upon scanning the middle-level essay, Ana points out that it has "a proper introduction… a supporting paragraph, and a conclusion at the end," which she describes as "nice because you can actually see them." Furthermore, participants also noted that they had an expectation of writers using transition words. throughout the TAP, Dan noted the presence or absence of "transition signals" and stated that these are very important to him. Ana also took issue with the low-level essay writer using "for example" in their introductory paragraph. Additionally, participants specifically focused on the essays' thesis statements. When rating the high-level essay, Sara critiques the writers' thesis statement by explaining that the introduction "does not directly address the prompt clearly, and then it leaves room for confusion." In other words, even though the writer attempted a thesis statement, it did not conform to Sara's expectations.

The Turkish participants made similar comments. Melda, Giray, and Filiz frequently mentioned concepts they perceived to be the key to effective rhetorical organization. Filiz, for example, asked if she needed to look for a thesis statement. After reading one of the stimulus essays, the first thing Giray said was, "oh so, there is no thesis statement, no hook, and no topic sentence."

Language accuracy and range/complexity emerged as a common theme but was markedly more salient in the KRI-NES group. Specifically, spelling was discussed among all participants despite the fact spelling is not explicitly mentioned in the rubric (though the rubric does include "word forms"). However, participants had differing opinions on the importance of spelling. On the high-level essay, Ana points out that there is only one spelling error, but that it did not affect her evaluation the otherwise high level of language accuracy. Whitney and Dan underscore the importance of spelling in their evaluation of student writing. Whitney noted that, despite her preference to not prioritize language errors, "spelling plays a factor" in her scoring decisions. She indicates that the writers' misspelling of "Christmas" influenced her evaluation of language accuracy for one essay. On the other hand, Sara considers "spelling a little less" than other errors and Molly noted that, while in the low-level essay there were errors "like spelling, but I don't care about spelling." Additionally, comments were made regarding the writers' word choice. Whitney took issue with the use of "certainly" by one of the essay writers: "When they say, 'globalization will certainly benefit...' I would just tell them to be careful with certain words because there's always going to be somebody that says… you don't know for a fact."

Turkish participants also voiced their opinions on their linguistic expectations when rating, but to a notably less specific degree. Mercan, who was the strongest proponent of accuracy and range and complexity, commented that her primary expectation from her students was them "not making mistakes when using basic tenses and not using the same words like 'important' repeatedly". When comparing the language criteria, Filiz said, "accuracy is maybe a little important but complexity… plainness and understandability are more important to me than complexity."

4.1.6 In-Text Focus: Context-Specific Discussions

A recurrent in-text focus among multiple KRI participants was the writers' ability to provide textual support for their assertions. For the high-level essay, Sara commented that the writer did not "pull quotes… or information specifically from [the source text]," but that it connects well all the way through." Therefore, she assigned a high organization score. Whitney noted instances where the writer of the middle-level essay did not make clear connections between the main idea and the supporting evidence. She noted that the writer seems to be "making assumptions." Furthermore, multiple raters felt the low-level essay writer did not use the supporting text effectively. Molly states that the quote "[the writer] used was not relevant."

Several Turkish participants, despite not being asked specifically, referred to genre expectations and perceived norms of academic writing in a way to further contextualize their reasoning on specific aspects of essay rating. To illustrate, comparing the writing pedagogy in her previous institution and the current one, Melda explained:

[EAP writing pedagogy in my previous institution] wasn't as academic. It was very general and easy. But this context takes it more seriously, and the writing is more academic. We cover many genres like description, process writing. There were no such things in my previous institution.

She equated a more academically oriented curriculum with the assessment of genre conventions. Similarly, Giray often pointed to the importance of "essay types," which he also exemplified by commenting, "if I assign an opinion essay, I want my students to follow the format of an opinion essay." Mercan and Giray also discussed their perceptions of academic writing norms in the most detail, likely because they had the most disciplinary writing experience, which may have influenced their rating behaviour. Lastly, it is also important to keep in mind that all participants mentioned their programs' curricula were centred around genre conventions, essay types and organizational structure of academic essays, which showed how their instructional practices were closely aligned with the institutional assessment.

In sum, the in-text essay components that raters focused on were generally divergent, which supports findings from previous rater variability studies that different subgroups of raters may have different priorities when scoring essays (Cumming et al., 2002; Eckstein, Casper, Chan, & Blackwell, 2018; Marefat & Heydari, 2016; Shi, 2001). The discrepancy may stem from a variety of factors such as the differences in the types of courses taught (i.e. composition versus English language) (Eckstein et al., 2018) or language background (Marefat & Heydari, 2016; Shi, 2001). On the other hand, focusing on organizational features emerged to similar degrees of salience for both groups. This commonality supports previous research that suggests that organizational features are closely related to the quality of academic writing (Mauranen, Pérez-Llantada, & Swales, 2010). Overall, these findings show that the evaluation of writing per what is traditionally conceptualized as "language" and "rhetoric" maybe be more simplistic than raters' elicited behaviours. The NES raters in this sample evaluated essay organization, in part, by the words that writers chose to use, and the Turkish raters seemed to conceptualize "essay types" as a separate phenomenon from content and organization.

4.2 Insights from Post-TAP Interviews

For the post-TAP interviews, participants were asked to discuss their academic and professional experiences in order to contextualize their rating behaviour and identify possible connections between their experiences and behaviours.

4.2.1 Administrative Dynamics

While administrative factors were mentioned for both sets of participants, the issue was much more salient in the Turkish context, as the NES participants from the KRI context gave the impression that the administration had a relatively hands-off approach when it came to how they rated students' writing. However, Dan did note that writing outcomes are important to his programme's administration. Ana explained that the lack of direct involvement may be due to the background discrepancies between the administrators and teachers. In other words, as Ana stated, she is "in teaching mode," while the programme's administrators have been "in administration for so long" that they tend to be less connected to the classroom.

The Turkish participants, however, often mentioned the organizational structure of writing pedagogy and assessment in their institutions, with which they seemed to comply to a great extent. It was clear from Ceyda's and Filiz's responses that they trusted their institutional decision-making processes, such as the evaluation of curriculum and the development of end-of-year tests through asking for teachers' input. Another institutional factor was the use of standardized tests before and after each academic year to ensure uniform decisions of proficiency and placement. Because of these tests, participants felt they could not make extensive changes to their classroom curriculum and testing. While Giray and Melda were clear opponents making curricular changes in order to minimize differences between teaching and standardized testing, Melda felt restricted by the administrative control of, and pressures on, writing assessment. However, she added that "no [teacher] really objects." Thus, not only was it implied from the discussions that assessment practices influenced their writing pedagogy, Giray also openly stated, "unfortunately, we make decisions based on testing."

Another factor that emerged from the interviews with the Turkish participants is the observable links between the degree of the participants' administrative involvement and their stance on institutional policies and practices of writing instruction and assessment. For instance, both Ceyda and Giray had administrative duties and were part of the decision-making mechanisms, which lead to more detailed explanations of the development, administration, and rating of the tests, use and revision of rubrics, and the workings of problem-solving processes. In addition, Filiz and Giray taught degree courses (unlike the other who taught pre-degree courses), and, therefore, had relatively more autonomy, meaning faster processes of and fewer parties involved in decision-making.

4.2.2 Teaching Experiences

Participants also noted how their teaching experiences generally influenced what they focused on in essay rating. Ana described how, when she first started teaching, she highly prioritized task completion. She states, "in the beginning, when I started teaching writing and grammar, I used to focus so much on 'did he answer the question?' and it would drive me away from [actually] seeing the students' work." In other words, early in her career, Ana would assign scores first considering whether the writer answered the question and then consider other aspects of writing; however, through years of experience, she moved away from this practice and began conceptualizing each essay component uniquely, which was evident in the TAP. Furthermore, Dan believed that his experience in KRI has taught him which language errors to focus on and noted that students struggle with "spelling, verb agreement and paragraph writing," so he tends to be more sensitive to these issues when assessing student writing, and he indeed primarily commented on language errors during the TAP. Furthermore, several participants indicated that collaborating with colleagues was a major influence on how they assessed writing. Both Ana and Dan stated that they learned from working with other teachers. Ana mentions these collaborations taught her "what to look for" when assessing writing. Whitney specifically mentioned discussing the expectations of instructors of the higher levels in the programme and letting "what they needed" guide how she assessed student writing.

The Turkey-NNES participants were also very clear about how their professional teaching and testing experience positively impacted their essay rating behaviour, more so than any other factor including pre-service and in-service training. Giray said, "I learned [how to rate essays] mostly when I started working," and added that with experience, his "self-confidence when making rating decisions increased, and marking anxiety and indecisiveness decreased." While Ceyda said her rating, speed increased as she gained more experience, Mercan similarly considered herself to be a relatively slow rater due to her limited experience rating essays. Although she had rating experience in her previous two jobs, because the latter was not an active teaching position and she only occasionally rated essays; therefore, she felt as though she had been "starting from scratch."

4.2.3 Academic/Pre-Service Training Experiences in Isolation

When asked about potential influences of their academic/pre-service training experiences on how they evaluate student writing, all KRI-NES participants indicated that they perceived it to be entirely divorced from their current assessment behaviours. When asked if she took a testing course during her TESOL MA programme, Molly stated that it was "a long time ago," so she "can't remember." Whitney noted that, although she took an assessment course, she has "not implemented any of that" because "if it said anything in a book, it really didn't apply to my students." Dan also perceived that his pre-service training did not influence his rating behaviour as his CELTA was focused on spoken communication. Furthermore, Sara points out that, during her MA, she had an assessment class, but was young and "didn't pay attention." She also believes that "one course does not make you an assessment master" and felt she "didn't know what I was doing" despite the assessment course. Finally, Ana expressed frustration with the assessment component of her master's degree. She states that she "wouldn't say it taught us much." She gives the example of learning about rubrics: she did not feel like her programme "show[ed] us... what they needed to look for."

Similarly, despite having taken assessment courses during their pre-service training at the undergraduate level, no Turkish teacher considered this experience to have been beneficial especially for their essay rating practices due to limited applicability of what they learned. Filiz said, "My undergraduate course wasn't hands on. I don't remember actually rating student essays using rubrics". Melda and Giray also did not recall any specific attention to essay rating in their training, and Ceyda's TEFL certificate training included only a short, theoretical course on principles of educational testing. Although Mercan also mentioned that her training was primarily theoretical, and "essay rating, rubric use were not areas covered in depth," she also said that it laid the foundation of her knowledge in the area.

4.2.4 Simultaneous Teaching and Training Experiences

While participants perceived their isolated academic/pre-service training experiences as largely irrelevant, several participants from both groups reflected positively on training experiences that occurred in conjunction with teaching. For example, Molly mentioned her undergraduate work in her university's writing centre as being especially instrumental to how she rates writing. She noted that she was simultaneously enrolled in a course where they "read lots of books on writing theory," which she then implemented in her work as a writing tutor. Sara discussed her teaching experiences during her masters' degree. While teaching in the local community, she would approach her writing pedagogy professor for advice on how to grade students' writing, but these conversations were extracurricular and not part of the assessment course. Finally, Ana explains that she completed her master's dissertation on genre-based writing instruction while teaching. She made pedagogical decisions based on her research, which she believes has influenced how she conceptualizes learner academic writing to date. Additionally, both Molly and Sara have engaged in independent learning regarding assessment while teaching. Molly undertook a formal online course and Sara engaged in independent academic reading. Both participants stated that these independent professional development activities have had an impact on their writing assessment behaviours.

Similar connections were made between academic and professional experiences by the Turkish participants. Mercan and Giray, who took graduate-level testing courses when they were at least partly involved in essay rating practices in their institutions, expressed their appreciation of the training for expanding their knowledge of language testing in general. The areas in which Giray said his knowledge improved were, "testing principles," "writing test specifications" and "item design." Furthermore, there were connections between participants' research and essay rating. Mercan, for instance, stated that her own research on lexical aspects of L2 academic writing led to her having "higher awareness" of lexical accuracy and range when rating essays. Having specialized in curriculum design during their graduate education, Ceyda and Filiz were more focused on the interaction between institutional essay rating considerations and curricular policies and practices. Giray, whose research was on English as a Lingua Franca (ELF)-aware teacher education, was the only participant who was clearly opposed to such connections between his research and writing assessment, commenting that unlike in speaking, "ELF-aware writing" was a challenge mainly because he believed that ELF "prioritizes content over grammar," which conflicted with his expectations from his students to "write accurately" and "follow the format of" specific essay types taught in classes.

Data from the semi-structured interviews further support that administrative considerations were more influential to Turkish participants' writing assessment beliefs than the KRI-NES participants. This phenomenon can be related to their TAP rating behaviours in that Turkish participants more often referred to their institutional dynamics, while institutional constraints were rare in the KRI-NES data. Furthermore, the present study confirms previous research that finds that professional experiences have a more salient influence on raters' scoring behaviours than pre-service experiences (Erdosy, 2004; Vogt & Tsagari, 2014); however, if the training experience had a concurrent teaching context in which they could practically implement what they learned, participants considered it to be influential. While it is important to note which experiences have a more overt connection to raters, there may also be an unperceived influence of academic experiences on raters' behaviours. As argued in Öz and Atay (2017), ELT graduate education can be partially related to teachers having clearer perceptions and expectations of academic writing.

5 Implications for the Context and Conclusion

In sum, while several rating behaviours were common between groups of raters, there were also key differences (see Table 1). Additionally, for both groups, their professional experiences seemed to have a more salient impact on their rating behaviour than their pre-service training, as was true in Erdosy's (2004) study. However, Turkey-NNES participants more so felt their administrative dynamics influenced their rating decisions, whereas KRI-NES participants did not.

There are several practical implications regarding rater training that can be drawn from these findings. The present study provides evidence

Table 1 Summary of TAP findings

	Commonalities	KRI-NES	Turkey—NNES
Beyond-text focus	Evaluating relationships between rubric criteria	Envisioned personal characteristics of writers	Confusion about rubric use
	Compare stimulus essays to own students'	Compared essays to previous ones	
	Reflecting on severity/leniency	Relied on NES intuition	
In-text focus	Organization	Evaluated writer's use of source text	Academic writing norms and conventions
	Language issues[a]		

Note [a] Present in both, but notably more so in KRI-NES group

that raters use their present teaching context as a base of comparison if they do not undergo a rigorous rater training session (e.g. Vogt & Tsagari, 2014). If an institution values standardization in student writing evaluation, it may be prudent to have teachers undergo training sessions, otherwise they can interpret and apply rubric criteria subjectively. However, it may also be possible for teachers to have too much top-down oversight, which may result in their institutional concerns becoming overly influential in their general rating behaviours (Barkaoui, 2007; Latif & Haridy, 2018). Teachers and administrators should be aware of the needs of their context in order to train raters in a way that is effective and appropriate to their setting, thereby enhancing the validity argument of writing assessment in a given context. Furthermore, this study also illuminated that academic/pre-service training experiences that are disconnected from practical implementation may not have a memorable impact on teachers. Therefore, for training to have a long-term, salient impact on teachers, there should be a meaningful, practical component in addition to language testing theory and concepts.

To conclude, as we can see from the data, essay raters are not tabulae rasae: they employ a variety of essay rating behaviours that are influenced by their unique experiences. Understanding raters' behaviours and influences thereof can enhance understanding of the construct validity of writing assessment per setting. While our aim is by no means to generalize our findings to describe profiles of essay raters, we do hope to add to the understanding of essay rating as a context-specific practice. Furthermore, our findings suggest that there may be more variety in rater behaviours than outlined in Cumming et al. (2002). Further research in this area could identify additional strategies that raters employ, which could then be used to inform rater training for both classroom assessment and standardized test contexts. Questions about the influence of context and background factors remain. A large-scale quantitative study should be performed in order to better identify connections between raters' previous experiences and their rating decisions.

As for limitations, we acknowledge the imperfect comparison between our two participant groups due to vast contextual discrepancies in, for example, cultural contexts, institutional dynamics, types of classes taught, language backgrounds, and so on. Further research is needed on specific rater subgroups within KRI, Turkey and throughout the ME. We are aware that having two different interviewers may have affected the data that were collected; however, we felt that talking to a former colleague would allow participants to feel freer in their responses. However, despite these limitations, we believe the findings of this study can contribute to a more comprehensive understanding of the complex dynamics involved in essay rating.

Acknowledgements We would like to thank Dr. Sara Cushing for her valuable and constructive suggestions during the design and the writing of this study. We are also grateful to the editors who helped us improve the quality of this manuscript with insightful comments.

References

Ahmed, H. H., Puteh-Behak, F., & Sidek, H. M. (2015). Examining EFL secondary reading curriculum in Iraqi Kurdistan: A review. *Journal of Applied Sciences, 15*(3), 377–391.

Altınmakas, D., & Bayyurt, Y. (2019). An exploratory study on factors influencing undergraduate students' academic writing practices in Turkey. *Journal of English for Academic Purposes, 37,* 88–103.

Attali, Y. (2016). A comparison of newly-trained and experienced raters on a standardized writing assessment. *Language Testing, 33*(1), 99–115.

Barkaoui, K. (2007). Participants, texts, and processes in ESL/EFL essay tests: A narrative review of the literature. *Canadian Modern Language Review, 64*(1), 99–134.

Barkaoui, K. (2011). Think-aloud protocols in research on essay rating: An empirical study of their veridicality and reactivity. *Language Testing, 28*(1), 51–75.

Borg, S. (2016). *English medium instruction in Iraqi Kurdistan.* London: British Council. Retrieved January 13, 2020, from https://englishagenda.britishcouncil.org/sites/default/files/attachments/teaching_english_publication_en_web_version_v1.pdf.

Bourke, B. (2014). Positionality: Reflecting on the research process. *The Qualitative Report, 19*(33), 1–9.

Boyd, C. O. (2001). Phenomenology the method. In P. L. Munhall (Ed.), *Nursing research: A qualitative perspective* (3rd ed., pp. 93–122). Sudbury, MA: Jones and Bartlett.

Charters, E. (2003). The use of think-aloud methods in qualitative research an introduction to think-aloud methods. *Brock Education: A Journal of Educational Research and Practice, 12*(2), 68–82.

Creswell, J. W. (2014). *Research design: Qualitative and quantitative approach* (4th ed.). Thousand Oaks, CA: Sage.

Crusan, D., Plakans, L., & Gebril, A. (2016). Writing assessment literacy: Surveying second language teachers' knowledge, beliefs, and practices. *Assessing Writing, 28,* 43–56.

Cumming, A., Kantor, R., & Powers, D. E. (2002). Decision making while rating ESL/EFL writing tasks: A descriptive framework. *The Modern Language Journal, 86*(1), 67–96.

Davidson, P., & Coombe, C. (2019). Language assessment literacy in the Middle East and North Africa (MENA) region. *Arab Journal of Applied Linguistics, 4*(2), 1–23.

Diallo, I. (2014). Emirati students encounter western teachers: Tensions and identity resistance. *Learning and Teaching in Higher Education: Gulf Perspectives, 11*(2), 1–14.

Doğancay-Aktuna, S. (1998). The spread of English in Turkey and its current sociolinguistic profile. *Journal of Multilingual and Multicultural Development, 19*(1), 24–39.

Eckstein, G., Casper, R., Chan, J., & Blackwell, L. (2018). Assessment of L2 student writing: Does teacher disciplinary background matter? *Journal of Writing Research, 10*(1), 1–23.

Erdosy, M. U. (2004). Exploring variability in judging writing ability in a second language: A study of four experienced raters of ESL compositions. *ETS Research Report Series, 1,* i–62.

Gebril, A., & Hidri, S. (2019). Language assessment in the Middle East and North Africa: An introduction. *Arab Journal of Applied Linguistics, 4*(2), i–iv.

Han, T., & Huang, J. (2017). Examining the impact of scoring methods on the institutional EFL writing assessment: A Turkish perspective. *PASAA: Journal of Language Teaching and Learning in Thailand, 53,* 112–147.

Holliday, A. (2005). *The struggle to teach English as an international language.* Oxford, UK: Oxford University Press.

Ismael, D. A. I. (2013). The influence of TESOL teacher assessment literacy on the ethicality of English language assessment and the position of Kurdish

TESOL teachers. *International Journal of Bilingual & Multilingual Teachers of English, 1*(2), 911–104.

Jenkins, J. (2011). Accommodating (to) ELF in the international university. *Journal of Pragmatics, 43*(4), 926–936.

Jenkins, J. (2014). *English as a Lingua Franca in the international university.* London, UK: Routledge.

Jenkins, J., & Leung, C. (2019). From mythical 'standard' to standard reality: The need for alternatives to standardized English language tests. *Language Teaching, 52*(1), 86–110.

Kakabra, K. K. (2015). English language learning anxiety among foreign language learners in Kurdistan region of Iraq: Soran University as an example. *International Journal of Education and Research, 3*(1), 485–494.

Kırkgöz, Y. (2009a). Globalization and English language policy in Turkey. *Educational Policy, 23*(5), 663–684.

Kırkgöz, Y. (2009b). Students' and lecturers' perceptions of the effectiveness of foreign language instruction in an English-medium university in Turkey. *Teaching in Higher Education, 14*(1), 81–93.

Latif, M. M. A., & Haridy, A. (2018). High-Stakes English writing assessment in Egyptian secondary schools: Historical testing orientations and current instructional practices. *The politics of English second language writing assessment in global contexts* (pp. 85–99). London, UK: Routledge.

Marefat, F., & Heydari, M. (2016). Native and Iranian teachers' perceptions and evaluation of Iranian students' English essays. *Assessing Writing, 27,* 24–36.

Marefat, F., & Heydari, M. (2018). English writing assessment in the context of Iran: The double life of Iranian test-takers. In T. Ruecker & D. Crusan (Eds.), *The politics of English second language writing assessment in global contexts* (pp. 77–92). London, UK: Routledge.

Mauranen, A., Pérez-Llantada, C., & Swales, J. M. (2010). Academic Englishes: A standardized knowledge? In A. Kirkpatrick (Ed.), *The Routledge handbook of World Englishes* (pp. 656–674). London, UK: Routledge.

McKay, S. L. (2009). Introspective techniques. In J. Heigham & R. A. Croker (Eds.), *Qualitative research in applied linguistics: A practical introduction* (pp. 220–241). London, UK: Palgrave Macmillan.

Miles, M., Huberman, A. M., & Saldaña, J. (2014). *Qualitative data analysis* (3rd ed.). Los Angeles, CA: Sage.

Muhammed, A. A., & Ameen, C. A. M. (2014). Idea transformation between L1 and L2 as a writing problem for Kurd EFL learners at different university levels. *International Journal of Scientific & Engineering Research, 5*(7), 353–359.

Ölmezer-Öztürk, E., & Aydın, B. (2019a). Voices of EFL teachers as assessors: Their opinions and needs regarding language assessment. *Journal of Qualitative Research in Education, 7*(1), 373–390.

Ölmezer-Öztürk, E., & Aydın, B. (2019b). Investigating language assessment knowledge of EFL teachers. *Hacettepe University Journal of Education, 34*(3), 602–620.

Öz, S., & Atay, D. (2017). Turkish EFL instructors' in-class language assessment literacy: Perceptions and practices. *ELT Research Journal, 6*(1), 25–44.

Ruecker, T., & Crusan, D. (2018). The intersections of politics and second language writing assessment: What we know. In T. Ruecker & D. Crusan (Eds.), *The politics of English second language writing assessment in global contexts* (pp. 1–12). London, UK: Routledge.

Shi, L. (2001). Native-and non-native-speaking EFL teachers' evaluation of Chinese students' English writing. *Language Testing, 18*(3), 303–325.

Vogt, K., & Tsagari, D. (2014). Assessment literacy of foreign language teachers: Findings of a European study. *Language Assessment Quarterly, 11*(4), 374–402.

Yastıbaş, A. E., & Takkaç, M. (2018). Understanding language assessment literacy: Developing language assessments. *Journal of Language and Linguistic Studies, 14*(1), 178–193.

How Writing Teachers' Beliefs Influence Grading Practices

Najoua Ben Hedia

1 Introduction

Achieving objective and reliable assessment has long been the main objective of research on writing assessment. The main challenge for a considerable number of studies was the investigation of rater variability and its effect on validity. Rater effects, errors, and bias have been traditionally pointed to as the main causes of rater variability (Eckes, Müller-Karabil, & Zimmermann, 2016). Research has recently shown interest in investigating teachers' beliefs as another possible cause of rater variability. A considerable number of studies have investigated the extent to which teachers' beliefs influence the evaluation of students' compositions. This is also the aim of the present study which intends to explore the possible association between Tunisian EFL writing instructors' beliefs and their grading practices. This field of study is still under explored in the Tunisian and North African context. This chapter aims to address this research gap. Research that addresses writing teachers' grading practices

N. Ben Hedia (✉)
University of Tunis El Manar, Tunis, Tunisia

© The Author(s) 2020
L. McCallum and C. Coombe (eds.), *The Assessment of L2 Written English across the MENA Region*, https://doi.org/10.1007/978-3-030-53254-3_7

is much needed in a Tunisian context which aspires to reach international teaching and testing standards. Tunisia also faces the challenge of a growing international need for effective writing ability in the global community. Another important incentive is that writing in the Tunisian educational system occupies a central place in assessment. Thus, looking into scoring validity, "the bug of all bears" as Gamaroff (2000) calls it, is a pressing goal. In fact, the study hopes to trigger more research on different aspects of writing assessment in the MENA region.

The study seeks answers to the following research questions:

RQ 1: What are the Tunisian tertiary level writing instructors' beliefs about writing and grading?

RQ 2: What are their grading practices? What do they reveal about writing assessment in public Tunisian universities?

RQ 3: Do Tunisian writing instructors' professed beliefs match their grading practices?

2 Literature Review

2.1 Rater Variability

Rater variability can be of two types: *inter-rater variability* which refers to a lack of agreement between raters and *intra-rater variability* which occurs in case of inconsistencies in judgments by the same rater. Rater variability in any form is a threat to validity as it is a component of construct-irrelevant variance (Messick, 1993) and a source of measurement error. "Faulty criteria or scales, unsuitable raters or procedures, lack of training or standardization, poor or variable conditions for rating, inadequate provision for post exam statistical adjustment, and unsystematic or ill-conceived procedures for grading and awarding" (Shaw & Weir, 2007, pp. 143–144) are some of the factors that may lead to construct-irrelevant variance. Researchers have explored several factors, among them the use of grading scales. Some empirical studies have presented the use of scoring rubrics as a solution to reduce bias and increase reliability of scoring (e.g., Campbell, 2005; Jonsson & Svingby, 2007). However, several other studies (e.g., Eckes, 2008) have reported that scoring rubrics and training in using them have not always led to increased inter-rater reliability. Other related factors such as rater characteristics (e.g., McNamara, 1996), rater severity and the halo effect (e.g., Engelhard, 1994), raters' perceptions of grading criteria (e.g., Eckes, 2012; Gamaroff, 2000) also influence rater behaviour. Interest in the role of raters' cognition and perceptions leads us to the focus of the present study, the link between teachers' beliefs and essay scoring practices.

2.2 Teachers' Beliefs

Though the concept of beliefs has been the subject of investigation in different fields, it has not yet been clearly defined (Borg, 2001). In fact, several expressions are used to refer to the concept. Beliefs, for instance, have been defined as *propositions* (Rokeach, 1968), *perspectives* (Goodman, 1988), *unconscious assumptions* (Kagan, 1992), *conceptions* (Lloyd & Wilson, 1998; Thompson, 1992) and *mental constructs* (Skott, 2013). Fives and Buehl (2017, p. 26) suggest a wider perception of beliefs. They perceive beliefs "as part of a system, an integrated multi-dimensional web of perspectives (beliefs), conceptions (knowledge), and values (affects /emotions) held by the individual that govern cognitive and external actions".

Research in teaching has provided evidence that beliefs can control teachers' actions, decision making, and even how they interpret and teach the content. Fives and Buehl (2012), identified three main functions of teachers' beliefs: filters for interpretation, frames for defining problems, and guides or standards for action. A wide range of studies investigated different aspects of the influence of teachers' beliefs on their teaching practice. In the field of language teaching, for instance, Kern (1995) and Siebert (2003) compared teachers' and students' beliefs about language learning. Utami (2016) explored EFL teachers' beliefs and their teaching practices, while Gabillon (2012) focused on EFL/ESL teachers' peripheral and core beliefs, Lipa and Harlin (1993) also studied differences between teachers' beliefs about the process approach and its classroom implementation, and Richards, Gallo, and Renandya (2001) probed belief change among pre-service and in-service teachers.

In the Tunisian context, very few studies (e.g., Barkaoui, 2007; Hidri, 2015; Ounis, 2017, 2019) have dealt with teachers' cognition. The present study shares some common points with Barkaoui's (2007) as both studies are about writing assessment beliefs and grading practices, but the latter focuses just on the rating scale impact, whereas this chapter explores other factors such as teaching practices and written corrective feedback.

Interest in understanding the interplay between beliefs, cognitive processes, and essay evaluation started with Diederich, French, and Carlton (1961) who analyzed teachers' comments on essay scores and suggested five rater types. More recent studies (e.g., Eckes, 2008, 2012; Humphry & Heldsinger, 2019) considered raters' perceptions of criterion importance as a factor of rater categorization. These studies reflect Wolfe, Kao, and Ranney's (1998) concept of *scoring focus* which assumes that lack of agreement among raters may be caused by differences in focus on grading criteria. For instance, some raters may believe that content is the most important component while others focus more on language.

Widiastuti (2018) reported some teachers' reliance on their philosophy of teaching and learning while grading the students' writing assessment. The concept of teaching and learning philosophies is also addressed in this study which attempts to understand the foundations of the participants' knowledge and beliefs about writing assessment. A related issue is the concern with the impact of writing assessment literacy also referred to as competence in assessment (Stiggins, 1995). Studies like those carried out by Min (2013) and Crusan, Plakans, and Gebril (2016) call for a need to develop writing teachers' assessment knowledge, which will lead to a change in some wrong beliefs and practices and, therefore, reduce error measurement and rater variability.

A further key aspect of writing assessment research is the influence of teachers' beliefs on written corrective feedback (WCF). Despite the conflicting positions on the role, type, and effectiveness of WCF (see Bitchener & Ferris, 2012), research has provided ample evidence for the impact of WCF on the development of L2 learners' writing ability. Studies of the influence of teachers' philosophies and perceptions on

WCF reflect a belief in the important role of this aspect of writing assessment. A number of studies have been devoted to different features of EFL writing instructors' beliefs on WCF in order to understand teachers' perspectives on the issue. For example, Diab (2005) and Alshahrani and Storch (2014) compared teachers' and students' perceptions of WCF. Lee (2009) and Mao and Crosthwaite (2019) investigated matches and mismatches between teachers' perceptions and practices of WCF. Ferris, Brown, Liu, and Stine (2011) and Al-Bakri (2016) focused on the connection between teachers' beliefs, practices, and context challenges.

Providing an exhaustive overview of the research published on writing assessment and teachers' beliefs is beyond the scope of this section which just sought to present a brief review of published research that presented ample evidence that teachers' beliefs can be a source of rater variability and may affect scoring validity.

3 Methodology

3.1 The Study Context

The study is concerned with the grading practices of essays written by undergraduate Tunisian students of English. The student writers are studying for a degree in English language and literature in departments of English in Tunisian state universities. Writing is an important component of their education. It takes a central place in instruction and assessment. All the students who major in English have to take a writing class for three years. They first learn the different types of paragraphs, and then they learn how to write a five-paragraph essay and the different rhetorical modes. There is a special focus on argumentative writing as this is believed to be the genre most needed by university students.

The writing tests are generally in-class timed essays or paragraphs. Officially writing assessment is both continuous and summative but in practice it is mainly summative. With summative assessment, though dominant, as in most EFL contexts (Lee, 2017), the grades do not just serve the need for accountability. Grades can be used for decision making or to inform content course instructors about the students' progress.

Table 1 Participants' teaching experience

Teaching experience	No. of subjects
5 years	1
6–10 years	6
More than 10 years	3

3.2 Participants

Ten female writing instructors took part in the study. There were no selection criteria, they were a convenience sample but quite representative of the profile of writing instructors in the departments of English in the Tunisian universities. They are all university instructors in different universities in Tunis. They teach writing to different levels of undergraduate students of English. None of them were novices in the field (see Table 1), they have at least 5 years of teaching experience at the university level and have taught writing for at least 3 years. One of them is a Ph.D. holder, all the other participants have a Masters' degree and some of them are Ph.D. candidates. The teachers were not informed of the research aims.

3.3 Methods

Since beliefs are not observable and can just be inferred (Pajares, 1992), the study design required the use of different types of data sources. To garner as much information as possible, three data collection instruments were used: classroom observation, a sample of graded essays, and a semi-structured interview. The use of different data sources helps check the consistency or inconsistency of findings of each instrument and "enable the most accurate attribution of beliefs possible" (Speer, 2005, p. 388).

The data were collected over two sessions. The first session was devoted to classroom observation. This is one of the most commonly used instruments in the study of teachers' beliefs (Philipp, 2007). Observing the participants in their "natural settings", allows the researcher to interpret the phenomenon under study "in terms of the meanings people bring to them" (Denzin & Lincoln, 2005, p. 3). For the current study, observing the teachers in their classrooms provided information about the adopted approach. It also helped infer the teachers' beliefs and check the degree of congruity between the espoused beliefs and classroom practice.

The writing classes lasted between one hour and a half to two hours. 6 out of the 10 observed lessons were taught to first year students of English, 2 to second year students, and 2 to third (final) year students. The lessons were not videotaped, I transcribed the steps followed during the lessons, I noted the types of activities, and kinds of supporting materials, and I observed the teachers' and learners' behaviour during the whole lesson. I also paid attention to the amount and types of feedback, as well as to the amount of time allocated to the practice of writing.

Collection of the second instrument started at the end of the first session. Immediately after the lesson observation, the teachers were provided with an argumentative essay written by a third-year student of English (see Appendix 1) and they were asked to grade it at home and write comments to justify the grade. This essay will be referred to as *essay 1* henceforth. The participants were also asked to provide the researcher with a graded copy of one of their students' essays. One of them provided me with an electronic copy and the other participants asked their students to provide me with a sample graded essay. These essays were not written for research purposes, they were not about the same topic, and were written by students in different levels. The essays written by the participants' students will be referred to as *essay 2*, hereafter. Essay 2 was used to control the participants' bias, i.e. it was a way to check the instructors' consistency in providing WCF. Comparing the WCF in essay 1 and essay 2 was also meant to contribute to the objective attribution of beliefs. Speer (2005) warns against the use of an inappropriate research design that may lead to a discrepancy between the professed and attributed beliefs.

The third data collection instrument was a semi-structured interview. The choice of this tool was dictated by the study objectives and the assumption that teachers may be unaware of their beliefs or unable to state them explicitly. This type of interview allows for probing and digging deeper into the participants' thoughts to get richer information that will be used to corroborate the information inferred from the classroom observation and the WCF analysis. The interview

(Appendix 2) consisted of open-ended and closed-ended questions. All the open-ended questions, with the exception of one, were followed by a request to explain and provide further information. The interview aimed at gathering information about the subjects' teaching experience, the training they received in teaching and testing writing, their teaching and grading practices, changes in beliefs, and causes of the changes. The interviews were carried out during the second session. They lasted between 15 and 30 minutes.

3.4 Data Analysis

Analysis of the data obtained from the classroom observations and interviews consisted of three steps: transcription, drafting a summary sheet, and data categorization. The graded essays underwent different types of analysis. The grades awarded to essay 1 were compared to check if there were any discrepancies between the participants. Three participants provided a grading scale to explain how they reached the final grade. These scales were compared and closely analyzed to help infer beliefs about the participants' grading practices and writing ability conceptions. The last step was devoted to the analysis of the teachers' WCF. There were two types of feedback: comments written on the students' texts or in the margins, these will be referred to as *corrective feedback* because the aim from such comments was generally to draw attention to errors. The second type of comments refers to the teachers' observations, which are generally provided after the students' texts. These two categories underwent different types of analysis. The feedback typology suggested by Ellis (2008) was used to identify and classify the participants' corrective feedback. The comments, which were used to justify the grades, were classified under 5 categories: content, organization, cohesion, language, and mechanics. This categorization was imposed by the themes of the comments. A frequency count of the instances of corrective feedback was carried out to compare the participants' use of WCF.

The same steps were followed in the analysis of the WCF of essay 2. The results were used to compare individual participants' practices during and before the research.

4 Results and Discussion

4.1 Data from the Classroom Observations

All the observed lessons were about academic essay writing but, as indicated in Table 2, they focused on different aspects of essay writing. In all the lessons the teachers focused on essay/paragraph structure and explained or reviewed the linguistic features of that essay/paragraph. Analysis of the different steps of the lessons indicated two different ways of lesson organization: reading-writing integration and rule-based instruction leading to composition practice. Seven participants integrated reading and writing. The reading activities, though important components of the lessons, did not last long and served either to provide the students with a topic or ideas (3 teachers) or as a sample essay that illustrates a specific organizational pattern (5 teachers). The rule-based lessons consisted of two main phases: a review or introduction of some specific text features and a writing practice phase.

All the lessons sought to develop the students' knowledge about specific text features and the steps of the writing process. The participants used different aspects of the process approach to writing. The students were asked to brainstorm, select and organize ideas, develop a thesis statement or a topic sentence. Some of the activities were done individually but there was also a lot of group and pair work in most of the observed lessons, especially during the writing tasks. The students spent on average 35 minutes writing (they had to work on different stages of the writing process). This corresponds to 30% of the writing class time. Just 2 participants devoted 50% of their class time to writing, one of them spent

Table 2 Lesson focus

Essay type	No. of lessons
Academic essay structure (practice/review)	3
Refutation of the opponents' arguments	2
Literary essay	1
Ethos, logos, and pathos	1
Narrative essay (organizational pattern)	1
Problem solution pattern (body paragraph structure)	1
Functions and structure of a concluding paragraph	1

half of the time lecturing about writing rules and academic essay structure. There were three other lessons where the teacher talking time was quite high. In fact, most of the participants showed some concern with writing rules and text organization patterns. Another common feature in the observed lessons was that all the participants played the role of a guide and a facilitator during the writing and feedback phases of the lesson. Feedback sessions were in the form of class activity and input from peers was mainly on content and organization, even when the students corrected their peers' language mistakes, the instructors just consented without explaining the error or talking about its gravity. There were very few instances where the teachers themselves corrected language mistakes. This happened mainly when the students brainstormed and were unable to provide the appropriate words or expressions. In fact, the main focus during the practice phase was on relevance, strength of the arguments, appropriate support, and strict conformity to the text organization conventions.

Based on the lesson observations, one can claim that most of the lessons fit the process genre approach to writing as described by Badger and White (2000). The observed writing classes involved linguistic knowledge, awareness of the context and purpose of writing, skills development through the use of the different stages of the writing process, and input from the teachers, the students, and sample texts. It is important to note here that though not all the observed lessons contained sample texts; nine out of the ten participants noted during an informal discussion after the lesson observation that they do provide texts to illustrate organizational patterns. The teachers seem to be on the right track, because the process genre approach is believed to be a suitable choice for modern classrooms (Tudor, 2017).

4.2 Data from the Graded Essays

While the class observation results indicate some homogeneity between the participants, analysis of the graded essays revealed some disagreement on the grading criteria. Table 3 shows that grades assigned to essay 1 varied between 6 and 12.5 out of 20, indicating, thus, a high standard

Table 3 Grades awarded to essay 1

Participant No.	1	2	3	4	5	6	7	8	9	10
Score	8	7	12.50	8.5	9	6	12	11	6	9.5

deviation (2.32). Three participants awarded a grade higher than average and the others estimated that the essay was rather poor. This discrepancy could be due to the absence of a grading scale and differences in grading criteria. Seven participants did not indicate whether they used holistic or analytic grading. The other participants, however, explicitly stated their grading scales. The scales consisted of 3–4 rubrics which had different labels, but they were about language, content, and organization. "Content", for instance, was referred to as "development" by one participant and "organization" was labelled "structure" by two participants. The common point between these scales is the remarkably high weight of the language rubric: 50% of the overall score in one case and 40% in the two other cases. In addition to that, language is stated as the first component of the three scales. These scales, as McNamara (1996) suggests, are an embodiment of the raters' perception of the importance of linguistic accuracy for the writing ability.

There was a special focus on grammar, vocabulary, word choice, spelling, punctuation, and style errors. In fact, 86.5% of the identified instances of corrective feedback were about language mistakes and just 13.5% were about content and organization. The participants used the three types of feedback suggested by Ellis (2008): direct, indirect, and metalinguistic feedback. In direct feedback, the teacher corrects the errors, but there is no error correction in indirect feedback which consists of two subcategories: *indicating and locating errors* and *indication only*. The participants used just the first subcategory; they underlined the errors or used cursors to draw the students' attention to their language errors. Metalinguistic feedback, too, consists of two subcategories: *use of error codes* (abbreviations, such as *sp* for spelling) and *brief grammatical description* in the form of explicit comment on the errors. Table 4 shows that about 60% of the provided corrective feedback was metalinguistic. The brief grammatical description was more used than error codes. The

Table 4 Types of corrective feedback

Participant	Direct feedback	Indirect feedback	Metalinguistic feedback – Error code	Metalinguistic feedback – Brief description	Total
1	11	2	21	6	40
2	6	23	13	14	56
3	9	21	16	17	63
4	4	17	20	12	53
5	2	6	6	2	16
6	11	11	6	17	45
7	17	16	9	9	51
8	2	15	2	8	27
9	2	0	1	28	31
10	2	4	29	29	62
Total	66	115	123	142	446
Percent	14.80%	25.78%	27.58%	31.84%	100%

latter consisted almost exclusively of language errors while 42% of the former category consisted of feedback on content and organization.

Direct error correction was the least used category. The teachers used this category to correct language mistakes. The limited use of this type of feedback and the heavier use of the two other types suggest that the teachers want the students to correct their own mistakes and thus help them achieve better linguistic accuracy. These findings confirm the teachers' concern with linguistic accuracy and indicate their desire to raise the students' awareness about their weaknesses.

The strong focus on linguistic accuracy was not confirmed by the analysis of the comments written at the bottom of the essays. Based on the number of occurrences of comments on different features, content seems to be the most important feature. All the participants but one wrote at least one statement about the content (relevance, sound reasoning, development of ideas, etc.). Seven teachers started their feedback with comments on content. Some of the observations suggest an interest in the audience and a belief that an essay is an act of communication. For instance, many participants insisted on the clarity of the message through asking the students to provide support and two participants noted that the use of the religious arguments was not convincing.

Organization of the content was also an important feature, but it occupied the second rank. Out of the nine participants who wrote feedback about essay organization, just one instructor started her feedback with comments on information structuring. The teachers' comments were sometimes technical, too broad, and rarely contained indications as how to overcome the weaknesses. Feedback, as in the examples below, points to a belief in assessment of learning and not assessment for learning. Such comments seem to hold the students responsible for not learning and putting in practice what they were taught in class (e.g. *'No argumentation', 'Weak introduction and conclusion', 'No thesis statement', 'No topic sentences'*).

Eight participants' comments showed again concern with clarity of expression, appropriate word choice, and grammatical correctness but such comments were often placed after the comments on content and organization. Punctuation was the least considered feature, just two participants commented on this aspect of writing.

Comparison of the subjects' comments on the two essays revealed a striking intra-rater consistency; most of the participants' comments on essay 2 were about the same aspects as in essay 1. Some participants used even the same order. For instance, participant number three started her feedback, in both essays, with comments about the students' language. In fact, she followed the order of items suggested in her grading scale. This can be considered as a proof that the participants behaved as usual and there was no Hawthorne effect. There was just one case where the participant provided a much more detailed feedback on essay 1 than on essay 2. This might be due to time constraints or the fact that teachers could discuss the feedback on essay 2 in class and during writing conferences. The few other noted differences in the participants' feedback seem to be due to differences in the students' performance. For instance, participant number 7 noted a cohesion problem in essay 2, but not in essay 1.

4.3　Data from the Interviews

The striking finding about the participants is that none of them had professional training in teaching, testing, and grading writing. 8 out of the 10 participants had a very brief introduction to teaching writing during their pre-service training. The two other participants did not get any training at all. The only form of professional training, reported by just 2 participants, was through the TKT and CELTA training programmes organized by the Tunisian Ministry of Higher Education with the cooperation of the US Embassy or the British Council. Even here, training in teaching and testing writing was just one component of the programme. Another participant reported that she also attended workshops organized by the university.

In some cases, the participants' post graduate studies helped them acquire some theoretical knowledge about testing. Teaching experience and self-development have also helped some participants acquire some knowledge about the theory and practice of teaching and grading writing.

The participants' lack of training was reflected in their responses to some of the interview questions. For instance, question number three was about the teaching approach adopted in class. It was noted earlier that all the participants used the process genre approach in their classes; however, three teachers stated that they used the process approach and seven teachers were unable to name an approach, they just described the steps they followed in class. This might also be partly due to the fact that they did not use a specific textbook. In response to question number four, they noted that they used files compiled from different sources. A specific textbook would have probably been helpful because the preface or the introduction would mention and explain the adopted approach. Materials selection does not seem to be theoretically grounded. It is important to note, though, that some participants might not have taken part in the materials selection. They just adopted the files prepared by senior colleagues.

Question number five was about the amount of time devoted to the practice of writing in class. The responses suggest that on average, each instructor devotes approximately 57 minutes to writing practice, which corresponds to 47.5% of class time. This figure exceeds the one suggested by the lesson observation report, but it should not be taken as signalling a mismatch since the activities vary from one session to another and time planning is also subject to change.

Change in teaching practice was the concern of question number six which sought to check the claim that changes in beliefs and practice are the result of a change in knowledge. While all the participants admitted that they had changed their teaching practices, just the two participants who had the TKT and CELTA training acknowledged the influence of the training they had. Another participant who has been teaching for 18 years pointed to her teaching experience as the source of learning and change in practice.

The changes in the participants' teaching practice, summarized in Table 5, indicate a move towards a better implementation of the writing process. For instance, 6 participants noted that they involved the learners more during the writing classes and they relied a lot on group work and interaction with the students. Another interesting change was the fact that some participants learnt not to "abide by the book" and introduce some changes in the curriculum. This change seems to be the result of awareness of the students' specific needs and learning preferences. It also expresses a desire to make the course more motivating. There is just one response that reflects the concern with linguistic accuracy.

Questions seven to nine were about assessment practices. The results indicate that two assessment tools were used by the participants: essay tests and portfolios. All the participants made use of the timed essay based on a prompt and all, but one believed that essays provided them with objective evaluation of the students' writing ability. One participant expressed her reservations about the objective evaluation and noted that "*the essay topic could sometimes be binding*" and, thus, affect the students' performance. She believed that portfolios allowed a better evaluation. Three other participants made use of portfolios in order to get a more objective evaluation of the students' writing proficiency. In response to question nine which was about the change in assessment practices, two of these participants noted that they recently introduced the use of portfolios. Three other participants believed that they changed their assessment practices. One of them stated that she learnt to write more specific questions, but the others did not provide enough information. The other participants (05) stated that the exam system allowed for no change. In an attempt to dig deeper, four of these participants were asked why they tested writing. They suggested three reasons: accountability to the

Table 5 Changes in teaching practices

Interactive class/Use of group work (6)
Changes in the course content//I no longer "abide by the book" (4)
Awareness of the students' different learning styles
Less theory and more writing practice in class (3)
I use brainstorming and peer-editing
I think about how to motivate the students (2)
I have become more meticulous
I think more about the students' needs
I pay more attention to the students' level
I carried out error analysis
I rely a lot on social media

administration, assessment of learning, and assessment for learning. The last reason was suggested by just one participant.

Grading practices, the focus of this study, were dealt with in questions 10–14. Nine out of the ten participants used analytic scoring and believed that a grading scale allowed for more objective evaluation. Despite the few differences in the rubrics labelling, there was a consensus about the components of the grading scale. The responses indicate, however, a lower degree of agreement as to the order of importance of the rubrics. There was a slight disagreement among the participants about the value of *Content* and *organization*; the two criteria were perceived as equally important or one being slightly more important. The main disagreement was about the subgrade allocated to correct language use. Five participants assigned a higher subgrade to language, because they considered it the most important feature of good writing. Among these participants was the one who never used analytic scoring because "*it inflates grades*". She noted that language correctness was the main criterion of evaluation. This lack of consensus among the teachers explains the discrepancy in the grades awarded to essay 1.

A comparison of the scales suggested during the interview and the ones used during the evaluation of essay 1 yielded a competent degree of consistency among the participants who stated their grading scales.

The use or non-use of analytic grading, as shown in Table 6, does not seem to greatly affect the grading procedure. Just one participant stated that she usually read the essays only once; she just re-read when

Table 6 Essays grading practices

	Rate	No. of participants
Number of times the participants read the essays	Once	1
	Twice	3
	2–3 times	6
Drawing attention to mistakes	sometimes	1
	Always	9
Providing feedback	Always	10

she could not get the student writer's ideas. This participant noted earlier that she recently started using analytic grading. The other participants read the essays at least twice before assigning grades. The need for more than one reading was justified by a concern with objectivity, a better understanding of the content and organization, providing pertinent comments, and a preoccupation with language mistakes. Three participants noted that they devoted a second or third reading to spot mistakes. Drawing the student writers' attention to their mistakes seems very important to all the participants. Table 6 indicates that nine participants always highlighted errors. According to responses to question twelve, all types of errors were spotlighted but special attention was paid to language mistakes. All the participants believed that language mistakes were the most serious errors since they obstructed meaning and indicated a lack of mastery of the English language. Content and organization flaws were also considered as serious errors by two participants.

Once the errors are spotted, teachers write their overall impressions at the end of the compositions. This seems to be common practice among all the participants. They all commented on the different aspects of the essays with a special focus on language. Three participants noted that in addition to the traditional written feedback, they also relied on one-to-one writing conferences, i.e. face to face communication because it allowed them to better explain the problems to the students. The aim from providing written and oral feedback, according to the participants, was mainly to draw the students' attention to their mistakes and help them raise awareness about their writing weaknesses. The striking finding here was the general tendency among most of the participants to equate feedback with weaknesses and mistakes. Just three participants presented a different view, one talked about feedback as a process and she stated that she dealt with the students "as cases", which means that she made use of personalized feedback. The two other participants talked about providing negative as well as positive feedback. One of them even insisted on the need to select words and expressions that would not sound too negative so that she would not block and demotivate her students. This participant and another one noted that they also relied on peers' feedback in the classroom. This confirms the claim made earlier about the use of process writing in the classroom and students' involvement in the feedback sessions during the observed lessons.

Analysis of the participants' comments on essays 1 and 2 confirms the claim about the tendency to provide mainly negative comments. Negative comments are concerned with weaknesses in the students' essays and positive comments are about good features in the students' texts. There were 104 negative comments in the analyzed data while there were just 14 instances of positive comments. This means that 88% of the comments were negative. On average, there were 5 negative comments on each essay while the highest occurrence of positive comments is 4 in just one essay. Out of the 20 analyzed essays, nine essays contained positive feedback. Another important finding was that eight out of the ten participants used a red pen to highlight mistakes and write feedback and some of them opted for a negative tone, as illustrated by the comments: "*Some shocking mistakes*", "*No hook!*" and "*No interesting motivator!*".

The last question in the interview was also about feedback. It was meant to further explore the participants' beliefs and practices. The participants were given a list of items (see Appendix 2, question 14) and were asked to select the ones they focused most on. Their responses indicate some congruence. Table 7 shows that linguistic accuracy was their

Table 7 Feedback focus

Item	No. of participants
Language	9
Organization	7
Content	6
Cohesion	4
Punctuation	4

main concern: 9 participants reiterated their belief in the importance of correctness. Organization and content were also presented as important objectives, though they were not given the same weight as language correctness. Cohesion and punctuation were not perceived as important components of a good writing proficiency. In fact, just two participants noted that they focused equally on all the aspects.

The results suggest that the most commonly reported core belief centred on the role of linguistic accuracy. A good piece of writing must exhibit mastery of the language: correct grammar, correct sentence structure, appropriate and varied word choice, and correct spelling and punctuation. This belief is based on a peripheral one; the belief that lack of accuracy affects the message and, thus, impedes communication. This claim is justified by the high subgrade allocated to language in the grading scales, the evaluation of language errors as the most serious type of errors, and the high percentage of marginal corrective feedback about language. The participants' claim that language correctness was important for the clarity of the message is another evidence for the claim. Concern with accuracy seems to be quite common among writing teachers. Previous research (such as Furneaux, Paran, & Fairfax, 2007; Zamel, 1985) reported that writing teachers dealt with the students' essays as language teachers and showed little concern with the communicative side of the piece of writing.

These beliefs reflect some influence of the product approach to writing. Another possible cause is the use of the summative approach to assessment which is characterized by accountability (Lee, 2007). The summative approach leads writing instructors to perceive the students' essays as a product to be graded and the comments are used to justify the grades.

The teachers' lack of training and its resulting limited rating literacy seem to have greatly contributed to the adoption of these beliefs. The participants' experience helped them develop some literacy, but their grading practices seem to be at least partly influenced by the beliefs they developed during their education. This is alarming because, as Kagan (1992) noted, such preconceptions cannot be easily changed.

The second key belief is incompatible with the previous ones. The results suggest that the participants hold a conviction that writing is an act of communication. Despite the important role ascribed to language, content, organization, and audience were not neglected by the participants. These aspects of essay writing formed the focus of the comments written at the bottom of the students' essays and were also taken into consideration in the metalinguistic corrective feedback. Further evidence for the existence of this belief is the use of the writing process in class, the teachers' minimal feedback about the linguistic mistakes during the observed sessions, and their desire to empower the students to develop good writing strategies. This is a case of conflicting beliefs leading to a clear mismatch between the teaching and grading practices: the use of the writing process while teaching and a focus on linguistic accuracy during the evaluation of the students' essays. The teachers seem to be torn between the approach suggested in textbooks and their preconceptions.

The results pointed to another mismatch between professed beliefs and practice. There is incongruence between the participants' claim that feedback provision aimed at helping the students learn and the negative feedback they wrote. The data also contained very few instances of directive feedback that indicated to the students how to overcome the weaknesses. Such feedback cannot empower the students, nor can it promote their confidence and motivation in writing. This mismatch, too, is the result of lack of training. An awareness of the different approaches to teaching writing and training in testing and grading could have helped the teachers adopt an approach appropriate for their sociocultural context and develop a more competent degree of assessment literacy.

5 Implications for the Context and Conclusion

The first research question of the study was about the kinds of beliefs held by the teachers. The findings indicate there are two main conflicting beliefs. The first is a belief that linguistic accuracy plays a very important role in writing development. This belief is backed by the belief that lack of linguistic correctness can impede clarity of the message. The second key belief is the conception of writing as an act of communication that has to consider purpose and audience. This conflict is a sign of mixed conceptions and serves to explain the mismatch between the teaching and grading practices.

The teachers' grading practices formed the concern of the second question posed in the study. In fact, the results pointed to a huge gap between the participants' teaching and grading practices. In class, the teachers adopted the process genre approach to teaching writing and focused on the different stages of the writing process. Writing seems to be perceived as a communicative event that takes into consideration the purpose of communication, the participants, and the socio-cultural context. This belief is just partly reflected in the teachers' grading practices. The participants dealt with the essay as a final product; they believed that their main task was to spot errors and point to weaknesses.

Research question number three was about congruity between the professed beliefs and the grading practices. The results indicated some congruity as well as mismatches. As previously noted, the congruity concerned the beliefs about the importance of linguistic accuracy and the perception of writing as a communicative event. The mismatches resulted from the conflicting beliefs about teaching and grading objectives. The process-product dichotomy led to a mismatch between the teaching and grading practices. The teachers' classes focused on writing as a process while their grading practices indicated a focus on the product and language accuracy. This also led to a mismatch between the espoused aim from feedback provision and the high percentage of negative feedback the participants provided.

The study findings point to an urgent need to provide the writing teachers with training in teaching, testing, and grading writing. The literature on teaching writing has stressed the importance of training. For instance, Weigle (2007, p. 207) argues that "a solid understanding of assessment issues should be part of every teacher's knowledge base, and teachers should be encouraged to equip themselves with this knowledge as part of their ongoing professional development." Training can lead teachers to change their beliefs (Wilson & Cooney, 2002). Had the teachers had solid background knowledge about theories of teaching writing and adequate assessment literacy, they would have noticed the mixed and conflicting beliefs they held, and they would have focused on the message contained in the students' essays more than on the language and stylistic errors.

Assessment literacy will also enable teachers to reflect upon the disadvantages of summative assessment and probably opt for assessment for learning that might fit better their teaching objectives. This type of assessment will also help advance the teaching and learning. A complete change in the system is a requirement but this is beyond individual teachers' control. Writing teachers can; however, make a wider and more effective use of portfolios during the term and use impromptu essays for the end of term tests.

In the absence of institutional training, self-directed professional development is a solution, it can influence beliefs. One of the participants in this study mentioned that she reads books to access knowledge about teaching writing. Another important road to change in beliefs is collegial interaction. There is ample evidence in the literature (for instance, Schubert & Ayers, 1992; Siciliano, 2016) about teaching colleagues' potential influence on knowledge and beliefs change.

The present study has attempted to shed some light on the role of teachers' beliefs in writing assessment grading. This area of research is still unexplored in the MENA region and there is a need for further in-depth research. For instance, replication of the present study may increase our understanding of the association between the teachers' beliefs and their grading practices. Future research should involve a larger sample to allow for more generalizable findings. A longitudinal study of teachers' beliefs is also required; it will provide insights into the development of beliefs and change over time. There is also an urgent need to investigate the learners' perceptions of feedback. Such studies will provide a clearer picture of writing assignment in the Tunisian context and help in the development of sound writing instruction and appropriate testing and grading practices.

Appendix 1: Essay 1

Topic: Self-immolation has become a very frequent form of protest in post-revolutionary Tunisia. Explain your position on the issue.

Essay:
As a result of dictatorship, many people rebelled and break out with silence. Self-immolation wasn't as efficient as many people thought it to be for many reasons. it represents a way to violence, it doesn't calm down problems and religiously prohibited.

Self-immolation is a kind of violence since it requires the use of fire. Immolating oneself represent a sort of showing people how to use violence against the government. In fact, it is a pressure made on the government to show political leaders the power of violence that a citizen can produce. Apart from this, Self-immolation contributes in teaching children how to use violence against their parents. So, Self-immolation is not only a sort of physical violence but also a psychological one on children.

Socially estimated, Self-immolation is not considered as a solution to stop problems. In contrast, this violent act will increase tension within the society. People will feel pity for the dead person. Others will disagree with the issue. Thus, Self-immolation was far from being a solution, it may cause strikes and other protests. It may cause anger within people who will not take an easy or peaceful way to solve the problem. The government as well, will not make logical decisions since it is under horrible pressure.

Religiously speaking, Self-immolation was considered illegal by many religious people. In the islamic religion, Self-immolation is killing oneself which ultimetly considered as committing suicide. As it is well known, the islamic religion views suicide as something forbidden. In fact, our souls are gifts given to us to protect them and give them the best thing they deserve and not to extinct them. For many religious, killing oneself is among the horrible sins that a human being can commit. Therefore, Self-immolation was religiously unacceptable in many societies.

To sum up, Self-immolation is far from being a peaceful way to express oneself or protest. Instead, self-expression may be another solution for peaceful state and avoiding dictatorship.

Appendix 2: Prompts for the Teacher Interview

1. How long have you been teaching writing?
2. Did you get any training in teaching, testing and grading writing?
3. Which approach to writing do you adopt in your classes? Why?
4. Do you use a specific textbook or a compiled file?
5. How much time do your students spend writing during the writing classes?
6. Have your teaching practices changed over the years? How?
7. Which assessment tools do you use (essays, portfolios, objective tests, indirect test/timed tasks, free writing)?
8. Do you think that these tools help you provide accurate/objective evaluation?
9. Have your assessment practices changed over the years?
10. How do you score the students' writing?
11. How many times do you read the essay? Why?
12. Do you correct/highlight errors? What type of errors? What are the most serious errors?
13. Do you provide your students with feedback? Why? What do you often comment upon?
14. Which of the following items do you focus most on: content, organization, language, cohesion, punctuation, and spelling? Why?

References

Al-Bakri, S. (2016). Written corrective feedback: Teachers' beliefs, practices and challenges in an Omani Context. *Arab Journal of Applied Linguistics, 1*(1), 44–73.

Alshahrani, A., & Storch, N. (2014). Investigating teachers' written corrective feedback practices in a Saudi EFL context: How do they align with their beliefs, institutional guidelines, and students' preferences? *Australian Review of Applied Linguistics, 37*(2), 101–122.

Badger, R., & White, G. (2000). A process genre approach to teaching writing. *ELT Journal, 54*(2), 153–160.

Barkaoui, K. (2007). Rating scale impact on EFL essay marking: A mixed-method study. *Assessing Writing, 12*(2), 86–107.

Bitchener, J., & Ferris, D. R. (2012). *Written corrective feedback in second language acquisition and writing.* New York: Routledge.

Borg, M. (2001). Teachers' beliefs. *ELT Journal, 55*(2), 186–188.

Campbell, A. (2005). Application of ICT and rubrics to the assessment process where professional judgment is involved: The features of an e-marking tool. *Assessment & Evaluation in Higher Education, 30*(5), 529–537.

Crusan, D., Plakans, L., & Gebril, A. (2016). Writing assessment literacy: Surveying second language teachers' knowledge, beliefs, and practices. *Assessing Writing, 28,* 43–56.

Denzin, N. K., & Lincoln, Y. S. (Eds.). (2005). *The Sage handbook of qualitative research* (3rd ed.). CA: Sage.

Diab, R. L. (2005). Teachers' and students' beliefs about responding to ESL writing: A case study. *TESL Canada Journal, 23*(1), 28–43.

Diederich, P. B., French, J. W., & Carlton, S. T. (1961). Factors in judgments of writing ability. *ETS Research Bulletin, RB-61-15,* i–93.

Eckes, T. (2008). Rater types in writing performance assessments: A classification approach to rater variability. *Language Testing, 25*(2), 155–185.

Eckes, T. (2012). Operational rater types in writing assessment: Linking rater cognition to rater behavior. *Language Assessment Quarterly, 9,* 270–292.

Eckes, T., Müller-Karabil, A. & Zimmermann, S. (2016) Assessing writing. In D. Tsagari, & J. Banerjee (Eds.), *Handbook of second language assessment* (pp. 147–164). Boston: De Gruyter Mouton.

Ellis, R. (2008). A typology of written corrective feedback types. *ELT Journal, 63*(2), 97–107.

Engelhard, G., Jr. (1994). Examining rater errors in the assessment of written composition with a many-faceted Rasch model. *Journal of Educational Measurement, 31*(2), 93–112.

Ferris, D., Brown, J., Liu, H. S., & Stine, M. E. A. (2011). Responding to students in college writing classes: Teacher perspectives. *TESOL Quarterly, 45*(2), 207–234.

Fives, H., & Buehl, M. M. (2012). Spring cleaning for the "messy" construct of teachers' beliefs: What are they? Which have been examined? What can they tell us? In K. R. Harris, S. Graham, T. Urdan, S. Graham, J. M. Royer, & M. Zeidner (Eds.), *APA handbooks in psychology: APA educational psychology handbook, Vol. 2. Individual differences and cultural and contextual factors* (pp. 471–499). Washington: American Psychological Association.

Fives, H., & Buehl, M. (2017). The functions of teachers' beliefs: Personal epistemology on the pinning block. In G. Schraw, J. Lunn, L. Olafson, & M. VanderVeldt (Eds.), *Teachers' personal epistemologies: Evolving models for transforming practice* (pp. 25–54). NY: Information Age Publishing Inc.

Furneaux, C., Paran, A., & Fairfax, B. (2007). Teacher stance as reflected in feedback on student writing: An empirical study of secondary school teachers in five countries. *International Review of Applied Linguistics, 45*, 69–94.

Gabillon, Z. (2012). Revisiting foreign language teacher beliefs. *Frontiers of Language and Teaching, 3*, 190–203.

Gamaroff, R. (2000). Rater reliability in language assessment: The bug of all bears. *System, 28*, 31–53.

Goodman, J. (1988). Constructing a practical philosophy of teaching: A study of preservice teachers' professional perspectives. *Teaching & Teacher Education, 4*, 121–137.

Hidri, S. (2015). Conceptions of assessment: Investigating what assessment means to secondary and university teachers. *Arab Journal of Applied Linguistics, 1*(1), 19–43.

Humphry, S., & Heldsinger, S. (2019). Raters' perceptions of assessment criteria relevance. *Assessing Writing, 41*, 1–13.

Jonsson, A., & Svingby, G. (2007). The use of scoring rubrics: Reliability, validity and educational consequences. *Educational Research Review, 2*, 130–144.

Kagan, D. M. (1992). Implications of research on teacher belief. *Educational Psychologist, 27*(1), 65–90.

Kern, R. G. (1995). Students' and teachers' beliefs about language learning. *Foreign Language Annals, 28*(1), 71–92.

Lee, I. (2007). Assessment for learning: Integrating assessment, teaching, and learning in the ESL/EFL writing classroom. *The Canadian Modern Language Review, 64*(1), 199–213.

Lee, I. (2009). Ten mismatches between teachers' beliefs and written feedback practice. *ELT Journal, 63*(1), 13–22.

Lee, I. (2017). *Classroom writing assessment and feedback in L2 school contexts*. Singapore: Springer Nature.

Lipa, S. E., & Harlin, R. (1993). Assessment: Insights into teachers' beliefs and practices. *Reading Horizons, 33*(3), 195–208.

Lloyd, G. M., & Wilson, M. (1998). Supporting innovation: The impact of a teacher's conceptions of functions on his implementation of a reform curriculum. *Journal for Research in Mathematics Education, 29*, 248–274.

Mao, S. S., & Crosthwaite, P. (2019). Investigating written corrective feedback: (Mis)alignment of teachers' beliefs and practice. *Journal of Second Language Writing, 45*, 46–60.

McNamara, T. F. (1996). *Measuring second language performance.* London; New York: Longman.

Messick, S. (1993). *Foundations of validity: Meaning and consequences in psychological assessment.* Princeton, NJ: Educational Testing Service.

Min, H. T. (2013). A case study of an EFL writing teacher's belief and practice about written feedback. *System, 41*, 625–638.

Ounis, T. (2017). Exploring secondary teachers' perceptions of classroom assessment in a Tunisian context. *International Journal of Language and Linguistics, 4*(2), 116–124.

Ounis, T. (2019). Tunisian EFL teachers' beliefs and perceptions about oral corrective feedback. *Communication and Linguistics Studies, 5*(2), 45–53.

Pajares, M. F. (1992). Teachers' beliefs and educational research: Cleaning up a messy construct. *Review of Educational Research, 62*(3), 307–332. https://doi.org/10.3102/00346543062003307.

Philipp, R. (2007). Mathematics teachers' beliefs and affect. In F. K. Lester (Ed.), *Second handbook of research on mathematics teaching and learning* (Vol. 1, pp. 257–318). Charlotte, NC: Information Age.

Richards, J. C., Gallo, P. B., & Renandya, W. A. (2001). Exploring teachers' beliefs and the processes of change. *The PAC Journal, 1*(1), 41–62.

Rokeach, M. (1968). *Beliefs, attitudes, and values: A theory of organization and change.* San Francisco: Jossey-Bass.

Schubert, W. H., & Ayers, W. A. (Eds.). (1992). *Teacher lore: Learning from our own experience.* New York: Longman.

Shaw, S. D., & Weir, C. J. (2007). *Examining writing: Research and practice in assessing second language writing.* Cambridge: Cambridge University Press.

Siciliano, M. D. (2016). It's the quality not the quantity of ties that matters: Social networks and self-efficacy beliefs. *American Educational Research Journal, 53*(2), 227–262.

Siebert, L. L. (2003). Student and teacher beliefs about language learning. *The ORTESOL Journal, 21*, 7–39.

Skott, J. (2013). Understanding the role of the teacher in emerging classroom practices: Searching for patterns of participation. *ZDM Mathematics Education, 45*, 547–559.

Speer, N. M. (2005). Issues of methods and theory in the study of mathematics teachers' professed and attributed beliefs. *Educational Studies in Mathematics, 58,* 361–391.

Stiggins, R. J. (1995). Assessment literacy for the 21st century. *Phi Delta Kappan, 77*(3), 238–245.

Thompson, A. G. (1992). Teachers' beliefs and conceptions: A synthesis of the research. In D. A. Grouws (Ed.), *Handbook of research on mathematics teaching and learning* (pp. 127–146). New York: Macmillan.

Tudor, E. (2017). *The process genre writing approach; an alternative option for the modern classroom.* Retrieved from: https://files.eric.ed.gov/fulltext/ED571522.pdf. Last accessed: 20.4.2020.

Utami, D. N. (2016). The EFL teachers' beliefs and their teaching practices. *OKARA Journal of Languages and Literature, 2,* 134–144.

Weigle, S. C. (2007). Teaching writing teachers about assessment. *Journal of Second Language Writing, 16,* 194–209.

Widiastuti, I. A. (2018). Teachers' classroom assessment and grading practices. *SHS Web of Conferences, 42,* 00052.

Wilson, M., & Cooney, T. (2002). Mathematics teacher change and development. In G. C. Leder & E. Pehkonen (Eds.), *Beliefs: A hidden variable in mathematics education* (pp. 127–148). Doordrecht, The Netherlands: Kluwer Academic Publishers.

Wolfe, E. W., Kao, C. W., & Ranney, M. (1998). Cognitive differences in proficient and nonproficient essay scorers. *Written Communication, 15,* 465–492.

Zamel, V. (1985). Responding to student writing. *TESOL Quarterly, 19*(1), 79–101.

Designing Scoring Rubrics for Different Writing Tasks: The Case of Resume Writing in Iran

Mojtaba Mohammadi and Jaber Kamali

1 Introduction

Assessing writing is one of the thorniest and the most perennial issues among language teachers and researchers in the field of English language teaching (e.g. Crusan, 2010; Crusan & Matsuda, 2018; Hamp-Lyons, 2001). Besides controversies on defining the construct, scoring writing tasks is among the most challenging issues. These two—defining the construct and scoring—both go hand-in-hand to make writing assessment more complex and contentious. Looking back at the history of assessment, in general, and assessment of writing, in particular, reveals a trend towards presenting typologies of stages and generations of writing assessment. This ranges from Spolsky's (1979) three stages of traditional/pre-scientific, psychometric-structuralist and integrative-sociolinguistic assessments to Hamp-Lyons' (2001) four

M. Mohammadi (✉)
Islamic Azad University, Roudehen, Iran

J. Kamali
Farhangian University, Tehran, Iran

generations of direct testing, indirect testing, portfolio-based assessment and humanistic/technological/political/ethical assessment. They all underpin a metamorphosis from an objective, single-trait, decontextualized, language-based to a subjective, integrated, contextualized, need-based type of writing assessment. On the practical side, writing teachers are teaching the syllabi which require them to work on writing tasks covering, sometimes, a wide variety of functions and genre. The assessment method/instrument needed for different tasks cannot be a one-size-fits-all one but rather the one which can fit the purpose of the activity and the needs of the learners. Moreover, training on how to develop and use an effective rubric, as several scholars (e.g. Andrade & Du, 2005; McCormick, Dooley, Lindner, & Cummins, 2007) have put forth, can improve the degree of consistency, reliability and validity of the measurement. Based on these accounts, this chapter, following a brief literature review on the rubric as a tool to assess writing tasks, aims to describe how to design a rubric to rate a resume writing task and see how functional it is when adopted by the teachers in the Iranian EFL context.

2 Literature Review

2.1 Rubric: The What

Rubric, originally means "red" in Latin which is used to highlight legal decisions and directions for religious services, is commonly defined in education as "a document that articulates the expectations for an assignment by listing the criteria or what counts, and describing levels of quality from excellent to poor" (Andrade & Du, 2005, p. 1). According to Mertler (2001, p. 1), rubrics are "scoring guides, consisting of specific pre-established performance criteria, used in evaluating student work on performance assessments". Crusan (2015, p. 1) also viewed a rubric as "a guide listing specific criteria for grading or scoring academic papers, projects, or tests, and an instrument that describes a specific level of performance within a scale". These definitions underline two major features: a set of pre-determined criteria and a levelled quality definition (gradation of quality) based on which language performance is measured. These are, in fact, the building blocks of a typical rubric.

Rubrics are generally divided into three different categories. The first category is the generic vs. task-specific rubrics which handle either many tasks or just one. The second category is primary-trait vs multiple-trait rubrics where one or various characteristics of a specific task are evaluated. The last category is holistic vs analytic rubrics which are the most common rubric types. In holistic rubrics, one task is evaluated without considering its detailed components and only based on the overall impression of the evaluator. In analytic rubrics, on the other hand, different components of the performance are evaluated separately in quantifiable criteria. Although holistic and analytic rubrics have their own affordances and constraints (e.g. Brown, 2017), recent studies bid farewell to the holistic approach in favour of multiple-trait and argues that writing is not a single ability and "it is hard to build a house with only one brick" (Hamp-Lyons, 2016a, 2016b, p. A3).

2.2 Rubric: The Why

Besides their use as instruments for evaluating learners' performance construed by many scholars (e.g. Campbell, 2005; Reddy & Andrade, 2009), the use of rubrics in education and language assessment is reportedly manifold. They can be used for teaching and learning especially when adopted within an instruction based on the formative assessment approach (Jonsson, 2008; Stiggins, 2001), for programme evaluation (Dunbar, Brooks, & Kubicka-Miller, 2006), and for measuring the efficacy of the courses (Dunbar et al., 2006; Reddy & Andrade, 2009). Rubrics are also reliable and valid assessment tools for multidimensional complex performances (Andrade & Valtcheva, 2009). Also, most recently, studies have confirmed that using rubrics in a task can improve the reliability, validity, and consistency of the assessment (Crusan, 2015; Dempsey, PytlikZillig, & Bruning, 2009).

2.3 Writing Scales and Rubrics

Rubrics are largely developed and used for assessing the productive skills (speaking and writing) since their evaluation outcome has always been known to be subjective and unfair. Rakedzon and Baram-Tsabari (2017) listed a number of writing scales and rubrics which rely on either human or computer rating systems. Such scales as the Test of English as a Foreign Language (TOEFL), the Test for English for Educational Purposes (TEEP), the ESL Composition Profile (Jacobs, Zingraf, Wormuth, Hartfiel, & Hughey, 1981) and the DELNA (Diagnostic English Language Needs Assessment) are instances of writing task rubrics for undergraduate levels. For graduate levels, the Graduate Record Examination (GRE) has a measurement scale for its writing section which is developed to analyze an issue and an argument. Computer rating systems have also been designed in the past four decades to score the writing performance tasks. According to Zhang (2013, p. 3), one of the high-stakes tests automated scales is called e-rater® engineered by Educational Testing Service, the TOEFL iBT developer, which "can provide feedback on grammar, word usage, mechanics, style, organization, and development of a written text". Zhang (2013, p. 1) also notes that Pearson's Intelligent Essay Assessor™ can also "provide feedback on six aspects of writing—ideas, organization, conventions, sentence fluency, word choice, and voice". Some of the scales for low-stakes tests are those for such tests as ETS's TOEFL® Practice Online (TPO), College Board's ACCUPLACER® and ACT's COMPASS®.

2.4 Approaches to Rubric Development

Rubrics are used as a tool to measure test takers' performance in criterion-referenced tests (CRT), where the achievement of the examinees is important, or norm-referenced tests, where evaluators wish to measure the relative performance of the learners along a continuum. Janssen, Meier, and Trace (2015) have introduced different classifications to rubric development or revision. One is Fulcher's (2003) framework with two intuitive and quantitative processes in which the former is more expert- or experience-based while the latter is mostly data-based or data-driven. Another classification is presented by Hawkey and Barker (2004) in which there are three methodologies of intuitive, quantitative, and qualitative. Rubrics adapted from other existing rubrics or those based on the expertise of the developers are included in the first one. Rubrics developed based on the expertise of a group of informants (e.g. in a workshop) on the features of the writing at different proficiency levels is qualitative. Quantitative methodology is based on experimental data and data analysis methods to rate the performance based on the rubric descriptors in the form of an integer scale.

2.5 Needs for Developing a Rubric

A huge body of research studies has made efforts to improve the functionality of rating scales (e.g. Barkaoui, 2007; Li, 2018; North, 1995) in rating situations. However, these studies have adopted a very universal view on rubric development. Writing assessment in an EFL context has been criticized for adopting an impressionistic rating (Barkaoui, 2010) where raters rely on their intuitions. Ghanbari and Barati (2015, p. 204) went further to cast doubt upon the existence of an explicit rating scale in the Iranian context. The results of their study revealed that "lack of a common rating scale caused the raters to draw on ad hoc rating criteria".

Therefore, in order to respond to this need in the context of language learning/teaching in Iran, the present study tries to design and develop a rubric for rating writing tasks which can be used objectively in assessing learners' resume writing. Hence, the research questions are proposed as follows:

RQ1: What steps should be taken in designing a scoring rubric for Iranian learners?

RQ2: How do Iranian EFL teachers reflect on the use of the newly developed rubric for rating resume writing tasks?

3   Developing a Rubric

There are a number of ways to develop a new rubric. Crusan (2010) proposes five stages to design a rubric: developing course goals, choosing assessment tasks to fit these goals, setting the standards for these tasks and goals, developing criteria to assess performance and rating values for analytic scoring. Vahdani and Mohammadi (2020) also introduced four steps in the process of rubric development, namely planning, drafting, assessing, and editing. Each of these phases is further divided into certain steps. Recently, Brown (2017) proposed seven stages to develop a rubric: planning the rubric, designing the rubric, developing assessment procedures, using the rubric, giving feedback with the rubric, evaluating the rubric and revising the rubric.

However, the rubric development steps we employed were from Mertler (2001) since it is the most examined and trusted model and is more compatible with our purposes—to provide an example of a rubric development. The steps are summarized as follows (Mertler, 2001, p. 4):

Step 1: Match up the task and learning instruction so the rubric can act as a clear measure of learning and task achievement.

Step 2: Identify observable attributes that you do not want/want to see your students demonstrate in their performance.

Step 3: Brainstorm characteristics that describe each attribute. Identify ways to distinguish between levels of performance for each attribute.

Step 4a: For holistic rubrics, write clear descriptions that guide how to distinguish between levels of performance. These should describe the highest and lowest levels of performance.

Step 4b: For analytic rubrics, write clear descriptions that guide how to distinguish between levels of performance. These should describe the highest and lowest levels of performance.

Step 5a: For holistic rubrics, describe other levels on the continuum that range from excellent to poor work for the attributes.

Step 5b: For analytic rubrics, describe other levels on the continuum that range from excellent to poor work for each attribute.

Step 6: Collect samples of student work that exemplify each level. These will help scoring by serving as benchmarks.

Step 7: Be prepared to reflect on the effectiveness of the rubric and revise it prior to its next implementation.

3.1 Sample Rubric Development: A Resume

Based on different English coursebooks, one of the topics of writing in English classes is resume writing (e.g. Richards, Hull, Proctor, & Bohlke, 2013; Soars & Soars, 2006). In the EFL context of Iran, most students have felt the importance of resume writing since they need to apply either for universities overseas, jobs or immigration and they all need a convincing resume. Hence, in this study, we are attempting to design a rubric for rating a resume writing task in the Iranian EFL context. Methodologically, the newly designed rubric, as mentioned above, is based on Mertler's (2001) steps. Regarding contents and organization, the researchers with years of teaching English experience exerted all their efforts to develop a rubric based on the needs of the learners and teachers. It is worthwhile mentioning that two previously developed rubrics from Amherst College and California State University, Northridge were consulted to help decide the content of the rubric. The steps and the concerns in each and every one of these steps to develop the rubric are presented as follows:

Step 1: Re-examine the learning objectives to be addressed by the task

To apply this step, we needed to define the learning objectives of the target language i.e. the resume. The objectives of resume writing are as follows:

1. To include all skills and abilities
2. To be accurate
3. To be appropriate
4. To sound persuasive.

Step 2: Identify specific observable attributes that you want to see

Considering all these aims, we identified the following four attributes on which to focus our rubric: content, accuracy, appropriacy and persuasiveness. The objectives for content are as follows:

- To ensure an employer can easily contact you.
- To convey academic qualifications and training.
- To contextualize your skills and qualifications in a concise manner, showing their relevance to your candidacy.

The accuracy objective can be scrutinized by these elements:

- To include skills or content that are relevant and do not appear elsewhere on the resume.
- To ensure your document is easily read and appears polished [orderly and neat].
- To ensure the resume is polished regarding mechanics, spelling and punctuation.
- To group content, drawing attention to experiences that resonate with your target audience and increase readability.

The objectives of accuracy which are divided into level of formality and audience should follow the following objectives

- To ensure the right level of formality of the text (not too formal, not too informal).
- To ensure your strengths are strategically highlighted for your specific audience.

The last attribute—persuasiveness, is how convincing the resume is. The feature is as follows:

- To ensure the persuasiveness of the text.

To design this part, we changed the attributes to measurable entities. To do so, we had to define the components of different attributes by brainstorming the components we would like to measure in each. Thus, we have to move to step three.

Step 3: Brainstorm characteristics that describe each attribute
Different factors were discussed and the factors we wanted to measure in content were:

1. Contact Information which should be informative enough with all the detailed information such as name, email, phone, etc.
2. Education by which we mean academic qualifications and training.
3. Work experience.
4. Skills, interests and personal hobbies.

For accuracy, style and appearance, mechanics, spelling and punctuations were agreed upon.

For appropriacy, audience and level of formality were taken as components.

And for persuasiveness, overall impression of the resume was considered as the only element.

Step 4b: write thorough narrative descriptions for excellent work and poor work for each individual attribute.

In this part, all of the narrative descriptions should be defined. To reach this aim, three scores were defined. 1. Above standard 2. Acceptable 3. Not acceptable.

1. Above standard

This score represents meeting the high standards of writing a resume e.g. in organization of content it represents:

- Section headers accurately reflect content
- Adequate content exists within a section to substantiate the heading.

2. Acceptable

This score exemplifies an acceptable resume with some considerations. For instance, in organization of content it represents:

- Section headers could more accurately reflect content
- Content of a section is not best placement of information.

3. Not acceptable

The last score is the one which means the resume does not meet the minimum standards. For example, in organization of content it represents:

- No use of sections or one "experience" section lists all entries
- Too many sections—not enough content to warrant a section
- Section titles don't reflect content.

Step 5b: the rubric by describing other levels on the continuum that range from excellent to poor work for each attribute.

In this part all the components went through different levels from above standard to not approved.

Steps 6 and 7: *They should be done by the teachers to see if they need any change in their rubrics.*

It should be borne in mind that like any other tool, the success in welcoming and using this rubric by the end-users is how effectively it works. That is why the best strategy can be to involve them in the process of preparing it. If the evaluators who are using the rubric have had a say in its development, they are more likely to buy into it as they see their voice in it. Moreover, the developers can benefit from their experience and see how other rubric-users view the assessment and the latent traits that need to be considered for the purpose of assessment. Having developed the first draft and having it proofread by two experienced teachers, the researchers trialled the final draft (see Appendix 1) to investigate its efficacy.

4   Methodology

After designing the rubric, it was administered to 20 EFL teachers. They were all teaching at a language institute in Tehran, Iran. They were all between 22 and 38 years old and taught *Cutting Edge* (3rd edition) (Cunningham & Moor, 2014) coursebook to adult learners. They all had a degree in English such as B.A., M.A. in Teaching English as a Foreign Language (TEFL), English literature or English translation.

12 of them were TESOL certificate holders and the rest had received domestic English Teacher Training Course (TTC) certificates.

A session was conducted by one of the researchers to discuss the scoring rubrics and what the teachers needed to know about it such as words, categories, etc. The teachers asked questions regarding the rubrics. They asked questions such as: Will the rubric be used for all levels of students? can the rubric be printed? what should we do if the result is unacceptable? and is it time-consuming? The questions were answered, and the teachers were asked to do a resume writing task in their classes, provide feedback on the resumes using the newly developed rubric and share their experience in an interview.

5   Results and Discussion

After in-depth oral interviews with 20 teachers, the interviews were transcribed and analyzed through thematic coding. Seven themes emerged which are discussed in turn in this section.

5.1   The Rubric Built Confidence for Raters

The first construct extracted from the teachers' interviews was "the rubrics build confidence for raters". All the teachers believed that rubrics could give them more confidence in both scoring and student's consultation. As is evident in extract 1, One teacher stated:

Extract 1

Of course, it is very good because it made us sure about what we should look at in rating their writing. It made me confident in giving the score to my students.

As can be seen in extract 1, the teacher obviously discussed the confidence the rubrics has built in them especially when giving scores. The reason behind it might be having a pre-established set of benchmarks for both the students to learn and the teachers to rate accordingly.

5.2 The Rubric Increased Students' Satisfaction

A number of the teachers claimed that "the rubrics can increase student's satisfaction". They believed that a measurement tool can make it clear what to score and what not to. One of the teachers expressed that:

Extract 2

> I had problems always, always I had problems with some students who thought this is not their writing, but themselves, which is judged, you know. So, I was always searching for a way to overcome this problem and I have found it. Many thanks to you. Nobody complained about their score because everything was clear for them.

One of the causes of student's dissatisfaction in language classes is being treated unfairly. However, the rubrics can clarify the reasons for losing marks for the students; this, thus, prevents dissatisfaction on the part of the students. Extract 2 evidently clarifies this issue and shows how the teacher could see satisfaction in students' behaviour.

5.3 The Rubric Created a Sense of Consistency

Reliability is the degree to which an assessment tool produces stable and consistent results. Three of the teachers believed that the rubrics provide the raters with the same guidelines; hence, they will score the same. 9 teachers stated that it can improve internal consistency. Extract 3 makes this point evident.

Extract 3

> I had a lot of students who came to me and told me that you focused on the parts that we had never before worked on or been corrected upon. And it made me think that if all of us [teachers] correct the part harmoniously, I mean having a unity in feedback and which part we provide feedback for, learners can learn easier because they have focused attention and the rubric does that. It provides a sense of unity. We all have a standard based on which we can check the writing.

It is evident in extract 3 that the teacher feels a difference after using the rubrics since it created a standard based on which the students are scored with different teachers (raters). Therefore, it can be concluded that this tool can help the reliability of scoring which refers to how consistently a test measures a characteristic.

5.4 The Rubric Increased the Validity of the Scoring

It is sometimes difficult to know if the scale is measuring the intended construct it is designed for. A few teachers mentioned how effective the rubric was since they know what they really want to measure which did improve the validity of the instrument. Extract 4 is an evident example.

Extract 4

When I have to correct more than 20 papers, my eyes get used to the mistakes and I sometimes don't see them. you know what I mean? when I look at the rubrics it works as a conscious … awareness … consciousness raising tool for me. It draws my attention to different aspects I have to consider in writing feedback.

As can be seen in extract 4, the given rubric can work as a *validity booster* since it can provide a clear definition of what we are measuring. This can add to the validity of the score on the grounds that all aspects which should be taken into account have been considered.

5.5 The Rubric Raised Students' Awareness About Different Components of a Proper Resume

By providing the teachers with the rubrics, not only do they know what they should consider in checking the resumes, but they are also able to learn how to teach resume writing. This impact of testing on teaching is called the washback effect (McKinley & Thompson, 2018). By giving the rubrics to the students, they also learn what aspects of resume writing they have to focus on. Extract 5 is clear about this point.

Extract 5

By looking at the rubric I learnt even how to teach resume writing. For example, I have never thought about the audience for resume writing and this rubric made me think about it. So, I can say the rubrics can act as a teaching tool, too.

Extract 5 underlines the washback effect of the rubric. As the teacher urged it can be used as a teaching tool and can be considered as a consciousness raising device.

Despite these positive points extracted from the interviews on the adoption of the rubric in class, they pointed out two shortcomings of the rubrics:

5.6 It Is Difficult for Learners to Understand

Eight of the teachers argued that the rubrics could cause confusion for learners. They claimed that the students had problems understanding what the rubric was and what it focused on. One of the teachers stated that:

Extract 6

They [learners] couldn't understand it. I think it was better to make it easier or have less words in it.

As can be seen from the extract, the teacher expresses that learners had problems understanding the rubric. The solution for this problem can be *training*. Training learners to use rubrics and being corrected based on the rubrics can be a remedy to this confusing problem. Another issue regarding this shortcoming is the learners' level of language proficiency. A solution to this problem can be designing different versions of the rubric for students of different levels of proficiency.

5.7 It Is Overloaded with Information

The other shortcoming stated by 5 of the teachers is that it was overloaded with information. They argued that having too much information can be counterproductive.

Extract 7

> It contains a lot of information and becomes a bit frightening for the learners. I was worried that they don't take enough time to read it and some of them told me so. They said it is too long and they don't have enough time to read it.

Regarding extract 7, we can conclude that level adaptation might be a solution here. We may use a shorter version for the learners which makes it easier for them to understand.

6 Implications for the Context and Conclusion

Overall, although there are some obstacles to employing designed scoring rubrics according to Iranian teachers' beliefs and practices, namely being difficult for leaners to understand and being overloaded with information, its use was considered a positive trend in scoring resumes by Iranian teachers since it can build confidence for raters, increase students' satisfaction, create a sense of consistency, increase the validity of the scoring, and raise students' awareness about different components of a proper resume.

Designing the rubric helped us figure out the importance of having a standard for measuring writing. Hence, it helped the validity and reliability of the scoring since the teachers know what they should look for in the writing task and they have the same standards. It could make the teachers more confident as well.

In conclusion, scoring a constructed response test has attracted considerable attention in different fields, ELT is no exception. Weigle (2002) pointed out that the two major concerns in this regard are the defining of the scale and the training of the raters. This chapter has tried to review different rubric development models such as Fulcher (2003), Hawkey and Barker (2004), Janssen et al. (2015), and Vahdani and Mohammadi (2020). It employed Mertler's (2001) framework to design a rubric for resume writing.

This chapter posits that the process of rubric development is a collective and iterative effort in which every stakeholder's voice plays a role. Although the process is a lengthy one, there is no doubt that the effort one puts into it and the benefits one reaps will make it a worthwhile process.

7 Appendix 1 : Resume Writing Rating Rubric

See Table 1.

Table 1 Resume rubric

Criteria	Above-standard (3)	Acceptable (2)	Not Acceptable (1)
Contact Information Objective: To ensure an employer can easily contact you.	• Includes name, email, phone • Name is the largest/most pronounced • Email address used is professional	• Includes name, email, phone • Name is not most pronounced • Email address is too casual	• Information is missing one of the following: name, email, phone • Email address is unprofessional/inappropriate
Education Objective: To convey academic qualifications and training. *Study abroad should be included, if applicable.	• Degree is spelled out • Major/minors (if declared) and graduation month/year is indicated • Each institution attended includes name, location, dates • Institutions are listed in reverse chronological order • Honours and scholarships listed and include dates (may be separate section)	• Degree is abbreviated • Major/minors (if declared) and graduation month/year is indicated • Each institution attended includes, name, location, dates • Institutions are listed in reverse chronological order • Honours and scholarships listed and dated	• Incorrect degree listed • Declared major/minor not indicated • Grad date not listed • Each institution does not include name, location, dates • Institutions are not listed in reverse chronological order • Honours/scholarships are not listed

(continued)

Table 1 (continued)

Criteria	Above-standard (3)	Acceptable (2)	Not Acceptable (1)
Experience Objective: To contextualize your skills and qualifications in a concise manner, showing their relevance to your candidacy.	• Each entry lists organization name, dates, position title, location and accomplishment statements • Statements begin with strong action verbs • All verbs reflect the correct tense • Statements are concise, direct and indicate one's impact on the organization • Statements are not written in complete sentences and appropriately omit extra words and personal pronouns • Statements are listed in order of importance • Results are quantified when possible • The most relevant entries include at least one statement	• 1-2 entries omit organization name, dates, position title or location • Resume has a pattern of a single error (e.g. no position titles) • Action verbs could be stronger • 1-2 individual errors in verb tense • Statements could be more concise, direct and indicate one's impact on the organization • Statements are written in complete sentences • Statements are listed in order of importance within an experience • Results are quantified when appropriate • The most relevant entries include at least one bullet point	• 3 + entries do not include organization name, dates, position title or location • Statements begin with weak action verbs • Multiple verb tenses are inconsistent with dates • Statements are wordy, vague or do not indicate one's impact on the organization • Statements contain personal pronouns • Statements are not listed in order of importance within an experience • Results are not quantified when appropriate • Statements are not included on relevant entries • Irrelevant/outdated high school information listed • Entries not listed in reverse chronological order

Criteria	Above-standard (3)	Acceptable (2)	Not Acceptable (1)
Skills/Interests/Language/ Certifications (optional) Objective: To include skills or content that are relevant and do not appear elsewhere on the resume.	• Listings are concise • Level of proficiency is indicated for skill-based entries (language, technology)	• N/A	• Listings are wordy • No level of proficiency indicated for language or computer skills
Overall Style/Appearance Objective: To ensure your document is easily read and appears polished.	• Fills one page without overcrowding • Order of information presented is consistent within each section • Information is presented only once • Appropriate margins and font size • Consistency in formatting (use of bold, italics)	• Page appears crowded • Order of information is consistent within sections • Information is only presented once • Appropriate margins and font size • Less than 2 errors in formatting consistency	• Document does not use space appropriately (too long or too short) • Inconsistency in the order of information within one or more sections • The same information is presented more than once • Margins and font size too big/too small • Inconsistency in formatting
Spelling, Punctuation and Mechanics Objective: To ensure resume is polished.	• Resume has no errors (spelling is correct, punctuation and spacing are consistent)	• Resume contains 1-2 minor errors (punctuation, spacing, formatting) • Resume has a pattern of a single error (e.g. some bullets have periods, some don't)	• Resume contains 3 or more individual errors • Resume has a pattern of two or more errors
Organization of Sections Objective: To group content, drawing attention to experiences that resonate with your target audience and increase readability.	• Section headers accurately reflect content • Adequate content exists within a section to substantiate the heading	• Section headers could more accurately reflect content • Content of a section is not best placement of information	• No use of sections or one "experience" section lists all entries • Too many sections—not enough content to warrant a section • Section titles don't reflect content

(continued)

Table 1 (continued)

Criteria	Above-standard (3)	Acceptable (2)	Not Acceptable (1)
Audience Objective: To ensure your strengths are strategically highlighted for your specific audience.	• Language is relevant to the reader (section titles, descriptions) • The most relevant information is grouped and appears on the first half of the page • The most relevant information is highlighted by formatting (bold, etc.) • Listed coursework (optional) is tailored to the target field	• Audience is addressed, but more focus is required • Language could be more relevant to the reader (sections, descriptions) • The most relevant information is grouped on the second half of the page • The most relevant information could be highlighted by formatting • Coursework (optional) is tailored to the targeted field	• Resume does not show evidence of being targeted to field of interest (NOTE: This rating pertains to all general resumes) • Section titles and descriptions do not support targeted field • The most relevant information is not grouped, does not appear on the first half of the page, or highlighted by formatting • Coursework (optional) is not tailored to specific field
Level of formality Objective: To ensure the right level of formality of the text (not too formal, not too informal)	• There is no use of slangs • There is optimal use of abbreviations • There is an optimal use of contractions	• Some slangs are used sporadically but do not hinder communication • There is under/overuse of abbreviations • There is an under/overuse of contractions	• The language is too informal
Overall impression Objective: to ensure the persuasiveness of the text	• It persuades the reader that the candidate possesses sufficient qualifications	• It persuades the reader to invite the candidate for interview although the reader is hesitant about the qualifications	• It does not show the qualifications needed for the purpose the resume is written for

References

Andrade, H., & Valtcheva, A. (2009). Promoting learning and achievement through self-assessment. *Theory Into Practice, 48*(1), 12–19.

Andrade, H., & Du, Y. (2005). Student perspectives on rubric-referenced assessment. *Practical Assessment, Research & Evaluation, 10*(3), 1–11.

Barkaoui, K. (2007). Rating scale impact on EFL essay marking: A mixed-methods study. *Assessing Writing, 12*(2), 86–107.

Barkaoui, K. (2010). Do ESL essay raters' evaluation criteria change with experience? A mixed-methods, cross-sectional study. *TESOL Quarterly, 44*(1), 31–57.

Brown, J. D. (2017). Developing and using rubrics: Analytic or holistic. *Shiken (JALT Testing & Evaluation SIG Newsletter), 21*(2), 20–26.

Campbell, A. (2005). Application of ICT and rubrics to the assessment process where professional judgement is involved: The features of an e-marking tool. *Assessment & Evaluation in Higher Education, 30*(5), 529–537.

Crusan, D. (2010). *Assessment in the second language writing classroom*. Ann Arbor, MI: University of Michigan Press.

Crusan, D. (2015). Dance, ten; looks, three: Why rubrics matter. *Assessing Writing, 26,* 1–4.

Crusan, D., & Matsuda, P. K. (2018). Classroom writing assessment. In J. I. Liontas (Ed.), *The TESOL encyclopedia of English language teaching*. New York: Wiley.

Cunningham, S., & Moor, P. (2014). *Cutting edge* (3rd ed.). Boston: Pearson Education.

Dempsey, M. S., PytlikZillig, L. M., & Bruning, R. H. (2009). Helping preservice teachers learn to assess writing: Practice and feedback in a web-based environment. *Assessing Writing, 14*(1), 38–61.

Dunbar, N. E., Brooks, C. F., & Kubicka-Miller, T. (2006). Oral communication skills in higher education: Using a performance-based evaluation rubric to assess communication skills. *Innovative Higher Education, 31*(2), 115–128.

Fulcher, G. (2003). *Testing second language speaking*. London, UK: Pearson Longman.

Ghanbari, N., & Barati, H. (2015). Iranian EFL writing assessment: The agency of rater or rating scale? *Iranian Journal of Language Testing, 4*(2), 204–228.

Hamp-Lyons, L. (2001). Fourth generation writing assessment. In T. Silva & P. K. Matsuda (Eds.), *On second language writing* (pp. 117–125). Mahwah, NJ: Erlbaum.

Hamp-Lyons, L. (2016a). Farewell to holistic scoring. *Assessing Writing, 100*(27), A1–A2.

Hamp-Lyons, L. (2016b). Farewell to holistic scoring. Part Two: Why build a house with only one brick? *Assessing Writing, 100*(29), A1–A5.

Hawkey, R., & Barker, F. (2004). Developing a common scale for the assessment of writing. *Assessing Writing, 9*, 122–159.

Jacobs, H. L., Zingraf, S. A., Wormuth, D. R., Hartfiel, V. F., & Hughey, J. B. (1981). *Testing ESL composition: A practical approach*. Rowley, MA: Newbury House.

Janssen, G., Meier, V., & Trace, J. (2015). Building a better rubric: Mixed methods rubric revision. *Assessing Writing, 26*(4), 51–66.

Jonsson, A. (2008). *Educative assessment for/of teacher competency*. Doctoral dissertation. Malmö University, Malmö, Sweden.

Li, C. (2018). *Constructing and applying rubrics in college-level EFL writing assessment in China*. Unpublished MA Thesis, Syracuse University. Retrieved from https://surface.syr.edu/thesis/241.

McCormick, M. J., Dooley, K. E., Lindner, J. R., & Cummins, R. L. (2007). Perceived growth versus actual growth in executive leadership competencies: An application of the stair-step behaviorally anchored evaluation approach. *Journal of Agricultural Education, 48*(2), 23–35.

Mckinley, J., & Thompson, G. (2018). Washback effect in teaching English as an international language. In J. I. Liontas, M. DelliCarpini, & S. Abrar-ul-Hassan (Eds.), *TESOL encyclopedia of English language teaching* (pp. 30–37). Hoboken, NJ: Wiley

Mertler, C. A. (2001). Designing scoring rubrics for your classroom. *Practical Assessment, Research & Evaluation, 7*(25), 1–8.

North, B. (1995). The development of a common framework scale of descriptors of language proficiency based on a theory of measurement. *System, 23*(4), 445–65.

Rakedzon, T., & Baram-Tsabari, A. (2017). To make a long story short: A rubric for assessing graduate students' academic and popular science writing skills. *Assessing Writing, 32*, 28–42.

Reddy, Y. M., & Andrade, H. (2009). A review of rubric use in higher education. *Assessment & Evaluation in Higher Education, 35*(4), 435–448.

Richards, J. C., Hull, J., Proctor, S., & Bohlke, D. (2013). *Interchange: 3*. Cambridge: Cambridge University Press.

Soars, J., & Soars, L. (2006). *American headway* (2nd ed.). Oxford: Oxford University Press.
Spolsky, B. (1979). Introduction: Linguists and language testers. In B. Spolsky (Ed.), *Approaches to language testing* (pp. v–x). Arlington, VA: Center for Applied Linguistics.
Stiggins, R. J. (2001). *Student-involved classroom assessment* (3rd ed.). Upper Saddle River, NJ: Merrill/Prentice-Hall.
Vahdani, R. V., & Mohammadi, M. (2020). Rubric-based assessment of the productive skills. In S. Hidri (Ed.), *Changing language assessment: New dimensions, new challenges* (pp. 77–94). London: Palgrave Macmillan.
Weigle, S. C. (2002). *Assessing writing*. Cambridge: Cambridge University Press.
Zhang, M. (2013). Contrasting automated and human scoring of essays. *R & D Connections, 21*. Retrieved from https://www.ets.org/Media/Research/pdf/RD_Connections_21.pdf. Last accessed: 10.5.2020.

Primary Trait Rubric: The Case of MENA Countries

Reza Vahdani-Sanavi

1 Introduction

MENA is the acronym for the Middle East and North African countries. According to the World Atlas (2019), the region includes 19 countries and accounts for 6% of the world population, 60% of the world's oil reserves and 45% of natural gas reserves in the world. The countries included in the MENA region might vary from one organization to the next, for example, according to International Organization for Migration (IOM) (2016), the countries included in the region are Algeria, Bahrain, Egypt, Iraq, Jordan, Kuwait, Lebanon, Libya, Morocco, Occupied Palestinian Territories, Oman, Qatar, Saudi Arabia, Sudan, Syrian Arab Republic, Tunisia, United Arab Emirates and Yemen. According to the International Monetary Fund (1996), some MENA countries have up to two thirds of their labour force from other MENA countries or

---

R. Vahdani-Sanavi (✉)
Social Sciences University of Ankara, Ankara, Turkey
e-mail: reza.vahdani@asbu.edu.tr

even outside this circle. Migration is another issue in the MENA countries as IOM's (2016) report suggests a 150% increase in the number of migrants to the region: The number of international migrants, including registered refugees, in the MENA region reached 34.5 million in 2015, rising by 150% from 13.4 million in 1990. In contrast, global migrant stocks grew by about 60% over the same period. Just over one-third of all migrant stocks in the region are of people from other MENA countries. Emigrants from MENA account for 10% of migrant stocks globally, and 53% of emigrants from MENA countries remain in the region.

Although the more recent movements to the region have been due to the refugee crisis (IOM, 2016), labour movement in the region is partly because of the working conditions in their home countries, according to the International Monetary Fund (1996): Reflecting employment conditions at home as well as special historical relations with other countries, many Arab workers, especially from North Africa, have also migrated outside the MENA region—mainly to Europe. Concurrently, the MENA region has received inflows of migrant workers from outside the region, especially south and east Asia. Asian nationals account for a growing share of the nonnational labour force in the GCC countries and in Israel. Israel has also absorbed in recent years a significant inflow of immigrants from the former Soviet Union.

According to the World Bank (2019a, 2019b), the growth outlook in the region shows a dip of 0.6% in 2019. This is claimed to be mostly because of oil output cut and Iran's "shrinkage" of economy. The World Bank experts further claim the growth from 2019 to 2021 is projected to be somewhere between 1.5 and 3.5%. However, notwithstanding this decline in the economic growth, the business world demand in the MENA region for labour force and constant employment call for a system in place for the recruitment of the most qualified applicants.

All this labour movement and increased trade dictate a lingua franca as the people who come "in contact with each other must find some way of communicating" (Wardhaugh & Fuller, 2015, p. 115). Although most of the inhabitants in the MENA region speak Arabic except for those in Iran and Israel, the work force from other countries whose language is not Arabic requires that everybody uses a lingua franca. Similarly, those who wish to continue their education in the region will have to know English to enter the English Medium Instruction (EMI) universities. When businesses and educational settings wish to admit the prospective candidates, they need to use some reliable tools that can inform them about the candidates' level of knowledge in that particular language. This is when assessment tools can be of use and applied to businesses and schools.

This workforce displacement among others has also given rise to the teaching of English as a medium of instruction (EMI) in many universities worldwide. Although some claim that the use of EMI has adversely affected the use of the native language (Gun, 2018; Khalaf, 2018; Kılıçkaya, 2006; Mense, Lemoine, Garretson, & Richardson, 2018) and even national identity (Amandolare, 2010), the force of circumstances seems to dictate its use as it is believed to substantially contribute to the internationalization of the educational settings and afford opportunities for the actual communicative use of the English language besides the internalization of concepts in another language (Sert, 2008).

Spring (2015) argued that the internationalization of education has been mostly expedited by the World Trade Organization's (WTO) 1995 General Agreement on Trade and Services (GATS), considering educational services as a commodity. This can mean the economic benefits and gains reaped from internationalization can act as a catalyst in this increasingly globalized world economy. Some of the countries in the MENA region are also affected by this change. Likewise, some more recent changes in the global political climate warrants more attention to English as a lingua franca (ELF) in the MENA countries. Badry (2019) claims:

> By the beginning of the twenty-first century, the changing political environment resulting from the 9/11 events in 2001, and later, Brexit, Trumpism and the ascendance of nationalist and anti-immigration movements in Europe and the US, shifted its direction and led to a decrease in student mobility westward and an increase in the movement of Western educational providers eastward. (pp. 2–3)

All the work force displacement, eastward shift of immigration and use of English in the educational settings in the MENA region make evaluation a must, be it in the educational context or the business one. Although there are some internationally recognized high-stakes tests to use to assess the test takers proficiency, different institutions use their own in-house exams. Naturally, a sub-section of any form of assessment should include sections for the evaluation of the test takers' performance and using a scale to rate their performance. When it comes to productive skills, one widely accepted technique to measure such skills is to use a rubric to measure the candidates' proficiency in productive skills as reliably as possible. However, the choice of the right rubric itself can be a point of contention. In the following sections of this chapter, we will explore some underpinnings in assessment endeavors, the different tools that can be used to assess writing, the pretexts why primary trait rubrics are unheeded and some possible solutions.

2 Review of Assessment Concepts

2.1 The Context of Language Use

Language use is a function of linguistic and situational factors called context. Hamp-Lyons (1995) stated that to know what good writing means and who a good writer is, we need context. The Common European Framework of Reference for languages (Council of Europe, 2001) enumerates five aspects of context: (a) domain, (b) situations, (c) conditions and constraints, (d) user's mental context and (e) the mental aspect of the interlocutors. Similarly, Weir (2005) emphasized a paradigmatic shift in favour of context, which comprises task setting, tasks demands and setting and administration. As language is highly dependent on context, test developers and users will have to heed these aspects to have a sound theoretical definition for their context, be it educational or vocational, and then build on that to know how they are able to operationally define the construct using the rubric that best fits the model. Additionally, the test creators will need to know what communicative competence model to refer to as the descriptors in the cell should accommodate it (see Bachman & Palmer, 2010, for examples of communicative competence models).

2.2 Argument Use Assessment (AUA)

We use assessment to make decisions. These decisions depend on the purpose for which an assessment is designed. Some might be for diagnostic and others for prognostic purposes. However, every decision we make based on the test scores obtained from the test-takers' assessment results might have consequences for the stakeholders. It is these purposes that might also affect our choice of the rubric we employ to assess the test takers' performance.

Bachman and Palmer (2010) proposed Argument Use Assessment (AUA) as an approach to create links between test takers' performance and the consequences of the decisions we make with them. By AUA, Bachman and Palmer mean the links that need to be made from a test taker's performance to the consequences ensuing an assessment, which also involves the decisions taken for individuals and the interpretations made about the candidates' language ability. They use Toulmin's (2003) argument for establishing and rationalizing all the links among these concepts.

Bachman and Palmer (2010), following Toulmin's (2003, p. 103) approach, claimed that to establish any link between, for instance, the interpretations we make about test takers' language ability and assessment records, we need to provide support. Such support can be called claims, which include an entity, or a topic and one or more qualities about that entity. Using this line of reasoning, they proposed that language assessment should have four claims:

1. The consequences of the decisions that we make should be beneficial;
2. The decisions based on the interpretations should be values sensitive and equitable;

3. The interpretations that we make based on the assessment records should be meaningful, impartial, generalizable, relevant and sufficient and finally
4. The assessment records should be consistent.

As can be drawn from the claims above, the qualities Bachman and Palmer proposed for AUA are beneficence, values sensitivity, equitability, meaningfulness, impartiality, generalizability, relevance, sufficiency and consistency. Although more than two claims might be relevant to the topic of this chapter, I will basically put generalizability and consistency into perspective.

Generalizability signifies one important quality of the interpretations we make from the test scores and allow the test users to make more valid judgments and decisions. It is this quality of an assessment that warrants that the test takers are able to perform in real life situations as well as they do in the test conditions. This is to be achieved should the test tasks used in the assessment replicate and correspond as closely to the Target Language Use (TLU) tasks within the target language domain in question (Bachman & Palmer, 1996, 2010). When employers wish to employ staff for their business, they should make sure of their prospective employees' successful achievement of their tasks. This can only be achieved if they can make sure the tasks employed in the screening match those in the real world. Likewise, the educators in an academic context have to make sure the tasks they use in the test represent those the test takers will be exposed to in their departments.

Having ensured that the right tasks have been employed to measure prospective candidates' competency in the language, the next step is to strive for reliability of the scores obtained. As for consistency, using a rubric can help test developers achieve records which are less pervious to fluctuations that could threaten this quality of assessment. Although this quality is mainly about the consistency of scores, it also has half an eye on other aspects of tasks as they seem highly pertinent: "the assessment records (scores, descriptions) are consistent across different assessment tasks, different aspects of the assessment procedure (e.g. forms, occasions, rates), and across different groups of test takers" (Bachman & Palmer, 2010, p. 103). Essentially, a consistent assessment generates the same information regardless of the tool we use to assess a test taker's ability, the tasks, the time, and raters. Obviously, a rubric can help us achieve part of this consistency by having raters who are trained on how to employ the respective rubric (Blaz, 2001; Brookhart, 2013; Brown, 2012; Coombe, 2010), but we need to decide what rubric to use to that end.

2.3 The Skill of Writing

Writing can be studied through textual, contextual and cognitive approaches (Weir, 2005). Traditionally, the lion's share of the focus in writing has been on its textual dimensions. However, considering the context validity of any assessment endeavour, we should not divert our attention away from the context. Writing is a cognitive endeavour, but we need to consider the context in which it occurs as without considering it, we might fail to pay due attention to the purpose for which we are assessing the test takers' performance as well as other contextual factors such as the response format, known criteria, weighting, order of items and time constraints.

When it comes to the assessment of writing, however, there is always the possibility of some kind of scoring pollution as there are such threats as construct-irrelevant variances due to the presence of other skills. Apart from this challenge, the design of test tasks and the assessment of the candidates' performance seem to be some other challenges test developers face (Fulcher, 2003; Luoma, 2004). Weigle (2012) stated that the assessment of writing hinges upon defining the construct should the test developers plan to make an informed decision.

As for the test tasks, test takers should know what tasks should be employed to maximize the likelihood of the test takers' use of the expected response which represents the knowledge that needs to be evaluated. This is especially important as the test takers might use their strategic competence to avoid the target linguistic forms. For instance, if the goal is to measure certain discourse makers taught in a course, the examinees can simply circumvent them by adopting their synonyms. Thus, test tasks that can elicit the required quality to be measured play a major part in any assessment endeavour (Brown & Abeywickrama, 2010).

A similarly considerable challenge is that of measuring the creative product of the test takers consistently. Here the major concern is how to avoid compromising the reliability of the test. Clearly, one major player in the game of reliability is the scale that is to be used for measuring the skill as reliably as possible. The choice of what type of rubric to ply hinges upon a host of factors such as the time allotted or necessary for correction, criteria adopted for scoring, the expertise of the scorers, the need for feedback provision to the test takers, generalizability of use over tasks and genres, clarity of the criteria and the availability of training for the examiners, just to name a few. These reasons have given rise to the use of multiple types of rubrics.

2.4 Reviewing Rating Scales and Rubrics in Assessing Writing

Assessment has gained importance in helping decision makers reach better decisions. There are multiple ways to assess a candidate's product. Over the past five decades, the increasingly extensive use of essay type questions has given rise to the use of less objectively scored test tasks, which require a different method of scoring other than the simple tallying of the right answers. Different ways to score these subjectively scored tasks have been proposed to minimize the setback of a less reliable scoring system. However, what method to employ is a point of contention.

Green and Hawkey (2012) enumerate impression scoring, error counting and rating scales as three ways to assess language in use. In impression scoring, the rater assigns a score based on the quality of the product within depending on the total number that can be awarded for a candidate's performance. This can be 92 out of 100 or 14 out of 50 depending on what the maximum score is. The problem with impression scoring is that the raters might act according to different standards. One might pay more attention to one aspect of writing more than another and yet another rater's definition for poor performance might be qualitatively different from that of another. All in all, impression scoring might not be as fair and objective as one expects the test results to be.

In error counting the raters are supposed to tally the number of errors in the candidates' performance and assign a score accordingly. Green and Hawkey (2012) believe that although it was originally thought to be more objective, error coding turned out to have the same problem as impression scoring in that the raters at times disagreed on what to count as an error. A further downside of this method of rating performance was that the test takers tended to use avoidance strategies when they were unsure of a structure. This meant they did not take risks to produce some grammatical structures or lexical items; hence, simpler prose devoid of more advanced lexical or grammatical intricacies.

Another assessment tool, although it is not only used to measure test taker's performance (Reynolds-Keefer, 2010) is a rating scale or rubric, consisting of grading scales. Rating scales help experts make more reliable decisions. They have several advantages over other forms of grading. Andrade (2000) presented some of these merits. He asserted that rubrics are user-friendly and can help learners understand how they can improve their performance. Rubrics can also enhance the educationalists' accountability to their learners as they clearly state what is to be expected from them (Andrade, 2000; Crusan, 2010). Brookhart (2013) also maintained that rubrics can facilitate learning, while Stevens and Levi (2013) claimed that rubrics can boost students' performance by giving feedback.

Rating scales have their share of disadvantages too (Hamp-Lyons, 2003; Vahdani-Sanavi & Mohammadi, 2020; Weigle, 2002). However, to delve more deeply into each of them, we will first have to review their different types and decide which to use despite their caveats.

3   Types of Rubrics

The literature on rubrics suggests different classifications for this tool. Some researchers categorize them into holistic, analytical and primary trait (Brown, 2004; Brown & Abeywickrama, 2010; Cumming, 1997; East & Young, 2007), while others have proposed other classifications such as measurement-driven versus performance data-based rubrics (Fulcher, Davidson, & Kemp, 2010); "constructor-oriented, assessor-oriented, and user-oriented" scales (Alderson, 1990); or, task-specific versus task-independent rubrics (Brown, 2012). The responsibility of choice of/among the different rubrics lies with the users (Weigle, 2002, 2012). However, Weigle believes the decision makers will also have to decide who to choose as raters and how to train them. Moreover, our choice of what type of rubric to use largely depends on the purpose for which the assessment is used (Becker, 2010/2011). The author's personal correspondence and communication with faculty members from twelve universities and four human resources directors in eight countries in the MENA region revealed the use of holistic and analytic rubrics in universities and impression scoring in businesses. No institution reported the use of primary trait rubrics.

3.1 Holistic Rubrics

The most prevalent types of rubrics are the holistic ones. Vahdani-Sanavi and Mohammadi (2020) explained that holistic scoring requires assigning a single score where the score is not broken into the concepts that form the construct. In other words, scores are not assigned to every single concept that forms the whole. In this approach, the rater will take the overall performance of the candidate into consideration rather than each of the descriptors or criteria in question (see Table 1).

This type of rubric has some advantages and disadvantages. Brown (2004, p. 242) detailed the advantages of holistic rubrics when used to score writing as:

1. It is time-efficient;
2. It enjoys a higher inter-rater agreement (especially for expert raters, Barkaoui, 2011, p. 290);
3. It is more user-friendly especially for non-experts (Weigle, 2002, p. 114);

Table 1 Holistic rubric used for an integrated writing task (Reprinted with permission from the School of Foreign Languages, the Social Sciences University of Ankara)

B2 Global Scale: Can produce clear, detailed text on a wide range of subjects and explain a viewpoint on a topical issue giving the advantages and disadvantages of various options.
Overall Written Production-B2: *Can write clear, detailed texts on a variety of subjects related to his field of interest, synthesizing and evaluating information and arguments from a number of sources.*

Score	Task description
5	An excellent response to the prompt
	Effectively addresses the task including all the main ideas in the passage
	Is well organized and well developed, using clearly appropriate explanations, exemplifications and/or details
	Displays unity, progression and coherence
	Displays consistent facility in the use of language, demonstrating syntactic variety, appropriate word choice and idiomaticity, though it may have minor lexical or grammatical errors
4	Good response to the prompt
	Addresses the task well, though some minor omissions
	Is generally well organized and well developed, using appropriate and sufficient explanations, exemplifications and/or details
	Displays unity, progression and coherence, though it may contain occasional redundancy, digression or unclear connections
	Displays facility in the use of language, demonstrating syntactic variety and range of vocabulary, though it will probably have occasional noticeable minor errors in structure, word form or use of idiomatic language that do not interfere with meaning
3	Adequate response to the prompt
	Addresses the task, though some major omissions
	Displays unity, progression and coherence, though connection of ideas may be occasionally obscured
	May demonstrate inconsistent facility in sentence formation and word choice that may result in lack of clarity and occasionally obscure meaning
	May display accurate but limited range of syntactic structures and vocabulary

(continued)

Table 1 (continued)

Score	Task description
	B2 Global Scale: Can produce clear, detailed text on a wide range of subjects and explain a viewpoint on a topical issue giving the advantages and disadvantages of various options. **Overall Written Production-B2**: Can write clear, detailed texts on a variety of subjects related to his field of interest, synthesizing and evaluating information and arguments from a number of sources.
2	Limited response to the prompt Limited development in response to the task with significant misrepresentations and omissions Inadequate organization or connection of ideas Inappropriate or insufficient exemplifications, explanations or details to support or illustrate generalizations in response to the task A noticeably inappropriate choice of words or word forms and an accumulation of errors in sentence structure and/or usage
1	Very limited response to the prompt Serious disorganization or underdevelopment of the task; little or no relevant information from the text Little or no detail or irrelevant specifics or questionable responsiveness to the task Serious and frequent errors in sentence structure or usage
0.5	Too little text to grade Contains only very short 2 or 3 sentences that is somewhat related to the topic or is blank Attempts to answer the prompt but the text poses serious problems for the reader Frequent language errors—poor control of basic structures Very limited vocabulary
0	No answer or totally irrelevant response or plagiarism Merely copies words from the topic, rejects the topic, or is otherwise not connected to the topic Is written in a foreign language Contains plagiarism (in existence of hard evidence) Contains only one sentence that is somewhat related to the topic or is blank

4. It underlines writer's strengths (Cohen, 1994, p. 315) and
5. It can be employed for different tasks.

Hamp-Lyons (1995) suggested holistic rubrics do not supply sufficient information regarding a test takers' knowledge as one composite score is reported for performance. Brown (2004) pinpointed the downsides as follows:

1. It "masks" the criteria within each score;
2. It does not provide very valuable feedback for the candidates (no washback);
3. It does not work equally well across different genres and
4. It requires rigorous and extensive training for raters.

3.2 Analytic Rubrics

In analytic scoring, productive skills are assessed according to the different criteria that the rubric developers have identified. These criteria are placed on one axis and scores are assigned for each of those criteria on the other axis (Table 2). The cells that are formed within such a table are then filled with what is known as descriptors. The raters are to study the descriptors carefully to see what score to assign to the candidates. Should a candidate's performance fail to be on par with the descriptors in each cell, they will be awarded a lower score on the grid.

For pedagogical purposes, analytic rubrics are more fruitful as they lend themselves better to teaching and learning (Blaz, 2001; Brown, 2012). The learners are able to discover the areas that need further improvement in that the scores they are assigned suggest where they need to strategically invest their time. This can help learners to zero in on their problem areas.

Overall, it is believed that while holistic rubrics increase the validity of the measurement (White, 1984), analytic ones increase the reliability of the measurement (Knoch, 2009). Analytic rubrics are further claimed to help learners' critical thinking sub-skills (Saxton, Belanger, & Becker, 2012) and improve their writing skills in general (Dappen, Isernhagen, & Anderson, 2008).

Table 2 Critical Thinking Value Rubric (VALUE Rubric, 2020)

	Capstone 4	Milestones 3	Milestones 2	Benchmark 1
Explanation of issues	Issue/problem to be considered critically is stated clearly and described comprehensively, delivering all relevant information necessary for full understanding	Issue/problem to be considered critically is stated, described, and clarified so that understanding is not seriously impeded by omissions	Issue/problem to be considered critically is stated but description leaves some terms undefined, ambiguities unexplored, boundaries undetermined and/or backgrounds unknown	Issue/problem to be considered critically is stated without clarification or description
Evidence *Selecting and using information to investigate a point of view or conclusion*	Information is taken from source(s) with enough interpretation/evaluation to develop a comprehensive analysis or synthesis Viewpoints of experts are questioned thoroughly	Information is taken from source(s) with enough interpretation/evaluation to develop a coherent analysis or synthesis Viewpoints of experts are subject to questioning	Information is taken from source(s) with some interpretation/evaluation but not enough to develop a coherent analysis or synthesis Viewpoints of experts are taken as mostly fact, with little questioning	Information is taken from source(s) without any interpretation/evaluation Viewpoints of experts are taken as fact, without question

	Capstone 4	Milestones 3	2	Benchmark 1
Influence of context and assumptions	Thoroughly (systematically and methodically) analyzes own and others' assumptions and carefully evaluates the relevance of contexts when presenting a position	Identifies own and others' assumptions and several relevant contexts when presenting a position	Questions some assumptions. Identifies several relevant contexts when presenting a position. May be more aware of others' assumptions than one's own (or vice versa)	Shows an emerging awareness of present assumptions (sometimes labels assertions as assumptions) Begins to identify some contexts when presenting a position
Student's position (perspective, thesis/hypothesis)	Specific position (perspective, thesis/hypothesis) is imaginative, taking into account the complexities of an issue Limits of position (perspective, thesis/hypothesis) are acknowledged. Others' points of view are synthesized within position (perspective, thesis/hypothesis)	Specific position (perspective, thesis/hypothesis) takes into account the complexities of an issue Others' points of view are acknowledged within position (perspective, thesis/hypothesis)	Specific position (perspective, thesis/hypothesis) acknowledges different sides of an issue	Specific position (perspective, thesis/hypothesis) is stated, but is simplistic and obvious

(continued)

Table 2 (continued)

	Capstone 4	Milestones 3	Milestones 2	Benchmark 1
Conclusions and related outcomes (implications and consequences)	Conclusions and related outcomes (consequences and implications) are logical and reflect student's informed evaluation and ability to place evidence and perspectives discussed in priority order	Conclusion is logically tied to a range of information, including opposing viewpoints; related outcomes (consequences and implications) are identified clearly	Conclusion is logically tied to information (because information is chosen to fit the desired conclusion); some related outcomes (consequences and implications) are identified clearly	Conclusion is inconsistently tied to some of the information discussed; related outcomes (consequences and implications) are oversimplified

Reprinted with permission from "Critical Thinking VALUE Rubric". VALUE: Valid Assessment of Learning in Undergraduate Education. Copyright 2020 by the Association of American Colleges and Universities. http://www.aacu.org/value/index.cfm

3.3 Primary Trait Rubric

To evaluate constructed responses where the focus is on one major criterion such as task achievement, test developers propose primary trait rubrics (Brown, 2004; Davis, 2019). This kind of rubric was first employed in the US National Assessment of Educational Progress (NAEP) by Lloyd-Jones and his colleagues. Lloyd-Jones's (1977) model had four levels starting from 1 as the least to 4 as the highest. This method of holistic scoring is mostly employed when one major goal is to be achieved as the purpose of performance. For instance, having the test takers summarize the main ideas in expository writing. The score on this scale will probably change according to the number of main ideas identified and presented from the original passage. In other words, raters will know how to penalize the candidates who have missed out on one, two or more of the ideas which are to be presented. As another example, if the test takers are supposed to read, summarize and evaluate a passage, the trait-based rubric will probably mention what concepts or components the ideal summary will include and how the test takers will have to evaluate the concepts thereof.

Unlike holistic task-independent rubrics, primary trait rubrics are prepared and specifically designed for every single task. Therefore, each task requires a different rubric as the primary trait to be assessed might vary from one task to the next. For example, if the function of the test is to measure test takers' competency in narrative writing, their ability to give details about the setting, characters or the events count, but for higher levels of competency, the rubric might stipulate more advanced features of narration as a climax in the story, plot twists or complications. It is axiomatic that a different set of functions can as such dictate a different rubric.

In the original format of Lloyd-Jones's model (1977), he proposed three segments of discourse: explanatory, expressive and persuasive. He claimed that writers might be good at one segment and yet not another. The purpose of the primary trait rubric, therefore, is to decide which of these functions are to be evaluated (Lloyd-Jones, 1977). Tables 3 and 4 show what primary trait rubrics look like and how they change although they are both used for expressive discourse. Table 3 is for the following

Table 3 Primary Trait scoring for expressive discourse (Adapted from Lloyd-Jones, 1977, pp. 60–63)

0	No response, a fragmented response
1	Does not clearly state their stance, or does not cite reasons for their stance Only paraphrasing the stem Stance adopted but not maintained
2	Adopts a stance but fails to fully develop it
3	Adopts a stance and gives one fully supported reason, one fully supported and one unsupported reason or two or three unwarranted reasons
4	Adopts a stance and gives two or more fully supported reasons, one fully supported and two or more underdeveloped reasons or four or more reasons not fully supported

Table 4 Draft Version of Primary Trait Rubric (Adapted from Lloyd-Jones, 1977, pp. 47–50)

	Cannot be scored: irrelevant to the picture; does not attempt or fully memorized
1	The response fails to address the imaginative aspect of the photo although the writer manifestly attempts to describe the picture
2	Clear point of view, Incorporating the imaginative aspect of the picture despite some inappropriate structures for the genre; Alternatively, good structure but lack of the imaginative aspect of the picture
3	These papers are generally competent in creating a realized point of view towards the world of the picture
4	Shows clear ability to sustain temporal and spatial point of view; Fully detailed; clear narrative style; Clear positive or negative attitude, Clear position
5	The response shows all the positive aspects of band 4. It fully addresses all parts of the task. Presents a fully developed statement that can be interpreted explicitly

prompt: "Some people believe that the place of a woman is in the home. Others do not. Take ONE side, Write an essay in which you state your position and defend it" (Lloyd-Jones, 1977, p 60).

Table 4 evinces a higher level of specificity for a pictorial prompt where test takers can see five children jumping playfully on a capsized boat. The table is a draft version of the primary trait rubric used before it is revised (see Lloyd-Jones, 1977, pp. 52–53 for the final scoring rubric), suggesting that the rubric is devised as two phases. The respondents are to imagine they are one of the kids or a passer-by seeing the setting and express how any one of those in the picture would relate the story to a close friend. In other words, the writer is supposed to see things through someone else's spectacles: one of the players or the observer. The respondents are also supposed to express strong feelings such that their audience could empathize with the narrator. Obviously, the prompt suggests that although the primary trait is the test taker's command of the expressive discourse, the item writers expect the respondents heed the degree of formality/informality because of familiarity with the audience.

Like other types of rubrics, primary trait rubrics have certain strengths and drawback that can be portrayed as their characteristics:

1. They are difficult and time-consuming to prepare;
2. There should be sample essays to anchor or benchmark performance for each score;
3. They are more detailed yet more user-friendly as they are specific to one task;
4. There are multiple rubrics for multiple tasks; hence, more difficult or unwieldy;
5. They require many raters for the benchmarking to achieve agreement;
6. They are generalizable to only the same discourse segment and not the pool of discourse
7. Stronger validity claims for the task and the discourse segment but less external validity/generalizability.

4 Constructing Rubrics: Validity and Reliability

In constructing rubrics, irrespective of its type, test makers will have to consider some points such as the development of the rubric, its improvement and rater training. Regarding rubric development, some experts claim that writing the rubric from scratch is reinventing the wheel and therefore propose adopting and adapting the extant ones (Crusan, 2010). Brown (2012, pp. 18–30) proposed the nuts and bolts of developing a rubric. He tabled six stages, the first three of which, planning, designing and planning the assessment procedures and using the rubric, form the construction of a rubric. Each of these phases is further broken down into some stages to know how to initiate the rubric and create one.

Once a rubric has been developed, it should be constantly and systematically revised to ensure valid inferences and subsequent decisions will be made. For example, Janssen, Meier and Trace (2015) used the Rasch model to revise one rubric for the admission to Ph.D. programs. They studied Jacobs, Zinkgraf, Wormuth, Hartfiel, and Hugley's (1981) rubric for their research. Having detected certain inconsistencies in the rubric, Janssen, Meier, and Trace (2015) tried to discover how the model could be improved. They claimed that using the Rasch measurement model made the rubric more accurate and efficient. They claimed that the Rasch model can be employed to revise the rubric. Alternatively, Brown (2012) mentioned how the reliability and fairness of the rubric can be improved by training the raters and how rubric developers should try to revise the quality of their rubrics.

As mentioned above, one way to enhance the fairness and dependability of the decisions based on the scores, is training the raters. After the construct has been theoretically defined, scoring rubrics are developed to operationally measure the construct in question. However, raters are highly likely to construe the band descriptors in each of the rubric cells differently. Rater agreement on the concepts and their interpretation thereof highly depend on rater training (Herman & Winters, 1994). To have a more functional training session, Johnson, Penny and Gordon (2009) mentioned what the training session should include (see sequence of training activities, p. 214). High-quality training can enhance both inter-rater and intra-rater reliability (Malini Reddy & Andrade, 2010), which can mean multiple ratings by either the same or different raters. This suggests the rating of the writing performance more than once which can increase the reliability of the measure (Coombe, 2010).

5 Primary Trait Rubric: To Use or Not to Use

In workplaces, it is important for employers to know whether they can extrapolate from the applicants' test scores a likely successful actual performance in the target language use domain. The author's personal communication with some enterprises suggests that despite theoretical justifications for the use of authentic tasks (Bachman & Palmer, 1996, 2010), the Human Resources directors interviewed displayed a lack of expertise in assessing the language proficiency of the candidates.

When using an instrument to measure the test takers' performance, decision makers need to know what matters most. Task achievement is usually more important to decision makers than any other multiple linguistic traits that linguists are largely concerned about. Most activities in the business world include negotiations or persuasions whereby the interlocutors are expected to evince their knowledge of manipulative or heuristic functions. This involves, therefore, the employers' intent to know about their prospective employees' performance to make the best decisions for their enterprises, as failing to do so might have profound adverse consequences ranging from losing clients to the possibility of going out of business. Primary trait rubrics can be more useful if the segment of discourse is limited to certain functions the knowledge of which can be the difference between failure and success.

Obviously, test tasks that correspond to those in the target language use domain carry weight, but what equally concerns test developers is the issue of consistency as the assessment of test takers' performance is subject to fluctuations because of the inherent nature of assessing productive skills. In this vein, testing and assessment experts have long used rubrics as a tool to evaluate the test takers' performance. However, what type of rubric serves what purpose needs to be meticulously taken into consideration. Drawing on the extant literature, it can be argued that the primary trait rubric can be used for different tasks as it takes one major criterion as the most important one in business communications: task achievement. Primary trait rubric can enhance the validity of the measurement as it helps measure the construct which is purported to be measured. However, as the preparation of primary trait rubrics is a complicated process as it is task dependent (Lloyd-Jones, 1977), one solution would be the use of domain-specific rubrics.

The complexity or the quality of writing does not need to be analyzed in the business world. Therefore, with an eye on the task achievement, using the primary trait rubric can help decision makers make better decisions when employing applicants. As long as the task is achieved, the quality of the writing and the complexity of lexical and structural accuracy can play second fiddle to it. As developing rubrics for use in the business world, the developers of the rubric should consult previous data available from the candidates' samples as it can be conducive to higher validity (Turner & Usher, 2002).

In an educational setting, the purpose of assessment might be different. The faculty members I interviewed asserted the use of both analytic and holistic rubrics for the assessment of the learners' writing performance. None of them reported the use of the primary trait rubric as they claimed they were using what the school has decided they should use.

When the purpose is to diagnose the areas that need improvement, an analytic rubric might be more advantageous (Brown, 2005). As in such cases, teachers can provide learners with feedback on their performance and help them discover what needs to be remedially done to dispense with the problem areas. In achievement or diagnostic assessment, therefore, analytic rubrics work better and can be more informative. However, in proficiency and placement exams where the function of the test is not to give feedback, holistic rubrics are more functional.

All in all, it is important to raise awareness of HR directors and ELF instructors in the MENA region of the purpose of different tasks and different rubrics available so that they can create the optimum conditions for effective assessing, which can include the use of the authentic tasks and consistent scoring of those tasks.

6 Implications for the Context and Conclusion

Primary trait rubric is a much-neglected rubric in the MENA region context. In this article, the author tried to focus on some of the underpinnings of this type of rubric, and it was by no means to suggest that it has to be used in this context, but rather to consider. As pointed out by Coombe and Evans (2009), the choice of the right rubric depends on the context of use. It is imperative that before embarking on the development of any rubric, we decide what the construct to be measured comprises so that we will not incur under-representativeness of the construct, nor construct-irrelevance. Decision makers will also have to decide what the purpose of the assessment is or what uses they are planning to have for the assessment as failing to do so might result in the wrong choice of rubric. Whether it is for professional or educational purposes, one thing is definitive: rubrics are useful and informative for measuring the candidates' performance (Brown, 2012).

References

Alderson, C. (1990). Bands and scores. In C. Alderson & B. North (Eds.), *Language testing in the 1990s* (pp. 71–86). London: Modern English Publications and British Council.

Amandolare, S. (2010, June). *Arabic's uncertain future has troubling cultural implications. How we use Arabic today!* Retrieved from: http://www.findingdulcinea.com/news/international/2010/mar/Arabic-s-Uncertain-Futurehas-Troubling-Cultural-Implications.htm. Last accessed: 10.5.2020.

Andrade, H. (2000). Using rubrics to promote thinking and learning. *Educational Leadership, 57*(5), 13–18.

Bachman, L. F., & Palmer, A. S. (1996). *Language testing in practice: Designing and developing useful language tests* (Vol. 1). Oxford: Oxford University Press.

Bachman, L. F., & Palmer, A. S. (2010). *Language assessment in practice: Developing language assessments and justifying their use in the real world*. Oxford: Oxford University Press.

Badry, F. (2019). *Internationalization of higher education in the countries of the Gulf Cooperation Council: Impact on the national language*. Paper commissioned for the Arab States 2019 Global Education Monitoring Report, Migration, displacement and education: Building bridges, not walls. Retrieved from: https://unesdoc.unesco.org/ark:/48223/pf0000371703. Last accessed: 10.5.2020.

Barkaoui, K. (2011). Effects of marking method and rater experience on ESL essay scores and rater performance. *Assessment in Education: Principles, Policy & Practice, 18,* 279–293.

Becker, A. (2010/2011). Examining rubrics used to measure writing performance in U.S. intensive English programs. *The CATESOL Journal, 22,* 113–130.

Blaz, D. (2001). *A collection of performance task and rubrics: Foreign language*. Larchmont: Eye on Education.

Brookhart, S. M. (2013). *How to create and use rubrics for formative assessment and grading*. Alexandria, VA: ASCD.

Brown, H. D. (2004). *Language assessment: Principles and classroom practice*. San Francisco: San Francisco State University.

Brown, H. D., & Abeywickrama, P. (2010). *Language assessment: Principles and classroom practice* (2nd ed.). New York: Pearson Longman.

Brown, J. D. (2005). *Testing in language programs: A comprehensive guide to English language assessment*. New York: McGraw-Hill.

Brown, J. D. (2012). *Developing, using, and analyzing rubrics in language assessment with case studies in Asian and Pacific languages*. National Foreign Language Resource Center at University of Hawaii. 1859 East-West Road# 106, Honolulu, HI 96822-2322.

Cohen, A. D. (1994). *Assessing language ability in the classroom* (2nd ed.). Boston: Heinle & Heinle.

Council of Europe. (2001). *Common European framework of reference for languages: Learning, teaching, assessment*. Cambridge, UK: Press Syndicate of the University of Cambridge.

Coombe, C. (2010). Assessing foreign/second language writing ability. *Education, Business and Society: Contemporary Middle Eastern Issues, 3,* 178–187.

Coombe, C., & Evans, J. (2009). Writing assessment scales: Making the right choice. In C. Coombe, P. Davidson, & D. Lloyd (Eds.), *The fundamentals of language assessment: A practical guide for teachers* (2nd ed., pp. 106–111). Dubai, UAE: TESOL Arabia Publications.

Crusan, D. (2010). *Assessment in the second language writing classroom*. Ann Arbor, MI: The University of Michigan.

Cumming, A. (1997). The testing of writing in a second language. In C. Clapham & D. Corson (Eds.), *Encyclopedia of language and education: Language testing and assessment* (Vol. 7, pp. 131–139). Norwell, MA: Kluwer Academic.

Dappen, L., Isernhagen, J., & Anderson, S. (2008). A statewide writing assessment model: Student proficiency and future implications. *Assessing Writing, 13*, 45–60.

Davis, L. (2019). Primary trait scoring. In B. B. Frey (Ed.), *The SAGE encyclopedia of educational research, measurement, and evaluation* (pp. 1296–1297). Thousand Oaks: Sage. https://doi.org/10.1002/9781118784235.eelt0365.

East, M., & Young, D. (2007). Scoring L2 writing samples: Exploring the relative effectiveness of two different diagnostic methods. *New Zealand Studies in Applied Linguistics, 13*, 1–21.

Fulcher, G. (2003). *Testing second language speaking*. London: Pearson Education.

Fulcher, G., Davidson, F., & Kemp, J. (2010). Effective rating scale development for speaking tests: Performance decision trees. *Language Testing, 28*(1), 5–29.

Green, A., & Hawkey, R. (2012). Marking assessments: Rating scales and rubrics. In C. Coombe, P. Davidson, B. O'Sullivan, & S. Stoynoff (Eds.), *The Cambridge guide to second language assessment* (pp. 299–306). Cambridge: Cambridge University Press.

Gun, S. (2018). Review of English language education policy in the Middle East and North Africa. *Eurasian Journal of Applied Linguistics, 4*(2), 409–415. https://doi.org/10.32601/ejal.464207.

Hamp-Lyons, L. (1995). Rating nonnative writing: The trouble with holistic scoring. *TESOL Quarterly, 29*, 759–762.

Hamp-Lyons, L. (2003). Writing teachers as assessors of writing. In B. Kroll (Ed.), *Exploring the dynamics of second language writing* (pp. 162–189). Cambridge: Cambridge University Press.

Herman, J. L., & Winters, L. (1994). Portfolio research: A slim collection. *Educational Leadership, 52*(2), 48–55.

International Monetary Fund. (1996). https://www.imf.org/external/pubs/ft/mena/04econ.htm.

International Organization of Migration. (2016). *Migration to, from and in the Middle East and North Africa Data snapshot*. Retrieved from: https://www.iom.int/sites/default/files/country/mena/Migration-in-the-Middle-East-and-North-Africa_Data%20Sheet_August2016.pdf. Last accessed: 10.5.2020.

Jacobs, H., Zinkgraf, S., Wormuth, D., Hartfiel, V., & Hughey, J. (1981). *Testing ESL composition: A practical approach*. Rowley, MA: Newbury House.

Janssen, G., Meier, V., & Trace, J. (2015). Building a better rubric: Mixed method rubric revision. *Assessing Writing, 26,* 51–66.

Johnson, R. L., Penny, J. A., & Gordon, B. (2009). *Assessing performance: Designing, scoring, validating performance tasks*. New York: The Guilford Press.

Kiprop, V. (2019, May 8). *What are the MENA countries?* WorldAtlas. https://www.worldatlas.com/articles/what-are-the-mena-countries.html.

Khalaf, S. (2018). *A language in decline*. Retrieved from: https://en.qantara.de/content/the-uncertain-future-of-modern-standard-arabic-a-language-in-decline. Last accessed: 10.5.2020.

Kılıçkaya, F. (2006). Instructors' attitudes towards English-medium instruction in Turkey. *Humanizing Language Teaching, 8*(6), 1–16.

Knoch, U. (2009). Diagnostic assessment of writing: A comparison of two rating scales. *Language Testing, 26,* 275–304.

Lloyd-Jones, R. (1977). Primary trait scoring. In C. R. Cooper & L. Odell (Eds.), *Evaluating writing: Describing, measuring, judging* (pp. 33–68). Urbana, IL: National Council of Teachers of English.

Luoma, S. (2004). *Assessing speaking*. Cambridge, MA: Cambridge University Press.

Malini Reddy, Y., & Andrade, H. (2010). A review of rubric use in higher education. *Assessment & Evaluation in Higher Education, 35,* 435–448. https://doi.org/10.1080/02602930902862859.

Mense, E. G., Lemoine, P. A., Garretson, C. J., & Richardson, M. D. (2018). The development of global higher education in a world of transformation. *Journal of Education and Development, 2*(3), 47–60. https://doi.org/10.20849/jed.v2i3.529.

Reynolds-Keefer, L. (2010). Rubric-referenced assessment in teacher preparation: An opportunity to learn by using. *Practical Assessment, Research, and Evaluation*, Vol. 15, Article 8, 1–9.

Saxton, E., Belanger, S., & Becker, W. (2012). The critical thinking analytic rubric (CTAR): Investigating intra-rater and inter-rater reliability of a scoring mechanism for critical thinking performance assessments. *Assessing Writing, 17,* 251–270.

Sert, N. (2008). The language of instruction dilemma in the Turkish context. *System, 36,* 156–171.

Spring, J. (2015). *Globalization of education: An introduction*. New York: Routledge.

Stevens, D. D., & Levi, A. J. (2013). *Introduction to rubrics: An assessment tool to save grading time, convey effective feedback, and promote student learning.* Stylus Publishing, LLC.

Toulmin, S. E. (2003). *The use of argument.* Cambridge: Cambridge University Press.

Turner, C. E., & Usher, J. (2002). Rating scales derived from student samples: Effects of the scale marker and the student sample on scale content and student scores. *TESOL Quarterly, 36*(1), 49–70.

Vahdani-Sanavi. R, & Mohammadi, M. (2020). Rubric-based assessment of the productive skills. In S. Hidri (Ed.), *Changing language assessment: New dimensions, new challenges* (pp. 77–92). London: Palgrave Macmillan.

Wardhaugh, R. & Fuller, J. M. (2015). *Introduction to sociolinguistics* (7th ed.). Malden, MA: Willey Blackwell.

Weigle, S. C. (2002). *Assessing writing.* Cambridge: Cambridge University Press.

Weigle, S. C. (2012). Assessing writing. In C. Coombe, P. Davidson, B. O'Sullivan, & S. Stoynoff (Eds.), *The Cambridge guide to second language assessment* (pp. 218–224). Cambridge: Cambridge University Press.

Weir, C. J. (2005). *Language testing and validation.* Hampshire: Palgrave Mcmillan.

White, E. M. (1984). Holisticism. *College Composition and Communication, 35,* 400–409.

World Bank. (2019a). *Economic profile of the MENA.* Retrieved from: https://www.worldbank.org/en/region/mena/publication/mena-economic-update-april-2019-reforms-and-external-imbalances. Last accessed: 10.5.2020.

World Bank. (2019b). *World Bank Information on the MENA.* Retrieved from: https://www.worldbank.org/en/region/mena. Last accessed: 10.5.2020.

World Trade Organization. (1995). *The General Agreement on Trade in Services (GATS): Objectives, coverage and disciplines.* Retrieved from: https://www.wto.org/english/tratop_e/serv_e/gatsqa_e.htm. Last accessed: 10.5.2020.

Teaching and Assessment Connections: Exploring Learner Performance and the Impact of Instruction

Assessing L2 Argumentation in the UAE Context

Jingjing Qin

1 Introduction

In this rapidly changing, complex global context, argumentative and critical thinking skills are becoming increasingly important for the new generations of Emirati students. According to one of the national priorities listed in the UAE Vision (2021), namely, aiming for a competitive economy driven by knowledgeable and innovative emirates, it is no exaggeration to state that equipping students with these critical skills lays the groundwork to achieve this goal. In today's modern workplace, the mechanical blue-collar jobs are decreasing dramatically, more job opportunities require students to develop and evaluate propositions by employing disciplinary knowledge and evaluative abilities when reading and writing (Ferretti & De La Paz, 2011). As a result, the students have to be prepared for the modern workplace by enhancing their argumentative writing abilities.

J. Qin (✉)
Zayed University, Abu Dhabi, UAE
e-mail: Jingjing.Qin@zu.ac.ae

© The Author(s) 2020
L. McCallum and C. Coombe (eds.), *The Assessment of L2 Written English across the MENA Region*, https://doi.org/10.1007/978-3-030-53254-3_10

In light of the increasing demand of the use of English in both academic and professional settings in the UAE, university students are often expected to be able to achieve a level of English language proficiency to allow them to communicate in writing clearly at local, regional, and international levels. As described clearly in one of the six major learning outcomes regarding the language in the English-medium government university where the researcher is currently working, it states that graduates will be able to "demonstrate competence in understanding, evaluating, and using both qualitative and quantitative information to explore issues, solve problems, and develop informed opinions". This explains the importance of the ability to frame and defend one's point of view after considering and integrating a constellation of propositions and present it in a written form. This chapter is intended to examine how Emirati students perform in English argumentative writing in a UAE government university and how the argumentative writing is assessed in an English academic writing class.

2   Literature Review

Despite its importance in today's academic world and professional settings, research regarding argumentation and the related critical thinking skills is lacking in the UAE. Within the context of English as the first language (L1) education, the Toulmin model of argument structure (henceforth, the Toulmin model), proposed by the British philosopher Toulmin (1958, 2003), has been widely used in teaching and researching argumentative writing. Specifically, this framework has been used extensively in accounting for the various elements marking the progress of an argument in English argumentative writing. According to Toulmin (1958, 2003), every argument is composed of three main elements: claim, data, and warrant. It is worth noting that not all three elements are explicit, and sometimes warrants may not need to be stated in real-life arguments. Toulmin et al. (1979, 1984) go on to assert that in an extended argument structure, there may be some second-level elements such as qualifier, backing, and rebuttal, the uses of which are determined by the exigencies of the argument. (See Toulmin, 1958, 2003; Toulmin, Reike, & Janik, 1979, 1984 for more detailed information.) Toulmin's logic of reasoning maintains that claims must be supported and explained to convince or persuade an audience. Those teaching from this orientation emphasizes that the students understand the core elements of logic (i.e. claim, data, warrant, qualifier, counterargument, and rebuttal) and use them to construct convincing arguments as product.

One important factor to be taken into consideration in researching the concept of argumentation in the second language contexts is the influence of students' native language culture and rhetorical traditions. Kaplan's (1966) seminal work on contrastive rhetoric asserts that inevitably students have brought their own culturally shaped notions of writing in their native language to write argumentation in English. In Arab contexts, a number of research studies point out that L1 Arabic speaking students experience great difficulty in writing western-style argumentation in English (Al-Abed Al Haq & Ahmed, 1994; Kamel, 2000). Specifically, it is reported that often there is no refutation of counter arguments which makes the texts more descriptive and less convincing (Al-Abed Al Haq & Ahmed, 1994; Al Jubouri, 1995; El-Seidi, 2000; Hamdan, 1988). The famous "doodles" pattern featuring the rhetorical pattern of Arabic written texts shown in Kaplan (1966) depicts the digression of ideas which often times are not fully developed and/or supported. All these studies indicate that it is difficult for L1 Arabic students to both understand and produce the English argumentative writing.

Based on the researcher's years of experiences in teaching English argumentative writing in the UAE, it is observed that the educational system in UAE, especially at the government-run public schools, is characterized by rote-memorization, and that students' abilities to express their own thoughts and to make judgements of ideas before making decisions are often neglected. Furthermore, the Arabic cultural disposition emphasizing social harmony and respect for the authority may also make Arabic students reluctant to voice their own opinions/ideas independently. Thus, this educational practice and cultural inclination unavoidably hampers the students' development of argumentative writing skills, which emphasize forming one's own point of view.

As a result, an increasing number of studies focus on explicit instruction of argumentative principles and writing, which would be expected to be adapted and transferred to students' academic study as well as real-life contexts. (Connor, 1987; Connor & Lauer, 1985; El-Seidi, 2000; Kamel, 2000). As a case in point, this chapter examines whether students in a UAE government university improved in their argumentative writing skills after taking a mandatory English argumentative writing course in their first two years of general education courses. A timed in-class argumentative essay was given to the students at the 8th week of the 16-week semester. Through a detailed analysis of students' written samples, these students' argumentative skills were uncovered and critically analyzed. Furthermore, the chapter describes how the feedback gleaned from this common assessment would be mapped to the teaching curriculum to shed light on the teaching effectiveness and to provide directions for future teaching. The chapter ends with suggestions of research-based activities on how to assess argumentation, and thus critical thinking skills, to university students in this region.

3 Methodology

3.1 Participants and Writing Instructional Context

All 23 participants were enrolled in an academic writing class where the researcher was teaching and had completed two academic writing classes prior to this one when the data were collected. They were mostly second-year university students around a similar age, 18–21 years old, studying in a variety of disciplines ranging from natural sciences to social sciences. In their previous English writing classes, they had learned to write in different genres, such as narrative, rhetorical analysis, and persuasive essays. By the second year of the general education courses, they were required to complete the third academic writing course, which focused on research-based argumentative writing. The course goals are listed as: (1) learn to develop balanced arguments in the form of academic writing, and (2) be taught to think critically about information and evidence and to become better information users. These goals highlight the importance of balanced argument.

During the first seven weeks of the semester, the students were introduced to the concept of argumentation and understanding different perspectives of controversial issues. Partly due to the influence of Arabic rhetorical patterns and cultural preferences, the students struggled with presenting a clear point of view on a controversial issue; they would rather take a middle position. In response to this persistent problem, explicit instruction had focused on encouraging them to take a stance on a debatable issue while recognizing its opposing viewpoints. Likewise, they often experienced difficulty in understanding counterarguments and rebuttals, the two crucial elements in constructing a well-balanced argument. As a result, a number of teaching strategies were applied to help the students understand the complexity of argumentation and the interplay among arguments, counterarguments, and rebuttals. These strategies included organizing class debates and asking the students to analyse the Toulmin model elements in sample argumentative papers.

3.2 In-Class Timed Writing Assessment

During the middle of the semester (week 8), students were asked to write an in-class argumentative essay (80 minutes) based on an assigned topic and a reading text provided to them (see Appendix 1 for the writing prompt). The assigned topic is current and related to the students' personal life (i.e. whether online shopping is harmful to the environment or not). The readability of the reading text (594 words) was controlled to be accessible to the students' levels, with Flesch reading ease of 50.6, and Flesch-Kincaid Grade level of 10.8. The text presented differing views on the topic, namely, whether online shopping helps or worsens the environment. In the argumentative writing, students were expected to present their viewpoints on the controversial issue and were explicitly required to incorporate at least two pieces of information from the reading text. Furthermore, counterarguments and rebuttals were expected in the students' essays.

3.3 Assessment Criteria

To examine the details of argument structure, specific elements of argument were analyzed based on the adapted Toulmin model of argument structure (1958, 2003), namely, claim, data, counterargument claim, counterargument data, rebuttal claim, and rebuttal data.

To assess the quality of argumentative writing specifically, the study adopted an analytic scoring rubric for argumentative writing (ASRAW) proposed in Stapleton and Wu (2015) with the intention of integrating the assessment of both argumentative structural elements and the quality of reasoning, one of the few in the field of L2 argumentative writing assessment. In the ASRAW (Appendix 2), the different elements are weighted differently, with claim accounting for 5%, data 25%, counterargument claim (10%), counterargument data (25%), rebuttal claim (10%), and rebuttal data (25%).

4 Results and Discussion

Out of 23 essays, 19 essays presented a clear point of view at the surface level by providing a clear thesis statement about the controversial issue and it was placed in the introductory paragraph, typically towards the end of the paragraph. Only three essays were either off-topic or the viewpoint was unclear. It should be noted that the topic was proved to be controversial, as approximately half of the students argued that online shopping helped the environment and the other half argued against it.

In terms of the use of Toulmin argument structure, frequency counts of each argumentative element for the 19 essays were tallied to identify those elements. As seen in Table 1, out of 19 essays, all the essays presented the basic argument structure, which consists of claims

Table 1 Description of the use of argumentative elements

Argumentative elements	N	Mean	SD	Min	Max
Claim	19	1.53	.77	1	4
Data	19	2.32	.82	1	4
Counterargument claim	19	1.21	.71	0	2
Counterargument data	19	.34	.67	0	2
Rebuttal claim	19	.84	.77	0	2
Rebuttal data	19	.21	.75	0	2

supported by some sort of data; 18 essays (94.74%) presented counterarguments; 13 essays (68.42%) were able to challenge the counterarguments by providing the rebuttals. These findings seem to show that the students had grasped the understanding of the basic argument structure after the 7-week instruction period, and the majority of them learned the importance of showing awareness of opposing viewpoints by including the counterarguments. Numerous studies of argumentative discourse show that both children and adults are predisposed to neglect other perspectives, which is also called my-side bias (Kuhn, 1991; Perkins, Farady, & Bushey, 1991). After the instruction, the students seemed to have improved their argumentative ability by considering other viewpoints.

As mentioned before, a critical thinker should be able to consider different viewpoints and weigh the pros and cons of each viewpoint. The reading text provided sufficient numbers of opposing viewpoints on the controversial issue of whether online shopping is harmful to the environment or not. It was at each students' discretion as to which perspective they wanted to support in their argumentative writing. It follows that students were given the chance to incorporate the counterarguments in their papers and also to rebut them, as long as they were aware of the necessity of doing so. It is encouraging to see that the majority of the students started to pay attention to the use of counterarguments and demonstrated them in their essays. However, some of the students failed to challenge them with appropriate rebuttals. Without the use of rebuttal, the overall effectiveness of argument would suffer or even be diminished, as shown in the following excerpt:

Amazon have suggested to change their delivery trucks into ones that run by electricity, This will indeed make online shopping more environmentally friendly (Adapted from James Baldwin, 2017). However, this does not help in reduce nor resolve the issue additional packaging. (Text sample 11)

Another aspect associated with good argumentation is the need to show that alternative views, which are also called counterarguments, are shown via rebuttals to be less convincing or effective than the main arguments. However, sometimes the rebuttals in the students' essays were seen as not stronger than the counterargument or not relevant.

There are some people argues that online shopping is reducing carbon footprint by having electronic trucks for delivery. Your thinking is wrong because not all the companies have electronic trucks, I guess only amazon who have those trucks and not everyone is ordering from them. (Text sample 1)

It is argued that online retailers such as amazon are replacing their vdelivery trucks with more energy efficient like the electric vehicles which can make online shopping more greener. However, there are around hundreds of online shopping, not all of them are using the electric vehicles, and there is no evidences that shows how theseelctric vehicles are reducing the carbon footprint or does it really make the planet greener. (Text sample 8)

As shown in the text samples, it seemed that the students tried their best to provide evidence to support their claims. However, a closer look at this support/evidence suggested some deficiencies in the student's ability to argue. More specifically, students sometimes had issues with the data and evidence to support the claims and their counterargument claims. Their rebuttals claims were sometimes inaccurate or irrelevant, or lacking in logical coherence and structure. Stapleton and Wu (2015) argue for more research in the quality of argument beyond just the presence of argument element; they pointed out that many studies (e.g. Nussbaum & Kardash, 2005; Wolfe, Britt, & Butler, 2009) only focused on assessing the success or failure of argumentative ability by valuing the

Table 2 Description of the quality of argumentative writing

Argumentative elements	N	Mean	SD	Min	Max
Claim	19	5.00	.00	5.00	5.00
Data	19	15.79	7.31	.00	25.00
Counterargument claim	19	8.95	3.15	.00	10.00
Counterargument data	19	9.47	7.43	.00	20.00
Rebuttal claim	19	5.26	5.13	.00	10.00
Rebuttal data	19	6.05	8.26	.00	25.00
Overall Quality	19	47.62	19.91	15.90	90.90

presence of the argument elements rather than the quality of reasoning or substance contained within the argumentative elements. To this end, to further understand the quality of argumentative writing, the quality of argumentation was assessed with an analytic scoring rubric (Stapleton & Wu, 2015). Table 2 presents the results of the quality of argumentative writing regarding the different elements and its overall quality. It seems that the quality of data, counterargument claim, counterargument data, rebuttal claim, and rebuttal data varied greatly among the essays, and the quality of these elements are to be improved.

The study also examined the relationship between the overall quality of the essays and the use of argumentative elements. As mentioned earlier, the essays had been assessed with an analytic rubric. A composite score was given to each essay. Overall, a good essay is the one with a clear point of view supported with relevant and sufficient data, presenting counterarguments challenged by effective rebuttals (A sample essay attached as Appendix 3). In addition, the correlation shows that the use of claims and data are significantly positively correlated with the overall quality of essays, $r(19) = .62$, $p = .005$, and $r(19) = .48$, $p = .037$. It implies that the more claims and data an essay presented, the more likely its overall quality would be higher.

5 Implications for the Context and Conclusion

This chapter has examined how Arabic-speaking university students developed their argumentative abilities after seven weeks of instruction and whether the instruction had helped them achieve the curriculum learning outcomes described in the course description. In general, the students learned the basic argument structure of claims and data/evidence. Furthermore, they learned how to include opposing viewpoints and refute them so as to strengthen their own argument.

It should also be pointed out that the examination of students' essays showed that the quality of reasoning still warrants more improvement. Students still need instruction on what is considered as good quality evidence/data, which is missing in the curriculum. In today's competitive world, a crucial skill is to be able to corroborate one's view with effective evidence to convince others to adopt his or her view in the academic setting and the workplace. The study showed that it is insufficient to just teach the students to incorporate these argumentative elements; more attention should be given to help students understand the different quality of data, counterargument claims, counterargument data, rebuttal claims, and rebuttal data. Only after equipping the students with a more complex understanding of the quality of these different elements, can they thrive in today's complex global context where the ability to evaluate different kinds of propositions and to develop their own arguments is so crucial. The argumentation and critical thinking are such unprecedentedly important skills for the UAE students to master that it is never an overstatement that they build the foundation for cultivating the new knowledgeable and innovative generation.

Appendix 1: Writing Prompt

Instructions:
Do you agree or disagree with the statement below? Write a clear and organized essay supporting your opinion. A well-developed answer should be at least 300 words long.

Your essay should include two or more citations from the source below, with correct in-text APA citations. You do not need to include a list of references at the end of your essay.

Appendix 2: Analytic Scoring Rubric for Argumentative Writing (ASRAW)

See Table 3.

Appendix 3: A Student Sample of Effective Argumentation

Online shopping has been a wide trend these days. Many people prefer to buy online because either it is cheaper or less time consuming. However consumers do not really think about the negative consequences of it on the environment. An environmentalist expert said that delivery trucks of online markets that use gas, and cut a journey for just one item, is actually helping in increasing the carbon dioxide emissions, compared to when a person chooses to go to the mall and shop (Adapted from James Baldwin, 2017). Another environmental issue is the packaging of online products. These materials that are used to package and protect the product increase waste on our planet. This paper will argue that we should reduce online shopping because it rises carbon dioxide release in the air and waste in the world. As mentioned above using trucks that rely on gas can effect the quality of air. According to Jerry Storch chief of Storch Advisor (as cited in Baldwin, 2017), online delivery to the

Table 3 Analytical scoring rubric

1. Claim (5%)	Score: 5 States a point of view		Score: 0 Does not state a point of view	
2. Data (25%)	Score: 25 a. Provides multiple reasons to support the claim, and b. All reasons are sound/acceptable and free of irrelevancies	Score: 20 a. Provides multiple reasons for the claim, and b. Most reasons are sound/acceptable and free of irrelevancies, but one or two are weak	Score: 15 a. Provides one to two reasons for the claim, and b. Some reasons are sound/acceptable, but some are weak or irrelevant	Score: 10 a. Provides only one reason for the claim, or b. The reason provided is weak or irrelevant	Score: 0 a. No reasons are provided for the claim; or b. None of the reasons are relevant to/support the claim
3. Counterargument Claim/Alternative Point(s) of View (10%)	Score: 10 Provides counterargument claim(s)/alternative view(s)		Score: 0 Does not provide counterargument claim(s)/alternative view(s)	
4. Counterargument Data/Supporting Reasons for Alternative Point(s) of View (25%)	Score: 25 a. Provides multiple reasons for the counterargument claim(s)/alternative view(s), and b. All counterarguments/reasons for the alternative view(s) are sound/acceptable and free of irrelevancies	Score: 20 a. Provides multiple reasons for the counterargument claim(s)/alternative view(s), and b. Most counterarguments/reasons for the alternative view(s) are sound/acceptable and free of irrelevancies, but one or two are weak	Score: 15 a. Provides one to two reasons for the counterargument claim(s)/alternative view(s), and b. Some counterarguments/reasons for the alternative view(s) are sound/acceptable, but some are weak or irrelevant	Score: 10 a. Provides only one reason for the counterargument claim/alternative view, or b. The counterargument/reason for the alternative view(s) is weak or irrelevant	Score: 0 a. No reasons are presented for the counterargument claim/alternative view; or b. None of the reasons are relevant to/support the counterargument claim/alternative view
5. Rebuttal Claim (10%)	Score: 10 Provides rebuttal claim(s)		Score: 0 Does not provide rebuttal claim(s)	
6. Rebuttal Data (25%)	Score: 25	Score: 20	Score: 15	Score: 10	Score: 0

a. Refutes/points out the weaknesses of all the counterarguments, and b. All rebuttals are sound/acceptable c. The reasoning quality of all the rebuttals are stronger than the counterarguments	a. Refutes/points out the weaknesses of all the counterarguments, and b. Most rebuttals are sound/acceptable, but one or two are weak c. The reasoning quality of most rebuttals are stronger than the counterarguments, while one or two are equal to the counterarguments	a. Refutes/points out the weaknesses of all the counterarguments, and b. Some rebuttals are sound/acceptable, but some are weak c. The reasoning quality of some rebuttals is stronger than the counterarguments, while some are weaker than the counterarguments	a. Refutes/points out the weaknesses of some counterarguments, or b. Few of the rebuttals are sound/acceptable; most of them are weak, or c. The reasoning quality of most rebuttals is weaker than the counterarguments	a. No rebuttals are provided; or b. None of the rebuttals can refute the counterarguments

customers house is only causing additional emission of carbon dioxide. This shows that the process of delivery to a customers residence may be very convenient but not necessarily good for the environment. However this could be reduced if a person delays the delivery so he or she could get all her items in one go (Adapted from James Baldwin, 2017). People could also go to the mall instead. People could do multiple things when going to the mall, including shopping to the list may help make the process more green (Adapted from James Baldwin, 2017).

Another issue to discuss is packaging. As Storch says "But there is no way to get around the fact that you are taking something that is already packaged for consumer sale and putting it in additional package in order to deliver it" (Adapted from James Baldwin, 2017, para. 3). In other words additional packaging is only additional waste added to the pill of things humanity trying to get rid off.

Amazon have suggested to change their delivery trucks into ones that run by electricity, This will indeed make online shopping more environmentally friendly (Adapted from James Baldwin, 2017). However this does not help in reduce nor resolve the issue of additional packaging. A number of people state the opinion of consumers that shopping in malls could just drive to buy one item most of the times which in turn not help but increase the problem of carbon dioxide in the air (Adapted from James Baldwin, 2017). This could be a major problem but only if it were true. As Storch argues "the only problem with that is consumers dont behave that way" (Adapted from James Baldwin, 2017, para. 4).

In conclusion the delivery process carried by online retailers to their consumers can damage the environment. This paper argued that online shopping should be reduced. Because gas trucks can increase carbon dioxide in the air thus lowering its quality.

References

Al Jubouri, A. (1995). *Teaching and learning argument*. London: Cassell Publishers.

Al-Abed Al Haq, F., & Ahmed, A. (1994). Discourse problems in argumentative writing. *World Englishes, 13*(3), 307–323.

Baldwin, J. (2017, September 15). E-commerce goes green. *The Guardian*. Retrieved from Opposing Viewpoints in Context.

Connor, U. (1987). Argumentative patterns in student essays: Cross-cultural differences. In U. Connor & R. B. Kaplan (Eds.), *Writing across languages: Analysis of L2 text* (pp. 57–71). Reading, MA: Addison-Wesley Publishing Company.

Connor, U., & Lauer, J. (1985). Understanding persuasive essay writing: Linguistic/rhetorical approach. *Text, 5,* 309–326.

El-Seidi, M. (2000). Metadiscourse in English and Arabic argumentative writing: A cross-linguistic study of texts written by American and Egyptian university students. In I. Zeinab, S. Aydelott, & N. Kassabgy (Eds.), *Diversity in language: Contrastive studies in Arabic and English theoretical and applied linguistics* (pp. 111–126). Cairo: The American University in Cairo Press.

Ferretti, R. P., & De La Paz, S. (2011). On the comprehension and production of written texts: Instructional activities that support content-area literacy. In R. O'Connor & P. Vadasy (Eds.), *Handbook of reading interventions* (pp. 326–355). New York, NY: Guilford Press.

Hamdan, A. S. (1988). Coherence and cohesion in texts written in English by Jordanian university students. Unpublished Ph.D. Thesis, Manchester University, England.

Kamel, S. A. (2000). Categories of comprehension in argumentative discourse: A cross-linguistic study. In I. Zeinab, S. Aydelott, & N. Kassabgy (Eds.), *Diversity in language: Contrastive studies in Arabic and English theoretical and applied linguistics* (pp. 193–235). Cairo: The American University in Cairo Press.

Kaplan, R. B. (1966). Cultural thought patterns in inter-cultural education. *Language Learning, 16,* 1–20.

Kuhn, D. (1991). *The skills of argument*. New York, NY: Cambridge University Press.

Nussbaum, E. M., & Kardash, C. M. (2005). The effects of goal instruction and text on the generation of counterarguments during writing. *Journal of Educational Psychology, 97,* 157–169.

Perkins, D. N., Farady, M., & Bushey, B. (1991). Everyday reasoning and the roots of intelligence. In J. F. Voss, D. N. Perkins, & J. W. Segal (Eds.), *Informal reasoning and education* (pp. 83–106). Hillsdale, NJ: Erlbaum.

Stapleton, P., & Wu, Y. (2015). Assessing the quality of arguments in students' persuasive writing: A case study analyzing the relationship between surface structure and substance. *Journal of English for Academic Purposes, 17,* 12–23.

Toulmin, S. (1958). *The uses of argument.* Cambridge: Cambridge University Press.

Toulmin, S., Reike, R., & Janik, A. (1979). *An introduction to reasoning.* New York, NY: MacMillan.

Toulmin, S., Reike, R., & Janik, A. (1984). *An introduction to reasoning* (2nd ed.). New York, NY: MacMillan.

Toulmin, S. (2003). *Return to reason.* Cambridge, MA: Harvard University Press.

UAE Vision 2021, H.H. Sheikh Mohammed bin Rashid Al Maktoum (2016). Retrieved from: https://www.vision2021.ae/en/our-vision. Last accessed: 21.04.2020.

Wolfe, C. R., Britt, M. A., & Butler, J. A. (2009). Argumentation schema and the myside bias in written argumentation. *Written Communication, 25,* 183–209.

Integrated Summarizing Read-to-Write Tasks: Patterns of Textual Borrowing and the Role of the Written Genre

Katayoun Rezaei and Elaheh Sotoudehnama

1 Introduction

In an academic setting, writing one's own viewpoints relevant to a particular subject is merely one of the tasks frequently practiced. In a typical classroom, skills are highly conjoined; students may listen to a lecture or read a particular article and later transfer the information into an essay (Cumming et al., 2005; Weigle, 2004). In fact, as Chapelle et al. (2008) put forward, writing in an academic domain requires synthesizing sources of information learned previously and constructing valid arguments based upon them. However, composing written texts from source materials while acknowledging them, has always been a perplexing task for foreign language learners to accomplish. Abasi et al. (2006) believed that academic writing passages of learners reveal inappropriate textual borrowing behaviour which is considered as an act of plagiarism in the academic milieu. This may be due to the fact

---

K. Rezaei (✉) · E. Sotoudehnama
Department of English Language and Literature, Faculty of Literature, Alzahra University, Tehran, Iran

that synthesizing and summarizing tasks demand quite elaborate cognitive procedures both to comprehend the source materials and further write a meaningful text using stylistic conventions to acknowledge the sources (Cumming et al., 2005). Moreover, the learners' L1 background (Cheong et al.,2019), learners' culture (Pennycook, 1996), learners' language proficiency (Weigle & Parker, 2012), and source text characteristics (Cho et al., 2013; Weigle & Parker, 2012) can all affect the performance of learners while composing an integrated writing task.

With the advent of integrated writing tests, this particular concern has found its way into the field of writing assessment as well. These task types have gained popularity among test developers and can also be traced in high-stakes tests such as TOEFL iBT, IELTS, Canadian Academic English Language Assessment, and Trinity College Reading-into-Writing task. The reason behind this trend is that integrated tasks are a better representation of academic real-life writing; hence, are claimed to be more authentic (Gebril & Plakans, 2009; Weigle & Parker, 2012) and can enhance a positive washback effect in the academic setting (Cumming et al., 2005). Another merit of these tasks lends itself to the fact that they compensate for learners' lack of topic or background knowledge and provide content for learners to use in their writing (Plakans, 2009). Nevertheless, the extent to which the writing of the testees is affected by the inappropriate use of input source materials and various textual borrowing patterns can have a detrimental effect on validity of the integrated writing tasks; as the scores achieved in this test may not exhibit the testees' true language proficiency level (Weigle & Parker, 2012).

In light of these effects, the present study looks at the textual borrowing patterns in the under-studied context of an Iranian university. The research proceeds by considering how this study contributes to the existing literature on textual borrowing and in doing so generates several implications for the teaching and assessment in this context.

2   Literature Review

The common core component, when defining the underlying construct of all integrated writing tasks, includes bringing the language of sources in one's own written words (Knoch & Sitajalabhorn, 2013). Thus, summarizing, synthesizing and paraphrasing are embedded in completing these tasks (Shi, 2004). Summarizing is defined as reducing a text based on its main sentences and presenting its important ideas in a nutshell (Shi, 2012). When summarizing, learners comprehend, interpret and reconstruct the ideas mentioned in a text. The synthesizing task is similar to summary, but it is cognitively more demanding. While synthesizing, students are required to construct their own macro propositions or rather super propositions from different or even sometimes contradictory propositions of multiple sources (Plakans, 2009). These types of tasks include three processes of organizing, selecting, and connecting (Spivey & King, 1989). On the other hand, paraphrasing can be defined as, 'restating a source text in one's own words with a credit to the original author' (Shi, 2012, p. 135). A true process of paraphrasing; however, rarely occurs while summarizing, due to the complicated academic literacy it requires, and if it does, it stands in need of substantial knowledge about that content (Shi, 2012), rules relevant to referencing (Pecorari, 2006), and deductive as well as analogical thinking (Yamada, 2003). Therefore, the construct of integrated writing tasks as well as the underlying factors affecting performance of the writers are truly complicated and intertwined.

The source material characteristics, i.e. task type, prompt, length, organizational pattern and discourse features, may add to the difficulty level of integrated writing tasks. As Cumming et al. (2006) concluded, different input sources can induce the amount and level of copying from source materials. Shi (2004) purportsed that textual borrowing origins form the complicated nature of tasks while composing an integrated written text. In his study, the participants were given two types of integrated writing tasks; namely summarizing and opinion writing. The findings affirmed that learners copied more words from the source material in the former task. Moreover, compared to the L1 English students, citing and referring to the source material was foremost overlooked by the L2 learners. Further, Weigle and Parker (2012) examined the extent to which the learners were able to paraphrase the source materials without copying. In their study, the effect of learners' educational status and the topic of the tasks were evaluated. Their results revealed that there was a significant interaction between students' status and the prompt; nevertheless, they did not find any statistical effect of topic on the percentage of words borrowed. This finding was only true at the macro-level of analysis, however. In fact, a closer look at the strings of borrowed words indicated that the patterns of textual borrowing varied across the topics given.

The role of the embedded genre of input sources is another essential factor which may affect the writing performance of testees as well as the amount or patterns of textual borrowing. According to Hyland (2007, p. 149):

> Genre refers to abstract, socially recognized ways of using language. It is based on the idea that members of a community usually have little difficulty in recognizing similarities in the texts they use frequently and are able to draw on their repeated experiences with such texts to read, understand, and perhaps write them relatively easily.

As he stated, when taking the role of readers/writers, we are constantly using our past experiences of similar written works to try and understand/convey the meanings of a text. These experiences are not merely relevant to the linguistic features of a specific genre, but more importantly, to our context, the purpose, and the audience to whom we are communicating with. Therefore, the readers/writers usually refer to the formed schema they share with their audience to digest/express the viewpoints embedded within a text successfully. He further insisted on the importance of genre-based writing instruction and the benefits it brings to both the teachers and learners. One of the most salient advantages of this instruction is the way it raises their knowledge of genre and aids the learners to comprehend the structure of different genres, relevant contextual features and social discourse behind the written text as well as its underlying linguistic elements (Hyland, 2007). These will only be learned through experiencing, practicing and awareness raising. Tardy (2009) also introduced a genre knowledge framework which is composed of four components. Formal knowledge refers to textual features of the genre, such as the common lexical and grammatical features within a genre. Process knowledge revolves around the conventional practices required in carrying out a specific genre. Rhetorical knowledge deals with the understanding of socio-historical aspects of different genres. Finally, subject-matter knowledge indicates the users' content knowledge in a discipline which enables one to construct and convey meaning. In order for learners to comprehend and decode the ideas of a text and reproduce a summary, they should have the knowledge of these four components, or else, they may find it difficult to understand the conventions of the written genre and to write it in their own words while avoiding copying. All these concerns regarding genre practice proves that genre awareness is a prerequisite to the understanding of texts as a source of input in an integrated task (Gentil, 2011) and can have a particular impact on the performance of test takers. Narrative texts generally lend themselves more to summarizing; hence, are easier to summarize (Yu, 2009). It is claimed that the narrative genre is embedded in people's everyday life experience (Yu, 2009) and may be more tangible and easier to comprehend; therefore, easier for the learners to put it into their own words as well. On the other hand, at the micro-linguistic level, usually the argumentative text genre contains more complex structures and technical vocabulary which makes it difficult to understand the meaning of the text. Moreover, at the macro-level organization of argumentative genre, ideas or arguments are arranged more coherently and interrelated (Qin & Uccelli, 2016) and easy to follow. These characteristics may also hinder or mitigate the summarizing process of learners when composing their summaries.

A small number of studies have shed light on how reading texts of different genres may influence the outcome of integrated writing tasks (Keck, 2014; Jiuliang, 2014; Yu, 2009). Yu (2009) provided the EFL Chinese learners with three distinct text genres to summarize; expository, narrative and argumentative. His results displayed the significant impact of source texts on the summarizing tasks of learners. This was even to some extent higher than the effect of learners' language proficiency. Moreover, in the interviews conducted, learners considered length of the texts, topic familiarity, micro-linguistic as well as macro-organization characteristics of the texts as the main factors affecting their summary writing process. In a more recent study, Jiuliang (2014) examined the performance of undergraduate Chinese in two summarizing tasks, one providing an expository and the other a narrative text as the input source. The Many-Facet Rasch analysis indicated that learners performed better in the expository summarizing task. Nevertheless, the results of the interviews were in contradiction with the findings and the learners perceived the expository task more difficult. In their point of view, lexical difficulty of the expository text, informal register used in the narrative source, learners' schemata knowledge being more prepared for the narrative genre, and students' own affective filters were among the factors which facilitated the process of summarizing the narrative text. Keck (2014) also studied the patterns of textual borrowing and selection strategies of novice as well as experienced L1/L2 learners of English in composing three argumentative summarizing tasks with different topics. Based on the findings of this study, L1 and L2 writers selected the same ideas of the texts to be included in their summaries with the emphasis on the ones mostly stated in introductory and concluding paragraphs. Moreover, it was revealed that the novice L2 learners were the only group whose exact copied strings of words were long in their summarizing task, whereas, the experienced L1 learners avoided using this pattern in their writings.

When it comes to the source text genre type in summarizing tasks, only a few studies have studied the effect of different genre types on testees' written performance and the patterns of textual borrowing. According to Yu (2009), the role of text genre type on the performance of summarizing tasks has rarely been the concern of researchers, in particular, the argumentative genre which is the most salient discourse in an academic context. These studies may be even more essential and informative for the EFL instructors and test developers. In Iran, for instance, the emphasis of the curricula and assessment at tertiary level of education has been more on reading comprehension and translation skills in most majors not relevant to English literature, translation and TEFL (Farhady & Hedayati, 2009) and wherever writing is practiced at the ESP/EAP undergraduate courses, composing independent writing essays takes control of the teaching and assessment process. This seems to be no longer in line with the current academic needs of the students. These days, learners have access to numerous on/offline sources in various written genres, based on which they compose their articles and present their research projects in English. Hence, more attention should be drawn to the integration of skills, genre-based approaches to writing, and more recent types of writing assessment, in the academic milieu of Iran and similar EFL contexts. The following research seeks to examine the difference in the number and patterns of textual borrowing of foreign language writers, with English as their foreign language, while composing from sources with two different academic genres, i.e. expository and argumentative.

To this end the following research questions are formulated:

RQ 1: What are the patterns of textual borrowing and the extent of use of each pattern among the testees, while summarizing two different writing genres, i.e. expository and argumentative?
RQ 2: Is there any significant difference in the amount of textual borrowing while using two different written genres namely; expository and argumentative, as source materials?
RQ 3: What are the citation strategies used by the testees while composing their two written summarizing tasks?

3 Methodology

3.1 Participants

The participants of the study comprise 26 EFL undergraduate Iranian learners studying at a private university in Tehran. They ranged in age from 18 to 30 and came from three different majors, including TEFL, English literature and English translation. These three majors are the existing English majors at undergraduate level in Iran. The national curriculum designed for the undergraduate English majors in Iran introduces two writing courses to be covered at universities, n advanced writing course and, upon its accomplishment, an essay writing course.

The participants were passing their essay writing course at the time of the study. The concept of plagiarism was part of the course instruction; however, integrated writing tasks were not included in their class assessment prior to this research. Due to the complicated process involved in completing the integrated writing tasks and the level of the source texts of the study which were not suitable for low language proficiency learners, students at the intermediate level or above were selected based on the results of a language proficiency test, First Certificate in English(FCE), to take part in this research project. After screening the written summaries, four participants were excluded, since their writings were a mere copy paste of the source materials or were too short and meaningless, in which the ideas of the source texts were not mentioned sufficiently to be considered as an acceptable summary of the source. Therefore, the data analysis procedure was run with 22 female ($n = 13$) and male ($n = 9$) participants, and in sum 44 writings were accepted for further evaluation.

3.2 Instrumentation and Procedures

In this study, the focus of the integrated task was on summary writing from reading source materials. To this end, two reading texts, one an expository and the other an argumentative text were selected. These two genres are among the most commonly used texts in an academic setting (Weigle, 2002). The criterion used in selecting the passages was based on Alderson's (2000) classification of reading genres. The length of the two passages and their readability level were evaluated to reduce the level of discrepancies between the two texts. Fog's readability criterion was used to assess the readability of the texts. The topics of the texts were relevant to the academic context and relevant to the general daily life discussions and the learners were all familiar with them, thereby increasing their face validity. This ensured that the source texts would not raise the issue of content bias or underestimate the validity of the study. Features of the texts are shown in Table 1.

To fulfil the purpose of this study, the participants were asked to write two summary tasks based on two reading passages, i.e. the expository and argumentative texts, provided as the input source materials. First

Table 1 Features of the source reading texts

Topic	Genre	Purpose	Length	Fog's readability criterion
The Risks of Cigarette Smoke	Expository	Explain the effects/reasons	552 words	17
Equal Acceptance of Male and Female at Universities	Argumentative	Discuss a viewpoint or an argument	582 words	16.5

a piloting session was conducted prior to the main test with a group of learners, representative of the main testees of the study. Although at first the word limit was not essential to the researchers, after piloting the tasks in advance, we found out that some participants wrote summaries of the texts that were too short which would lead to difficulties in conveying the meaning and main ideas explained in the source texts. These extremely short summaries were not comprehensible and were hard to rate. Hence, on the sheets given, the testees were asked to write at least 200 words for each task. A brief introduction was also stated in the instructions on the basic requirements of the summarizing task the testees were about to complete. Based on the findings of the piloting session, the testees were asked to spend 30 minutes to complete each task. The order of completing the summarizing tasks started with the expository text followed by the argumentative reading passage. The texts were available while the testees completed their summaries. Afterwards, the writing of the testees underwent the process of content analysis. The purpose of this procedure was to find the number and patterns of textual borrowing within the writings of testees in each genre. The coding was done according to Shi's (2004) model. This method was also used by Weigle and Parker (2012) in their research to extract the source borrowing patterns applied by their testees. One rater who was a PhD student in TEFL and had experience in scoring the writing performance of EFL learners, was trained to run the coding process of the data in two consecutive sessions within a two-month period. The intra-rater reliability calculated using the correlation coefficient for the expository task was $\alpha = .86$ compared to the Alpha value achieved for the argumentative task $\alpha = .89$. Consistency measures greater than .70 are considered acceptable in the literature (Saxton et al., 2012).

3.3 Data Analysis

In the data analysis phase of this study, the writings of the testees were reviewed. Through content analysis, levels of paraphrasing of the testees and the amount of textual borrowing patterns were examined. In the present coding procedure, the use of (1) two or more content words, (2) three successive words which make a syntactic constituent and (3) every four consecutive words from the same clause was considered as evidence of textual borrowing (Shi, 2004). For example, in the summarizing task entitled 'The Risks of Cigarette Smoke'; (1) *physical strength,* is a copied extract as it includes two consecutive content words (a noun followed by an adjective) taken from the same clause of the source text. (2) Again, in the same text, *reason of death,* is considered a borrowed string as it forms a syntactic constituent. (3) Finally, from the other source entitled 'A university should accept male and female students equally', *to achieve equilibrium among women and men,* is a mere copy of more than four words from the same clause of the source text. Moreover, in his coding pattern, Shi (2004) introduced four levels of paraphrasing. The first category is mere copying where the writer completely copies the words from the source verbatim. In the second category, one can find a slight change while making use of source material and paraphrasing it, such as using synonyms or disregarding and/or adding a word. The third category indicates close paraphrasing where the writer modifies the syntax and wording of the source material. The last category represents flawless paraphrasing where nothing is borrowed and copied from the source texts. Since the last category is not a sign of text borrowing or copying and shows that the writer has acknowledged the author of the source materials while summarizing, it is not included in this research (see Table 2). The amount of the testees copy pasting will be released through these levels of paraphrasing, as the levels of paraphrasing move from strong levels of copying toward lesser amounts of copying. However, it has to be mentioned that Shi (2004) also classified the textual borrowing patterns based on their being referenced to the source material by quotes. We eliminated this classification in our study due to the fact that our participants occasionally revealed it while summarizing. They mainly neglected quoting and citation of the source material. This is dealt with as a separate question in the form of detailed analyses of the summaries later in the results section.

Furthermore, the statistical analysis of repeated measure ANOVA was conducted where the independent variable was genre type with two levels, namely expository and argumentative, and the dependent variable was the mean percentage of textual borrowing patterns, to examine whether there exists a significant difference between the two genres in the amount of textually borrowed strings of words.

4 Results and Discussion

4.1 Patterns of Textual Borrowing Detected

The first research question of the study aimed to evaluate the extracted patterns of textual borrowing in the summarizing tasks of the testees in order to investigate whether the testees' performance in two distinct genres was different considering the amount of word strings they had borrowed from the reading passages in the patterns drawn out. To this end, the summarized written texts of the participants were coded according to an adaptation of Shi's (2004) model of paraphrasing levels. The borrowed strings in the writings were distinguished and coded under three main patterns of textual borrowing; (1) mere copied, (2) modified copied and (3) reformulated. The example extracts from the source materials as well as patterns of borrowing in writings of the testees are provided in Table 2.

Furthermore, to gain an in-depth look at the possible differences in the patterns of borrowing between the two genres, the length of the strings detected for each pattern of borrowing was calculated. According to Shi (2004), the length of the borrowed strings was determined by counting the total number of successive words borrowed from a clause in

Table 2 Sample extracts of textual borrowing patterns

Patterns of borrowing	Genre type	Paraphrase attempt extracts	Source material extracts
(1) Mere copied	(1) Expository (2) Argumentative	The report further suggests that *cancer is not caused or developed by a single element in smoke* *Pupils often show some sort of talent* toward particular subjects in early age	This report emphasizes that *cancer is not caused by a single element in* cigarette *smoke* *Pupils often show some sort of talent* from their very childhood toward learning…
(2) Modified copied	(1) Expository (2) Argumentative	They believe that *the impact of passive smoking is much more on non-smokers* For instance, *jobs requiring physical power are more suitable for boys than girls*	Consequently, *the effects of passive smoking are far greater on non-smokers* than on smokers We cannot deny that the *jobs which require more of physical strength are best suitable for boys*
(3) Reformulated	(1) Expository (2) Argumentative	In cigarettes carbon monoxide fights with oxygen in blood and destroys the oxygen in the cells and … In some countries like India *as women aren't allowed to continue study, they take the responsibility of house work*	In the red cells of blood, Carbon monoxide found in cigarette, competes with oxygen and interferes with the blood's ability… It is accustomed *that the women of the community are bound to do home duty where they are not allowed to study* after …

the source text and adding the number of other content words borrowed from the text within the same clause to that number. After measuring the length of the borrowed strings, the total percentage of borrowed words in each of the three main patterns in both summarizing genres was computed (see Table 3). As the results of descriptive statistics in Table 3 pinpoint, the number of textual borrowing patterns was not the same between the two genres among the participants. In general, the participants wrote longer summaries for the second genre, i.e. argumentative text. As illustrated, the mean of the total word count for this genre was $M = 213.09$ compared to $M = 199.18$ for the expository written summaries.

Findings further showed that the mean score for the patterns of textual borrowing was higher for the expository genre. This indicates that most participants borrowed longer strings from the source materials in the expository genre and failed to paraphrase the ideas mentioned in the source text successfully. Moreover, the most salient textual borrowing

Table 3 Descriptive statistics of textual borrowing patterns

	N	Minimum	Maximum	Mean	Std. Deviation
Total words genre Exp	22	100	299	199.18	48.465
Total words genre Arg	22	126	292	213.09	45.580
Total percent borrowed Genre Exp	22	1	49	29.32	11.704
Total percent borrowed Genre Arg	22	2	44	20.14	12.299
Percent of copied patterns Genre Exp	22	1	38	14.41	10.112
Percent of copied patterns Genre Arg	22	0	40	9.36	3.608
Percent of modified patterns Genre Exp	22	0	24	9.32	6.862
Percent of modified patterns Genre Arg	22	0	25	8.50	6.795
Percent of reformulated Patterns Genre Exp	22	0	16	5.59	3.608
Percent of reformulated Patterns Genre Arg	22	0	8	2.18	2.239
Valid N (listwise)	22				

pattern elicited with the mean score of $M = 14.41$ was mere copying in the expository genre. In fact, the smallest mean was related to the percentage of reformulated patterns ($M = 2.18$) in the argumentative genre. The maximum string length borrowed was as well attributed to the mere copied textual pattern. On average, participants' length of copied words and constituents from the source materials appeared to be greater for the expository writing genre. However, as can be seen in Table 3, there were a few participants who avoided copying from sources in both genres.

While examining summaries of the testees in more detail, it was discovered that there was not any special contradiction between the two genres with regard to the place of occurrence of the patterns of textually borrowed word strings. Borrowing words as mere copied or modified copied expressions and reformulated structures were tracked in different paragraphs of the testees' writings, including introduction, body, and conclusion in both genres. It is worth mentioning that testees foremost borrowed strings of words from the sources to state the main ideas of the texts in their writings. The findings showed that, 20 testees out of 22 used the main points of the source texts in their argumentative summary writing tasks, while 18 testees out of 22 also did the same in their expository genre summaries. This highlights that the testees were able to understand the main ideas of the texts in general and the necessity to express them in their summaries, even if they have not all been successful in summarizing or paraphrasing the main ideas in an acceptable way and may have committed plagiarism. Modified copied expressions and reformulated structures were, respectively the most common and least used patterns of textual borrowing in summarizing main ideas in both genres. Furthermore, in the expository genre 18 out of 22 testees also used mere copying and modified copied patterns in writing the supporting details of the expository reading passage. As the structure of this passage included defining statements, number of examples, and few reports, the testees tended to use more borrowing patterns while summarizing. In particular, paraphrasing the definitions embedded in the expository texts seemed to be a challenging task to accomplish and most of them have reformulated or simply modified the definitions. Nevertheless, the testees were more successful in summarizing the supporting arguments in the argumentative task and used fewer mere copied strings from the source text. On the contrary, the thesis statement of the argumentative passage was more frequently prone to mere or modified copying.

4.2 Role of Different Genres of Source Materials in Summarizing Tasks

To answer the second research question and find out whether different genres presented in source materials had an effect on the amount of textually borrowed words from the source texts, four repeated measure ANOVAs were conducted. The two types of genre, i.e. expository and argumentative texts, were the independent variables in this statistical analysis. The percentage of borrowed words in total and the percentage of borrowed words in each three patterns of textual borrowing in the two summarizing genres composed, were regarded as the dependent variable in the ANOVAs conducted. This analysis of variance was run due to the fact that every participant had written two summarizing tasks; both for the expository and argumentative reading sources. The Kolmogorove–Smirnov test proved normality for the percentage borrowed distributions in all four analyses of both genres ($p > .05$).

Results shown in Table 4 indicate that there was a significant difference between the total mean percentage of textual borrowing patterns while summarizing texts with different genres (Wilks' Lambda $= .514$, $F (1, 20) = 19.879$, $p < .001$, $\eta^2 = .486$). Moreover, findings revealed that genre type had statistically significant effects for mere copied patterns (Wilks' Lambda $= .787$, $F (1, 20) = 5.690$, $p = .027$, $\eta_p^2 = .213$) and reformulated patterns (Wilks' Lambda $= .579$, $F (1, 20) = 15.283$, $P = .001$, $\eta_p^2 = .421$. However, this was not the case for modified copied patterns ($F (1, 20) = .350$, n.s.). According to Cohen (1988), the effect sizes which are greater than .4 are considered large. This means that both the total mean percentage of textual borrowing patterns and reformulated patterns achieved high effect sizes as well.

Table 4 Multivariate tests for the patterns of textual borrowing

Effect		Value	F	Hypothesis df	Error df	Sig.	Partial Eta squared
Genre	Wilk's Lambda (Total percent borrowed)	.514	19.879[a]	1.000	21.000	.000	.486
	Wilks' Lambda (Mere copied)	.787	5.690[a]	1.000	21.000	.027	.213
	Wilk's Lambda (Modified copied)	.984	.350[a]	1.000	21.000	.560	.016
	Wilk's Lambda (Reformulated)	.579	15.283[a]	1.000	21.000	.001	.421

[a] Exact statistics

4.3 Citation Strategies and Voice

More in-depth analysis into the summarizing written texts of testees was conducted to analyze the third research question. As mentioned earlier, the patterns of textual borrowing can also be classified as being cited through quotes (Shi, 2004) or other citation strategies. Since most of our testees neglected these strategies in their summaries and refused to acknowledge the ideas mentioned in the reading texts, citation was not included in our categorization of textual borrowing patterns. The testees just tried to summarize or paraphrase the texts in their writing process without referring to the author of the source text or the input source itself and ended up copying strings of words while not mentioning any citations. Among the 22 participants of this study only 8 testees used citation strategies in their writings. In general, the testees avoided using quotes as a citation strategy. Only 3 out of 22 testees exhibited this strategy. On the other hand, the testees used citing words in their paraphrasing to indicate their awareness of citing and appreciating the authorship of the original writer of the source text. Instances of the citing words written by the testees include; 'according to the author', 'the author of the passage explains that', 'the writer believes', 'the author states', 'he later discussed that', etc. Below is an example of this type of citation:

Extract 1: The writer of this text believes that [academic grades *mere copy*] and [pupils' skills and interests *reformulated*] are the key factors, as education's main purpose is to eventually [help the people to enjoy their future. Pupils often show some sort of talent toward *mere copy*] particular subjects in early ages. Here the writer suggests that [the main criteria of major selection *reformulated*] should be based on the [skills or grades that the students achieve in that specific major *mere copy*].

Another strategy used in citing among the testees was referring to the text or reading passage itself using expressions such as 'the main concern of the passage is', 'as mentioned in the text', 'the text says that', etc., to show that the ideas reflected in their summarizing text do not belong to themselves and are borrowed from elsewhere.

Extract 2: After that, the document states that [a very large amount of deaths caused by lung cancer are because of smoking cigarettes and not only that; many other cancers like mouth or kidney are also caused by smoking cigarettes *reformulated*].

The mentioned citation strategies can be traced more frequently in the expository text compared to the argumentative passage. This may be due to the purpose of this particular written genre which provides explanation to the causes and outcomes of an issue, here smoking cigarettes. Thus, macro-organization of this text genre consists of a number of citations itself from a few studies and records relevant to the topic in order to clarify and explain the ideas mentioned. These citations may have inevitably triggered the testees to use citation strategies as well to summarize the text. This, nevertheless, was not the case with the argumentative reading text in which the original author has merely brought few examples to support the main argument of the text. This text did not contain any citations and the ideas were further elaborated from the author's point of view. Therefore, not being exposed to any citations in this reading passage may have led to the learners using fewer citation strategies in their writing as well. Moreover, contrary to the expository text genre, the testees mostly applied citations in the introduction paragraph of their argumentative summarizing task. Whereas, in the expository summaries, the citations were detected in all paragraphs and were even more salient in the body when explaining reasons and bringing detailed information. The following extract is taken from a testee's summary of the expository text. This is the body paragraph of the summary where the testee brings explanations and reasons to support the idea stated in the text.

> Extract 3: As mentioned in the text, if we want to have a precise look to the process of oxygen absorption in human body, we can find out that cigarette components like [carbon monoxide compete with oxygen in blood cells *mere copy*]. Therefore, the risk of creating blood clots increases and [the blood circulation has been affected as a result *reformulated*].

In the further analysis of written summaries, it was detected that the testees used personal voice in their argumentative summaries. This was exhibited in the summary writing of 10 out of 22 testees. However, this does not indicate that they had added their own opinions to the ideas stated in the reading text as it has to be done in an opinion-based integrated writing task. They had observed the instruction of the tasks which informed them to merely write a summary without providing their own ideas. They had embedded their own voice in their summaries by using the pronoun 'I', while mentioning the viewpoints of the original author of the text. This use of the personal pronoun was not discerned in the expository genre.

> Extract 4: I believe that the power of women can be caused by [same number of acceptance of men and women *modified copy*]. Also, regardless of gender, people should have the same opportunity for studying.

According to Zhao (2013), illustration of voice in writing is context-dependent and authors may use various strategies to construct their voice in a written text. In the context of this study, the testees mostly employed the first-person pronoun to identify their voice in their argumentative written genre. This can be related to the structure of the argumentative writing in which the sentences and supporting ideas contribute to the main arguments pointed out by the author and are built upon them. This may have been one of the reasons why the testees tried to use the personal pronoun 'I' in their summaries. They also understood the importance of the personal voice in the argumentative reading text and felt the necessity to express it as well in their own writings, in particular, when concluding their written summaries as well as stating the main argument of the text in their introduction paragraph. As the findings indicated, testees exhibited different citation strategies in their summarizing tasks depending on the genre type of the reading passages.

4.4 Discussion

The present study aimed to determine the frequency and patterns of textual borrowing that students used across two written genres. The results of the repeated measure ANOVAs and content analysis confirmed that the number and patterns of borrowing differed between the two genres; nevertheless, in the modified copied pattern the mean difference between the two genres did not yield a significant value. Mere copied strings were by far the most used pattern in both genres; the reformulated patterns of borrowing were very low among the testees in composing the argumentative genre; however, their presence among the written summaries of the testees was better for the other genre. In general, the testees rarely made use of the reformulated pattern compared to the other two patterns. This may be related to the complicated procedure of reformulating the syntactic features of a clause compared to modified copying pattern where few words are replaced with their synonyms in a clause in an attempt to paraphrase it or compared to the mere copying of a clause. It may be quite demanding for the testees and engages their linguistic knowledge to reorder and/or manipulate the parts of speech or alter the structure of a clause. That is why the occurrences of modified copied patterns were higher than reformulated ones. The learners' lack of an extensive lexical repertoire can also impede the process of correct paraphrasing. This may be the reason why the mere copied patterns were the most salient patterns used by the learners in both genres regardless of the lexical and structural features of the genre type. A number of researchers have as well purported that linguistic knowledge of learners has an impact on their paraphrasing and patterns of textual borrowing

(Cumming et al., 2005; Shi, 2012). However, in their research Weigle and Parker (2012) did not find a significant effect for the proficiency level of learners while completing their integrated tasks. Furthermore, a lot of the strings borrowed by the testees were general terms, words or as Weigle and Parker (2012) stated, 'collocations'. This finding is in accordance with Keck's (2006) study. These word strings seemed to be more complicated to paraphrase in general.

The departure found in the number and patterns of textual borrowing between the two genres may be due to the fact that although both of these genres are foremost read and used in an academic context, the argumentative one is practiced more often among foreign language learners in Iran. The learners are regularly required to write their argumentation on a special topic as an independent task of writing. Hence, they are more familiar with this genre. This can raise their awareness regarding the regulations, outlining and structure of an argumentative text and make it easier for them to comprehend the source materials written in this specific genre and better summarize it. Jiuliang (2014) also found that schematic knowledge of the participants in his research was among the factors affecting the performance of testees. Their daily life encounters of the narrative genre and the activated schematic knowledge of narrative texts made it easier for them to summarize the narrative text compared to the expository text.

Moreover, we can attribute the difference in the number of textually borrowed patterns extracted in this study to the distinct features of the provided genres. The lexical complexity and syntactic properties of the source passages could have affected the understanding and summarizing process of the testees. For example, in this study, the expository text contained lots of details, definitions and specific terms. The presence of certain numerics and key lexical terms could have forced the learners to borrow them in their summaries despite their being aware of acknowledging the source materials. The testees may have found these key combinations of words existing in the definitions more difficult to paraphrase. At the same time, they were determined to transfer their meaning precisely. That's why the number of short strings, less than four words, of mere copied patterns were noteworthy. This is in line with Gebril and Plakans' (2009) findings which indicated that vocabulary and syntactic structure of the reading input source hinders the comprehension and writing performance of writers in integrated tasks. Abasi et al. (2006) also stated that the learners are obliged to take advantage of the textual borrowing patterns when the difficulty level of a source text is considerable. Moreover, the clear outlining and macro-organization of the argumentative text helped testees to understand the main ideas of the text easily in the introduction and conclusion parts of the passage. Therefore, they borrowed more extracts from these main arguments in their summaries compared to the supporting details embedded in the text.

The findings of our study also indicated that there was a discrepancy in citation strategies used by the testees in two writing genres. Testees displayed their personal voice in the argumentative task through the use of the pronoun 'I' and used fewer citation strategies in their summaries compared to the expository summarizing task. One possible reason for this variation between the genres may be rooted in the characteristics of the genres. As each of these genres possess their own conventions, structures, and macro- organizational elements, the differences between the genres can bring up their own difficulties in comprehension of the source or patterns of textual borrowing in the summaries. In line with our finding, Yu (2009) and Jiuliang (2014) emphasized the role of the macro-organization of a text in understanding and the selection of source texts as well as the process of summarizing them. The presence of self-voice in the structure of an argumentative text is very common, as the writers try to find their way to support and clearly declare their claim or argumentation while the text moves on. Further, the use of the first singular pronoun by testees while stating the ideas of the author of the source material without citing or providing any quotes can be relevant to the cultural issues. This is where we can refer to Pennycook (1996) who believed that cultural differences among the western and eastern countries and disciplinary practices such as rote learning as well as construction of identity (Abasi et al., 2006) may trigger the attitude of borrowing or copying the source materials in one's writing. These issues are critical and should not be neglected. It will take time for a novel learner who is not from a western culture to create their own identity and authorship in writing (Shi, 2012). From a critical point of view, even some foreign language learners may intentionally borrow words in the texts without citing due to their negative attitude toward plagiarism (Pennycook, 1996). Thus, the concept of plagiarism and source text borrowing strategies is an interdisciplinary and cultural entity which can be affected by various factors.

5 Implications for the Context and Conclusion

Altogether, we can conclude that genre type can affect summary writing performance of the foreign language learners. Thus, it brings a word of caution for the teachers as well as test developers when judging the textual borrowing attitude of the learners or in composing a summarizing task on a specific genre, particularly in EFL contexts with different rhetorical knowledge of the written genres. This introduces further evidence for the importance of academic integrated writing tasks such as summarizing or opinion tasks in the EFL context where novel approaches to teaching and assessing writing is not adequately included in the course syllabi. Since it may be taken for granted that talking about borrowing from sources and inhibiting students from copying sources is enough, the concept of plagiarism may not be practiced as effectively as expected in some EFL academic milieu like Iran and this may be the main reason the learners are not aware of how much textual borrowing or which patterns of it is tolerable. As a result, the majority of them may inadvertently borrow large amounts of source materials in their writings and plagiarize. According to their culture and beliefs, the sources provided to them are considered as the 'repositories of impersonal truths' (Abasi et al., 2006); therefore, they prefer to pick up those styles and patterns rather than create their own writing values.

As the definition of writing skill has evolved gradually to reflect the real life needs of learners, changes have to be implemented and practiced in the EFL writing courses similar to the context of the present study to help the students learn and improve their disciplinary writing at higher levels of education. This requires a shift from the product-oriented English writing curriculum to practices which engage the learners in every step of their writing process. Further, as the washback of assessment types, utilized in the classrooms, on the teaching of writing is also considered as an important factor, the instructors and test developers in these EFL contexts need to move toward other task types to assess the writing skill of the learners in accordance to the construct of the academic setting. These tasks may include paraphrasing and summarizing. Through assessing and teaching various academic writing tasks to the learners, teachers can compensate for their pitfalls and aid them in the process of building their own identity in their writings which will further stop them from copying and borrowing the source materials in their own writings. However, instruction in plagiarism and integrated tasks shouldn't be restricted to discussions around different cultural attitudes toward plagiarism or a number of useful strategies. Among the other useful subjects which can be taught in the academic setting are paraphrasing, synthesizing and genre awareness. Li and Casanave (2012) and Keck (2006) insisted that learning and teaching paraphrasing skills, although difficult, is truly beneficial to the learners. These skills should also be taught in the EFL academic context along with the independent writing tasks to help learners survive in their academic roles. In line with the fact that paraphrasing can be learned, Johns (2011) expressed that genres and their principles are also deeply seated in the culture and raising learners' awareness about various genres is another essential skill required in an academic context, particularly in academic writing courses. Hyland (2007) discussed the importance of genre instruction in academic settings and claimed that it engages learners with real-life tasks. This will become even more critical when it comes to the learners of a foreign language, such as the testees of this study. Cultural differences and practices of the first language written genre's conventions can have an impact both on their comprehension of the written texts of another language with different genres and the production of various written genres. Thus, we believe all these techniques and problematic issues should be presented to the Iranian and other similar EFL learners or we shouldn't expect them to avoid using unacceptable patterns of textual borrowing in their writings.

Considering the cultural differences, the great camp of the educated generation, and the growing number of EFL students taking part in international English proficiency tests or publishing their works in English, the need to introduce the conventions of different written genres, familiarize EFL learners with the concept of plagiarism and teach them the regulations of writing to represent themselves in their articles written based on a number of input sources is irrefutable. Similarly, Pecorari (2006) stated that research on plagiarism and inappropriate textual borrowing should put aside its pitfalls and turn toward the potential opportunities it provides for learners to practice their academic writing style, learn its rules and conventions, and finally become an independent writer. The results of the present study support this viewpoint as well and elucidate the role of various factors such as genre type in composing from input sources.

There were a few limitations in this study which can provide further suggestions for research related to this particular concern. First, the number of participants in this study was not large enough to allow us to generalize our findings to other contexts. Furthermore, in our study we merely focused on two genres as source materials which were mainly the genres used in the academic context. Other studies can be conducted to include various genres and evaluate their effects on learners' performance. As mentioned before, summarizing is one example of the integrated writing task and our results are limited to this particular task type. It would be informative to examine the patterns of textual borrowing in other task types with different genres as well. Finally, research designed to detect the comments and reflection of the learners themselves on the occurrences of their textual borrowing patterns can prove beneficial to the teachers as well as the test developers.

References

Abasi, A., Akbari, N., & Graves, B. (2006). Discourse appropriation, construction of identities, and the complex issue of plagiarism: ESL students writing in graduate school. *Journal of Second Language Writing, 15*(2), 102–117. https://doi.org/10.1016/j.jslw.2006.05.001.

Alderson, J. C. (2000). *Assessing reading.* Cambridge, UK: Cambridge University Press.

Chapelle, C. A., Enright, M. K., & Jamieson, J. M. (Eds.). (2008). *Building a validity argument for the test of English as a foreign language.* New York: Routledge.

Cheong, Ch. M., Zhu, X., Li, G. Y., & Wen, H. (2019). Effects of intertextual processing on L2 integrated writing. *Journal of Second Language Writing, 44,* 63–75. https://doi.org/10.1016/j.jslw.2019.03.004.

Cho, Y., Rijmen, F., & Novak, J. (2013). Investigating the effect of prompt characteristics on the comparability of TOEFL iBT integrated writing tasks. *Language Testing, 30*(4), 513–534. http://doi.og/10.1177/0265532213478796.

Cohen, J. (1988). *Statistical power analysis for the behavioral sciences.* Hillsdale, NJ: Lawrence Erlbaum Associates.

Cumming, A., Kantor, R., Baba, K., Eouanzoui, K., Erdosy, U., James, M. (2006). *Analysis of discourse features and verification of scoring levels for independent and integrated prototype written tasks for the new TOEFL* (TOEFL Monograph No. MS-30). Princeton, NJ: Educational Testing Service.

Cumming, A., Kantor, R., Baba, K., Erdosy, U., Eouanzoui, K., & James, M. (2005). Differences in written discourse in independent and integrated prototype tasks for next generation TOEFL. *Assessing Writing, 10*(1), 5–43. https://doi.org/10.1016/j.asw.2005.02.001.

Farhady, H., & Hedayati, H. (2009). Language assessment policy in Iran. *Annual Review of Applied Linguistics, 29,* 132–141. https://doi.org/10.1017/S0267190509090114.

Gebril, A., & Plakans, L. (2009). Investigating source use, discourse features, and process in integrated writing tests. *Spaan Fellow Working Papers in Second or Foreign Language Assessment, 7,* 47–84.

Gentil, G. (2011). A biliteracy agenda for genre research. *Journal of Second Language Writing, 20*(1), 6–23. http://doi.org/10.1016/j.jslw.2010.12.006.

Hyland, K. (2007). Genre pedagogy: Language, literacy and L2 writing instruction. *Journal of Second Language Writing, 16*(3), 148–164. https://doi.org/10.1016/j.jslw.2007.07.005.

Johns, A. M. (2011). The future of genre in L2 writing: Fundamental, but contested, instructional decisions. *Journal of Second Language Writing, 20*(1), 56–68. https://doi.org/10.1016/j.jslw.2010.12.003.

Jiuliang, L. (2014). Examining genre effects on test takers' summary writing performance. *Assessing Writing, 22,* 75–90. http://doi.org/10.1016/j.asw.2014.08.003.

Keck, C. (2006). The use of paraphrase in summary writing: A comparison of L1 and L2 writers. *Journal of Second Language Writing, 15*(4), 261–278. http://doi.org/10.1016/j.jslw.2006.09.006.

Keck, C. (2014). Copying, paraphrasing, and academic writing development: A re-examination of L1 and L2 summarization practices. *Journal of Second Language Writing, 25*(1), 4–22. https://doi.org/10.1016/j.jslw.2014.05.005.

Knoch, U., & Sitajalabhorn, W. (2013). A closer look at integrated writing tasks: Towards a more focussed definition for assessment purposes. *Assessing Writing, 18*(4), 300–308. https://doi.org/10.1016/j.asw.2013.09.003.

Li, Y., & Casanave, C. P. (2012). Two first-year students' strategies for writing from sources: Patchwriting or plagiarism? *Journal of Second Language Writing, 21*(2), 165–180. https://doi.org/10.1016/j.jslw.2012.03.002.

Pecorari, D. (2006). Visible and occluded citation features in postgraduate second-language writing. *English for Specific Purposes, 25*(1), 4–29. https://doi.org/10.1016/j.esp.2005.04.004.

Pennycook, A. (1996). Borrowing others' words: Text, ownership, memory and plagiarism. *TESOL Quarterly, 30*(2), 201–230. https://doi.org/10.2307/3588141.

Plakans, L. (2009). Discourse synthesis in integrated second language writing assessment. *Language Testing, 26*(4), 561–587. https://doi.org/10.1177/0265532209340192.

Qin, W., & Uccelli, P. (2016). Same language, different functions: A cross-genre analysis of Chinese EFL learners' writing performance. *Journal of Second Language Writing, 33,* 3–17. https://doi.org/10.1016/j.jslw.2016.06.001.

Saxton, E., Belanger, S., & Becker, W. (2012). The Critical Thinking Analytic Rubric (CTAR): Investigating intra-rater and inter-rater reliability of a scoring mechanism for critical thinking performance assessments. *Assessing Wiring, 17*(4), 251–270. https://doi.org/10.1016/j.asw.2012.07.002.

Shi, L. (2004). Textual borrowing in second-language writing. *Written Communication, 21,* 171–200. https://doi.org/10.1177/0741088303262846.

Shi, L. (2012). Rewriting and paraphrasing source texts in second language writing. *Journal of Second Language Writing, 21*(2), 134–148. https://doi.org/10.1016/j.jslw.2012.03.003.

Spivey, N. N., & King, J. (1989). Readers as writers: Composing from sources. *Reading Research Quarterly, 24* (1), 7-26. https://doi.org/10.1598/RRQ.24.1.1.

Tardy, C. M. (2009). *Building genre knowledge*. West Lafayette, IN: Parlor Press.

Weigle, S. C. (2002). *Assessing writing*. Cambridge, UK: Cambridge University Press.

Weigle, S. C. (2004). Integrating reading and writing in a competency test for non-native speakers of English. *Assessing Writing, 9*(1), 27–55. https://doi.org/10.1016/j.asw.2004.01.002.

Weigle, S. C. & Parker, K. (2012). Source text borrowing in an integrated reading/writing assessment. *Journal of Second Language Writing, 21*(2), 118–133. http://doi.org/10.1016/j.jslw.2012.03.004.

Yamada, K. (2003). What prevents ESL/EFL writers from avoiding plagiarism? Analyses of 10 North-American college websites. *System, 31*(2), 247–258. https://doi.org/10.1016/S0346-251X(03)00023-X.

Yu, G, (2009). The shifting sands in the effects of source text summarizability on summary writing. *Assessing Writing, 14*(2), 116–137. https://doi.org/10.1016/j.asw.2009.04.002.

Zhao, C. G. (2013). Measuring authorial voice strength in L2 argumentative writing: The development and validation of an analytic rubric. *Language Testing, 30*(2), 201–230. https://doi.org/10.1177/0265532212456965.

Changing Practices to Overcome Writing Difficulties in EFL Courses at University: A Lebanese Case Study

Tamara Al Khalili

1 Introduction

I have taught English as a Foreign Language (EFL) to Arab students at the tertiary level for several years. At one of the private universities in Lebanon, EFL is offered with the four language skills taught as an integrated course. Based on my experience, I have noticed that many EFL students dislike the writing sessions the most. They skip writing classes and they prefer to submit already written compositions prepared at home. When I investigated this further, some students admitted that their writing "is horrible". Others stated that they have problems with starting to write, developing and concluding their compositions and few reported that they lack ideas and they need to read about the topic extensively before writing. Little has been written about this issue in Lebanon and therefore this study is an attempt to shed light on these problems and attitudes within an exam-based university context.

T. Al Khalili (✉)
University of Exeter, Exeter, UK
e-mail: tk335@exeter.ac.uk

© The Author(s) 2020
L. McCallum and C. Coombe (eds.), *The Assessment of L2 Written English across the MENA Region*, https://doi.org/10.1007/978-3-030-53254-3_12

Academic writing is one of the skills tested in university entrance exams in Lebanon and it is considered essential for student success at undergraduate and graduate levels (Esseili, 2016). However, many EFL students fail the exam because of the writing section and they are obliged to take remedial courses to enhance this competency (Esseili, 2014). Clearly, academic writing is a complex skill and it requires time, effort and perseverance to be mastered. The literature has shown that the process writing approach gives students the chance to elaborate thoroughly on their writing and develop it in a prolonged systemic way (Harmer, 2004). Accordingly, and based on the above requirements, this study was conducted to investigate the following research questions:

RQ 1: How do pre-university EFL students' perceive academic writing at the tertiary level in Lebanon?
RQ 2: How did an intervention based on the PWA affect EFL students' academic writing grades and attitudes at university in Lebanon?

2 Literature Review

Writing is one of the four language skills that are taught in ESL/EFL classes in Lebanon. It gains special importance since it is the main medium used to write assignments and projects in different subjects at university (Esseili, 2016). Despite this reality, second language writing (SLW) is considered a difficult task and one of the hardest skills to teach and learn (Al Kamli, 2019). Hashemnezhad (2012, p. 722) considers writing as one of the least understood subjects in applied linguistics and he confirms that "many linguists still depict writing as an orthographic demonstration of speech and product approach". Similarly, Al Hamandi (2015, p. 5) admits that many EFL teachers in Lebanon still follow traditional approaches and most of their instruction is focused on "rules of language, organization, and mechanics which made many ESL/EFL students face difficulties in learning how to write in English". These factors in addition to several cultural backgrounds have made SLW competency in Lebanon a difficult task confined to talented and creative souls (Hamandi, 2015).

To minimize the writing difficulty and boost students' grades in writing tests several approaches were introduced into the new Lebanese English writing curriculum. Primarily, the product approach dominated the writing classes until the end of the 1990s. Then, the process approach took over and recently the genre process approach has been gaining popularity (Badger & White, 2000). However, several studies have shown that the process writing approach is still leading and is succeeding in enhancing second language learners' writing competency particularly in countries that use English as a medium of instruction including Lebanon (Hamandi, 2015; Esseili, 2014; Mourssi, 2013).

According to Badger and White (2000), the product approach consists of four main stages: the familiarizing stage, the controlled writing stage, the guided writing stage and the free writing stage. Since the emphasis of the product approach is on the composed product, teachers in the 1970s and 1980s adopted methods and materials they assumed would positively influence their students' writing (Zamel, 1982). These methods did not consider the act of writing, the purpose of writing, the audience and the process of composing. This lack of attention to the process of composing itself encouraged Zamel (1982) to investigate the issue further and to ask questions about how to write, how to pre-write and re-write.

The PWA appeared in the early 1970s as a response to the supremacy of a product- pedagogy in ESL contexts. Flower and Hayes (1981) as cited by Graham (2006), describe the PWA as a unit in the cognitive process approach that consists of three stages; planning, translating and reviewing. The first stage includes generating ideas and organizing them. The second stage involves translating the ideas into written details with attention to syntax, spelling and grammar. The third stage includes reading for developing and editing the text. This division was later modified by Hayes (1996) into separate stages including prewriting, drafting, editing, revising and publishing. Determining topics and generating ideas are in the prewriting stage. Arranging generated ideas and transferring lexical and syntactic elements on paper occur in the drafting stage. Revising and improving these elements arise in the revision stage, and finally sharing it before publication (Johnson, 2008; Simpson, 2013). Atkinson (2003) affirms that the writing process is outlined in several stages that consist of a set of writing behaviours. It is divided into brainstorming, planning, mind mapping, drafting, peer revising, editing, final drafting and producing a well-developed version that is evaluated by the mentor. Principally, writers in process approaches are independent producers of texts and the teachers' main role is to help learners enhance their abilities to plan, define a problem, suggest and evaluate solutions (Hyland, 2003). They are low key facilitators, activity and resource directors, collaborators and joint co-authors (Florio-Ruane & Lensmire, 1989).

Literature has shown that the PWA has many benefits. It enhances cooperation between students and teachers and removes pressure from students because when their knowledge is combined with other sources it results in quality prewriting information (Lappo, 1985). Moreover, when they re-read their papers, they become strong evaluators and capable of helping others in developing and revising their contents. Even after publishing, students can read and evaluate the final text and learn from it (Keh, 1990).

In contrast, few researchers write about the limitations of the PWA. Badger and White (2000, p. 157) illustrate that the PWA considers all writing as produced by "the same set of processes and it offers learners insufficient input, particularly in terms of linguistic knowledge to write successfully". According to Reid (2001), as cited by Bayat (2014), process approaches do not account for mental processes used by the writer during text production. They disregard grammar and structure and the written product causes inconvenience. They emphasize the use of drafts and consequently students are more inclined to fail exams (Horowitz, 1986). Moreover, the functionalists, consider the process approaches as asocial. They observe learners as individuals and the writing process as something abstract which contains internal processes (Ezza, 2010). Likewise, Hamandi (2015, p. 8) observes that some non-native English teachers reject the PWA because of their cultural background. As authority figures, they may not want to "jeopardize their authority by giving up their control over their students through implementing the process approach strategies like response groups, peer conferences, and share sessions". Thus, they do not embrace the process approach to writing instruction because of cultural bounds.

Despite the few challenges mentioned in the literature, the majority of research studies on writing pedagogies supported the PWA in ESL/EFL contexts in particular. For instance, Hamadouche (2010) investigated the effectiveness of the PWA on Algerian EFL university students. The results of his study supported the importance of proceeding through the different stages of the PWA to write better compositions. Sheir, Zahran, and Koura (2015) also investigated the effectiveness of PWA in developing EFL engineering students writing performance in Egypt. The results of their study revealed that the development of their students' writing skills requires dealing with writing as a process that follows different stages and not as a product of accurate use of grammar and vocabulary. Adopting PWA helped their EFL students overcome the difficulties they face, produce well-written tasks and realize their potential. Also, Al-Sawalha and Chow (2012) conducted a study in Jordan and showed that the PWA has the potential to assist Jordanian EFL students in written communication in a holistic way and it increased their enjoyment while writing. Therefore, this case study is intended to add to what is already written about using the PWA in the Arab world in terms of its effectiveness on improving students' attitudes towards academic writing and in raising their marks in the timed writing assessments at university in the Lebanese context.

3 Methodology

This research study is a single holistic case study that is primarily interpretive in nature. It is intended to investigate the effectiveness of an intervention based on the process writing approach in an English remedial course in a pre-university programme in a private university in Lebanon. The course is offered as a prerequisite for Remedial III and IV that prepares students to study their majors later in English and the writing section of this course constitutes a large portion of the syllabi. During the sessions, students read articles and passages related to different topics and they collaboratively brainstorm these topics in class. Then they are asked to choose between three different topics to write about. The data collected in the study is derived from a variety of sources (students' writings, students' perceptions and field notes) to investigate the case further and to analyse intensively the "multifarious phenomena that constitute the life cycle of this unit" (Cohen & Manion, 1989, p. 124). In this case study, there was close cooperation between the researcher and the participants that allowed the researcher to better understand their attitudes and draw conclusions.

3.1 Participants

Convenience sampling was employed in this case study. The participants are seven EFL learners at the tertiary level in Lebanon aged between 18 and 20. These learners, who were given pseudonyms for ethical purposes, are Arab students, mainly Lebanese but they exhibit a wide range of educational experiences (L2 or L3), language capabilities and interests.

3.2 Data Collection and Analysis

This research study is based on an intervention that differs from the traditional way of teaching writing in its cyclical process and systematic way. It provides students with a set of writing strategies that help them generate ideas, collect data, assemble them and activate plans. This intervention is adopted from basic research on learning writing and has revealed positive effects on diverse populations in several ESL settings (Hashemnezhad, 2012). The study was conducted over eight sessions and the students were learning session by session new things and applying them in class. The sessions ran smoothly, and considerable attention was given to all the stages of the intervention.

Data gathering is crucial in any research study, and three data collection tools were used to answer the research questions in this study. First, students' diagnostic writings and post-tests were administered and compared. The topics of the tests were the same in the pre and post-tests. The actual teaching time for every session in Remedial English II is 90 minutes. The writing task was often in the last 40 minutes of the session. This time was adequate for doing what I intended to do for the research study. Five to ten minutes were spent in every single session for class instruction. In the first instructional session, students were asked to sit for a diagnostic test (expository paragraph/essay) about one of three topics that I provided (see Appendix 1). The topics were about exercise, sleep habits and festivals. Presumably, the students have enough information and vocabulary to write about one of these topics but at the beginning of the first session, I reviewed with them the characteristics of good paragraphs to refresh their memory. In general, 30–40 minutes is considered enough time for beginners to write a short paragraph. The pre-test was collected and evaluated according to an analytical scale that I adopted from previous research conducted by Gomez, Richard, Rafael, and Gomez (1996). The rubric is based on 1–5 analytic ratings that assess topic development, organization, meaning, sentence construction and mechanics and all the papers were scored out of twenty-five (see Appendix 2 or Table 2 for more information). I kept the pre-test with me to compare the results with the post-test. In the second session, the prewriting techniques were explained based on Emig's (1971) four major dimensions; prewriting, composing, revising and post-writing and students were asked to write about the same topic they wrote about in the pre-test. Students selected one of the five techniques and generated their ideas in 30 minutes. During this stage, I was guiding the students, observing them and taking notes. In the third session, I talked about drafting and students started their first draft by putting their generated ideas in a single paragraph. When the students mastered the skill of writing main ideas and supporting details in one clear paragraph, I explained how to develop the content into several paragraphs. After this session, some students were capable of writing a four-paragraph essay while others were not, but I witnessed gradual improvement in their writing skills. The last sessions were for peer review, teacher–student conference and revision. Students evaluated their peers' papers after I discussed with them a list of Do's and Don'ts (adapted from a peer review guide from Eksi (2012)). I advised them to objectively critique aspects such as content and sentence structure by commenting on their colleague's writing performance, rather than the person, helping their peers in improving the draft instead of making vague, marginal or global comments and focusing on how the argument is supported instead of agreeing or disagreeing with it. Parallel to peer review, teacher–student conferences were conducted to draw the students' attention to mistakes related to meaning, mechanics, grammar and spelling. Students made the corrections in the second and third drafts and edited their final one before the final submission for evaluation. The pre-tests and post-tests that were on the same topics were compared by using the same analytical rubric (see Appendix 2) and the course coordinator double-checked the results for credibility.

Second, field notes were used as another tool to document carefully and in detail what was happening while the students were writing over the eight sessions. All kinds of data including signs, gestures, face impressions, side talks, and conversations were observed and recorded to help me answer the research questions during the data analysis stage. Field notes were read carefully and analysed and based on the emerging issues of these documents, semi-structured interviews with the participants were conducted and then analysed. Semi-structured interviews were conducted with each of the 7 students individually in the classroom without any distractions. Permission was granted ahead of time to prepare the venue and ensure that all the interviews are conducted in a safe and comfortable setting. Each interview lasted 10–12 minutes and the same list of questions was asked of all interviewees (see Appendix 3 for more information on interviews). The opening questions were straightforward to encourage the interviewees to talk and to help them understand the discourse. The rest of the questions were about students' previous writing experiences, perceptions, motivation, assessment and finally their attitude about the topic investigated (Ritchie & Lewis, 2003). Students were given time in the interviews to finish and sometimes further questions were asked to help them make their points clearer. I reminded some students to continue saying what they left unfinished to get more detailed results. Moreover, I gave participants the option of choosing the interview language to help them express themselves more freely. All the interviewees preferred to be interviewed in Arabic, but scripts were translated into English. The interviews were audio-recorded, and notes were taken.

4 Results and Discussion

Pre and post-tests were administered, evaluated and compared by the researcher with the help of the course coordinator to ensure credibility. The results of the pre-tests and post-tests of each student were compared item by item and the findings of this instrument confirmed the effectiveness of the PWA in this context. The findings showed that the results of most of the elements in the rubric have improved in the post-test after the students were exposed to the PWA. Therefore, the PWA has helped the students systematically develop their writing abilities, attitudes, grades and produce well organized and focused assignments. Students used good descriptive language, different types of sentences and they presented their essays in a coherent manner. Therefore, the PWA has played an effective role in achieving the learning outcomes of the writing section of the course and this was basically revealed through the improvement in grades as Table 1 shows for the differences for the seven participants.

As mentioned earlier, semi-structured interviews supplemented the pre and post-tests and the field notes. The interviews were conducted individually, and the questions were carefully created to elicit as much data as possible. The data originated was transcribed and analysed thematically. The field notes were read thoroughly, and common topics were extracted. The emerging data were categorized, organized in tables, and coded. Then, it was reduced logically and analysed in an attempt to find answers to the research questions.

The data that emerged from these three tools were collected, categorized, labelled and synthesized manually. Then, descriptive accounts were prepared by identifying key dimensions and finally these forms of data were justified and explained. This was done systematically through the analytical hierarchy (Ritchie & Lewis, 2003). All in all, the PWA emphasized students' linguistic skills rather than linguistic knowledge and the results of the study showed that students who have better English schooling experiences benefited the most from this approach.

Table 1 Pre-post-test diagnostic results

Students	Topic development /5 Pre	Post	Internal organization /5 Pre	Post	Conveying meaning /5 Pre	post	Sentence construction /5 Pre	Post	Mechanics /5 Pre	post	Overall grade/25 Pre	Post	Overall difference
Rana	2	3	2	3	2	3	3	4	2	3	11	16	5 pts.
Sally	2	3	2	3	2	3	2	3	2	3	10	15	5 pts.
Maher	3	4	3	5	3	4	3	4	3	4	15	21	6 pts.
Adil	2	3	1	3	2	3	2	3	2	3	10	15	5 pts.
Saleem	2	4	2	4	3	4	3	4	3	4	13	20	7 pts.
Hadi	3	4	3	4	3	5	3	4	3	4	15	21	6 pts.
Rania	2	3	2	3	2	3	2	3	2	3	10	15	5 pts.

This process of using a multi-method approach and collecting multiple sources of evidence to pinpoint the same phenomena and improve the accuracy of observation achieved triangulation (Ashour, 2018). The emergent data deriving from the above-stated methods had undergone several phases of analysis to create a clear conceptual framework and to reduce a large amount of unneeded material. The raw data derived from these sources gave rise to three specific descriptive accounts and typologies that helped in answering the research questions: students' previous writing experiences, students' exposure to the writing process approach and student's attitudes towards the writing process approach.

4.1 Students' Previous Writing Experiences

Academic writing was not something new for students participating in the study. Based on the interviews, it was clear that the 7 students were used to writing academic tasks at school in Arabic, French or English. According to the data collected in this study, 5 out of 7 students dislike writing the most. The findings showed that students used to write in previous language classes though not frequently except for two students (Maher and Rami) who have been writing weekly compositions since grade 8. The others used to write on a monthly basis or when they had language tests. However, none of the students was familiar with all the stages of the PWA. Students were taught that they should plan and then write. Also, planning was not a requirement. Their teachers wanted the essay itself, not the process that yielded the product. Six students used the first two stages of the writing process at school: prewriting and drafting. According to Rana, language teachers taught them how to write an outline in middle school. As for Sally who got her formal school education in a school that follows the French system said:

> In grade 5 in French classes, they taught us there is an introduction and body with several main ideas and examples but in English classes, they did not explain that. In English, the teacher used to give us one essay and she used to say memorize it for the test.

Maher assured that at school, language teachers had taught them to brainstorm, make an outline, cluster and free write to gather ideas before writing. Adil was taught the basics which to him is listing ideas then writing the essay. Saleem agreed with his friends about being taught to generate ideas and then writing them in a well-developed essay but he had difficulty in applying this to papers. Hadi agreed with Sally that Arabic language teachers had taught them the first two stages in writing but not the English teachers. He stated that "We didn't learn it appropriately, we used to write in tests without being taught how or even practice for the test and the grades were always low".

One point that drew my attention is that Sally and Rania admitted that the teachers had used to give them the essay ready to memorize for tests. However, Rania had the chance to write and get her paper checked but the teacher wanted them to memorize her own sample for the final assessment. Therefore, the element of organizational pattern drill is followed in ESL/EFL classes in some schools in Lebanon. To summarize, I can say that all the students in my study were familiar with at least two stages of the writing process but the writing was not an ongoing exercise and when they used to write they wrote their essays in one single session and the product was the focus.

4.2 Students' Usage of the Process Writing Approach

During the period of the study, students were interested in applying what they have learned in the mini-lessons at the beginning of the sessions and this was shown in the field notes and later in the interviews. The stages of the PWA were taught explicitly and the students showed understanding and willingness to apply them. The prewriting stage was an easy stage for four of the seven students as the field notes showed. The students were excited about generating ideas and I witnessed during the prewriting sessions that most of the students preferred outlining to other techniques except for two students. The first used clustering and the second resorted to listing in the first writing exercise. In the second exercise, almost all of the students used outlining as their chosen prewriting strategy. It seems that students' attitudes towards outlining is affected by their previous learning backgrounds as was stated by Ashwell (2000) and this was confirmed in the interviews. Most of the students wrote informal outlines and I made it clear that it is not necessary to follow a parallel and concise structure at this level as Zamel (1982) stipulates. When students were outlining, they jotted down their ideas randomly, exchanged them, translated words from Arabic and borrowed some phrases from the book. The prewriting stage ran smoothly without strain and students did not find it difficult. It fostered classroom interaction and engaged the students. Adding to this, the fact that they were familiar with this stage since many of them had previous ideas about planning from school in L1 if not in L2. Moreover, writing in L1 is considered easier than writing in the L2 as mentioned by Sally who said, "Of course in Arabic, it is easy to write but it's difficult in English". I realized through observation that the students were exerting effort while writing especially the French-educated ones. They needed help and continuous guidance because they were still in the process of learning new conventions and their limited knowledge of vocabulary, language structure and content impeded their performance in writing. They expressed this feeling in the interviews as well. For instance, Sally said, "I dislike writing the most because I can't write a sentence properly. I know words but I don't know how to create sentences and sometimes I do not know the meaning of some words".

The second stage was a comparatively difficult task especially for the French-educated students who faced difficulties in writing comprehensive sentences. The actual act of going back to the prewriting technique used by each student and coming up with meaningful sentences was not that easy. This was referred to in the literature by many scholars (e.g. Bereiter & Scardamalia, 1987; Esseili, 2012) when they considered writing as a two-way communication at the heart of constantly developing knowledge and text and it is especially difficult for L2 and L3 writers. In the study, only Maher considered drafting easy probably because his language command is better than his colleagues. He explained that "The first draft is the easiest task because I know that the teacher will check my draft and I learn from doing my mistakes and then correcting them and get better grades".

The third stage was the revising stage which involved three strategies: peer review, teacher conference and review for content, for sentences and for editing. These strategies provided feedback for students to review their papers. According to 5 students, peer review was helpful and fruitful. It encouraged them to read with their friends as writers in mind (Raimes, 1991). In this stage, students tried to review for "higher-order concerns such as the development of ideas, organization, and the overall focus of what their friends are writing about" (Keh, 1990, p. 296). Moreover, peer review enhanced their communicative skills and engagement in the writing exercise. For instance, Saleem declared that:

> The peer review was very engaging because the information is already there, I just have to correct the mistakes whereas writing the first draft was harder because I had to exert a lot of effort to come up with ideas.

Moreover, in this strategy, students used higher-order thinking skills like critical thinking in sociable situations (Florio-Ruane & Lensmire, 1989) and got the chance to negotiate mistakes like the development of ideas and organization with their peers in clear comments and constructive criticism. Saleem said that "he learned more about writing through critically reading others' papers". However, not all the students welcomed this strategy. I had a few students who were unwilling to provide negative comments probably to save face and maintain harmony with their friends as Carson and Nelson (2000) and Li (2007) suggest.

As for student–teacher conferences, they were beneficial because students usually learn from their mistakes and the mistakes, in this case, were pointed out by the instructor, explained for all the students and corrected on the spot as was stated in the notes. In this sense, two students, Maher and Rania, considered student–teacher conferences very beneficial because they gave them the chance to negotiate their mistakes with a knowledgeable mentor who can draw their attention to different types of mistakes in terms of meaning, structure and grammar. Rania said:

> Teacher conferences were very helpful to me because I learn my mistakes from the teacher face to face and I discuss my concerns with her directly because she is the most experienced and knowledgeable person in this area in our course.

This emphasizes the positive role that explicit teachers' feedback plays in improving the quality of the students' writings (Ferris & Roberts, 2001). In addition to that, it is evident that there are cultural bounds in the Middle East that consider teachers a good source of knowledge in the classroom and their feedback is always taken for granted (Hamandi, 2015).

The last stage was the editing stage where surface errors and corrections were delayed for this stage. To Sally, this stage was the easiest. She said:

> The easiest thing to do in the writing sessions was the last draft and the hardest thing was writing the first draft when we had to transfer the generated ideas in the outline to complete meaningful and grammatically correct sentences and paragraphs.

During this last stage, students refined their ideas and got their papers ready to be evaluated and published. When students were asked about the stage, they preferred the most, the responses were varied. 3 out of 7 preferred the prewriting stage and this was clear in the observations. The students were relaxed and actively engaged in prewriting by sharing their voices and beliefs.

4.3 Students' Attitudes Towards the Process Writing Approach

According to the results derived from the interviews, 5 out of 7 students disliked SLW and considered it hard. However, after learning about the process approach several students changed their attitude towards writing. Sally used to panic while writing. After the intervention, she said: "I gained much from the process approach and writing became easier especially now because I am learning new vocabulary words at college which will help me write better papers". Similarly, Adil expressed his dislike towards writing because he lacks ideas. He said that "after learning about the process approach and with sufficient time for brainstorming and generating ideas, writing became much easier than expected". The main problem for this student was his weak command of the English language because he had not taken the English classes seriously at school as he admitted. Moreover, his previous teacher's traditional way of teaching writing was not helping him. That is why he said, "I was good but then I stopped being good, I got bored". The PWA empowered this student and helped him regain confidence in writing. It was effective because it improved his weaknesses without humiliating him. He said:

> Yes, the PWA changed my attitude toward writing and encouraged me to write my outlined ideas easily because I want to pass. I have a goal that I want to reach and without writing, I will not succeed at university in all the other subjects that need writing in English and achieve my goal.

Similarly, Saleem used to avoid writing at university. He explained that he disliked writing because he had not practiced writing much at school. He did not learn it in an appropriate way and his grades were always low. Now after the PWA his grades have improved. He got 21 out of 25 in the post-test and he has improved a lot in all the areas assessed as he said. He said, "I wish I had the chance to learn it before. It would have been beneficial, and I wouldn't have suffered now at university in the English courses". Also, Hadi disliked writing because he had not learned it in an appropriate way as he mentioned. He asserted that the teachers at school used to ask them to write without teaching them how and what to write. To him, the PWA simplifies writing for those who find it difficult. Rania agreed with her colleagues that before the process approach, she did not know how to start writing and what to talk about and how to organize her thoughts. Now she feels at ease because the outline helps her transfer her ideas easily into a well-developed essay. This study has increased the students' awareness of the PWA as was stated by them. Among all the participants, only one student (Maher) used to like SLW before the intervention. He stated that at school he used several prewriting strategies and it was obvious that his command of the English language is better than his colleagues because of better previous schooling experiences. The PWA enhanced his grades further and he improved a lot in terms of idea development. In the interview, he stressed on the importance of teaching this process at school because it empowers students and prepares them to write well at college and he made it clear that if he had the chance to learn it earlier, his writing would definitely have been better and he would have gotten better grades.

Therefore, based on the three sources used in this study, it seems that the PWA was beneficial in this context and has managed to change students' negative attitudes and perceptions towards writing. The tests' results and the notes showed improvement and the students themselves admitted this in the interviews. However, when students were asked about applying this process in timed writings at college, they all agreed that it is somehow a long process and requires time. There are several strategies in each stage that will definitely help students write effectively but the majority of the participants prefer to shorten the techniques and the stages used and review individually or with the teacher. To them, the PWA is very organized and systematic but time-consuming. They pointed out that at university students do not have much time to follow this process but at school, it would work perfectly well.

5 Implications for the Context and Conclusion

Teaching writing is complex. It demands wise observers and active teachers intervening in the whole writing process. To date, very few studies have been conducted in Lebanon on using the PWA to enhance students' attitudes towards writing at the university level. The findings of this study have emphasized the importance of teaching writing more like a workshop where students are taught several effective strategies in each of the four stages in the process approach to write with some control over what to write and how to write it. Curriculum designers and linguists in Lebanon introduced this approach to writing instruction at educational institutions and two writing conferences are held in Lebanon annually to familiarize teachers with the latest approaches in the EFL context but unfortunately not all teachers are embracing these student-centred approaches starting with the primary years. This study proved that learning how to write is a process that requires practice from the early stages and if students are motivated, they can master this skill easily and get good grades.

In conclusion, this study intended to investigate the effectiveness of an intervention based on the PWA and its effects on students' attitudes towards writing and developing their written communication skills in terms of topic development, internal organization, meaning, sentence construction and grammar. It also focused on how the PWA has boosted the students' grades and raised their moralities and confidence in academic writing. As a researcher, I was intervening in the case as an active actor in the issues being researched. I introduced the intervention, implemented it, collected data and organized it in a database for inspection, synthesis and analysis. The findings derived were fruitful and promising. The tests compared showed improvement in all the areas for all the participants, the interviews showed improved attitudes towards writing and the notes showed that the students have learned better organizational skills, have become more engaged in the writing sessions and have overcome the fear of getting bad grades in their writing assessments. Therefore, the findings of the study have proved the effectiveness of this intervention in a remedial English course at the tertiary level in Lebanon.

To ensure credibility, the results were discussed and interpreted by the participants before reporting them. Also, my thoughts and analysed data were all discussed, and peer checked by the course coordinator who was a neutral observer. In addition to credibility, I tried to achieve reliability by systematically designing the case, and by having a comprehensive research plan. I recorded all the evidence in a comprehensive way and

I fully documented all the analyses. The internal validity of each piece of evidence was assessed by comparing it with other evidence. Evidence was collected by using different research methods to sustain method triangulation and researcher triangulation was also fulfilled by audit trial. As for external validity, I conducted this case study with knowledge of the existing theories and my findings were relatively close to previous studies conducted in the Arab world (Hamandi, 2015; Al Kamli, 2019; Mourssi, 2013; Trabelsi, 2015).

Lincoln and Guba (1985) state there is no generalization in case studies, instead, they talk about the transferability of the findings from one context to another and fittingness in different contexts. In this case study, I applied the PWA in one English course at a pre-university level in Lebanon and based on the results, I can say that this student-centred approach was effective in this context in several ways. First, it helped the students overcome the obstacles to starting the writing task. Also, it increased their awareness of the PWA which is based on the process of improving the content and the ideas of the composition rather than the end product. Moreover, it improved their attitude towards making mistakes and empowered them by reviewing their friends' papers. Most important of all, it enhanced communication, increased interaction between students who were held responsible for providing constructive feedback to their peers and raised their moralities and self-confidence in producing good pieces of writing with good grades. Writing became more interesting and less pressurizing for the students participating in this study who used to avoid writing at school because of its negative effects on their overall grades.

Appendix 1: Test topics

Diagnostic test topics and Post-test topics
Option 1: Write a paragraph of 150 words on celebrating special occasions.
Option 2: Write a paragraph of 150 words on sleep habits.
Option 3: Write a paragraph of 150 words on exercise.

Appendix 2: Analytical rating scale

See Table 2.

Table 2 Analytical rating scale

Level	Topic development
5	Knowledgeable; supported, is well organized and logical. Clearly a superior paper
4	Knowledgeable; adequate details and elaboration provided; ideas are relevant to the topic and stated clearly
3	Adequate knowledge of subject; limited elaboration, limited range of thoughts and considerable lack of details;
2	Most phrases are difficult to understand; often times incoherent
1	Not enough text to permit evaluation
Level	**Internal Organization**
5	Minor problems with the sequencing of thoughts, details and topic development
4	Some problem evident with the sequencing of thoughts, details and topic development
3	Major problems with the sequencing of thoughts, details and topic development
2	Most phrases are difficult to understand; often times incoherent
1	Not enough text to permit evaluation
Level	**Conveying Meaning**
5	Excellent range of vocabulary; conveys meaning accurately; good use of descriptive language
4	Some use of descriptive language; conveys meaning adequately; words are broad, precise and literate
3	Limited and simple word choice; lacks descriptive language usage
2	Most phrases are difficult to understand; often times incoherent
1	Not enough text to permit evaluation
Level	**Sentence Construction**
5	Creates complex constructions; few errors with parts of speech; little or no evidence of fragmented or run-on sentences; native-like control of grammar
4	Has minor problems with complex constructions; some errors in agreement, tense number, word/order, function, pronouns, articles or prepositions; produces some fragments or run-on sentences
3	Has major problems with complex constructions; produces simple constructions; major problems with fragmented or run-on sentences
2	Most phrases are difficult to understand; often times incoherent
1	Not enough text to permit evaluation
Level	**Mechanics**
5	Mastery of conventions; very few errors in spelling, capitalization, punctuation and paragraphing
4	Some errors in spelling, punctuation, capitalization and paragraphing
3	Numerous errors in spelling, punctuation, capitalization and paragraphing
2	Most phrases are difficult to understand; often times incoherent
1	Not enough text to permit evaluation

Appendix 3: Interview questions

1. What is your first language?

   ما هي لغتك الأم؟
   _____

2. Do you use another language in communication at home or with friends?

   هل تستخدم لغة أخرى للتواصل في المنزل أو مع الأصدقاء؟
   _____

3. What medium of instruction is used at your school?

   وما هي اللغه المستخدمة في مدرستك؟
   _____

4. Did you study English before? If yes to which level?

   هل درست اللغة الإنجليزية من قبل؟ إذا كانت الإجابة بنعم الى أي مستوى؟
   _____

5. Which English language skill do you like most and why?

ما هي مهارة اللغة الإنجليزية التي تحبها أكثر ولماذا؟

_____

6. Which English language skill do you dislike and why?

ما هي مهارة اللغة الإنجليزية التي لا تعجبكم ولماذا؟

_____

7. Do you have a previous experience with any type of writing? How do you find it?

هل لديك خبرة سابقة في الكتابة؟ كيف تجد الكتابة؟

_____

8. Have you ever written an academic essay? If yes, how often did you do that?

هل سبق لك أن كتبت مقالا أكاديميا؟ إذا كانت الإجابة بنعم، كم مرة فعلت ذلك؟

_____

9. Did the writing or the language teachers teach you how to write?

هل علمك معلمو الكتابة أو اللغة كيفية الكتابة؟

_____

10. Did you follow a technique while writing?

هل اتبعت تقنية أثناء الكتابة؟

_____

11. What was the easiest thing to do in the writing sessions we had & what was the hardest part?

ما هو أسهل شيء يمكن القيام به في جلسات الكتابة التي قمنا بها وما هو أصعب جزء؟

12. How do you find the writing process approach?

كيف تجد نهج عملية الكتابة؟

13. Have you used any of its strategies or similar strategies before?

هل استخدمت أي من استراتيجياتها أو استراتيجيات مماثلة من قبل؟

14. Which strategy have you found more helpful to adapt to your writing?

ما هي الاستراتيجية التي وجدتها أكثر فائدة في كتاباتك؟

15. Was it difficult to follow any of the techniques and strategies in the process? Why?

هل كان من الصعب اتباع أي من التقنيات والاستراتيجيات في هذه العملية؟ و لماذا؟

16. Do you find the writing process approach an influential way that helps you write well?

هل تجد عملية الكتابة نهجا مؤثرا يساعدك على الكتابة ؟ لماذا؟

17. To what extent this process is practical in EFL classes?

إلى أي مدى تكون هذه العملية عملية في فصول اللغة الإنجليزية كلغة أجنبية؟

18. Will you follow it in your future writing exams? Why or why not?

هل ستتبع هذه العملية في امتحانات الكتابة الخاصة بك في المستقبل؟ لما و لما لا؟

19. Does using the writing process approach change your attitude towards writing?

هل استخدام نهج عملية الكتابة غير من موقفك تجاه الكتابة؟

20. Do you recommend using it in EFL classes? Why or why not?

هل توصي باستخدامها في فصول اللغة الإنجليزية كلغة أجنبية؟ لما و لما لا؟

References

Al Kamli, H. M. (2019). The effect of using mind maps to enhance EFL learners' writing achievement and students' attitudes towards writing at Taif university. *Arab World English Journal*: *Thesis Collection*, ID Number, 232, 1–92.

Al-Sawalha, A., & Chow, T. (2012). The effects of proficiency on the writing process of Jordanian university students. *Academic Research International*, 3(2), 379–388.

Ashour, M. (2018). Triangulation as a powerful methodological research technique in technology-based services. *Business and Management Studies: An International Journal*, 6(1), 193–208.

Ashwell, T. (2000). Patterns of teacher response to student writing in a multiple draft composition classroom: Is content feedback followed by form feedback the best method? *Journal of Second Language Writing*, 9(3), 227–257.

Atkinson, D. (2003). L2 writing in the post-process era. *Introduction*. *Journal of Second Language Writing*, 12, 3–15.

Badger, R., & White, G. (2000). A process genre approach to teaching writing. *ELT Journal*, 54(2), 153–160. https://doi.org/10.1093/elt/54.2.153.

Bayat, N. (2014). The effect of the process writing approach on writing success and anxiety. *Educational Sciences Theory and Practice, 14*(3), 1133–1141.

Bereiter, C., & Scardamalia, M. (1987). *The psychology of written composition.* Hillsdale, NJ: Lawrence Erlbaum Associates.

Carson, J. G., & Nelson, G. L. (2000). Chinese students' perception of ESL peer response group interaction. *Journal of Second Language Writing, 5*(1), 1–19.

Cohen, L., & Manion, L. (1989). *Research methods in education* (3rd ed.). Routledge: London.

Eksi, G. (2012). Peer review versus teacher feedback in process writing: How effective? *International Journal of Applied Educational Studies, 13,* 33–48.

Emig, J. (1971). *Composing processes of twelfth graders.* Urbana, Illinois 61801: National council of Teachers of English.

Esseili, F. (2012). *Faculty and EFL student perceptions of L2 writing at the University of Balamand* (1st ed.). Unpublished survey results. Beirut, Lebanon.

Esseili, F. (2014). English language teaching in Lebanon: Trends and challenges. In K. M. Bailey & R. M. Damerow (Eds.), *The teaching and learning of English in the Arabic speaking world* (pp. 101–114). New York: Routledge.

Esseili, F. (2016). The status of EFL/ESL writing in Lebanon. In T. Silva (Ed.), *L2 writing in the global context: Represented, underrepresented, and unrepresented voices.* Beijing, China: The Foreign Language Teaching and Research Press.

Ezza, E. (2010). Arab EFL learners' writing dilemma at tertiary level. *English Language Teaching, 3*(4), 33–39.

Ferris, D. R., & Roberts, B. (2001). Error feedback in L2 writing classes. How explicit does it need to be? *Journal of Second Language Writing, 10*(3), 161–184.

Florio-Ruane, S., & Lensmire, T. (1989). The role of instruction in learning to write. In J. Brophy (Ed.), *Advances in research on teaching* (1st ed., pp. 73–100). Greenwich, CT: JAI.

Flower, L. S., & Hayes, J. R. (1981). The pregnant pause: An inquiry into the nature of planning. *Research in the Teaching of English, 15,* 229–243.

Gomez, R., Richard, P., Rafael, A. L., & Gomez, L. (1996). Process versus product writing with limited English proficient students. *The Bilingual Research Journal, 20*(2), 209–233.

Graham, S. (2006). Strategy instruction and the teaching of writing. A meta-analysis? In C. A. MacArthur, S. Graham, & J. Fitzgerald (Eds.), *Handbook of writing research* (pp. 187–207). New York: Routledge.

Hamadouche, M. (2010). *Developing the writing skill through increasing learners' awareness of the writing process*. M.A. Thesis, University of Constantine.

Hamandi, D. H. (2015). *The relative effect of trained peer response: Traditional versus electronic modes on college EFL Lebanese students' writing performance, revision types, perceptions towards peer response, and attitudes towards writing.* M.A. Thesis. American University of Beirut. Retrieved from https://scholarworks.aub.edu.lb. Last accessed: 10.5.2020.

Harmer, J. (2004). *How to teach writing*. London: Longman.

Hashemnezhad, H. (2012). A comparative study of product, process, and post-process approaches in Iranian EFL students' writing skill. *Journal of Language Teaching and Research, 3*(4), 722–729.

Hayes, J. R. (1996). A new framework for understanding cognition and affect in writing. In C. M. Levy & Ransdell (Eds.), *The science of writing: Theories, methods, individual differences, and applications* (pp. 1–27). Mahwah, NJ: Law-rence Erlbaum.

Horowitz, D. M. (1986). Process, not product: Less than meets the eye. *TESOL Quarterly, 20*(1), 141–144.

Hyland, K. (2003). *Second language writing*. Cambridge: Cambridge University Press.

Johnson, A. P. (2008). *Teaching reading and writing: A guidebook for tutoring and remediating students*. New York: Roman and Littlefield Education.

Keh, L. C. (1990). Feedback in the writing process: A model and methods for implementation. *English Language Teaching Journal, 44*(4), 294–303.

Lappo, R. M. (1985). *The process approach to writing: Towards a curriculum for international students*. Unpublished Ph.D. thesis, University of Hawaii Manoa.

Li, X. (2007). Identities and beliefs in ESL writing: From product to processes. *TESL Canada Journal, 25*(1), 41–64.

Lincoln, E., & Guba, G. (1985). *Naturalistic inquiry*. Newbury Park. London: Sage.

Mourssi, A. (2013). Theoretical and practical linguistic shifting from product/guided writing to process writing and recently to the innovated writing process approach in teaching writing for second/foreign language learners. *International Journal of Academic Research in Business and Social Sciences, 3*(5), 732–749.

Raimes, A. (1991). Out of the woods: Traditions in the teaching of writing. *TESOL Quarterly, 25*, 407–430.

Reid, J. M. (2001). Writing. In R. Cater & D. Nunan (Eds.), *The Cambridge guide to teaching English to speakers of other languages* (pp. 23–33). Cambridge: Cambridge University Press.

Ritchie, J. & Lewis, J. (2003). *Qualitative research practice. A guide for social science students and researchers.* London, Thousand Oaks, New Delhi: Sage.

Sheir, A., Zahran, F., & Koura, A. (2015). The effectiveness of process writing approach in developing EFL writing performance of ESP college students. *Educational Sciences Journal, 23*(3), 1–23.

Simpson, A. (2013). *A process approach to writing.* Retrieved from http://www.developingteachers.com. Last accessed: 7.10.2019.

Trabelsi, S. (2015). An evaluation of Sohar university GFP students' performance in writing: A pedagogical perspective. In R. Al-Mahrooqi, V. Thakur, & A. Roscoe (Eds.), *Methodologies for effective writing instruction in EFL and ESL classrooms* (pp. 353–378). United States of America: IGI Global.

Zamel, V. (1982). Writing: The process of discovering meaning. *TESOL Quarterly, 16*(2), 195–209.

Integrating Computer- and Teacher-Provided Feedback in an EFL Academic Writing Context

Mojtaba Heydari and Fahimeh Marefat

1 Introduction

Large-scale conventions of writing assessment have traditionally preferred the utilization of timed impromptu writing tests (Weigle, 2002) in which examinees are asked to complete a writing task in a limited time. Its practicality (in terms of time, cost, and efficiency of administration and scoring) has encouraged most official high-stakes language tests and many universities to include timed essay writing tasks as a part of their assessment package (Ferris, 2009). However, this type of assessment has been criticized mostly from a process-oriented pedagogical point of view. From this perspective, time limitation makes it difficult for examinees to accomplish pre-writing and revising steps and urges them to focus more on the product, rather than the process, of writing.

An alternative to the traditional types of writing assessment would be formative assessment which requires providing ongoing support to students who are learning to write. However, overpopulated classes

M. Heydari (✉) · F. Marefat
Allameh Tabataba'i University, Tehran, Iran

and overloaded teachers cannot afford the time and resources required to implement formative assessment in their curriculum (Brady, 2012). Nevertheless, advances in the teaching tools specially designed for improving the writing skill has led to the development of digital writing tools which can automatically provide students with instant feedback on their performances. Examples of these tools include: *ETS Criterion*, *MY Access!*, *Cambridge Write & Improve*, and *Grammarly* which are now publicly available (but mostly not for free) in Iran and worldwide. Such automated writing tools can identify the problems and strengths of the writings and instantly provide feedback to help the writer resolve the problem, learn from their mistakes, and ultimately develop their English writing proficiency. They can take the burden off the teachers' shoulders and save a lot of time by not getting them involved in cumbersome proof-reading and error-correction feedback provision practices. That is, teachers can focus on more global concerns while the computer is taking care of word and sentence-level issues.

2 Literature Review

2.1 English Writing in the Context of Iran

Starting around more than a decade ago, as the booming population of Iranian millennials entered the universities, a very competitive environment in the Iranian higher education system began to take shape. Iranian families encouraged their children to pursue their education in university graduate degrees in hopes of having a higher economic and social status. The parents who had experienced the volatile conditions after the revolution and war in the 1970s and 1980s were ready to make any sacrifice to give their children a better future. They had witnessed a lack of educated workforce during the so-called "construction era" and were convinced that provided that their children receive higher graduate and post-graduate degrees in the fields of engineering and medicine, a secure financial future would be granted to them (Borjian, 2013). With this pervasive mentality, the children were predisposed to make any efforts they could to excel in their studies. The majority of teenagers inherited their parents' mindset at the onset of their adolescence and started to study hard so that they could succeed and excel in their exams. Limited academic resources were not able to accommodate the huge number of students who were now trying to get into universities. While there is no well-established account of the number of university students, according to unofficial government statistics, out of 1.5–1.8 million university student candidates in the first decade of the twenty-first century, only 200–300 thousand of them would be accepted in universities. Soon thereafter, gaining a bachelor's degree seemed insufficient for many job-seekers to find a career that could get them the future their parents and themselves had imagined. The competition was becoming stiffer and the students had no choice but to pursue their education at the graduate and post-graduate levels.

The policymakers underscore international publications as an index of the academic productivity of graduate students, professors, and universities. This makes the English writing skill a necessity for those who are looking for better educational and professional opportunities such as seeking admissions at higher levels, applying for scholarships, occupying academic teaching positions, or even receiving monetary rewards (Mansouri Nejad, Qaracholloo, & Rezaei, 2020). However, since universities do not generally offer courses in academic English writing to help the students with their publications, the students are left to themselves to self-study or seek assistance from private language schools to improve their writing skills (Borjian, 2013).

In addition, due to the lack of a positive career outlook and the volatile economic and political situation of the country, many graduate students are now seeing emigration as their first choice. In such a context, taking part in standardized English exams like IELTS and TOEFL (which are required by a majority of international universities to grant admission to non-English speaking applicants) is trending. In addition to the international tests, some higher education organizations in Iran have developed and promoted their own English proficiency tests. Considering the importance of these tests in the future life and career of the students and the relatively expensive costs of international tests such as TOEFL and IELTS in Iran, success in these tests has become very important for many test-takers.

As such, test-takers have started to look for shortcuts and overnight hacks to improve their scores. Teachers in the private sector have also started devising coaching strategies and making the students more test-wise in order to achieve higher scores. Despite the candidates' need to improve their general English proficiency, a majority of English classes are now focusing solely on the approaches to give the students a boost in their scores without improving their English skills (Marefat & Heydari, 2018).

As for the public education system, after almost 40 years of its introduction, Iran still has a centralized curriculum and assigns the same textbooks, teaching methods, and testing procedures to all parts of the country (Borjian, 2013; Riazi, 2005). Also, the official English syllabi in Iran are mainly rooted in the grammar-translation method and consists of activities like reading passages, sentence translation, vocabulary memorization, and lots of grammar drills. In such a context, students do not have the opportunity to practice English writing for real-world needs and they end up practicing for exam purposes.

2.2 Theoretical Framework

A corrective feedback study can perfectly fit within the socio-cultural theory of learning. According to Vygotsky (1978), human cognitive development can occur in a mediated social interaction where an expert (e.g., a teacher) provides appropriate assistance to a novice (e.g., student). From this perspective, the assistance and scaffolding (written corrective feedback in our case) needs to take into consideration both the learners' current and potential levels. Indeed, the extent of teacher scaffolding is gradually minimized so that the learner can act more autonomously. As Boggs (2019) rightly puts, "In practice, the less autonomous end of the scaffolding continuum might be teachers scaffolding understanding through instruction, while the opposite end is learners independently using resources to support their own learning" (p. 2). Given that the current and potential levels of performance are assessed properly; the learner can take the most advantage of the feedback offered. Consequently, the resource or mediating tool that best fits the learner is adopted. Mediating tools, as a key construct in socio-cultural theory, refer to any means or tools used to facilitate and shape actions, including the regulation of the thinking processes (Storch, 2018). For example, using digital written corrective feedback can be considered as a tool to help the writers develop their cognitive processes and improve their writing skills.

While there are still controversies on the effectiveness of feedback on improving students' writing skills (e.g., Ferris, 2006; Truscott, 2004), an ample body of research has shown its usefulness (Bitchener & Ferris, 2012; Ene & Upton, 2018). In a similar vein, a distinction is made between formative and summative evaluation. Formative evaluation provides writers with individualized feedback on their texts to help them learn writing (Philips, 2007). Contrary to summative assessment which draws students' attention to their final performance only, formative assessment gives them the chance to focus on their strengths and weaknesses so that they can improve their writing skills. That is, it is an assessment for learning rather than an assessment of learning (Taylor, 2005). Still, another distinction is often made between direct (e.g., crossing out a word, inserting a word, and writing the correct word) and indirect (e.g., highlighting an erroneous sentence without correcting it) feedback (Ferris, 2002, 2006; Truscott, 1996, 1999, 2004). Even more, some studies have focused on the implicit vs. explicit feedback distinction which is based on how overtly the feedback indicates that a part of the writing is not acceptable or needs improvement (e.g., Ellis, 2009). While it has been shown that written corrective feedback improves the fluency and accuracy of the writers, findings are mixed regarding which type of feedback can be more beneficial (Ellis, 2009). Despite the inconclusive results, one of the most viable conclusions states that direct and indirect feedback are complementary and both can be effective (Ferris, 2010).

2.3 Digital Writing Assessment Platforms

In the mid-1990s and early 2000s, desktop computers and the Internet were beginning to find their way into many aspects of our lives, and second language learning and assessment was not an exception (Fotos

& Browne, 2004). The concept of computer-provided feedback became an innovative way to help students improve their writing. In resonance with these developments, a distinction emerged in the field of second language writing assessment: computer- vs. teacher-provided feedback (Ene & Upton, 2018). This type of feedback, often in the form of scores, was originally used for assessment purposes in high-stakes tests like TOEFL. Today, commercial versions of the assessment engines are available to help writers not only to assess but also to improve their writing. As an example, services like ETS's *Criterion* and Cambridge *Write&Improve* are now publicly available (Lavolette, Polio, & Kahng, 2015; Yannakoudakis, Andersen, Geranpayeh, Briscoe, & Nicholls, 2018).

Most assessment engines are designed based on Supervised Machine Learning which is a class of artificial intelligence. In this method, the engine is trained by analysing a huge number of essays that have already been assessed by human raters. Then, it identifies all the numerous distinguishing features of each high-quality writing. These features are then used by the algorithms to predict the level of quality for any new given text. Such services share in common the aim of helping students to become better writers and thus provide them with instant feedback and multiple drafting opportunities to improve their writings based on the feedback they receive (Stevenson & Phakiti, 2014). This approach can save time and cost thus making formative assessment possible even in the context of populated classes and overloaded teachers. As a result, the teachers will be encouraged (and enabled) to cut off on the conventional timed writing practices and begin to evaluate and improve their students' writing skills benefitting from formative assessment.

2.4 Research Problem

Previous research has studied the role of traditional written corrective feedback in improving students' writings in the context of Iran and has emphasized the need to come up with practical suggestions for the teachers (e.g., Nemati, Alavi, Mohebbi, & Panahi Masjedlou, 2017). While innovative solutions like digital writing assessment platforms seem to be very promising, there is a dearth of evidence to support their effectiveness in the context of Iran. In addition, although past research in the international context has studied the efficiency of computer-generated feedback as an alternative assessment (Stevenson & Phakiti, 2014), researchers have suggested the need to study the combination of teacher-provided and computer-generated feedback types (Elola & Oskoz, 2016, 2017; Ene & Upton, 2018; Zhang & Hyland, 2018). Besides, as pointed out by Storch (2018), there is a direct need to consider the social context of learning as well as the individual factors that can affect the provision and effectiveness of feedback.

Another aspect that should be considered is the extent to which learners' needs and characteristics can influence the effectiveness of the feedback (Nassaji, 2016). Therefore, we need to know more about how, for example, a student's learning objectives or previous English training and second language writing habits might affect their uptake of the corrective written feedback. In most corrective feedback studies, students are treated equally irrespective of their background, which might affect whether or not and to what extent they benefit from the provision of corrective feedback. However, there is still a scarcity of understanding about whether students can benefit differently from the feedback they receive depending on their individual differences. It is indeed important to see how students' attitudes towards the use of corrective feedback, combined with their personal educational goals, can contribute to improvement in their writing skills.

The current study is therefore guided by the following research questions:

RQ 1: Do Iranian university students recruited to improve their written academic English skills benefit from +Class View, an online platform, where they receive automated as well as teacher feedback?

RQ 2: To what extent do Iranian university students recruited to improve their written academic English skills engage with the automated as well as teacher feedback?

RQ 3: What are the key parameters affecting the level and type of engagement in the feedback of the Iranian university students recruited to improve their written academic English skills?

3 Methodology

Five Iranian EFL university students enrolled to improve their written academic English skills participated in the study. While two students were trained and had already taken an IELTS test, the other three had never prepared for a standardized English proficiency test of any kind. They were all university students who had finished or were working towards their master's degrees in the fields of mechanics, computer programming, architecture, and management. Their ages ranged from 25 to 29. Two of them were female and three were male with the females being the youngest.

All the students took a placement test at the beginning of the course. They were all roughly classified into B1 and B2 Common European Framework of Reference (CEFR) levels based on the results of the Cambridge English Placement Test. All the participants had a personal computer connected to the Internet. In a short screening interview before the study, three of them identified their computer literacy knowledge as "Good" and the other two as "Very Good" when asked (on a five-point Likert Scale from Very Limited to Very Good) how they would rate their computer knowledge in regard to the use of the World Wide Web and word processing applications. A few follow-up questions also confirmed their ability to use a computer for such purposes. The questions elicited, for example, if they had ever used track-change feature of a word processing software or revised a written text based on the comments they had received from a reviewer.

3.1 The Writing Assessment Platform

The students were then asked to join + Class View platform which is a part of the *Write & Improve* platform which works in association with Cambridge English. This platform provides a variety of automated feedback with the option of adding a teacher's feedback. It also provides summative and formative feedback, progress graphs, word- and, sentence-level feedback, and a prompt relevance score. These features make it an ideal platform to monitor and improve the writing skills of

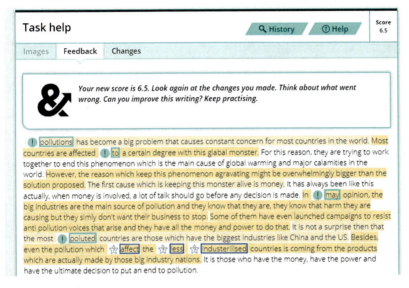

Fig. 1 Feedback provided by the Write & Improve platform

different students. Equally significant is the type of feedback the platform provides; it does not directly ask the writer to change a specific sentence element or consider a grammatical point. Rather, it is worded in a way to encourage the writer/learner to reflect on their writing and decide whether and how they want to make a change. Complementary to the computer-generated feedback, the teacher can leave comments and suggestions for the learners on the structure of the writing, the content, or even grammatical hints. Figure 1 presents a screenshot of the corrections provided by the platform.

3.2 Design

Over a course of eight weeks, the students were asked to write essays in response to prompts of general argumentative academic topics (see Fig. 2 for an example) on a weekly basis at a place of their convenience (e.g., home, library, café). After the students delivered their weekly tasks, they were instantly marked (from one to nine in .5 intervals) and received

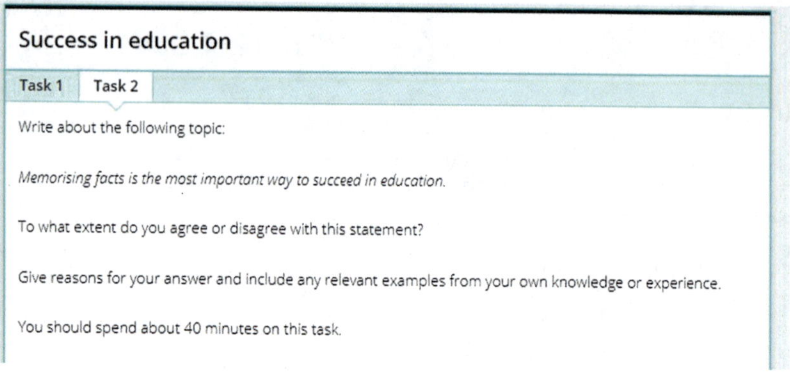

> **Success in education**
>
> Task 1 | Task 2
>
> Write about the following topic:
>
> *Memorising facts is the most important way to succeed in education.*
>
> To what extent do you agree or disagree with this statement?
>
> Give reasons for your answer and include any relevant examples from your own knowledge or experience.
>
> You should spend about 40 minutes on this task.

Fig. 2 A screenshot of one of the prompts assigned to the students

automated and teacher feedback. Sentence-level feedback was automatically generated by the platform's assessment engine. Having seen the comments made by the computer, the teacher (the first author) then read their essays and provided personalized feedback that focused on other aspects of their writings including content, organization, and tips on how to improve their writing. At this stage, the students were required to revise their drafts drawing upon the feedback and resubmit their manuscripts within 24 hours to be marked as a new submission.

Teacher and computer feedback along with students' uptake were stored by the automatic track-change feature of the platform. The data were then manually coded in terms of feedback type and uptake. We looked for the type of corrections made in the revision to identify whether the change was based on the automatic feedback, teacher feedback, or neither (student-initiated revision). For the purpose of coding, we followed Ene and Upton (2018)'s student uptake coding procedure which differentiated between successful, unsuccessful, unattended, and unverifiable uptake. This coding allowed us to quantify the types of student uptake in order to compare the efficiency of computer- vs teacher-provided feedback. However, we decided to eliminate the "unverifiable uptake" category because the interviews made it possible for us to make appropriate decisions for every example of the uptake. Table 1 shows some examples from our data for each category used in our coding.

Table 1 Examples for the categories of uptake used in the coding

Successful Uptake
- **Original sentence:** "... they are learning from their parents and the people who around them ... "
- **Feedback:** "Did you forget the verb after the word 'who'?"
- **Revised sentence:** The writer identifies the problem and fixes the issue: "... they are learning from their parents and the people who are around them..."

Unsuccessful Uptake
- **Original sentence:** "... money has drawbacks such as make youngsters more acquisitive... "
- **Feedback:** "There are some problems in this sentence".
- **Revised sentence:** The writer is not able to identify the problem and instead of changing the verb "make" to a gerund, he changes the phrase "such as" to "like" and thus fails to fix the issue: "... money has drawbacks like make youngsters more acquisitive... "

Unattended Uptake
- **Original sentence:** "... giving money as a gift helps teenagers make their economic sights more complete".
- **Feedback:** "The meaning is unclear. What do you mean by 'economic sights'?"
- **Revised sentence:** The writer does not revise the sentence by keeping the original sentence unchanged

What is unique to this study is combining the more traditional type of written feedback given by the teachers with the benefits of using sophisticated computer-based feedback and assessment. In the current project, we implemented numeric feedback (in the form of IELTS band scores from 1 to 9) on the students' performance as well as qualitative written feedback. The numeric feedback was generated immediately by the assessment engine of the platform accompanied by the qualitative written feedback provided both by the teacher and the engine.

Within three days after finishing the writing tasks, the five students were individually interviewed on their perceptions of the usefulness of the feedback and how they interacted with the feedback to improve their writing. The interview was semi-structured and included seven core questions and a few follow-up questions. The participants were questioned about their background education in English writing and the methods they used to develop their writing skills. They were also asked about their preference over the type of feedback they received, the type of feedback they found to be more beneficial to improve their writings, and the reason(s) why they responded or skipped certain comments.

4 Results and Discussion

Table 2 shows that a total of 784 comments were offered by the computer and the teacher on the 40 essays written and submitted by the five students during the eight weeks.

Overall, the automated comments outnumber those made by the teacher to 1.62 times. With regard to the overall quality, comments are equally distributed by 50% ($n = 40$). Surprisingly, no automated feedback is provided on organization and content, while those provided by the teacher are 100% ($n = 57$) and 100% ($n = 49$), respectively. The explanation could be that the engine is programmed to merely comment on word- and sentence-level. When it comes to sentence structure and word choice, and spelling and punctuation, the computer-generated feedback increases to 76.32% ($n = 145$), 63.18% ($n = 139$), and 85.64% ($n = 161$). Comparatively, the comments provided by the teacher fall short of the automated counterpart with respect to these rubrics to almost 23.68% ($n = 45$) one third, one half 36.82% ($n = 81$), and one sixth 14.36% ($n = 27$).

We summarized the data for each student to discover which student more successfully engaged with the comments and the feedback they received, the concern of the second research question. As depicted in Table 3, the highest number of attempts to address the feedback belongs to Student 2, by addressing 97% of the feedback and leaving only 3% unattended. This student also has the highest rate of successful feedback implementation, namely, 82%. Student 1 has the most unnoticed proportion of feedback 24%. However, the student with the lowest rate of successful attempts is Student 3 who attempted to address 94% of the feedback but was only successful in improving 49% of the feedback received. It is worth mentioning here that from among all the 784 comments, 284 comments were basically not addressing any problem and were, therefore, eliminated from our analysis here. Examples of such

Table 2 Frequency and percentage of comments and corrections made by the computer and teacher

	Sentence structure	Word choice	Organization	Spelling and punctuation	Content	Overall quality	Total # of feedback
Computer	145 (76.32%)	139 (63.18%)	0 (0%)	161 (85.64%)	0 (0%)	40 (50%)	485 (61.86%)
Teacher	45 (23.68%)	81 (36.82%)	57 (100%)	27 (14.36%)	49 (100%)	40 (50%)	299 (38.14%)
Total	190 (100%)	220 (100%)	57 (100%)	188 (100%)	49 (100%)	80 (100%)	784 (100%)

Table 3 Frequency and percentage of successful, unsuccessful, and unattended feedback

	Successful implementation	Unsuccessful implementation	Unattended	Total
Student 1	51 (57%)	17 (19%)	21 (24%)	89 (100%)
Student 2	80 (82%)	14 (15%)	3 (3%)	97 (100%)
Student 3	55 (49%)	51 (45%)	7 (6%)	113 (100%)
Student 4	56 (60%)	22 (24%)	15 (16%)	93 (100%)
Student 5	84 (78%)	14 (13%)	10 (9%)	108 (100%)
Total	326 (65%)	118 (24%)	56 (11%)	500 (100%)

comments were mostly motivational notes like "Good job", "I like this idea!", "Makes sense!" written by the teachers, or the comment "This seems to be a good sentence" used frequently by the platform to mark correct sentences.

An analysis of students' summative scores during the eight weeks suggested that the students did not improve the quality of their writings equally as indicated by the summative score provided by the platform's smart engine. Figure 3 shows the range of the scores gained by each student through the 8 writing tasks as well as their score for the first and the last weeks. An interesting observation in Fig. 3 is the different levels of variation in the scores achieved by the students for the writing tasks. For example, Student 4 enjoys an overall .5 band of improvement comparing week 1 to week 8 (while showing 1.5 band-score variations in their best and worst performances). On the other hand, Students 1 and 3 experience only .5 band-score variation throughout the tasks. Except for Student 1 who did not show any progress in their scores comparing week 1 to week 8 (while performing .5 band better in one of the tasks), four other students improved their scores by at least a .5 band-score during the eight weeks with Student 2 being an exception by an improvement from band 5.5 in the first to 6.5 in the last task.

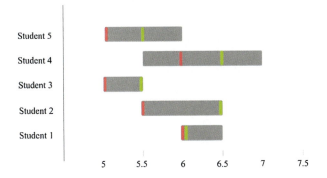

■ Range of the scores achieved by students through all the tasks
■ The score achieved by students for the first task
■ The score achieved by students for the last task

Fig. 3 The range of the scores gained by each student through the 8 writing tasks

4.1 Interviews

All the interviews were conducted in Persian and were audio recorded for further analysis. Each session took approximately 20 minutes. Students were all asked about their English learning background including the number of years studying English, types of courses, and preparation, as well as their aims and objectives for learning English. All the participants stated that they had been studying English on and off for more than 10 years, but two of them (Students 1 and 3) stated they had been preparing quite seriously for the IELTS test during the last two years. Both had been attending group and one-on-one classes to improve the four English skills for the test. Student 1 had already taken the test three times, but Student 3 had taken it only once.

When asked why they did not address certain received feedback, they mostly stated that some of the comments were so general and they were unsure as to how to revise the essay. The "general" feedback type was mostly generated by +Class View. Interestingly, the online platform was programmed to generate such feedback to encourage the learners to reflect on their writing and do their best to improve the sentence. For example, one type of sentence-level feedback provided by the computer highlights a sentence and states that the sentence may be improved instead of directly guiding to check the subject–verb agreement.

Figure 4 shows an example where one sentence is highlighted by the platform, suggesting that it could be improved in some way.

Figure 5 shows how different colors and highlighting used by the platform could be interpreted.

The authors were curious to discover whether general feedback would really push students towards more reflection on their sentence structure. Analysis of the data suggested that Student 1 experienced the lowest

> They talk about (!) succesful people's habits like sleeping, eating and excersicing to push peaople towrds success. But, who says evereyone should be a superstar? In my opinon, success in your family relationships is as important as the success in (!) ones career.
> Second, evereyone, even the bright

Fig. 4 Example sentence highlighted by Write & Improve that needs improvement

Sentence-level feedback

The colour of the sentences shows Write & Improve's opinion of the quality of each sentence. Sentences with a white background are sentences that Write & Improve considers good, whereas sentences with a solid coloured background have areas that could be improved. The crossed lighter-coloured background shows that the sentence is better but could still be improved.

> This seems to be a good sentence.
> This sentence could maybe be improved.
> There are some problems in this sentence.

Fig. 5 Feedback provided by Write & Improve to help writers understand the meaning of each color

amount of uptake regarding sentence structure. When interviewed, he stated that this type of feedback is not useful for him.

> I know my writing is not ideal and it needs improvement. I know every sentence I write can be improved. So, just telling me half of my sentences need improvement is not useful. I can't understand the problem. If I could, I would write a better sentence from scratch.

Then he continued:

> But I liked direct comments. For example, when it says "There is a missing word" I can think about it and figure out the missing word.

While this sense of uncertainty was prevalent among all the students to some extent, a few were more positive about their experience with indirect feedback. For example, Student 2 found it more of a challenge but generally helpful:

> …one-third of my sentences were highlighted as they could be improved. I was shocked to find out some of the sentences I was absolutely sure about, needed grammatical improvement. It was hard to find the problem sometimes, but I tried Googling the sentences and checking my verbs. Prepositions, etc.… that was helpful!

Students 3 and 5 showed more inclination towards the use of direct feedback as they stated it was easier for them to understand and implement. Considering their relatively lower proficiency levels, it can be pointed out that probably the level of proficiency could have influenced the way they reacted to the comments. Previous research has similarly reported that direct and explicit feedback is the most effective type of feedback particularly at lower proficiency levels (Ene & Upton, 2018).

Even with indirect feedback, it seems that the use of metalinguistic comments and explanations could be conducive to help the students identify the type of problem they are dealing with. Student 4 mentioned that the labels attached to each highlighted word or sentence helped her a great deal. The feedback provided by the computer included small icons across the problematic part of the essay giving the writers a sort of clue to spot the problem (see Fig. 6). Student 4 commented: "*I have a lot of problems with prepositions…whenever I saw the 'missing word' icon, I knew I probably had forgotten a preposition*".

We also found misalignment of the writers' perceptions with their performance as a recurring theme in the interviews. Three students claimed that they address almost every explicit and direct feedback; however, the data from our quantitative analysis showed they all had skipped a fairly considerable number of the comments. When we pointed

---

Feedback explained ✕

Word-level feedback

When Write & Improve finds a problem in your writing, a symbol next to the word that is affected is shown. There are four different types of symbols:

❗ **Incorrect word?** Is this word correct?

🔺 **Did you forget something before this word?**

🟢 **Did you forget something after this word?**

☆ **Suspicious word.** Something doesn't look right about this word.

You can find more information about the error by clicking on the symbol.

Sentence-level feedback

The colour of the sentences shows Write & Improve's opinion of the quality of each sentence. Sentences with a white background are sentences that Write & Improve considers good, whereas sentences with a solid coloured background have areas that could be improved. The crossed lighter-coloured background shows that the sentence is better but could still be improved.

This seems to be a good sentence.

This sentence could maybe be improved.

There are some problems in this sentence.

Fig. 6 Explanations for each type of icon to suggest a type of revision required

out the mismatch and presented to them some of the unattended comments, they were surprised not to have noticed them. Student 4, for example, was shocked to learn that she had not addressed 16% of the feedback she received. She commented: "It's very weird; maybe I was overwhelmed by the number of the comments or maybe I was just careless not to notice them".

Scrutinizing the rate of successful uptake from both computer and teacher feedback and the students' perceptions, it seems that the effectiveness of the feedback is more a matter of the "type" rather than the "source" of feedback. That is, as found in the interviews, the word-level feedback and explicit comments seem to be appreciated more by most students than sentence-level feedback and implicit comments regardless of whether they are provided by the teacher or the computer.

A major theme that emerged in the interviews was related to the type of students' previous English training. As mentioned earlier, two students had already taken specialized courses for the IELTS writing task. They had attended both a series of one-on-one tutoring classes and a 10-session workshop on IELTS academic writing. Students with the IELTS training background shared the view that direct feedback was much more effective than indirect feedback as in their tutoring sessions they were used to receiving an explanation of why a specific sentence needs improvement and how it could be revised and improved. For example, Student 3 said:

> The reason I registered in tutoring sessions was to have an experienced teacher correct my writings and tell me how to improve it. Before the classes, I used to write short essays to practice for IELTS, but I had no idea if I was improving and, if I was not, what kind of mistakes were keeping me behind.

Previous training seemed to affect the way the students employed external resources they had at their disposal. For example, both students with the IELTS training background mentioned that they tended not to refer to online dictionaries, wikis, grammar forums, etc. to look for their mistakes and found a way to get rid of them or improve their writing. They believed that in order to maximize the performance of the students in the writing, the test situation should be simulated in their practice writing sessions.

For example, Student 1 mentioned that as he is preparing for IELTS, he did not think if it was a good idea to rely on such sources as they will not be available during the exam.

> I've learned it from Konkour [1] preparation courses, to be successful you need to simulate the exam settings; the timing, the type of test, the way you answer, everything. Therefore, I do the same thing here. I don't spend more than 40 minutes on my writings. That's all the time I have on the exam.

When questioned on the way they addressed the feedback, they had a similar approach: relying on their existing knowledge to fix the problem or improve the highlighted parts of their written products. To them, making revisions were more like brushing up their text and improving the quality of their performance so that they could achieve a higher mark.

To the students with no prior IELTS training, however, responding to the comments using different resources seemed more rewarding. While they made some comments about the confusion they experienced with indirect feedback, they did not seemingly limit themselves to their own knowledge. Instead, they mentioned that this seemed like an opportunity to learn. Student 5, for example, states:

> ... it happened to me to look for a grammatical explanation or use of a word for half an hour. I was not sure if I could improve the text after, but I was happy because I learned many things through this search... Next time I was writing, I noticed I used a combination of words I had learned through my previous revisions.

The distinction between the two types of attitudes towards the use of feedback can be explained by the achievement goal theory, which makes a distinction between performance goals and learning goals. To Elliott

---

[1] Konkour is a nationwide entrance exam held once a year to qualify high school students for admission to universities. This is a comprehensive test comprising 200 multiple-choice questions on school subjects including Persian literature, English, Math, Physics, etc.

and Dweck (1988), learners with performance goals "seek to maintain positive judgments of their ability", while those with learning goals "seek to increase their ability or master new tasks" (p. 5). Previous research has shown that students with learning goals are more likely to look for strategies to improve their knowledge compared to those with performance goals (Waller & Papi, 2017).

This can explain why the students with no prior exam-oriented training perceived the revisions as lessons for ongoing learning rather than the students with performance goals (e.g., obtaining the highest score possible in their next IELTS test) who saw the revisions more like local tips to boost their exam marks.

In general, no student stated any strong preference over teacher or computer feedback. To them, a combination of content-level feedback provided by the teacher and word-level feedback provided by the computer seemed to be very beneficial. For example, student 4 stated that:

> I think I need both of them. A detailed correction of my mistakes and more general explanations about my arguments and organization. Some teachers have told me that parts of my writings can become unclear and difficult to understand; I want to know when and why do they happen and try to improve it.

In general, it seems that the participants were interested in getting involved in a form of feedback uptake. While this uptake seems more predominant in explicit, word-level feedback provided by the computer, when it comes to less-explicit higher-order comments, becomes very challenging for the students. Content and rhetorical features seem the most challenging for the students, and those who can deal better with this challenge are more likely to act on the feedback. Student 2 who showed a positive attitude towards the use of external resources seems to have benefitted more than Student 1 who strives on simulating the exam situation and relying on his existing knowledge to improve his writings. However, there is no clear evidence in this study regarding the effect feedback could have on the students' general, long-term writing proficiency. Previous findings on the effectiveness of automated writing feedback on the future writing performance of the students are also inconclusive (Stevenson & Phakiti, 2014).

Our participants perceived the digital feedback of both computer and teacher efficient. This is in consonance with previous studies reporting the usefulness of electronic feedback (Elola & Oskoz, 2016; Ene & Upton, 2018). It is also claimed that positive perception could predict student willingness to implement the feedback (Ducate & Arnold, 2012; Sheen, 2010). The positive attitude and the improvement in writings, as designated in our study, fits perfectly within this statement. However, we found that students had a strong preference for the feedback with a specified type of clue. Even for the teacher-provided feedback at the sentence-level, students had a better understanding when the teacher included some tips or directions on how to revise the writing.

5 Implications for the Context and Conclusion

Earlier in this chapter, we explained how important it is for the majority of the students to get good results in high-stakes national and international tests. Previous research has shown that teaching English writing in the context of Iran tends to be product-based and measurement-driven (Marefat & Heydari, 2018). To this end, many students and teachers are ready to cut corners and take shortcuts to save time and money and get acceptable test results. The dominance of this mentality has led to teaching and learning practices that do not instill long-term learning goals and focus on observable and achievable results in the short term. Therefore, even in the presence of proper feedback and revision time, some students might feel handicapped to decipher the feedback and look for solutions to fix the issues in their writings.

We found that although the students without prior IELTS training seemed more confused with the feedback than previously trained students, they showed a higher willingness to learn about their weaknesses and use their general problem-solving techniques to come up with solutions. These solutions were not successful in many cases, but it seems that the students participating in the study were satisfied with what they learned through the process and how it could eventually lead to improved writing skills.

This point can also be discussed from a socio-economic point of view. Sitting an international test is an expensive endeavor for many Iranian students, let alone the training and preparation costs. In addition, the highly competitive academic environment pushes more and more students to get better results in a shorter time span. In this context, it seems that educational policymakers can amend the negative effects by implementing a series of recommendations. First, incorporating English academic writing courses into the university curriculum should be valued. In this way, students will have enough time to familiarize themselves with the qualities of good writing and develop learning goals rather than performance goals. As a result, they would be more flexible. This, in turn, will help less privileged students to be more prepared for their future challenges by giving them access to free education.

It should be noted that official academic curriculum does not necessarily mean an exclusive traditional classroom-based instruction. In a large developing country like Iran, a fair distribution of physical and human resources across the country will be challenging. Therefore, digital learning/teaching platforms like Cambridge *Write&Improve* used in this study, can be developed on a national scale to provide affordable (or even free) and accessible quality material to students all over the country. The automated diagnostic feedback will enable the teachers to implement formative assessment in their classes and encourage learners to practice their writing skills beyond the limits of traditional product-based and timed writing tests. This can allow the learners "to reflect on their errors and simultaneously track their effect on their overall performance, thus facilitating self-assessment, self-tutoring and self-improvement through reflective use of feedback" (Yannakoudakis et al., 2018, p. 253). Besides, writing in modern academic settings seems to be mostly conducted via computers where digital literacy and digital strategies are intertwined with academic writing strategies. In this regard, digital education will give the students a better opportunity to develop their digital literacy and skills.

Another concern which still remains to be addressed at the national level is to revise and re-develop the existing high-stakes national tests based on the real academic needs of the students. The current tests encourage students to learn some grammar lessons at the sentence-level which has a negative washback effect. In the current situation, only a small percent of an entire cohort of students are being taught to write an essay while a great majority wind up practicing multiple-choice grammar questions in schools or universities. In a centralized education system like Iran, revising the high-stakes English tests, however challenging, will have a major positive effect on the teaching practices.

In conclusion, this study was the first attempt in the academic context of Iran to explore the effectiveness of an online platform to assess students' English writings and help them develop their writing skills. It was an opportunity to see if computer-provided feedback could be effective when combined with teacher-provided feedback. It also helped to investigate the social and individual factors affecting the students' uptake of feedback and its role in improving their writing skills. Using such a platform can not only be effective to improve student writings, but it also serves as a teaching venue where the writers can learn about the strengths and weaknesses of their writing, identify the problems, and actively engage in learning new words, grammar tips, and stylistic features.

We found that students who had been previously coached for the IELTS exam were efficient in addressing word-level feedback but were less willing to get involved in sentence-level feedback where they were required to be more patient and employ higher-level problem-solving skills to revise the text. Negative washback seems to be a dominant cause for these students' lack of motivation to spend more time on their writings and get involved in long-term learning goals rather than short-term performance goals.

Our study suffers from the relatively small number of students and the inclusion of only one teacher which accordingly limits the generalizability of the findings. Future studies with a higher number of participants and over a longer period of time would yield richer data and more generalizable findings.

References

Bitchener, J., & Ferris, D. R. (2012). *Written corrective feedback in second language acquisition and writing*. New York, NY: Routledge.

Boggs, J. A. (2019). Effects of teacher-scaffolded and self-scaffolded corrective feedback compared to direct corrective feedback on grammatical accuracy in English L2 writing. *Journal of Second Language Writing, 46,* 1–13.

Borjian, M. (2013). *English in post-revolutionary Iran: From indigenization to internationalization*. Bristol: Multilingual Matters.

Brady, B. (2012). Managing assessment in large EFL classes. In C. Coombe, P. Davidson, B. O'Sullivan, & S. Stoynoff (Eds.), *The Cambridge guide to Second Language Assessment* (pp. 291–298). New York, NY: Cambridge University Press.

Ducate, L., & Arnold, N. (2012). Computer-mediated feedback: Effectiveness and student perceptions of screen-casting software versus the comment function. In G. Kessler, E. Oskoz, & I. Elola (Eds.), *Technology across writing contexts and tasks* (pp. 31–56). San Marcos, TX: CALICO Publications.

Elliott, E. S., & Dweck, C. S. (1988). Goals: An approach to motivation and achievement. *Journal of Personality and Social Psychology, 54*(1), 5–12. https://doi.org/10.1037/0022-3514.54.1.5.

Ellis, R. (2009). A typology of written corrective feedback types. *ELT Journal, 63*(2), 97–107. https://doi.org/10.1093/elt/ccn023.

Elola, I., & Oskoz, A. (2016). Supporting second language writing using multimodal feedback. *Foreign Language Annals, 49*(1), 58–74. https://doi.org/10.1111/flan.

Elola, I., & Oskoz, A. (2017). Writing with 21st century social tools in the L2 classroom: New literacies, genres, and writing practices. *Journal of Second Language Writing, 36,* 52–60. https://doi.org/10.1016/j.jslw.2017.04.002.

Ene, E., & Upton, T. A. (2018). Synchronous and asynchronous teacher electronic feedback and learner uptake in ESL composition. *Journal of Second Language Writing, 41,* 1–13. https://doi.org/10.1016/j.jslw.2018.05.005.

Ferris, D. R. (2002). *Treatment of error in second language student writing*. Ann Arbor, MI: University of Michigan Press.

Ferris, D. R. (2006). Does error feedback help student writers? New evidence on the short- and long-term effects of written error correction. In K. Hyland & F. Hyland (Eds.), *Perspectives on response* (pp. 81–104). Cambridge: Cambridge University Press.

Ferris, D. R. (2010). Second language writing research and written corrective feedback in SLA. *Studies in Second Language Acquisition, 32*, 181–201. https://doi.org/10.1017/s0272263109990490.

Ferris, D. (2009). *Teaching college writing to diverse student populations*. Ann Arbor, MI: University of Michigan Press.

Fotos, S., & Browne, C. (2004). The development of CALL and current options. In S. Fotos & C. M. Browne (Eds.), *New perspectives on CALL for second language classrooms* (pp. 3–14). Mahwah, NJ: Lawrence Erlbaum Associates.

Lavolette, E., Polio, C., & Kahng, J. (2015). The accuracy of computer-assisted feedback and students' responses to it. *Language Learning & Technology, 19*(2), 50–68. http://dx.doi.org/10125/44417.

Mansouri Nejad, A., Qaracholloo, M. & Rezaei, S. (2020). Iranian doctoral students' shared experience of English-medium publication: the case of humanities and social sciences. *High Education*, Advance online Publication. https://doi.org/10.1007/s10734-019-00478-1.

Marefat, F., & Heydari, M. (2018). English writing assessment in the context of Iran: The double life of Iranian test-takers. In T. Ruecker & D. Crusan (Eds.), *The politics of English Second Language writing assessment in global contexts* (pp. 67–71). New York, NY: Routledge.

Nassaji, H. (2016). Anniversary article interactional feedback in second language teaching and learning: A synthesis and analysis of current research. *Language Teaching Research, 20*(4), 535–562. https://doi.org/10.1177/1362168816644940.

Nemati, M., Alavi, S. M., Mohebbi, H., & Panahi Masjedlou, A. (2017). Teachers' writing proficiency and assessment ability: the missing link in teachers' written corrective feedback practice in an Iranian EFL context. *Language Testing in Asia, 7*, 1–19. https://doi.org/10.1186/s40468-017-0053-0.

Philips, S. M. (2007). *Automated essay scoring: A literature review* (SAEE research series #30). Kelowna, BC: Society for the Advancement of Excellence Education.

Riazi, A. (2005). The four language stages in the history of Iran. In A. Lin & P. Martin (Eds.), *Decolonization, globalisation: Language-in-education policy and practice* (pp. 98–115). Clevedon: Multilingual Matters.

Sheen, Y. (2010). The role of oral and written corrective feedback in SLA. *Studies in Second Language Acquisition, 32*, 169–179.

Stevenson, M., & Phakiti, F. (2014). The effects of computer-generated feedback on the quality of writing. *Assessing Writing, 19*, 51–56.

Storch, N. (2018). Written corrective feedback from sociocultural theoretical perspectives: A research agenda. *Language Teaching, 51*(2), 262–277. https://doi.org/10.1017/S0261444818000034.

Taylor, A. R. (2005). *A future in the process of arrival: Using computer technologies for the assessment of student learning*. Kelowna, BC: Society for the Advancement of Excellence in Education.

Truscott, J. (1996). The case against grammar correction in L2 writing classes. *Language Learning, 46*(2), 327–369.

Truscott, J. (1999). What's wrong with oral grammar correction. *The Canadian Modern Language Review, 55*(4), 437–455.

Truscott, J. (2004). Evidence and conjecture on the effects of correction: A response to Chandler. *Journal of Second Language Writing, 13,* 337–343.

Vygotsky, L. S. (1978). *Mind in society: The development of higher mental processes* (eds & trans. M. Cole, V. John-Steiner, S. Scribner & E. Souberman). Cambridge, MA: Harvard University Press.

Waller, L., & Papi, M. (2017). Motivation and feedback: How implicit theories of intelligence predict L2 writers' motivation and feedback orientation. *Journal of Second Language Writing, 35,* 54–65.

Weigle, S. (2002). *Assessing writing* (Cambridge Language Assessment). Cambridge: Cambridge University Press. http://dx.doi.org/10.1017/CBO9780511732997.

Yannakoudakis, H., Andersen, Ø. E., Geranpayeh, A., Briscoe, T., & Nicholls, D. (2018). Developing an automated writing placement system for ESL learners. *Applied Measurement in Education, 31*(3), 251–267. https://doi.org/10.1080/08957347.2018.1464447.

Zhang, Z., & Hyland, K. (2018). Student engagement with teacher and automated feedback on L2 writing. *Assessing Writing, 36,* 90–102. https://doi.org/10.1016/j.asw.2018.02.004.

Research on Feedback in EFL Classes in the MENA Region: State of the Art

Moez Athimni, Safa Yaakoubi, and Hanin Bouzaiene

1 Introduction

Feedback is often defined as an instructional practice which allows learners and teachers to improve their performances and be better aligned with the learning targets. Chappuis, Stiggins, Chappuis, and Arter (2012) define feedback as the information provided to a learner in order to assess their performance in a certain learning task. Hattie and Timperley (2007) refer to feedback provision as an interactional process in which feedback is the information provided by an agent such as a teacher, peer, book, parent, self or experience as a response to an individual or a group performance or understanding. Winne and Butler (1994, cited in Hattie & Timperley, 2007, p. 82) emphasize the role of the learner in feedback provision. They define feedback as the information learners receive from a feedback provider and adapt to their own needs. This information often relates to a 'domain knowledge, metacognitive knowledge, beliefs about self and tasks, or cognitive tactics and strategies'.

Today, feedback can be considered as a well-established field in ELT thanks to the large amount of research conducted worldwide. The history of research in this field started in the middle of the previous century or even before. Hyland and Hyland (2006) state that research in feedback first started in L1 writing in the 1970s with the emergence of the 'learner-centred approach' in ELT. In the MENA region, however, research on feedback in EFL classes can be considered a novice field. A quick review of the research conducted in the region shows that almost all the works were published in the last decade. In addition, there seems to be a lack of research in the field. Ahmed (2020, p. 19), in a study conducted to review feedback research in L2 writing in the Arab world, concludes that '[t]he literature review demonstrates the paucity of research about feedback in EFL writing in some Arab countries'. This highlights the need for more research in the field and especially research studies which describe the state of art of research on feedback in EFL classes in the MENA region; a gap that this work purports to fill.

2 Literature Review

2.1 Feedback Effect on Instruction

Feedback plays a pivotal role in instruction. Several studies (e.g. Chan, Konrad, Gonzalez, Peters, & Ressa, 2014; Chappuis et al., 2012; Frear, 2010) consider feedback as a tool which has a significant impact on formative instructional practices. Most of these studies point to the existence of a positive correlation between feedback provision and the improvement of learner's achievement. Qi and Lapkin (2001; cf., Kang & Han, 2015) state that feedback provision boosts students' development in areas related to lexis, grammar and discourse. Sadler (1989) explains that feedback provision helps the learners bridge the existing gap between their own productions and the standards set by the curriculum. In the field of writing, Liu (2008) affirms that providing feedback helps reduce students' errors. Similarly, Bitchener and Storch (2016) assert that written feedback develops L2 writers' accuracy as well as their overall L2 level of command. They maintain that feedback equips students with the strategies necessary for the objective evaluation of their own production in terms of observing and monitoring the quality of their work. As for oral performance, Swain (2000) highlights the importance of teacher's feedback during speaking production through the use of empirical evidence.

In language learning, two views exist concerning the function of feedback provision: the cognitivist view and the constructivist view. According to Ellis (2009), the cognitivist view emphasizes the corrective nature of feedback. Feedback provision is perceived as a linear process in which information is transferred from the feedback provider, the expert, to a passive recipient, the learner. In the socio-constructivist view, however, feedback provision is an interactive process in which the feedback provider, the facilitator, provides information to help learners gain an understanding of their mistakes and make their own revisions (Evans, 2013). Despite these differences, these two views emphasize the importance of feedback in fostering language learning. Similarly, in the communicative approach, feedback is also viewed as a medium to boost motivation and develop linguistic accuracy (Ellis, 2009). Despite this wide agreement of the positive effect of feedback provision on the learning in general, and language learning, in particular; this process remains mostly constrained by the degree of knowledge teachers have about feedback in terms of available types and techniques.

2.2 Feedback Types

In relation to feedback types, the review of literature shows that different typologies exist. These typologies vary according to the feedback provider, mode of delivery and media of delivery (Wanchid, 2015). Feedback is often referred to as oral or written, implicit or explicit, positive or negative, direct or indirect, focused or unfocused and immediate or delayed.

Oral feedback refers to the information provided in an oral mode to the learner. This may include the comments directly provided during a classroom speaking activity or a discussion following a specific oral performance. Hadzic (2016, p. 6) affirms that 'when discussing oral feedback in the classroom, any kind of dialogue that provides information that will help students improve their learning can be included'. Written feedback is the information provided in a written mode on the learner's written performance. It may include written comments, correction of errors, or codes referring to specific types of mistakes. Sheen (2010) points to some differences between oral and written feedback. He explains that, compared to oral feedback, written feedback is more limited and individualized. While oral feedback is typically directed to individual learners and accessible for the rest of the learners as well; written feedback is individualized and only accessible to the recipient unless they wish to let others examine their corrections.

Feedback can also be classified as implicit or explicit. Sheen and Ellis (2011) explain that implicit feedback refers to the instances when the feedback provider requests clarifications from the learner about a specific error. Explicit feedback, on the other hand, consists in the direct correction of the error followed by an explanation. Oral feedback can be both implicit and explicit. Written feedback, however, is often described as explicit as there is little room for interaction between the feedback provider and the learner. Today, however, written feedback provision is becoming more interactive through the use of new technology, namely online feedback programs, social media and e-learning platforms. In a study conducted to compare the effects of implicit and explicit feedback on the learners' grammar accuracy, Zohrabi and Ehsani (2014) noticed that their students' grammar accuracy improved thanks to the provision of both implicit and explicit feedback. Explicit feedback, however, proved to be more effective as the groups who received explicit feedback outperformed the ones who received implicit feedback.

Feedback is also divided into positive and negative. Ellis (2009) states that while positive feedback refers to the instances when learners are rewarded for their correct use of the language; negative feedback relates to the provision of a correction of the error whether oral or written. The responses provided with the aim of correcting learners' errors are labelled 'corrective feedback' (CF). Ellis, Loewen, and Erlam (2006) maintain that CF is often used to point to the occurrence of an error, provide a correction, or supply some metalinguistic information concerning the nature of the error committed. These types of responses could be combined or separately provided.

Feedback can also be direct or indirect. Sheen and Ellis (2011) argue that the difference between direct and indirect feedback lies in the focus of the process itself. While the former focuses on the input provided to the learners, the latter prompts the output produced by the learners. Direct feedback consists in the provision of the correct form of the utterance in question to the learner. Indirect feedback, however, aims at eliciting such correct form from the learners. In terms of effect, Liu (2008) affirms that providing direct feedback helps reduce students' errors in their immediate drafts. In the same vein, Bitchener, Young, and Cameron (2005, p. 202) confirm that 'direct oral feedback in combination with direct written feedback had a greater effect than direct written feedback alone on improved accuracy over time'.

Feedback is also referred to as focused or unfocused. Unfocused feedback relates to the instances when teachers opt for correcting all the learners' errors, while focused feedback takes place when correcting only a few selected errors (Ellis, 2009). As far as focused feedback provision is concerned, several studies (e.g. Ferris, 1995; Ferris & Helt, 2000; Ferris, Chaney, Komura, Roberts, & McKee, 2000; Sheppard, 1992) highlight the need for a focused treatment of errors as different types of errors require different types interventions. In terms of effect, Farrokhi and Sattarpour (2011) argue that focused CF had more effect on their students' grammatical accuracy. Karimi and Fotovatnia (2010, cited in Alimohammadi & Nejadansari, 2014), on the other hand, maintain that focused and unfocused CF equally contribute to the development of their students' L2 writing grammatical accuracy.

Feedback can also be immediate of delayed. In oral feedback, teachers often have the choice between immediate/online and delayed/offline provision. In written feedback, however, the intervention is mostly 'offline' as teachers require time to correct the writing productions submitted by learners (Ellis, 2009; cf., Sheen & Ellis, 2011). Ellis (2009) refers to the disagreement between SLA researchers concerning the timing of oral feedback provision. While studies such as Harmer (1983) claim that immediate provision of feedback disturbs the learning context and thus hinders L2 learning; Ellis, Basturkmen, and Loewen (2001) contend that providing immediate feedback does not disrupt the communicative flow of the classroom activities.

2.3 Knowledge and Beliefs About Feedback Provision

The study of teachers' classroom feedback practices often leads to the investigation of their beliefs and knowledge about feedback provision. Lee (2008a, p. 69) affirms that:

> teachers' feedback practices are influenced by a myriad of contextual factors including teachers' beliefs, values, understandings, and knowledge, which are mediated by the cultural and institutional contexts, such as views about feedback and attitude to exams, and socio-political issues pertaining to power and teacher autonomy.

In a study conducted to explore feedback beliefs and practices among novice and experienced ESL teachers, Karaağaçzan and Yiğitoğlu (2018) conclude that teachers' provision of written feedback was mainly shaped by their attitudes towards writing as well as their beliefs about the roles of the teacher and the learners in their writing classes. In addition, many other studies (e.g. Eraut, 2000; Lee, 2008b; Parr & Limbrick, 2010) point to the discrepancy between teachers' knowledge and beliefs about feedback provision and their classroom practices. In most of these studies, teachers seemed to possess some theoretical knowledge about feedback provision, but they failed to translate that knowledge into concrete instructional practices.

The present study is undertaken to explore research activity about feedback in EFL classes in the MENA region. More specifically, it aims to describe the activity in terms of feedback areas investigated, findings and research gaps. The study is guided by the following questions:

RQ 1: What are the areas/aspects of feedback in EFL classes investigated by research studies conducted in the MENA region?

RQ 2: What are the main findings of these studies?
RQ 3: What are the gaps in the research activity about feedback in EFL classes in the MENA Region?

3 Methodology

To effectively review relevant studies about research on feedback practices in EFL classes in the MENA region, the study employed a scoping review. A scoping review is a study conducted to review available literature about a specific topic. More specifically it

> aim[s] to map rapidly the key concepts underpinning a research area and the main sources and types of evidence available, and can be undertaken as stand-alone projects in their own right, especially where an area is complex or has not been reviewed comprehensively before. (Mays et al., 2001, p. 194; emphasis in original)

Arksey and O'Malley (2005) specify that this type of study is often conducted to (a) explore research activity in a specific field in terms of extent, range and nature, (b) decide about the usefulness of undertaking a systematic review of the literature, (c) disseminate research results, and (d) spot research gaps in the field. In terms of research procedures, Pham et al. (2014) state that scoping reviews generally include five distinct phases. Phase one consists in the definition of the research questions. Phase two includes the identification of relevant studies. Phase three relates to the selection of relevant studies. Phase four consists in the extraction of data. The fifth and last phase includes data summary and synthesis.

In the present study, a scoping review is used to identify the areas of feedback investigated by research studies in the MENA region, summarize the e-studies and spot the research gaps in the field, if any. The time span was not set since the researchers are interested in defining the history of the research activity in the region. The search included peer-reviewed journal articles, chapters, academic books, theses and dissertations and conference papers. The selection of the relevant research works was guided by the following criteria:

a. the topic of the work is related to feedback, feedback provision, or feedback practices in the MENA region,
b. the study was conducted in the MENA region or about learners from the region, and
c. the work is published in English and available online.

Searches were performed in Google, Google-Scholar, Researchgate and Academia with a combination of the following search terms: 'feedback in the MENA region', 'feedback in the Arab world', 'feedback studies in the MENA region', 'feedback studies in the Arab world', 'feedback provision in the Arab world', 'feedback provision in the MENA region', 'feedback practices in the MENA region', and 'feedback practices in the Arab world'. The search of these terms identified 70 journal articles, book chapters, M.A. and Ph.D. dissertations and books. Titles and abstracts of these publications were scrutinized to select relevant studies to be included in the study. Finally, the research team agreed to base their scoping review upon 37 studies. These studies are indicated in the reference list with an asterisk (*).

4 Results and Discussion

4.1 Research on Feedback in EFL Classes in the MENA Region

In terms of the geographical distribution of research activity on feedback in the MENA region (see Table 1), the analysis of the articles collected for the study reveals that 27% of the feedback studies were conducted in Saudi Arabia, followed by Morocco (16%) and Iran (13%), Oman, Egypt and Libya are with 8% each, followed by Jordan and Tunisia (5%); and Kuwait and the UAE with 3%. These figures also reflect the amount of interest in feedback research in these countries. In addition to the small number of studies conducted in these countries, a close analysis

Table 1 Distribution of feedback research articles in the MENA region

Country	Number of articles	Percentage (%)
KSA	10	27
Morocco	6	16
Iran	5	13
Egypt	3	8
Oman	3	8
Libya	3	8
Tunisia	2	5.5
Jordan	2	5.5
Palestine	1	3
Kuwait	1	3
UAE	1	3
Total	37	100

Table 2 Research focus

Research focus	Number of articles	Percentage (%)
Feedback types	8	21.5
Feedback effect	13	35
Interaction	2	5.5
Knowledge, beliefs and practices	6	16
Students' attitudes	8	21.5
Total	37	100

of the dates of publication of the articles shows that this field of study does not have a long history in the region. Most of the articles selected for the study (32 out of 37) were published between 2015 and 2020, which indicates that the interest in this field started only in the recent years. In Saudi Arabia, for example, nine out of the ten articles included were published between 2018 and 2020, which shows that feedback is perhaps only just becoming established in the country.

In relation to the areas investigated by the feedback studies conducted in the region, the analysis revealed that these studies focused on different areas which include feedback types, feedback effect, interaction in feedback provision, teachers' knowledge, beliefs and practices, and students' attitudes towards feedback provision. Table 2 shows that these studies focused mainly on feedback effect (35% of the studies), followed by feedback types and students' attitudes with 21.5% each, and feedback knowledge, beliefs and practices with 16%. Little attention, however, was given to interaction which was the focus of only two out of 37 studies. These figures, however, provide a description of the articles based on their general research focus. In fact, most studies included more than one focus even though they claim, in their titles, that they focus on one aspect of feedback. For example, interaction during feedback provision, which was the focus of only two articles, was either mentioned or even investigated in many of the 24 other articles. In addition, some articles focus on different feedback aspects at the same time. Shaqaqi and Soleimani (2018), for instance, investigated the effects of two different types of feedback, namely the 'asynchronous and conventional paper-and-en metalinguistic feedback'. This work has been categorized as focussing on 'feedback effects'; however, it can also be categorized under 'feedback types' since it explores the effects of two feedback types.

4.2 Feedback Effect on Instruction

Out of the 37 studies, 19 investigated the effect of feedback on instruction. In terms feedback types, two studies focused on the effect of feedback in general, ten studies focused on written feedback, five studies on online feedback and two studies on oral feedback. All these studies concluded that feedback has a positive effect on the instructional process. No study referred to a negative or no effect. More specifically, these studies revealed that feedback has a positive impact on learners' achievement and motivation.

4.2.1 Effect on Learners' Achievement

12 studies refer to improvements in the learners' language skills thanks to the provision of different types of feedback. Some studies (e.g. AbuSeileek, 2013; Al Ajmi, 2015; Ali, 2016; Alhumidi & Uba, 2016; Al-Hazzani & Altalhab, 2018; Al-Saleh, 2018) rely on experimental designs to trace the effect of feedback on their learners. Their findings point to significant differences in the achievements of their experimental and control groups in written and oral tests. For example, in a study

conducted to trace the effect of online positive corrective feedback, Al-Saleh (2018, p. 1) refers to the existence of 'statistically significant differences between the performance of the experimental group and the control group on the post-writing test that showed the effectiveness of providing positive, written corrective feedback via Showbie on the students' English writing'. Other studies (e.g. Dehdary & Al-Saadi, 2020; Ouahidi & Lamkhanter, 2020; Sayed & Curabba, 2020; Shaqaqi & Soleimani, 2018) rely on the learners' accounts to measure the effect of feedback provision on their performance. The results reveal that most learners noticed some improvement in their writing and speaking skills thanks to feedback. For instance, Al-Sawalha (2016, p. 17) concludes that 'teachers' written feedback have a twin effect: the first one was improving and orientating students' revision skills and correcting their writing mechanisms, and the second was enhancing the Jordanian EFL students' overall writing quality while doing a different draft of the same essay and composition'. In another study conducted to measure the impact of 4D feedback, Dehdary and Al-Saadi (2020, p. 80) conclude that '[t]he participants approved of their progression while receiving 4D feedback. They found the sequence smooth and helpful'.

4.2.2 Effect on Motivation

Some studies (e.g. Daweli, 2018; Seliem & Ahmed, 2009; Zouaidi & Hermessi, 2019) mentioned that feedback has some effects on learners' motivation. Findings from these studies emphasize the role of some types of feedback, especially online feedback, in decreasing learners' inhibition and increasing their involvement in the classroom. In a study conducted about the provision of electronic feedback in Egyptian writing classes, Seliem and Ahmed (2009, p. 2) maintain that:

> E-feedback, as a new pedagogic practice, was generally effective in providing positive learning environment different from the physical rigid classroom environment, encouraging students' responsibility for their own written work, facilitating peer and lecturer collaboration, increasing student participation, sharing learned outcomes between students, and

giving writing feedback to students electronically was a well-received and helpful pedagogic practice.

The role of online feedback in creating a new motivating context for the learners is also reiterated by Daweli (2018) who explains that using this type of feedback involves the learners in a virtual social environment in which they feel free of any kind of inhibition or embarrassment. Focusing effect of oral corrective feedback (OCT), Zouaidi and Hermessi (2019) add that teachers' feedback practices do not only change the learner' immediate behaviour in the classroom but also their behaviour in the whole course.

4.3 Feedback Types

The analysis of the articles collected for the study shows that this aspect is of major concern for feedback research in the region. Almost all the articles focused on feedback types in terms of effect, related teachers' practices or students' preferences. Table 3 shows the existence of some differences in terms of researchers' interest in the types of feedback. Written feedback is by far the most commonly researched type (78.37%), followed by oral corrective feedback (29.72%), online feedback (27.02%) and peer feedback (11%).

4.3.1 Written Feedback

Among the articles included in the study, 29 focus on written feedback. Some articles (e.g. AbuSeileek, 2013; Al Ajmi, 2015; Al-Hazzani

Table 3 Research on feedback types

Feedback type	Number of articles	Percentage (%)[a]
Written feedback	29	78
Oral feedback	11	29
Peer feedback	4	11
Online feedback	10	27

[a]Some types were investigated in more than one article

& Altalhab, 2018; Alshahrani & Storch, 2014; Amara, 2017) highlight the advantages of written corrective feedback (WCF) provision and its effective role in the development of learners' language skills. AbuSeileek (2013, p. 330) affirms that WCF positively impacts learners writing skills. He explains that, in his study, 'participants who obtained written corrective feedback performed better on the writing post-test'. Al Ajmi (2015) adds that WCF provision helps improve students' performance on preposition use grammatical and lexical accuracy (Al-Hazzani & Altalhab, 2018) and verb tense accuracy (Shaqaqi & Soleimani, 2018). Al-Sawalha (2016, p. 63) adds that WCF plays an effective role in 'improving and orientating students' revision skills'.

Some studies, however, mention that despite its positive effects, WCF can sometimes be problematic in instructional settings. Alkhatib (2015, p. ii) refers to the degree of clarity of teachers' feedback. The author states that 'although students valued teachers' WCF and placed a great importance to it, they faced difficulties understanding some of their teachers' comments'. In the same vein, Amara (2015) and Said and El Mouzrati (2018) report that students complained about their teachers' feedback describing it as unclear and sometimes misplaced leading often to confusion and misinterpretation. Ouahidi and Lamkhanter (2020, p. 53) add that 'teachers' feedback, according to students, is more often than demotivating'.

4.3.2 Oral Feedback

10 studies out of 37 investigated oral feedback practices in the region. Some studies (Alahmadi, Alrahaili, & Alshraideh, 2019; Sakale, 2017; 2019; Zouaidi & Hermessi, 2019) refer to its positive effect on learning. Alahmadi et al. (2019) claim that oral feedback, when integrated as formative assessment tool, it improves the students' performance skills and enables them to understand the subject contents properly. Zouaidi and Hermessi (2019) emphasize that the use of some oral feedback techniques such as 'recast' increases the learners' motivation and involvement in the classroom activities. Sakale (2019) adds that helping students

make the necessary changes in their oral performance results in a density of negotiation leading to the improvement of student's oral performance.

Other studies (e.g. Alkhammash & Gulnaz, 2019; Karimi & Asadnia, 2015) refer to some limitations regarding the use of oral feedback in the classroom. Alkhammash and Gulnaz (2019, p. 51) point to the difficulty of customizing oral feedback to the individual needs of the learners. They report that '[t]eachers often encounter difficulties when dealing with spoken errors as they requires the use of appropriate techniques that best address particular types of error and are suitable for the type of learning activities and the learner' profile.'

In addition, oral feedback provision is mainly dependent on the student's level. In a study conducted to investigate teachers' use of feedback strategies, Karimi and Asadnia (2015) reveal that there was a significant difference in teachers' use of corrective feedback strategies between elementary and intermediate levels, and that more explicit correction, elicitation, metalinguistic clues, clarification request, and repetition are with learners at the elementary level.

4.3.3 Peer Feedback

Out of the 37 studies, four focus on peer feedback and five treat it as a secondary topic. Some of these studies (AbuSeileek, 2013; Alkhatib, 2015; Alnasser, 2018; Daweli, 2018) highlight the importance of this type of feedback in instruction. Alkhatib (2015, pp. 137, 138) mentions that teachers are aware of the necessity to allow students to obtain feedback from their peers. '[P]eer feedback helps them [students] exchange ideas' and to 'not to be over dependent on teachers'. Similarly, Seliem and Ahmed (2009) and Daweli (2018) affirm that peer reviews and comments helped participants improve and adjust their writings accordingly. For Ahmed (2020, p. 11), 'peer feedback did not only encourage students' revision but also benefited them linguistically, cognitively, and affectively.'

Other studies (e.g. Alkhatib, 2015; Alnasser, 2018), however, raise certain concerns about the use of this type of feedback in the classroom. Alkhatib (2015, p. 138) warns about replacing teacher's corrective feedback with peer feedback. She declares that 'although peer feedback is important and should be implemented according to teachers, it should however, neither replace nor compensate for teachers' WCF, and it should be guided by the teacher'. In the same vein, Alnasser (2018, p. 345) believes that despite the reported positive experience related to the used peer and computer-based feedback in the classroom; 'students are not yet ready to let go of teacher feedback'. Zyad and Bouziane (2020) point to the lack of trust in peer feedback. They argue that this type of feedback is questionable as the provider is perceived to be of 'equal footing' and capable of committing and overlooking mistakes.

4.3.4 Online Corrective Feedback

10 out of the 37 articles included in the study focus on online feedback. Results were varied but overall, online feedback is perceived as valuable and beneficial. Ali (2016) describes a study conducted to investigate the efficacy of incorporating 'screencast' feedback in a university EFL writing course. Students, in this study, demonstrated a positive attitude towards feedback and perceived it as clear and motivating, despite the problems related to internet connection. Seliem and Ahmed (2009, p. 20) affirm that

> E-feedback proved essential in the teaching and learning of essay writing for Egyptian student-teachers of English. Student-teachers revealed that it is instrumental in improving their essay writing skills. Besides, lecturers' experiences of e-feedback proved successful as they managed to respond to students' e-mails, but they found it exhausting.

4.3.5 Other Feedback Types

The articles included in the study also focus on other types of feedback. Direct and indirect feedback is investigated in 18 articles. Findings of these studies reveal the existence an agreement among students and teachers on the effectiveness of direct and indirect WCF. Alkhatib (2015, p. 135) contends that 'while all teachers believe in the effectiveness of the direct WCF, some teachers still believe that indirect WCF might be also used in three situations: when dealing with frequent errors, minor errors, and/or with stigmatizing errors'. Similarly, Ali (2016) stresses on the effectiveness of both types of feedback. In the same vein, Karimi and Asadnia (2015) propose a mixed approach in which both types of feedback are employed to maximize effectiveness. In terms of use, Al-Bakri (2016) claim that teachers mostly provide students with direct WCF. Zyad and Bouziane (2020) add that peer reviewers also provide direct feedback. In terms of preference, Alshahrani and Storch (2014) and Ouahidi and Lamkhanter (2020) assert that students prefer direct feedback as it is more accessible and can be easily implemented.

Focused and unfocused types of feedback are also investigated in the articles collected for the study. 9 out of 37 studies have mentions of focused (24.32%) and unfocused (21.62%) feedback types. In relation to students' preferences, Al Ajmi (2015) affirms that 88% of their informants [students] preferred focused WCF and saw it as facilitative, organized, effective and motivating. Additionally, Amara (2017) sheds the light on the effectiveness of focused WCF mainly on the improvement of students' writing and grammatical accuracy. In contrast, Alshahrani and Storch (2014) declare that teachers in their study were obligated by institutional guidelines to provide unfocused feedback to students.

In addition to the aforementioned types, some articles investigate implicit and explicit feedback. 12 out of 37 articles focus on this type of feedback. Al-Hazzani and Altalhab (2018) mention that explicit WCF has a significant positive effect on the development of students' grammatical and lexical accuracy. This is also reiterated by Farrokhi (2011), who admits that despite the low percentages of occurrence in actual teachers' practices, explicit correction has one of the highest percentages of effectiveness. Still with the frequency of occurrence, Khorshidi and Rassaei (2013) add that explicit feedback was the least frequent among the various feedback types included in their study. As for implicit feedback, studies show that it is not commonly used by teachers. Karimi and Asadnia (2015, p. 58) claim that '[a]lthough the teachers stated that they use both explicit and implicit CF according to error type, situation, and task, the teachers mostly relied on explicit feedbacks than implicit ones at both levels regardless of the error types and situation-based functions of the tasks'.

4.4 Interaction in Feedback Provision

The analysis of the feedback articles selected for the study revealed that interaction during feedback provision was of primary research concern in two articles and secondary research concern in 24 other articles. 25 articles dealt with teacher–students interaction, while only eight focused on peer interaction. In relation to teacher–students interaction in written feedback, Al-Harbi and Troudi (2020, p. 192) explain that the success of teacher–student interaction is based on the type of relationship established between the students and their supervisors. They argue that 'a good relationship between students and their supervisor will contribute to the successful completion of the students' research project and an improvement in their writing skills, in conjunction with effective and continual communication with their supervisors'.

Other studies (e.g. Al-Bakri, 2016; Al-Harbi & Troudi, 2020; Amara, 2015; Shawish & Al-Raheem, 2015) pointed to some challenges at the level of teacher–student written interaction, which mainly relate to the lack of communication, feedback misinterpretation and unrealistic expectations. Abu Shawish and Abd Al-Raheem (2015) point to the lack of communication between teachers and students regarding written corrective feedback provision. They explain that, due to the large number of learners, teachers were unable to appropriately communicate their feedback to all their students. For example, they were unable to have individual conferences with students who needed more care and guidance. Also some studies mention that marking and commenting on students' papers was problematic. Amara (2015) explains that students often misinterpreted their teachers' comments and perceived them as severe criticism or even accusations of plagiarism. Another problem with teacher–student written interaction relates to the unrealistic expectations of teachers and students. In a study conducted to explore Saudi postgraduate students' problems with academic English writing, Al-Harbi and Troudi (2020) found that many Saudi postgraduate students expect their supervisors to play the role of schoolteachers. For them, supervisors should provide close assistance and guidance to supervisees. Supervisees, on the other hand, should not give their own opinions or views or question those of their supervisors.

At the level of oral interaction, Sakale (2017, p. 276) focuses on the timing of teacher's intervention and more specifically on the wait-time necessary before feedback provision and its role in the development of the students' speaking skills. She states that '[a]ccording to research findings wait–time instruction might be determinant in letting learners more time to prepare their speaking and modify or add on new things which may lead to improvements in their oral production'. Alkhammash and Gulnaz (2019) point to some difficulties relating to the management of verbal interaction in the classroom. They maintain that successful provision of feedback requires the mastery of certain classroom management techniques that many teachers do not possess due to the absence of appropriate teacher training programs.

Some studies (e.g. AbuSeileek, 2013; Ahmed, 2020; Alnasser, 2018; Daweli, 2018; Reinders & Mohebbi, 2018) praised the use of peer interaction in the classroom as it enhances students' involvement and enables them to check their errors and correct them. Other studies (e.g. Alnasser, 2018; Athimni, 2020; Seliem & Ahmed, 2009; Zyad & Bouziane, 2020), however, mention some problems related to peer interaction. Athimni (2020, p. 149) mentions that this type of feedback is not preferred by students. He states that 'peer feedback did not seem to be preferred by many students. Only respondent 7 referred to this type of feedback. She explained that some of her students did not actively participate in peer feedback sessions as they are not willing to hear the evaluation of their peers'. In addition, Zyad and Bouziane (2020) and Seliem and Ahmed (2009) point to the lack of trust in peer correction. Most students question the value of this practice and consider it artificial and not valuable as all students nearly have the same language proficiency level.

4.5 Feedback Knowledge and Beliefs About Feedback Provision

Out of the 37 studies, nine focus teachers' feedback knowledge, beliefs about feedback provision. Most of the articles investigate the degree of congruence between the teachers' knowledge and beliefs about feedback and their feedback practices in the classroom. In terms of possession of theoretical knowledge about feedback, several studies (e.g. Al-Bakri, 2016; Alkhatib, 2015; Athimni, 2020) affirm that teachers seem to possess the theoretical knowledge necessary for good feedback practices in the classroom. Athimni (2020, p. 157) states that 'teachers' feedback practices were governed to an extent by theoretical knowledge and beliefs about feedback provision in writing classes'. In a study conducted to investigate EFL teachers' beliefs and practices about oral corrective feedback techniques, Alkhammash and Gulnaz (2019) claim that their findings are congruent with what is agreed upon in the literature concerning the most commonly used types of OCF techniques that are proved to help improve learners' spoken proficiency presenting. Teachers seem to possess the necessary knowledge about those techniques and properly use in their classrooms. Similar findings about congruence between teachers' beliefs and practices are also reported in studies (e.g. Alkhatib, 2015; Shawish & Al-Raheem, 2015) conducted, respectively, in Saudi Arabia and Palestine.

Other studies (e.g. Athimni, 2020; Farrokhi, 2011; Karimi & Asadnia, 2015; Said & El Mouzrati, 2018; Shawish & Al-Raheem, 2015), however, point to some discrepancies between teachers' knowledge and their actual classroom practices. Athimni (2020, p. 159) states that 'on some occasions and in relation to some aspects of feedback, teachers seemed to possess the theoretical knowledge, yet they failed to translate that knowledge into concrete instructional practices'. Equally, Abu Shawish and Abd Al-Raheem (2015) mention that, in their study, teachers opted for using unsound practices as well as sound ones despite their knowledge and awareness of sound feedback practices. More specifically and regarding OCF, Karimi and Asadnia (2015, p. 61) point to 'some areas of belief-practice mismatch in teachers' sensitivity to students' errors, their employment of different CF strategies, use of explicit and implicit CF, application of immediate and delayed CF, correction of global and local errors, focus on different linguistic targets, and reliance on self, peer, and teacher correction'.

Some studies (e.g. Al-Bakri, 2016; Alkhatib, 2015; Alshahrani & Storch, 2014) investigate the reasons behind this mismatch. Al-Bakri

(2016) explains that students' attitudes towards feedback could negatively impact teachers' emotional state, hindering their feedback practices. In the same vein, Alshahrani and Storch (2014) and Alkhatib (2015) consider the disagreement that may occur among teachers' beliefs, institutional guidelines and the teaching overall context among the factors that prevent teachers from enacting their beliefs into practices. Alshahrani and Storch (2014) add that, most often, there is a mismatch between the type of feedback recommended through institutional guidelines and that preferred by students. Alkhatib (2015) considers the issue from a wider perspective. She explains that teachers' feedback practices are influenced by a number of external factors including teachers' beliefs, understandings, theoretical knowledge, learning and teaching experience, students' behaviour and educational policy.

4.6 Students' Attitudes Towards Feedback

Out of the 37 studies, 8 studies investigated students' attitudes towards feedback. Some studies (Al Ajmi, 2015; Al-Sawalha, 2016; Ouahidi & Lamkhanter 2020; Shawish & Al-Raheem, 2015) mention that students have a positive perception of feedback. Ouahidi and Lamkhanter (2020, p. 42) report that '(62%) agreed that the teachers' feedback is very beneficial and, consequently, has a positive impact on improving their writing skill'. Sayed and Curabba (2020) also report similar results. They state that a vast majority of students perceived all types of feedback as worthwhile. In some studies, these attitudes seem to positively correlate with the use technology-assisted feedback. Ali (2016, p. 106) mentioned that when asked to evaluate 'Screencast' feedback, students' responses included adjectives like 'clear, personal, specific, supportive, multimodal, constructive, and engaging'. Similar results were also reported in other studies (e.g. Basabrin, 2019; Daweli, 2018; Seliem & Ahmed, 2009) about the use of other online programs such as Showbie, Google Docs, or e-feedback. Other studies (Alkhatib, 2015; Alnasser, 2018; Al-Saleh, 2018), however, report students' expressed preferences for teachers' WCF and highlight the role of the teacher as key feedback provider. Sakale

(2019, p. 350) praises 'the pivotal teachers' role' during speaking activities. She emphasizes 'the pertinence of teachers' feedback in the classroom particularly when pushing students to make modifications in their responses'.

In other studies (e.g. Amara, 2015; Ouahidi & Lamkhanter, 2020) students expressed a negative attitude towards the feedback provided by their teachers. They reported they faced difficulties in understanding some of their teachers' comments. Dehdary and Al-Saadi (2020) mentioned that students do not always find feedback to be facilitative; it is often described as 'restrictive' or even deficient. For Said and El Mouzrati (2018, p. 237), 'it seems that students rarely turn to teachers to discuss the content of the feedback with their teachers and prefer, instead, to discuss it with their peers. The majority of the respondents continue to complain that teachers' feedback is too vague and too general'.

4.7 Gaps in Feedback Research in the MENA Region

The present study provides an overview of research on feedback in EFL classes in the MENA region. It describes the areas investigated by researchers in the region. Some areas received extensive attention such as 'feedback effects' and 'feedback types'. Other areas received little or no attention; they constitute the 'gaps' of feedback research in the MENA region.

The analysis of the articles selected for the study shows that compared to other feedback areas; interaction received little attention from researchers. Only two articles focused on the interactional aspects of feedback, which represents a major gap in feedback research in the region. Investigating how teachers and students interact during the provision of written or oral feedback helps researchers spot the deficiencies that may occur in feedback communication. This involves the identification of teachers' and students' moves and roles attributed to each party during feedback provision. It also includes the description of the techniques and strategies used during the interaction. Furthermore, feedback interaction should be understood within the cultural context in which teachers and students operate, as it helps researchers identify the major cultural factors which affect the feedback interactional act. In broader terms, investigating how interactions are managed and how roles are attributed to teachers and students in a specific culture should be of prime concern to researchers as it helps them devise appropriate solutions to breakdowns in feedback communication which are properly adapted to the cultural contexts in which teachers and students operate.

Some feedback types received little attention by researchers, and this represents another gap in feedback research in the region. Compared to written feedback, which was the focus of 78% of the articles included in the study, the other types, namely oral, peer and online feedback were by far under-researched. This, to a certain extent, reflects a traditional view of language and language teaching. Language teaching, today, is learner-centred, communication-oriented and technology-assisted. The small number of studies conducted on oral, peer and online feedback report that these types are deemed to have positive effects on instruction. As such, further understanding is needed of how they should be effectively incorporated in the classroom in terms techniques and strategies appropriate to each type and teachers' and students' attitudes. More attention should also be provided to online feedback as more investigation is required to better understand the implications of incorporating this technology-assisted feedback in the twenty-first century's classroom, its limitations and any possible challenges as well as the ways to overcome them. This is becoming of prime concern today, especially after the COVID-19 pandemic.

Another gap in feedback research relates to the rift between teachers' feedback knowledge and their classroom practices. Among the 37 articles reviewed in the study, no attempt was made to investigate feedback provision in teacher-education programs and how they relate to real-life educational settings. Researchers need to examine the contents of these programs and find whether they equip teacher-trainees with the necessary knowledge on feedback provision, and more importantly provide them with the techniques that help them translate that knowledge into their daily classroom practices. Investigating this area may provide an answer to the everlasting incongruence between teachers' feedback knowledge and classroom practices reported in several studies conducted across the region.

5 Implications for the Context and Conclusion

The present study set out to review the available literature on research on feedback in EFL classes in the MENA Region. The review of 37 articles selected for the study revealed that interest in feedback research is a novice field in the region. The majority of the research works were conducted between 2015 and 2020 in Saudi Arabia, Morocco and Iran. These studies focused on different areas which include feedback types, feedback effect, interaction in feedback provision, teachers' knowledge, beliefs and practices and students' attitudes towards feedback provision. 'Feedback effect' and 'feedback types' were the main areas investigated by researchers in the region.

The findings of the feedback research studies provide information on the aforementioned areas. All the studies investigating the effect of feedback on instruction conclude that feedback has a positive effect on the learners' achievement and motivation. Empirical studies provide statistical evidence of improvement in learners' performance thanks to feedback provision. Other studies emphasized the role of some types of feedback, especially technology-assisted feedback, in decreasing learners' inhibition and increasing their involvement in the classroom.

Findings about feedback types reveal the existence of some differences in terms of researchers' interest in the different types of feedback. Written feedback is the most commonly researched type, followed by oral corrective feedback, online feedback and peer feedback. Written feedback is described as effective in developing learners' language skills. Some concerns, however, were raised about quality of teachers' comments in terms of clarity and responsiveness to learners' needs. Oral feedback is also perceived as effective in improving learners' oral performance and increasing their motivation, but some references are made relating to the ability of the teachers to customize their feedback to needs of individual learners and learners' willingness and degree of involvement. Peer feedback is also rated as important in feedback provision as it fosters learners' independence and boosts their motivation. Some criticisms, however, were levelled in relation to the frequency of its use in the classroom and the trust students have in their peers' comments. As for online feedback, it is described as valuable and beneficial, especially in motivating learners and providing alternative solutions for teachers. Some studies though, referred to some unacceptable practices students often resort to when they are under time constraints. Some studies also investigated other types of feedback such as direct and indirect feedback, focused and unfocused feedback, and explicit and implicit feedback. The findings point to the effectiveness of these types and the differences between them in terms teachers use.

Findings about interaction during feedback provision mainly refer to teacher–student interaction and peer interaction. In teacher–student interaction, the relationship established between the teacher and the students is perceived as a prerequisite for the success of written interaction. Some studies report failure in this process related to lack of communication, feedback misinterpretation and unrealistic expectations. In oral interaction, the focus is on the timing of teachers' intervention and the difficulties of the management of oral interaction in the classroom. As for peer interaction, some studies focus on the role of motivation in increasing students' participation, while others refer to the lack of trust students have in this process.

In terms knowledge and beliefs about feedback, several studies report that most teachers possess the theoretical knowledge necessary for good feedback practices. They point, however, to the large discrepancies between teachers' feedback knowledge and their classroom practices. Some studies investigate the reasons behind this rift. They refer to factors including time constraints, number of students in each class, students' level and attitudes, as well as their motivation and commitment.

Students' attitudes to feedback provision are also investigated in the research works included in the study. Some of them refer to the students' positive perception of feedback, especially technology-assisted one. Other studies refer to the students' negative attitudes towards the feedback provided, which mainly relate to difficulties in understanding some of their teachers' comments and lack of trust in the quality of their peers' feedback.

The study also provides an overview of the gaps of research on feedback in EFL classes in the MENA region. These include the feedback areas which received little or no attention from researchers, namely feedback interaction, oral, peer and online feedback, and feedback contents in teacher education. These areas require more investigation in order to improve feedback practices in the region.

Finally, the present study does not claim itself exhaustive as it does not include all the research works undertaken about feedback in EFL classes in the MENA region. Some studies were conducted as part of M.A. or Ph.D. programs but not published online, and other studies were published but not detected by the search filter. However, the added value of this study resides in the opportunity it provides for researchers inside and outside the region. Though not totally accurate, the study provides a general overview on feedback research activity in the region in terms of geographical distribution, history and feedback areas investigated. The description of the feedback areas investigated by research works provides guidance on the areas that should receive ample attention in future research studies. The summary of the findings of previous studies can be used in future comparative studies conducted in L1, L2 or EFL contexts. Early-career researchers can also benefit from the study, as it helps them easily locate the research gaps in the field and later compare their findings with the results of previous studies.

References

*AbuSeileek, A. F. (2013). Using track changes and word processor to provide corrective feedback to learners in writing. *Journal of Computer Assisted Learning, 29,* 319–333.
*Ahmed, A. M. (2020). Feedback in EFL writing: Arab world contexts, issues, and challenges. In A. M. Ahmed, et al. (Eds.), *Feedback in L2 English writing in the Arab world* (pp. 1–31). London, UK: Palgrave Macmillan.

*Alahmadi, N., Alrahaili, M., & Alshraideh, D. (2019). The impact of the formative assessment in speaking test on Saudi students' performance. *Arab World English Journal (AWEJ), 10*(1), 259–270.

*Al Ajmi, A. A. S. (2015). The effect of written corrective feedback on Omani students' accuracy in the use of English prepositions. *Advances in Language and Literary Studies, 6*(1), 61–71.

*Al-Bakri, S. (2016). Written corrective feedback: Teachers' beliefs, practices and challenges in an Omani context. *Arab Journal of Applied Linguistics, 1*(1), 44–47.

*Al-Harbi, N., & Troudi, S. (2020). Supervisors' written feedback on Saudi postgraduate students' problems with academic English writing in selected UK universities. In A. M. Ahmed, et al. (Eds.), *Feedback in L2 English writing in the Arab world* (pp. 171–200). London, UK: Palgrave Macmillan.

*Al-Hazzani, N., & Altalhab, S. (2018). Can explicit written corrective feedback develop grammatical and lexical accuracy of Saudi EFL learners? *International Journal of Education & Literacy Studies, 6*(4), 16–24.

*Alhumidi, H. A., & Uba, S. Y. (2016). The effect of indirect written corrective feedback to Arabic language intermediate students' in Kuwait. *European Scientific Journal, 12*(28), 361–374.

*Ali, A. D. (2016). Effectiveness of using screencast feedback on EFL students' writing and perception. *English Language Teaching, 9*(8), 106–121.

Alimohammadi, B., & Nejadansari, D.(2014). Written corrective feedback: Focused and unfocused. *Theory and Practice in Language Studies, 4*(3), 581–587.

*Alkhammash, R., & Gulnaz, F. (2019). Oral corrective feedback techniques: An investigation of the EFL teachers' beliefs and practices at Taif University. *Arab World English Journal (AWEJ), 10*(2), 40–54.

*Alkhatib, N. (2015). *Written corrective feedback at a Saudi university: English language teachers' beliefs, students' preferences, and teachers' practices*. Unpublished Ph.D. thesis, University of Essex.

*Alnasser, S. M. N. (2018). Exploring student-writers' views on replacing teacher feedback with peer feedback and computer-based feedback. *Arab World English Journal (AWEJ), 9*(3), 345–366.

*Al-Saleh, N. A. (2018). *The impact of positive and corrective feedback via Showbie on Saudi students' English writing*. Master's thesis. *Arab World English Journal* (pp. 1–121). Al Imam Muhammad ibn Saud Islamic University, College of Languages and Translation, Department of English Language and Literature, KSA.

*Al-Sawalha, A. M. (2016). EFL Jordanian students' reaction to written comments on their written work: A case study. *Arab World English Journal (AWEJ), 7*(1), 63–77.

*Alshahrani, A., & Storch, N. (2014). Investigating teachers' written corrective feedback practices in a Saudi EFL context: How do they align with their beliefs, institutional guidelines, and students' preferences? *Australian Review of Applied Linguistics (ARAL), 37*(2), 101–122.

*Amara, T. M. (2015). Learners' perceptions of teacher written feedback commentary in an ESL writing classroom. *International Journal of English Language Teaching, 3*(2), 38–53.

*Amara, T. M. (2017). The effect of focused corrective feedback on ESL learners' writing accuracy. *Sabratha University Scientific Journal*, 4–19.

Arksey, H., & O'Malley, L. (2005). Scoping studies: Towards a methodological framework. *International Journal of Social Research Methodology, 8*(1), 19–32.

*Athimni, M. (2020). Feedback practices in university English writing classes in Tunisia: An exploratory study. In A. M. Ahmed, et al. (Eds.), *Feedback in L2 English writing in the Arab world* (pp. 139–170). London, UK: Palgrave Macmillan.

*Basabrin, A. (2019). Exploring EFL instructors and students perceptions of written corrective feedback on blackboard platform: A case study. *Arab World English Journal: Special Issue: Application of Global ELT Practices in Saudi Arabia*, 179–192.

Bitchener, J., & Storch, N. (2016). *Written corrective feedback for L2 development*. Bristol: Multilingual Matters.

Bitchener, J., Young, S., & Cameron, D. (2005). The effect of different types of corrective feedback on ESL student writing. *Journal of Second Language Writing, 14*(3), 191–205.

Chan, P. E., Konrad, M., Gonzalez, V., Peters, M. T., & Ressa, V. A. (2014). The critical role of feedback in formative instructional practices. *Intervention in School and Clinic, 50*(2), 96–104.

Chappuis, J., Stiggins, R., Chappuis, S., & Arter, J. (2012). *Classroom assessment for student learning: Doing it right—Using it well*. Upper Saddle River, NJ: Pearson.

*Daweli, T. W. (2018). Engaging Saudi EFL students in online peer review in a Saudi university context. *Arab World English Journal (AWEJ), 9*(4), 270–280.

*Dehdary, N., & Al-Saadi, H. (2020). Students' perceptions of 4D feedback treatment on EFL writing in Oman. In A. M. Ahmed, et al. (Eds.), *Feedback in L2 English writing in the Arab world* (pp. 65–88). London: Palgrave Macmillan.

Ellis, R. (2009). Corrective feedback and teacher development. *L2 Journal, 1*(1), 3–18.

Ellis, R., Basturkmen, H., & Loewen, S. (2001). Learner uptake in communicative ESL lessons. *Language Learning, 51,* 281–318.

Ellis, R., Loewen, S., & Erlam, R. (2006). Implicit and explicit corrective feedback and the acquisition of L2 grammar. *Studies in Second Language Acquisition, 28*(3), 339–368.

Eraut, M. (2000). Non-formal learning and tacit knowledge in professional work. *British Journal of Educational Psychology, 70*(1), 113–136.

Evans, C. (2013). Making sense of assessment feedback in higher education. *Review of Educational Research, 83*(1), 70–120.

*Farrokhi, F. (2011). Teachers' stated beliefs about corrective feedback in relation to their practices in EFL classes. *Research on Foreign Languages Journal of Faculty of Letters and Humanities, 200,* 91–131.

Farrokhi, F., & Sattarpour, S. (2011). The effects of focused and unfocused written corrective feedback on grammatical accuracy of Iranian EFL learners. *Theory and Practice in Language Studies, 1*(12), 1797–1803.

Ferris, D. R. (1995). Can advanced ESL students be taught to correct their most serious and frequent errors? *CATESOL Journal, 8*(1), 41–62.

Ferris, D. R., Chaney, S. J., Komura, K., Roberts, B. J., & McKee, S. (2000, March 14–18). *Perspectives, problems, and practices in treating written error*. In Colloquium presented at International TESOL Convention, Vancouver, BC.

Ferris, D. R., & Helt, M. (2000, March 11–14). *Was Truscott right? New evidence on the effects of error correction in L2 writing classes*. Paper presented at Proceedings of the American Association of Applied Linguistics Conference, Vancouver, BC.

Frear, D. (2010). The effect of focused and unfocused direct written corrective feedback on a new piece of writing. *College English: Issues and Trends, 3,* 59–71.

Hadzic, S. (2016). *Oral and written teacher feedback in an English as a foreign language classroom in Sweden*. Dissertation, Linnaeus University, Sweden.

Harmer, J. (1983). *The practice of English language teaching*. London: Longman.

Hattie, J., & Timperley, H. (2007). The power of feedback. *Review of Educational Research, 77*(1), 81–112.

Hyland, K., & Hyland, F. (2006). Feedback on second language students' writing. *Language Teaching, 39*(2), 83–101.

Kang, E. Y., & Han, Z. (2015). The efficacy of written corrective feedback in improving L2 written accuracy: A meta-analysis. *The Modern Language Journal, 99*(1), 1–18.

Karaağaçzan, G., & Yiğitoğlu, N. (2018). Exploring novice and experienced teachers' beliefs and practices of written feedback. *Journal of the Faculty of Education, 19*(2), 355–369.

*Karimi, M. N., & Asadnia, F. (2015). EFL teachers' beliefs about oral corrective feedback and their feedback-providing practices across learners' proficiency levels. *The Journal of Teaching Language Skills (JTLS), 7*(2), 39–68.

*Khorshidi, E., & Rassaei, E. (2013). The effects of learners' gender on their preferences for corrective feedback. *Journal of Studies in Learning and Teaching English, 1*(4), 71–83.

Lee, I. (2008a). Ten mismatches between teachers' beliefs and written feedback practice. *ELT Journal, 63*(1), 13–22.

Lee, I. (2008b). Understanding teachers' written feedback practices in Hong Kong secondary classrooms. *Journal of Second Language Writing, 17*, 69–85.

Liu, Y. (2008). The effects of error feedback in second language writing. *Arizona Working Papers in SLA & Teaching, 15*, 65–79.

Mays, N., Roberts, E., & Popay, J. (2001). Synthesising research evidence. In N. Fulop, P. Allen, A. Clarke, & N. Black (Eds.), *Studying the organisation and delivery of health services: Research methods* (pp. 188–219). London: Routledge.

Ouahidi, M., & Lamkhanter, F. (2020). Students' perceptions about teachers' written feedback on writing in a Moroccan university context. In A. M. Ahmed, et al. (Eds.), *Feedback in L2 English writing in the Arab world* (pp. 35–63). London, UK: Palgrave Macmillan.

Parr, J. M., & Limbrick, L. (2010). Contextualising practice: Hallmarks of effective teachers of writing. *Teaching and Teacher Education, 26*(3), 583–590.

Pham, M. T., Rajić, A., Greig, J. D., Sargeant, J. M., Papadopoulos, A., & McEwen, S. A. (2014). A scoping review of scoping reviews: advancing the approach and enhancing the consistency. *Research Synthesis Methods, 5*(4), 371–385.

Qi, D., & Lapkin, S. (2001). Exploring the role of noticing in a three-stage second language writing task. *Journal of Second Language Writing, 10*(4), 277–303.

*Reinders, H., & Mohebbi, H. (2018). Written corrective feedback: The road ahead. *Language Teaching Research Quarterly, 6,* 1–6.

Sadler, D. R. (1989). Formative assessment and the design of instructional systems. *Instructional Science, 18,* 119–144.

*Said, K., & El Mouzrati, A. (2018). Investigating teacher written corrective feedback as a formative assessment tool. *Arab World English Journal (AWEJ), 9*(4), 232–241.

*Sakale, S. (2017). The impact of wait time instruction and teaching experience on teachers' feedback in Moroccan speaking classes. *Arab World English Journal (AWEJ), 8*(2), 268–278.

*Sakale, S. (2019). The important role of teachers' feedback during speaking activities in Moroccan classes. *Arab World English Journal (AWEJ), 10*(3), 344–351.

*Sayed, S., & Curabba, B. (2020). Harnessing the power of feedback to assist progress: A process-based approach of providing feedback to L2 composition students in the United Arab Emirates. In A. M. Ahmed, et al. (Eds.), *Feedback in L2 English writing in the Arab world* (pp. 89–110). London: Palgrave Macmillan.

*Seliem, S., & Ahmed, A. (2009). *Missing: Electronic feedback in Egyptian EFL essay writing classes*. Paper presented at CDELT 29th Conference, Conference Occasional Papers, Faculty of Education, Ain-Shams University, Egypt.

Sheppard, K. (1992). Two feedback types: Do they make a difference? *RELC Journal, 23*(1), 103–110.

*Shaqaqi, M., & Soleimani, H. (2018). Effects of asynchronous and conventional paper-and-pen metalinguistic feedback on L2 learners' use of verb tense. *Journal of Modern Research in English Language Studies, 5*(3), 55–72.

*Shawish, J. I. A., & Al-Raheem, M. A. A. (2015). Palestinian university writing professors' feedback practices and students' reactions towards them. *Journal of Teaching and Teacher Education, 3*(1), 57–73.

Sheen, Y. (2010). Differential effects of oral and written corrective feedback in the ESL classroom. *Studies in Second Language Acquisition, 32*(2), 203–234.

Sheen, Y., & Ellis, R. (2011). Corrective feedback in language teaching. In E. Hinkel (Ed.), *Handbook of research in second language teaching and learning* (2nd ed., pp. 593–610). New York: Routledge.

Swain, M. (2000). The output hypothesis and beyond: Mediating acquisition through collaborative dialogue. In J. P. Lantolf (Ed.), *Sociocultural theory and second language learning* (pp. 97–114). Oxford: Oxford University Press.

Wanchid, R. (2015). Different sequences of feedback types: Effectiveness, attitudes, and preferences. *Journal of Language Teaching and Learning in Thailand, 50,* 31–46.

Zohrabi, K., & Ehsani, F. (2014). The role of implicit & explicit corrective feedback in Persian-speaking EFL learners' awareness of and accuracy in English Grammar. *Procedia—Social and Behavioral Sciences, 98,* 2018–2024.

*Zouaidi, C., & Hermessi, T. (2019). The role of intrinsic motivation and oral corrective feedback in the EFL classroom. In S. Hidri (Ed.), *English language teaching research in the Middle East and North Africa* (pp. 431–454). Cham: Palgrave Macmillan.

*Zyad, H., & Bouziane, A. (2020). The effect of EFL correction practices on developing Moroccan students' English writing skills. In A. M. Ahmed, et al. (Eds.), *Feedback in L2 English writing in the Arab world* (pp. 113–138). London, UK: Palgrave Macmillan.

Using Research Methods to Capture the Nature of Writing Proficiency and its Assessment

Spelling Errors in the Preliminary English B1 Exam: Corpus-Informed Evaluation of Examination Criteria for MENA Contexts

Niall Curry and Tony Clark

1   Introduction

This chapter presents the analysis of written learner language in different MENA contexts in order to add to the literature on corpus linguistics for language testing and assessment. To do so, first this chapter presents relevant research on corpus linguistics, testing and assessment, and learner corpus research. Building on these broader linguistic contexts, research on spelling and assessment in Arabic-speaking contexts is then discussed. The novelty in this research pertains to the study of spelling errors in the error-annotated component of the *Cambridge Learner Corpus*, which is a 30-million-word corpus of learner language from the Cambridge English language examinations. This study focuses on comparing spelling errors from 5 subcorpora of the *Cambridge Learner Corpus* which capture

---

N. Curry (✉)
Coventry University, Coventry, UK
e-mail: niall.curry@coventry.ac.uk

T. Clark
Cambridge Assessment, Cambridge, UK

© The Author(s) 2020
L. McCallum and C. Coombe (eds.), *The Assessment of L2 Written English across the MENA Region*, https://doi.org/10.1007/978-3-030-53254-3_15

written examinations of Arabic speakers and a larger reference subcorpus of non-Arabic speakers. More specifically, these include subcorpora from Libya and the United Arab Emirates which are compared with other texts produced by other Arabic speakers, and all other speakers from the B1 preliminary exam subcorpora, in order to test for variation across variety of Arabic speaking contexts and different first language backgrounds.

In the context of the Preliminary English B1 exam, spelling errors are contrasted in order to illustrate that while similarities do occur in exam takers across and beyond MENA contexts, spelling errors are particularly salient among Arabic speakers. Spelling errors were chosen as they occur frequently in each subcorpus and are under investigated in Arabic speaking users of English (Abu-Rabia & Taha, 2006), at least from a corpus linguistics perspective. To address this gap, two case studies on spelling errors are presented, focussing on misspelled verbs and misspelled words that begin with 'wh/w'. The findings are then considered in terms of the assessment criteria for the Preliminary English B1 exam with the aim to produce and deliver guidance on how assessment criteria could be localised for MENA contexts.

2 Literature Review

2.1 Corpus Linguistics and Language Pedagogy

Corpus linguistics has made and continues to make strong contributions to many areas of language pedagogy. These contributions can be seen as indirect—informing materials used to teach/learn language—and direct—allowing users to directly access and analyse corpus data. This chapter is concerned with a lesser studied area of indirect applications of corpus linguistics to language pedagogy i.e. language testing and assessment. Looking back to the 'corpus revolution' of the 1980s (Rundell & Stock, 1992), corpus linguistics made significant contributions to lexicography and nowadays it is commonplace for reference material for language learning, such as dictionaries and grammars, to be corpus-informed (Hunston, 2002, p. 96). In fact, everyday teachers and learners, who may never have heard of a corpus, are using corpus-informed material. Lexicographers, for example, have profited extensively from corpora (Römer, 2011) which, according to Hunston (2002), can help lexicographers decide how to present entries, basing decisions on frequency, collocation and phraseology, variation, lexis/grammar, and authenticity among other things. Similarly, other reference materials, such as grammar, are also often informed by corpora and an extensive study of such grammar can be seen in McEnery and Xiao (2005) where non-corpus-informed grammar are seen to contain biases. The *Longman Grammar of Spoken and Written English* (Biber, Johansson, Leech, Conrad, & Finegan, 2012) or the *Cambridge Grammar of English* (Carter & McCarthy, 2013) are of particular note as, due to corpus intervention, they arguably give more accurate and authentic examples, contextualised examples and real descriptions, based, not on rationalistic thinking, but empirical research.

Beyond reference material, a corpus approach to syllabus development is also a noteworthy indirect application. Evidently, for corpus-based syllabi to be effective, corpus-based materials are a prerequisite (Mishan, 2005). Corpus-based materials such as the *Touchstone* series of English language textbooks (McCarthy, McCarten, & Sandiford, 2004–2006) are a good example of the indirect use of corpora in informing language teaching materials. They are based on the *Cambridge Reference Corpus* and the *Cambridge Learner Corpus* and 'present vocabulary, grammar and functions students encounter most often in real life' (McEnery & Xiao, 2011, p. 367).

A further indirect application of corpus linguistics can be seen in its incorporation into teacher training where it has exhibited extremely positive results. In such cases 'corpus evidence [can] address teachers' questions' (Tsui, 2006, p. 57) and raise awareness. Researchers like O'Keeffe and Farr (2012) have seen corpora as tools to improve teachers' knowledge, efficacy, and insight and in so doing develop teaching expertise. Knowledge, for example, may be acquired through increased awareness of how corpora work. Others such as Frankenberg-Garcia (2012) highlight how task-based approaches to teaching teachers about corpus linguistics can also raise awareness, for example. This improved awareness could help improve teaching efficacy as seen in studies such as

Abdelkader, Boumiza, and Braham's (2010) study, which highlights how corpora can help improve teaching efficiency in online Arabic learning environments. Finally, insight can be invoked through 'the study of naturally occurring classroom discourse [that can] provide student teachers with a valuable resource' (Amador Moreno Carolina, Chambers, & Riordan, 2006 p. 99).

Most pertinent here however, is the indirect application of language corpora to language testing. The field of language testing and assessment 'is concerned with the development of valid and reliable assessments that measure language ability through specific tasks for particular purposes' (Barker, Salamoura, & Saville, 2015). The role of corpora in language testing and assessment could be considered a relatively emerging field (Callies & Götz, 2015; Park, 2014) where corpora are now being used 'to make inferences about language ability and capacity for' learners to use a language (Chapelle & Plakans, 2013, p. 241). This movement allows us to move away from assessment based on more dated criteria towards a data-driven approach to language assessment (Callies & Götz, 2015). Some corpora, such as *the Cambridge Learner Corpus* (2016), *the Michigan Corpus of Academic Spoken English* (MICASE) (Simpson, Briggs, Ovens, & Swales, 2002) or *The Marburg Corpus of Intermediate Learner English* (MILE) (Kreyer, 2015) have been developed with language testing in mind (Kreyer, 2015). This has been a reaction to the movement to incorporate corpora in syllabi and materials development, where researchers believe that if we use corpora to inform our teaching, we must respond to this in our assessments (O'Keeffe, McCarthy, & Carter, 2007). In language testing, corpora have allowed us to build a collection of exam scripts which can help inform learner corpus research, as seen in Barker et al.'s (2015) work on language testing and assessment, and learner corpora. Their work is exemplary of how the role of corpora in language assessment has emerged, owing to previously theoretically weak approaches to the definition of the Common European Framework of Reference for Languages (CEFR) bandscale descriptors. Traditionally such descriptors were often based on teachers' perception of language and language skills that constituted a specific level. Corpora offered a more empirical and evidence-informed approach, based on examples of learner production. Other studies in the field have similarly used learner corpus research to develop test material, as seen in Qin, Du, Tao, and Qiu (2016) who look at corpora as a means to develop speech testing, or Banerjee, Yan, Chapman, and Elliott, (2015) who look at corpora as a means to effectively assess writing and standardise testing. Barker et al. (2015) discuss the role of *the Cambridge Learner Corpus* for informing language testing and assessment, by showing what learners can do at particular levels. They discuss how the corpus can be used to inform test design through demographic contextual metadata, and through task rating with error analysis and corpus annotation. Building on this and the many other studies referred to here, this chapter presents the analysis of spelling errors in written examinations in 5 subcorpora of the *Cambridge Learner Corpus* in order to inform assessment criteria specific to MENA contexts.

2.2 Spelling and Arabic-Speaking Contexts

Before the results are explored and discussed in detail, there are several points about the differences between English and varieties of Arabic to be noted—if their implications are to be understood in context. Firstly, all 28 Arabic letters represent consonants—the majority of the consonantal phonemes also appear in English, and most English phonemes feature in Arabic too (Allaith & Joshi, 2011). It should also be clarified that the language can be split into spoken Arabic and Standard Arabic; the latter has both spoken and written forms. Error analysis regarding spelling challenges among Arabic-speaking learners of English has indicated that phonological differences between Arabic and English can be used to predict spelling errors (Allaith & Joshi, 2011), and such errors can be categorised as insertion, omission, substitution or transposition errors. This means that learners might add a letter, omit a letter, change a letter for another or rearrange the order of letters in words, respectively (Al-Zuoud & Kabilan, 2013). Therefore, the role of the L1 in predicting errors is well established (Randall, 2005) and in their development of the BUiD corpus, Randall and Groom (2009) found evidence for many of the errors produced by Arabic speaking learners of English were categorised according to a range of orthographical and phonological possible causes for spelling errors. As such, the phenomenon of L1 interference for influencing spelling errors is deep-rooted; however, from another perspective, so too is the target language phonological interference, where the sounds of English impact on the accuracy of spelling among learners, and in the case of Alhaisoni, Al-Zuoud, and Gaudel (2015), to an even greater degree than L1 interference.

As the current study focuses on learners from Arabic-speaking contexts, these distinctions should be borne in mind. The research identified and described here offers a valuable insight into common spelling errors for these national groups, but it is not to be assumed that this can necessarily be transferred to other Arabic-speaking countries. Further investigation is required if that is to be conclusively established. This important caveat highlights the complexities of contemporary assessment in the MENA region. As will be described, research is beginning to help practitioners better understand the implications of linguistic variance. If test development is to be adequately informed, robust research is required to support decision making on aspects such as marking criteria. This research can potentially help assessment bodies to accommodate speakers of different first languages and from regional or national varieties of these first languages, and, in so doing, ensure appropriate test fairness. The Arabic-speaking world (and English education and exam practices within that) provide an excellent case study of the challenges this would entail. Before addressing these issues, the corpora used in this study must be described.

3 Data

3.1 Corpus Data: The Cambridge Learner Corpus

The *Cambridge Learner Corpus* is a 55-million-word corpus of keyed students' written responses to Cambridge English exams. This paper is based on the 30-million word error-annotated component of that corpus. The construction of this corpus has been ongoing for over 20 years and a detailed description of its construction is presented in Nicholls (2003).

Here, owing to limitations of space, a brief description of the corpus, its error annotation, and the subcorpora used herein are presented.

This corpus has been jointly constructed by Cambridge University Press and Cambridge Assessment and, to-date, amasses 55 million words of learner English. This learner English is taken from transcriptions of students' examination essays, which have been produced by over 200,000 students from 173 countries around the world. Alongside the text captured, the corpus also contains metadata, such as students' first language, nationality, exam, CEFR level of exam, CEFR level of student performance, year of taking exam, educational levels, age, years of English study, gender, and whether or not the student passed or failed. The error-coded component of the corpus currently contains 30 million words. It is on this error tagged part of the corpus that this analysis is based.

For error tagging, Hawkins and Buttery (2010), Hawkins and Filipovic (2012), and Nicholls (2003) outline in detail the annotation process and a taxonomy of errors tags in the Cambridge Learner Corpus, which are manually added by trained linguists. The corpus is also part-of-speech tagged by the Robust Accurate Statistical Parser (RASP; Briscoe, Carroll, & Watson, 2006), using the CLAWS2 tagset.

3.2 Subcorpora from the B1 Preliminary Exam

This study used the exam scripts from subcorpora containing the B1 Preliminary exam, formerly known as Cambridge English: Preliminary Exam Test (PET), in which learner performance was at B1 CEFR level. This excludes learners who scored below B1 and above B1 when taking this exam. The B1 Preliminary exam was chosen as the area of focus for a number of reasons. First, in the context of Arabic speakers, B1 Preliminary level texts in the *Cambridge Learner Corpus* account for the largest number of Arabic speaker texts in the corpus. As such, it makes sense to focus specifically on this level. Second, in order to avoid including too many variables in the subcorpora chosen, the decision was made to focus only on the B1 Preliminary level. This makes for a clearer comparison across varieties of Arabic and other first languages. Later in this section, Figs. 1, 2, 3, and 4 show that there are several metadata that account for variations within the samples the B1 Preliminary exam. Further examinations and levels, for example, would increase the differences in the samples studied, which would afford less clarity for comparison.

Within the *Cambridge Learner Corpus*, specifically, this study used a subcorpus of B1 Preliminary exam by Arabic speakers from Libya (PALB1), B1 Preliminary exam by Arabic speakers from the United Arab Emirates (PAUAEB1), B1 Preliminary exam by other Arabic speakers in

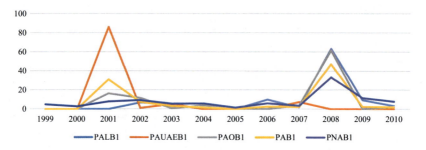

Fig. 1 Years of exam scripts per subcorpus in percentage

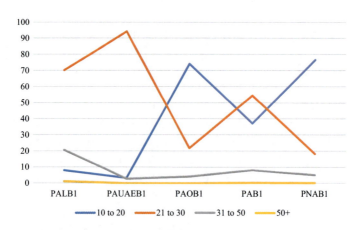

Fig. 2 Ages of exam takers per subcorpus in percentage

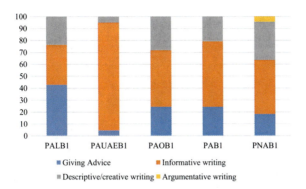

Fig. 3 Type of writing per subcorpus in percentage

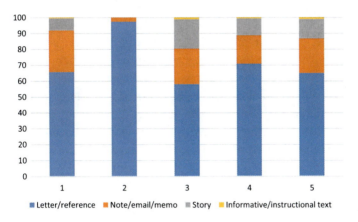

Fig. 4 Task type per subcorpus in percentage

the Cambridge Learner Corpus (PAOB1),[1] B1 Preliminary exam by all Arabic speakers in the Cambridge Learner Corpus (PAB1),[2] and all other B1 Preliminary exam by non-Arabic speakers (PNAB1).[3] Table 1 shows the size of each subcorpus studied. It was deemed important to also look across regions as a variable, as this can allow for considerations of varietal

---

[1] See Appendix 1 and Fig. 7 for a list of countries represented in PAOB1.
[2] See Appendix 2 and Fig. 8 for a list of countries represented in PAB1.
[3] See Appendix 3 and Fig. 9 for a list of first languages represented in PNAB1.

Table 1 Size of subcorpora of B1 preliminary for libyan Arabic, UAE Arabic, remaining Arabic speakers, all Arabic speakers and non-Arabic speakers

Corpus	Tokens
PALB1	10251
PAUAEB1	10542
PAOB1	17779
PAB1	38572
PNAB1	1633214

differences as well as contextualisation of education within geo-political boundaries.

While at first glance some of these subcorpora may appear small, they are extremely specialised owing to their explicit focus on subcorpora containing the B1 Preliminary exam from Arabic speakers. Following Aston (2001, p. 30), small specialised corpora can boast advantages and can be heavily patterned. As such, they can produce valuable insights into language use in the respective areas of language they represent (Aston, 2001, p. 30). Within these specialised subcorpora there are rich metadata which allow for a better understanding of the exam context. These metadata are now briefly presented, starting with Fig. 1, which shows the years in which the exam texts studied in each subcorpus were written.

Overall, most subcorpora peak in 2001 and 2008 with a steadier distribution in between and following these years. In terms of the ages of the exam takers in each subcorpus, Fig. 2 shows the range where most exam takers are aged between 10 and 30 in each subcorpus. While age does appear to be an important variable, the main difference is the absence of younger exam takers in PALB1 and PAUAEB1 when compared to the other subcorpora.

In terms of writing type, Fig. 3 shows the different types of writing completed across the subcorpora, where the majority of subcorpora here use informative writing. These ensures that the data are reasonably comparable. In terms of task type, most tasks completed were letter writing tasks, as can be seen in Fig. 4. Letter writing tasks are identified by the need for students to write a letter, often to a friend, as part of a writing task. This may contain elements of texts that are informative or instructional, for example. However, the key difference is the purpose of the task. Letter tasks serve to demonstrate students' ability to write in such a genre, while informative or instructional texts are tasks that require students to comment on topics or deliver advice and information in essay like formats.

Overall, these metadata serve to further illustrate the context in which the exam texts in each subcorpus were written. Next, the analysis of errors is presented, focusing on the identification of errors, the analysis of spelling errors, and the presentation of two case studies on misspelled words.

4 Analysis, Results, and Discussion

4.1 Corpus Analysis: Errors Identified

Using Sketch Engine, each corpus was searched for all errors by searching '#.*'. What was retrieved was used to identify highly occurring errors, which were then analysed using both quantitative and qualitative approaches. Table 2 shows the top 5 errors in each subcorpus of the *Cambridge Learner Corpus* in words per 10,000 words. What emerges is the shared nature of errors that occur most frequently in each subcorpus. This is especially interesting given the varied metadata presented in Figs. 1, 2, 3, and 4.

While frequency is certainly a guiding factor, it is important to consider these data, presented in Table 2, in the wider context. Many of these errors are of note and are worthy of consideration. However, the rationale for the focus on spelling errors in this chapter is based both on their frequency as an error type as well as spelling errors being an area of error research that has remained somewhat under investigated in studies on Arabic-speaking users of English, from a corpus linguistic perspective. Moreover, while syntax and lexical choice are likely to be influenced by the varied task types presented in Figs. 3 and 4, spelling is less likely to be impacted by the task type. As such, only spelling is considered here, which minimises the impact of differing corpus construction on the findings. For spelling, distribution across the corpora was checked in order to test for significance and dispersion tests were applied to bolster the

Table 2 Top 5 errors in each subcorpus

Errors identified

PALB1		PAUAEB1		PAOB1		PAB1		PNAB1	
Error	Freq. per 10k	Error	Freq. per 10k	Error	Freq. per 10k	Error	Freq. per 10k	Error	Freq. per 10k
#RP—replace punctuation	256	#RP—replace punctuation	157	#MP—missing punctuation	160	#RP—replace punctuation	140	#RP—replace punctuation	91
#MP—missing punctuation	106	#S.*—spelling error	135	#S.*—spelling error	104	#S.*—spelling error	113	#TV—incorrect tense of verb	59
#TV—incorrect tense of verb	91	#TV—incorrect tense of verb	98	#TV—incorrect tense of verb	98	#MP—missing punctuation	81	#S.*—spelling error	67
#S.*—spelling error	82	#R—replace error	94	#MP—missing punctuation	88	#TV—incorrect tense of verb	65	#MP—missing punctuation	47
#UP—unnecessary punctuation	67	#MP—missing punctuation	93	#RV—replace verb	60	#RV—replace verb	53	#RV—replace verb	47

statistical analysis and ensure that outliers did not skew the data. This is important as through these tests we can determine that the corpus did not contain texts that overly skewed the data, and we could determine that spelling errors were normally distributed across all the texts in the data. Subsequently, spelling errors were analysed in terms of word class and most common errors.

4.2 Spelling Errors: Corpus Findings

Focusing on spelling, Table 3 shows the number of errors in each subcorpus per 10,000 words.

Comparing the distribution of errors across these corpora, Fig. 5 shows the 95% confidence intervals for the distribution of errors across the 5 subcorpora and Fig. 6 shows a boxplot of distribution. The value of these dispersion tests is discussed next.

Focusing on Fig. 5, spelling errors appear to be distributed similarly in the Libyan and Emirati corpora and there is no significant difference in their dispersion within their texts. This is understandable given that spelling errors occur in 66.67% of texts in PALB1 and 69.09% of texts in PAUAEB1, and that their dispersion measured at a 0.88 and a 0.9 Julian's D score, respectively, 'which normalizes the coefficient of variation into the range (0,1)' (Coats 2019, p.24). This means that there is an even dispersion of errors across the two subcorpora and that they are not overly skewed by outliers. Focusing on the red line in Fig. 6, both subcorpora also show a similar mean of 2.36 and 2.45 spelling errors respectively per text in every 10,000 words. However, when considering

Table 3 Spelling errors per corpus per 10,000 words

Corpus	Spelling errors per 10,000 words
PALB1	82
PAUAEB1	135
PAOB1	104
PAB1	113
PNAB1	67

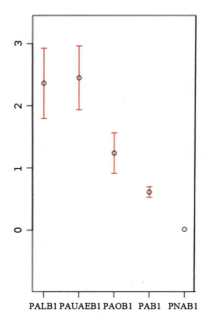

Fig. 5 95% confidence interval for spelling errors across subcorpora

spelling errors in PAOB1, PAB1, and PNAB1, there is a notable difference, where the significance of the spelling error drops for each corpus. This is especially interesting given that both PALB1 and PAUAEB1 contain texts written by exam takers who are largely of the age range 21–30, while PAOB1 and PNAB1 contain texts written by exam takers who are largely of the age range 10–20. In essence, this means that spelling errors in both PALB1 and PAUAEB1 represent a significant number of errors and spelling for these learners is potentially a greater challenge. Spelling errors in PAOB1 appear less significant and only occur in 44.58% of texts, at a mean value of 1.25 errors per text in every 10,000 words and with a normal distribution of 0.87 Julian's D. In PAB1 spelling errors are even less significant with a range of 24.04% of texts, a mean value of 0.61 errors per text in every 10,000 words, and a Julian's D score of 0.93 representing a normal distribution. Most noticeable here is PNAB1 which represents all Preliminary B1 exams completed by learners with languages other than English. PNAB1, comparably, does not see

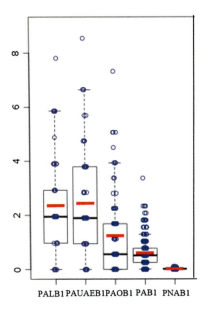

Fig. 6 Boxplot of spelling error distribution across subcorpora

spelling errors as particularly significant despite their normal distribution of 0.99 Julian's D score. Therefore, learners in Libya and the United Arab Emirates appear to encounter greater challenges with spelling at B1 level.

When looking at the specific spelling errors identified, Table 4 shows the top 5 errors per part-of-speech (PoS) per 10,000 words.

What emerges of note here is the consistency in the top 5 spelling mistakes being some ranking of nouns, adverbs, adjectives, verbs and prepositions, with nouns as the most commonly misspelled words in each subcorpus. Errors ranked from 2 to 4 are either adverbs, adjectives or verbs, with prepositions at number 5 in each subcorpus. Although other errors did occur, as in most corpus studies, we begin to see steep drop off on data as the list continues. Overall, consistent with the findings discussed in Figs. 5 and 6, PNAB1 contains relatively fewer examples of errors when compared to the 4 Arabic subcorpora. This further supports the view that spelling is a significant challenge for Arabic speakers. Given

Table 4 Top 5 parts of speech in which spelling errors occur in each subcorpus per 10,000 words

Parts of speech in which spelling errors occur

PALB1		PAUAEB1		PAOB1		PAB1		PNAB1	
PoS	Freq. per 10k	PoS	Freq. per 10k	PoS	Freq. per 10k	PoS	Freq. per 10k	PoS	Freq. per 10k
Nouns	41	Nouns	70	Nouns	42	Nouns	50	Nouns	1.2
Adverbs	16	Adjectives	21	Verbs	52	Adjectives	33	Adjectives	0.8
Adjectives	15	Adverbs	19	Adjectives	19	Verbs	26	Verbs	0.6
Verbs	14	Verbs	17	Adverbs	4	Adverbs	6	Adverbs	0.2
Preposition	11	Preposition	2	Preposition	4	Preposition	5	Preposition	0.1
Total	97	Total	127	Total	121	Total	120	Total	2.9

the infrequency of spelling errors in PNAB1, Table 5 shows the 10 most commonly misspelled words in PALB1, PAUAEB1, PAOB1, and PAB1 only. Note that in Appendix 4, Table 6 contains the top 10 spelling errors in PNAB1 in words per 10,000. Table 7 shows that the same spelling

Table 5 Top 10 most commonly misspelled words in each Arabic subcorpus per 10,000 words

PALB1		PAUAEB1		PAOB1		PAB1	
Word	Freq. per 10k	Word	Freq. per 10k	Word	Freq. per 10k	Word	Freq. per 10k
Whether	3	Centres	7	Centre	2.8	Centre	2.6
Programme	3	Here	5	Teacher	2.2	Centres	2.3
Centre	3	Museum	4	Because	2.2	Because	1.8
Because	3	Famous	4	Tomorrow	1.7	Beautiful	1.8
Town	2	Weather	3	Programme	1.7	Received	1.6
Together	2	Restaurant	3	Beautiful	1.7	Programme	1.6
Recommend	2	Mountains	3	Wearing	1.1	Famous	1.6
Received	2	Beautiful	3	Was	1.1	Museum	1.3
Later	2	Centre	3	Then	1.1	Here	1.3
Experience	2	Where	2	Sincerely	1.1	Whether	1.0

Table 6 Top 10 most commonly misspelled verbs in each Arabic subcorpus per 10,000 words

PALB1		PAUAEB1		PAOB1		PAB1	
Word	Freq. per 10k	Word	Freq. per 10k	Word	Freq. per 10k	Word	Freq. per 10k
Recommend	2	Centres	3	Wearing	1	Received	2
Received	2	Recommend	2	Was	1	Recommend	1
Realised	1	Received	2	Received	1	Centres	1
Qualified	1	Organised	2	Postpone	1	Wearing	1
Prepare	1	Climb	2	Believe	1	Was	1
Prefer	1	Waiting	1	've	1	Postpone	1
Jogging	1	Varied	1	Write	1	Organised	1
Is	1	Riding	1	Were	1	Introduced	1
Introduced	1	Read	1	Visit	1	Climb	1
Introduce	1	Describe	1	Understand	1	Believe	1

mistakes are much less frequent in all other B1 Preliminary examinations taken by non-Arabic speakers when compared to Table 5. This is unsurprising given that Figs. 5 and 6 show significant differences in the presence of spelling mistakes between Arabic and non-Arabic speakers.

Unlike the grouping of PoS in Table 4, Table 5 shows greater heterogeneity. There are fewer individual words that are frequently misspelled. Among those misspellings that recur are words like centre or centres, programme, whether, weather, museum, because, and received. Taking a more qualitative view, two errors are presented in greater detail. First, spelling errors in verbs are discussed and second, errors in words beginning with 'wh/w' are considered in more detail.

4.3 Case Study #1: Misspelled Verbs

In terms of verbs, in order to capture all spelling errors in verbs, the following search was queried: [tag = "V.*"] within < corr type = "#S.*"/> . This shows all verbs which are part of a correction tag where the error made was related to spelling. Normalised to 10,000 words, Table 6 shows the most commonly misspelled verbs in the 4 Arabic speaker subcorpora.

Initial reviews of the errors appear to show a range of words that are misspelled with no evident relationship between them. Taking a more qualitative view and following Al-Zuoud and Kabilan's (2013) taxonomy for categorising written errors as either insertion, omission, substitution and transposition—related spelling errors, some interesting trends were identified. While the likes of insertion errors did occur, there was only one example among these top 10 misspelled verbs:

> Well, if you prefere | prefer to go with your friends, I think you should talk to your parents about that. (PALB1)

Here the 'e' is added to prefer. However, more interesting are omission, substitution and transposition related spelling errors, which will now be briefly discussed.

In terms of omission, there were a number of examples with verbs like 'prepare', 'was', 'postpone', and 'have' in its contracted form 've'.

> I heard that you should prepar | prepare yourself before the final exam. (PALB1)

> I'm really sorry to tell you, but it is necessary to pospouon | postpone our meeting for a few hours. (PAOB1)

> Dear Mary, I'v | I've just arrived here on my holiday in India. (PAOB1)

In the case of these errors by omission, 'prepare', 'postpone' and 'have' in its contracted form 've' contain a letter which is not pronounced i.e. 'prepare' in standard British English /prɪˈpeər/[4] and standard American English /prɪˈper/ both end with the sound /r/where the grapheme 'e' is not pronounced. Similarly, the contraction 'I've' ends in standard British English as /-v/ or /-əv/ and in standard American English as /-v/ /-əv/, again with an 'e' not needing to be pronounced. For postpone, in the case of omission, it is the letter 't' that is problematic, where among the standard British English pronunciations /pəʊstˈpəʊn/ or /pəstˈpəʊn/ and the standard American pronunciation /poʊstˈpoʊn/ there is always a /t/ which is usually dropped in connected speech (Alameen & Levis, 2015, p. 155). Therefore, following Allaith and Joshi (2011) and Abu-Rabia and Taha (2006), the pronunciation of these words appears to interfere with their spelling by Arabic speakers. For the other examples of omission, there is spelling confusion where vowels are dropped in the place of a schwa /ə/:

> And I have orgnised | organised a lot of interesting things to do for the rest of the holiday. (PAUAEB1)

> In the morning I will vist |visit the centre and museum. (PAOB1)

---

[4]Note that the Cambridge Dictionary was used to capture phonetic transcriptions used in the chapter. This dictionary is available at: https://dictionary.cambridge.org/ [Last accessed: 1.8.2019].

Or, as in the following examples, where two vowels letters are used, often to represent a diphthong:

> I'm wating | waiting for you to write to me. (PAUAEB1)

> Suddenly, she saw a person waring | wearing the same hat that the man she was looking for was waring | wearing. (PAOB1)

> About the weather, you won't belive | believe how the weather is here. (PAOB1)

Therefore, vowels sounds that are reduced or combined seem to pose challenges for Arabic learners' spelling of the words in which they occur.

For substitution, a number of spelling errors occur, where consonant letters are replaced with other consonants, as in the following examples:

> So, why don't you go there with your friends? The food there id | is delicious as you know and the people are very friendly. (PALB1)

> Next week, I have decided to climp | climb some mountains and take some pictures from the top. (PAUAEB1)

> I hope you understant | understand. (PAOB1)

The errors with letters 'd', 'p', and 't' are consistent with Arabic learner errors reported in Allaith and Joshi (2011, pp. 1100–1101) who found that 'the absence of some phonemes from Arabic has a negative effect on its speakers' spelling of novel English phonemes'. Further substitution is evident in schwa /ə/related challenges, where an attempt to replicate graphically the sound of the schwa was made:

> We intreduced | introduced ourselves and then we started our lesson. (PALB1)

Finally, for transposition, a number of diphthong related spelling errors appear to occur in the subcorpora:

They interveiwed | interviewed our head-teacher and some good students. (PALB1)

I relaised | realised that after I was on the train. (PALB1)
   Dear friend, I was happy to have recieved | received your letter in which you explained to me about what your parents want. (PAUAEB1)

I'm really sorry to tell you this, but it is necessary to pospouon | postpone our meeting for a few hours. (PAOB1)

I went running to my friend to warn him but he didn't beleive | believe me and thought I was joking. (PAOB1)

Among these errors, again, there is a clear consistency surrounding errors with vowel sounds, where the vowels are inverted or in a different position to the corrected form. This again supports the relationship between phonological challenges and spelling errors among Arabic speaking learners of English (Al-Zuoud & Kabilan, 2013).

4.4 Case Study #2: Spelling Errors in Words Beginning with 'W/Wh'

Drawing on the most commonly misspelled words in Table 5, the word 'whether' has been misspelled in multiple ways, such as 'wether' and 'wheither'. The following examples illustrate this in practice:

Thanks a lot for your letter. I haven't heard from you for ages. You wanted me to give you advice about wheither | whether you should go with your family or with your friends. (PALB1)

I hope that you will have good time on your holiday wether | whether you go with your friends or with your parents. (PALB1)

PAUAEB1 also shows issues with the word 'weather', which is misspelled like whether with 'wether'

I bought some clothes for the cold wether | weather. PAUAEB1

Interestingly a further 'wh/w' spelling errors occur with 'where' in PAUAEB1, e.g.:

I would like to tell you more about the place were | where we are staying.

While of course these words differ, they do share phonological traits, which have been found to be a primary cause for spelling errors among Arabic learners of English (Abu-Rabia & Taha, 2006). As 'whether' and 'weather' are homophones in standard British English /ˈweð.ər/[5] and standard American English /ˈweð.ɚ/, it would appear that the 'wh/w' words are problematic for Arabic learners. Arguably, with the 'wh' consonant cluster at the beginning of 'whether' sounding the same as the 'w' at the beginning of 'weather', the errors appear to be linked to the relationship between phoneme and grapheme. The same can be seen with 'were' and 'where' where, although the pronunciations do differ, the initial sound for each word (/w/) is followed by vowel sounds such as /eə/, /e/, /ɜː/, /ə/, or, /ɚ/. As such, the 'h' in the 'wh' words is dropped. This omission of the 'h' grapheme is also consistent with Al-Zuoud and Kabilan (2013) who found that the majority of spelling errors among Arabic learners were omission errors. It is also of note that through conducting key word analyses of the subcorpora of PALB1, PAUAEB1, PAOB1, and PAB1 with PNAB1, none of the 'wh/w' are key to Arabic speakers. Therefore, Arabic speaking learners of English do not use these words in a noticably more frequent manner than non-Arabic first language speaking learners and it is not through increased usage that these omission errors were made.

---

[5]Note that the Cambridge Dictionary was used to capture phonetic transcriptions used in the chapter. This dictionary is available at: https://dictionary.cambridge.org/ [Last accessed: 1.8.2019].

4.5 Summary of Corpus Findings

Overall, this corpus analysis has shown that spelling errors are significant among Arabic first language speakers of English, and especially among those in Libya and the United Arab Emirates. Moreover, in these contexts, it appears that learners aged between 21 and 30 produce many of these errors, which is a finding not shared by the learners represented in the other subcorpora. Therefore, it is difficult to identify whether regional variety of Arabic, teaching and learning cultures, or age and learner profile render spelling for learners in this region particularly problematic. Naturally, this is beyond the scope of a corpus-based analysis. However, this does raise interesting questions that are worthy of academic pursuit.

In terms of the specific findings, a range of open class words are commonly misspelled i.e. nouns, adjectives, adverbs, and verbs. The two case studies of verbs and common words beginning with 'wh/w' take a more qualitative perspective and bolster the view that:

> Arab students, in general, have spelling problems because of the differences between English and Arabic sound systems (such as, the number and quality of vowels and diphthongs, consonant clusters in word initial, medial and final positions and the Arabic diacritic system is different for the English sound system). (Al-Zuoud & Kabilan, 2013, p. 173)

Among the errors identified, there is evidence of insertion, omission, substitution, and transposition errors, as defined earlier by Al-Zuoud and Kabilan (2013). These errors are associated with diphthongs, the use of the schwa, and silent letters in words. Of course, further analyses could be undertaken in in any one of these areas to gain a deeper view of phonology-related spelling errors in Arabic first language speakers of English. For now, what has been presented is sufficient to consider the implications of these findings on assessment.

5 Implications for Assessment: Reflections on Key Findings from the Corpus Analysis

In order to understand the significance of these results, it should be recalled that the identified error patterns contribute to a modest but emerging body of existing work on the challenges posed by spelling for Arabic first language speakers who are learning the English language. Owing to limitations of access to corpus metadata in the *Cambridge Learner Corpus*, further details on tagging, inter-rater agreement, and participant data are not available. This due to the nature of the texts, as international and authentic examinations, as being protected under policies such as GDPR. That being said, in spite of these limitations, the size and specialised nature of the corpus offers much in way of data that can be of value to the community of researchers who study learner errors, such as spelling.

As noted earlier, phonological errors appear to be the most common source of spelling difficulties for the wider Arabic first language group (Abu-Rabia & Taha, 2006), and certain phonemes in particular may diverge from established English usage (Allaith & Joshi, 2011). Our research adds to the above findings, demonstrating, from a corpus linguistic perspective, the range of spelling errors that occur in the data. It should now be determined what this means from an educational assessment perspective, and what possible action could be taken to better support English language testing in Arabic speaking contexts.

5.1 Research-Led Investigation and Informing Testing and Assessment in a Global Context

Two potential approaches to impacting assessment will now be discussed. These pertain to altering exam practices to fit local contexts and further targeted test preparation support, based on corpus studies. It is important to note that these approaches should not be considered to be mutually exclusive.

The first of these involves modifying English language examinations in order to better accommodate such groups as L1 Arabic speakers—a notion which should at least be considered in the design of future tests. This becomes particularly apparent when the finding that these learners differ from others in their spelling of certain phonemes is considered in more depth; the question may then be asked whether or not differing from others is necessarily 'incorrect'. In each of the above studies, Arabic students' spelling is defined against some form of established yardstick—be it L1 English usage, their non-Arabic L2 counterparts or other Arabic speakers. In the contemporary educational landscape this may not be an entirely fair comparison, especially as English is now a dominant language of instruction in a large number of tertiary study institutions in the region (Hopkyns, 2015). This development is not limited to the Arab world, and even those who question its merits can do little to deny its prominence (Bjorkman, 2011). Defining what 'English' *actually is* becomes problematic however, particularly how to accommodate international variations and decide what or who dictates acceptable academic usage. If Arabic students use alternative spellings for some of the phonemic features listed above, and the meaning of the expression remains clear, it should not necessarily be classed as an error. In case studies 1 and 2 described above, the spelling errors would not be described as incomprehensible or obfuscating meaning.

The continued need to share the English language and to accommodate international variety is evident, but how to do this is less clear. The term 'international English' may be used to refer to this shared concept, but such an expression leads to further confusion surrounding what international means; establishing which English variations are to be included under the term is far from straightforward (Flowerdew, 2012). Consequently, this presents a significant challenge for global assessment, if regional variations of usage are to be accommodated. This does not mean that it should be ignored, and it is advisable that the results of the above studies feed into discussions on how to approach spelling variation more inclusively in future.

5.2 Using Findings to Inform Assessment Practices: Recommendations

In relation to assessment practices, localised assessment variations may provide a viable solution, if practical matters such as cost and defining a manageable scope can be addressed. Future considerations might include:

- retraining examiners of candidates from certain regions not to penalise spelling or phonological errors which have been identified as attributable to L1 interference. This could be trialled on a small cohort in the first instance, and the implications monitored. Of course, this level of change would need to be directed at larger assessment bodies in order to practically effect change;
- altering existing writing band descriptors to reduce or mitigate any potentially punitive implications of areas which have been categorised as repeatedly problematic for specific learners, through research-led investigation; and
- collating established banks of writing scripts from candidates and analysing them to inform test content or marking practices. The potential benefits of this would not be limited to addressing spelling errors—however, this study demonstrates how consideration of linguistic and cultural contexts in international examinations is important, if an equitable examination experience is sought.

Each of the above notions should be considered, both as new tests are developed, and current models revisited and updated. Of course, the complexities of doing so should not be underestimated. One issue of which the current study reminds us is that the needs of an entire region cannot be addressed using a blanket approach. The challenges that Libyan and Emirati learners face at B1 level may differ considerably from Saudis at B2, for example. However, 30 such differences (and the admittedly somewhat daunting task of accurately documenting them) should not mean that the status quo is preserved, as this would effectively accommodate nobody in particular. Building a sufficient database of learner errors to ensure that the above suggested action can confidently be taken would neither be a quick nor a straightforward process. However, corpora such as the *Cambridge Learner Corpus* and *Trinity Lancaster Corpus* (Gablasova, Brezina, & McEnery, 2019) are noteworthy in this respect.

In the shorter term, it is perhaps more manageable to conceive of other means of helping first language Arabic learners to avoid having their exam scores reduced through these recurring spelling errors (if it is to be conceded that this is an accurate term, in the current climate at least). One approach is to intervene at the test preparation stage, and better equip candidates to meet acceptable spelling standards before taking the exam in question. Doing so may also require further reflection on the possible other contributing causes of the spelling difficulties described, and whether more could be done in response. It has been suggested that English education in the region has a tendency to focus on listening, speaking, writing, reading, development of lexis, and grammar—meaning that spelling receives relatively less attention (Al-Jarf, 2010). This - combined with the difficulties of phonology (Allaith & Joshi, 2011) and first language or 'phonological' interference (Alhaisoni et al., 2015), already outlined - may be exacerbating the issue. It may be more straightforward to address this, than alterations to global assessment policy. If local test preparation courses were able to incorporate sessions that specifically dealt with spelling and brought to candidates' attention that certain phonemes tend to cause Arab speakers problems in spelling (specifically identifying each one and explaining why it is different in English), it may help lower the frequency of errors.

6 Conclusions

In conclusion, this chapter has essentially raised a series of pertinent questions, and provided several answers, which serve as a starting point for future research. By adding to existing corpus linguistic work on Arabic speakers and spelling, it has become clear that there does appear to be a pattern for Arabic speakers as a group struggling with spelling. The notion that first language can predict spelling errors (Randall, 2005) is supported in this dataset; Libyan and Emirati students appear to be no exception. Understanding more about what these problems were in particular for these cohorts was the purpose of this research.

To summarise, it is now apparent that a series of open class lexical items are often misspelled, including nouns, adjectives, adverbs, and verbs. Furthermore, it has been documented that insertion, omission, substitution, and transposition were also recurring problems. The implications of this for assessment practices in the region were then discussed. It is evident that further work needs to be done on developing the existing knowledge bank of common spelling errors for the various groups of Arabic speakers, and that if this is done, there could be legitimate scope for adjusting marking approaches to accommodate these patterns of variation.

Promoting fairness for test takers would be at the centre of these suggested discussions, and although the considerable practical challenges of doing so should not be underestimated. Testing formats that can be adapted to local contexts are a highly appealing prospect. This may be considered an indirect application of corpus linguistics to assessment practices (particularly in the MENA region, but which should also be looked at elsewhere), two fields which should overlap more than they currently do. Finally, the implications of the study for the short-term have also been noted. The above findings can be used to improve test preparation practices in the countries featured and help test takers prepare for the examination using a pedagogical approach that accommodates their needs.

Acknowledgements We would like to thank Cambridge University Press and Cambridge Assessment for use of the Cambridge Learner Corpus.

Appendix 1: Countries in PAOB1

See Fig. 7.

Spelling Errors in the Preliminary English B1 Exam ... 387

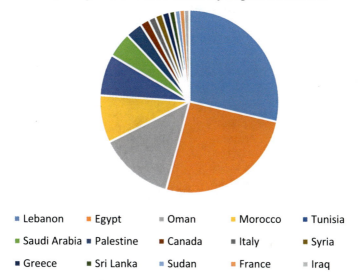

Fig. 7 Countries represented in PAOB1

Appendix 2: Countries in PAB1

See Fig. 8.

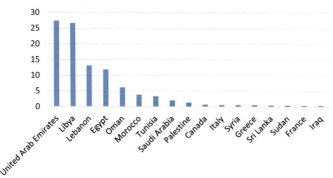

Fig. 8 Countries represented in PAB1

Appendix 3: First Languages

See Fig. 9.

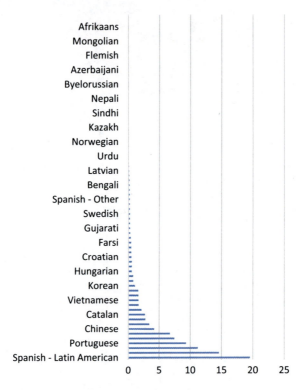

Fig. 9 First languages represented in PNAB1

Appendix 4: Misspelled Words

See Table 7.

Table 7 Top 10 misspelled words in PNAB1 per 10,000 words

Top 10 errors in PNAB1	
Word	Freq. per 10k words
Too	0.88782
Centre	0.863328
Programme	0.765362
Which	0.74087
Received	0.716379
Beautiful	0.704133
Believe	0.600044
Decision	0.557184
Favourite	0.514323
Thought	0.42248

References

Abdelkader, A., Boumiza, D. S., & Braham, R. (2010). An online Arabic learning environment based on IMS-QTI. In Proceedings—*10th IEEE International Conference on Advanced Learning Technologies* (pp. 116–118). ICALT 2010. http://dx.doi.org/10.1109/ICALT.2010.40.

Abu-Rabia, S., & Taha, H. (2006). Phonological errors predominate in Arabic spelling across grades 1–9. *Journal of Psycholinguistic Research, 35*(2), 167–188.

Alameen, G., & Levis, J. M. (2015). Connected speech. In M. Reed & J. M. Levis (Eds.), *The handbook of English pronunciation* (pp. 159–174) Sussex: Wiley Blackwell.

Alhaisoni, E. M., Al-Zuoud, K. M., & Gaudel, D. R. (2015). Analysis of spelling errors of Saudi beginner learners of English enrolled in an intensive English language program. *English Language Teaching, 8*(3), 185–192.

Al-Jarf, R. (2010). Spelling corpora in EFL. *Sino-Us English Teaching, 7*(1), 6–15.

Allaith, Z. A., & Joshi, R. M. (2011). Spelling performance of English consonants among students whose first language is Arabic. *Reading and Writing, 24*(9), 1089–1110.

Al-Zuoud, K. M., & Kabilan, M. K. (2013). Investigating Jordanian EFL students' spelling errors at tertiary level. *International Journal of Linguistics, 5*(3), 164.

Amador Moreno Carolina, P., Chambers, A., & Riordan, S. T. (2006). Integrating a corpus of classroom discourse in language teacher education: The case of discourse markers. *ReCALL, 18*(1), 83–104.

Aston, G. (2001). Learning with corpora: An overview. In G. Aston (Ed.), *Learning with corpora* (pp. 7–45). Bologna: CLUEB.

Banerjee, J., Yan, X., Chapman, M., & Elliott, H. (2015). Keeping up with the times: Revising and refreshing a rating scale. *Assessing Writing, 26,* 5–19. https://doi.org/10.1016/j.asw.2015.07.001.

Barker, F., Salamoura, A., & Saville, N. (2015). Learner corpora and language testing. In S. Granger, G. Gilquin, & F. Meunier (Eds.), *The Cambridge handbook of learner corpus research* (pp. 511–534). Cambridge: Cambridge University Press.

Biber, D., Johansson, S., Leech, G., Conrad, S., & Finegan, E. (2012). *Longman grammar of spoken and written English*. Harlow: Pearson Education.

Bjorkman, B. (2011). English as a Lingua Franca: Implications for EAP. *Iberica, 22,* 79–100.

Briscoe, E., Carroll, J., & Watson, R. (2006). The second release of the RASP system. In *Proceedings of the Coling/ACL 2006 Interactive Presentation Sessions* (pp. 77–80). Sydney, Australia.

Callies, M., & Götz, S. (2015). Learner corpora in language testing and assessment: Prospects and challenges. In M. Callies & S. Götz, (Eds.), *Learner corpora in language testing and assessment* (pp. 1–12). Amsterdam: John Benjamins.

Carter, R., & McCarthy, M. (2013). *Cambridge grammar of English: A comprehensive guide to spoken and written English grammar and usage*. Cambridge: Cambridge University Press.

Chapelle, C. A., & Plakans, L. (2013). Assessment and testing: Overview. In C. A. Chapelle (Ed.), *The encylopedia of applied linguistics* (pp. 241–244). New Jersey: Wiley-Blackwell.

Coats, S. (2019). Language choice and gender in a Nordic social media corpus. *Nordic Journal of Linguistics, 42*(1), 31–55. https://doi.org/10.1017/S0332586519000039.

Flowerdew, J. (2012). Corpora in language teaching from the perspective of English as an international language. In L. Alsagoff, S. L. Mckay, G. Hu, & W. A. Renandya (Eds.), *Principles and practices for teaching English as an international language* (pp. 226–243). Abingdon: Routledge.

Frankenberg-Garcia, A. (2012). Raising teachers' awareness of corpora. *Language Teaching,* 45(4), 475–489. https://doi.org/10.1017/S02614448 10000480.

Gablasova, D., Brezina, V., & McEnery, T. (2019). The Trinity Lancaster Corpus: Development, description and application. *International Journal of Learner Corpus Research,* 5(2), 126–158. https://doi.org/10.1075/ijlcr.190 01.gab.

Hawkins, J. A., & Buttery, P. (2010). Criterial features in learner corpora: Theory and illustrations. *English Profile Journal,* 1(1), 1–23. https://doi.org/10.1017/S2041536210000103.

Hawkins, J. A., & Filipovic, L. (2012). *Criterial features in L2 English: Specifying the reference levels of the Common European Framework.* Cambridge: Cambridge University Press.

Hopkyns, S. (2015). A conflict of desires: English as a global language and its effects on cultural identity in the united arab emirates. In R. Al-Mahrooqi & C. Denman (Eds.), *English education in the Arab world* (pp. 6–37). Newcastle: Cambridge Scholars Publishing.

Hunston, S. (2002). *Corpora in applied linguistics.* Cambridge: Cambridge University Press.

Kreyer, R. (2015). The Marburg corpus of intermediate learner English (MILE). In M. Callies & S. Götz (Eds.), *Learner corpora in language testing and assessment* (pp. 13–34). Amsterdam: John Benjamins.

McCarthy, M., McCarten, J., & Sandiford, H. (2004–2006). *Touchstone* (four levels). Cambridge: Cambridge University Press.

McEnery, A., & Xiao, R. (2005). Help or help to: What do corpora have to say? *English Studies,* 86(2), 161–187. https://doi.org/10.1080/001383804 2000339880.

McEnery, T., & Xiao, R. (2011). What corpora can offer in language teaching and learning. In E. Hinkel (Ed.), *Handbook of research in second language teaching and learning* (pp. 364–380). London: Routledge.

Mishan, F. (2005). *Designing authenticity into language learning materials.* Bristol: Intellect.

O'Keeffe, A., & Farr, F. (2012). Using language corpora in inital teacher education: Pedagogic issues and practical applications. In D. Biber & R. Reppen (Eds.), *Corpus linguistics* (Vol. 4, pp. 335–362). Los Angeles: Sage.

O'Keeffe, A., McCarthy, M., & Carter, R. (2007). *From corpus to classroom: Language use and language teaching*. Cambridge: Cambridge University Press.

Nicholls, D. (2003). The Cambridge learner corpus: Error coding and analysis for lexicography and ELT. In *Proceedings of the corpus linguistics 2003 conference* (pp. 572–581). Corpus Linguistics 16.

Park, K. (2014). Corpora and language assessment: The state of the art. *Language Assessment Quarterly, 11*(1), 27–44. https://doi.org/10.1080/15434303.2013.872647.

Qin, M., Du, X., Tao, J., & Qiu, X. (2016). A study on the optimal English speech level for Chinese listeners in classrooms. *Applied Acoustics, 104*, 50–56. https://doi.org/10.1016/j.apacoust.2015.10.017.

Randall, M. (2005). Orthographic knowledge and first language reading: Evidence from single word dictation. In B. Bassetti & V. Cook (Eds.), *Second language writing systems* (pp. 122–147). Clevedon: Multilingual Matters.

Randall, M., & Groom, N. (2009). The BUiD Arab learner corpus: A resource for studying the acquisition of L2 English spelling. In *Proceedings of the Corpus Linguistics Conference*, Liverpool, UK.

Römer, U. (2011). Corpus research applications in second language teaching. *Annual Review of Applied Linguistics, 31*, 205–225.

Rundell, M., & Stock, P. (1992). The corpus revolution. *English Today, 8*(3), 21–32. https://doi.org/10.1017/S0266078400006520.

Simpson, R. C., Briggs, S. L., Ovens, J., & Swales, J. M. (2002). *The Michigan corpus of academic spoken English*. Ann Arbor: The Regents of the University of Michigan.

Tsui, A. B. M. (2006). What teachers have always wanted to know—And how corpora can help. In J. M. Sinclair (Ed.), *How to use corpora in language teaching* (pp. 39–61). Amsterdam: John Benjamins.

Learning What Works in Improving Writing: A Meta-Analysis of Technology—Oriented Studies Across Saudi Universities

Lee McCallum and Mubina Rauf

1 Introduction

Writing proficiency in English has long been a sought-after skill in Saudi Arabia, as the country has developed international trade connections and the population has become increasingly educated (Elyas & Picard, 2018). However, developing this proficiency is arguably the greatest challenge for students who set out to master English language skills to join an increasingly young and ambitious Saudi workforce. In recognising this struggle, it has been an endeavour of many practitioners and researchers to deliver instruction that tackles many of the documented difficulties that students face in producing extended written English (e.g. Oraif, 2018).

L. McCallum (✉)
University of Exeter, Exeter, UK
e-mail: lm489@exeter.ac.uk

M. Rauf
Imam Abdurrahman bin Faisal University, Dammam, Saudi Arabia
e-mail: mrauf@iau.edu.sa

Among these interventions, technology is increasingly being promoted as an intervention that can bring about writing improvement. Yet, these studies have not been synthesised empirically, and the conflicting support for these studies makes it difficult to present a coherent picture that can be used to inform instructional practice across Saudi Arabia's Higher Education network. Given this lack of coherence, this chapter carries out a meta-analysis of these studies to empirically determine the effect technology has on writing improvement.

The chapter begins by setting out the general landscape of meta-analytic work that has focused on technology then it narrows to carry out a meta-analysis of studies that have been conducted over the last two decades (2000–2019). We hope this chapter serves as a robust overview of the literature that captures what technological interventions appear to be effective, but we also hope to encourage future work that is more transparently reported and more systematically designed with an acknowledgement of how study quality plays a role in the claims that are made about the effect of technology on writing improvement.

2 Literature Review

The literature review begins by looking at the current state of the literature on using technology to improve language learning as a whole with this discussion divided into two parts: first, an examination of past meta-analyses that have focused on the use of technology as a language-skills intervention and then what attempts that have been made to understand study quality within these meta-analyses and how moderator variables are acknowledged and analysed as influences on the effectiveness of technology. The review concludes by explaining why this effectiveness should be revisited with a focus on writing in the specific context of Saudi Arabia.

2.1 Past Technology-Oriented Meta-Analyses, Their Areas of Focus and Findings

Across the field of Second Language Acquisition (SLA), the notion of technology has been divided into several different sub-domains. Although attempts have been made to separate out such domains, these attempts have often blurred the lines in categorising technology types, modes of communication and uses. Scholars have categorised communication as either: synchronous or asynchronous. Synchronous communication means the technology is used to communicate in real-time with no delayed response (e.g. instant messaging) whereas asynchronous communication means the technology is used to communicate at different times where delayed response is possible (e.g. Moodle and other Learning Management Systems (LMSs), wikis, discussion boards and blogs) (Alghizzi, 2017).

Other distinctions have separated Computer-Assisted Language Learning (CALL) and Mobile-Assisted Language Learning (MALL). A number of different definitions exist for CALL including those referred to in Yang (2013) where CALL means the search for and study of applications of the computer in language teaching and learning or more widely CALL means learners learning language in any context with, through, and around computer technologies. Yang (2013) highlights the widening nature of CALL definitions and how the learning boundaries are blurred by what we consider a computer because many mobile devices now have access to previously desktop computer only applications. This point is also acknowledged by Burston (2015) in focusing on MALL. MALL is generally understood to include any learning that takes place with the sole or main technology being a handheld or palmtop device (Burston, 2015). This covers any portable device such as smartphones and handheld computers with wireless internet access.

Another term that frequents the literature is Computer-Mediated Communication (CMC). Chun (2016) lists the types of CMC as including: email, forums, chats, blogs, wikis, podcasts, videos, social media, virtual worlds and multiplayer online games. For the same reason why CALL and MALL are difficult to separate, there is also the possibility that the communication taking place under CMC also involves mobile devices. Given this, our chapter takes a broad overview of technology to include computer and mobile devices so as to provide a comprehensive picture of general technology use.

When we examine past CALL and MALL meta-analyses and their primary studies, we find consistently positive effects for the use of such interventions on language learning proficiency gains. Plonsky and Ziegler's (2016) review of 14 CALL meta-analyses covering 408 primary studies until 2016 indicates that there is a significant positive difference when comparing treatment (CALL learning contexts) and control groups (traditional learning contexts) (Cohen's $d = .84$). They also note a significant positive effect when they compare different technology treatments (Cohen's $d = .51$).

Across a similar time period in MALL meta-analyses and meta-syntheses, similar trends in effectiveness have been found. Taj, Sulan, Sipra and Ahmad's (2016) meta-analysis of the effect of MALL on vocabulary and grammar looked at a small sample of 13 studies and found MALL had a large positive effect on these areas of language learning (Cohen's $d = .80$).

Within this broad overview of language learning skills, other meta-analyses have looked closely at individual language skills. These meta-analyses have pointed out the consistently positive effect technology appears to have on different aspects of the skill of second language writing. Felix (2008) addressed L2 writing and found that technology had a positive effect on revision strategies as well as learners' ability to switch between formal and informal language. In Li and Hegelheimer's (2013) study of mobile-assisted grammar exercises, they found the exercises had a positive effect on the self-editing skills of writers.

From these meta-analyses, it appears that technology does have a largely positive effect on language learning. However, as the next sections will show, coming to this conclusion is undoubtedly influenced by issues of meta-analyses and primary study rigour and transparency as well as the acknowledgement and investigation of confounding or moderating research design and contextual learning variables.

2.2 Raising Issues of Study Quality and Reporting and Analysing Moderator Variables

Study quality in SLA has been broadly defined as 'the adherence to standards of contextually appropriate, methodological rigour in research practices, and the transparent and complete reporting of such practices' (Plonsky, 2013, p. 658). Plonsky (2013) identifies a number of important indicators of study quality in SLA. These can be grouped into indicators of analyses, settings and aspects of experimental research design and indicators of reporting practices. In the former group, example indicators include: reporting details of the sample sizes, details of the research context, and the reporting of the experimental design (e.g. random allocation of student groups) and in the latter group, example indicators include: the reporting of descriptive statistics and the incidence of missing data that influences the use and value of descriptive and inferential statistics.

Further to this point on study quality, a number of meta-analyses have also looked at the issue of study quality, rigour and transparency through moderator variables (e.g. Lin, 2012, 2014; Liu, Lu, & Lai, 2016; Plonsky & Ziegler, 2016; Sung, Chang, & Yang, 2015). Burston's (2015) synthesis and meta-analysis of MALL studies from 1994 to 2012 paints a disappointing picture for those studies claiming to use mobile devices. Burston (2015) highlights that only a small percentage of their 291 studies were actually fit for analysis because of poor statistical reporting. From 35 applicable studies, Burston (2015) emphasises that the studies suffer from research design flaws, namely small sample sizes (< 100 participants in many cases) and short intervention periods (< 10 weeks). Alongside these design flaws, the failure to adequately track the use of the intervention, the presence of uncontrolled and confounding variables, the inadequate description of the control group and scant statistical analyses were featured in 16 out of the 35 studies.

A further point of contention across these meta-analyses is their pooling together of all language skills to treat language learning holistically. We acknowledge from reviews (e.g. Plonsky & Ziegler, 2016) that some meta-analyses have focused on a single skill (e.g. reading) however holistic reviews are far more common. While this broad approach undoubtedly advances our knowledge of how effective technology is, we believe these reviews also mask potentially important insights we could gain from a fine-grained meta-analysis carried out on a specific language skill.

The next section of the review outlines why such a fine-grained analysis should be undertaken with the skill of writing and specifically why the domain of Higher Education in Saudi Arabia is a worthy context of study for such a fine-grained approach.

2.3 The Rationale for a Focus on Writing in Saudi Arabia

As noted in Sect. 2.1, the skill of writing has more often than not simply featured as an outcome measure alongside the other language skills of reading, listening and speaking.

However, the inclusion of writing in a holistic picture of language learning prevents us from fully understanding the effects of technology on this individual skill. In theoretical technology-oriented literature, several benefits have been put forward for how technology use can especially improve writing. In their research synthesis of 52 research articles from 2000 to 2016 on how CMC improves writing, Aslan and Ciftci (2019) report on learner perceptions and note how blogs, wikis and automatic chat platforms bring out different benefits. They highlight how blogs lead to learning new vocabulary items and allow writers to develop their understanding of topic, supporting and concluding sentences and summary writing. Wikis were also found to improve summary writing and allow writers to practise the various stages of process writing that they were taught in class. They also found wikis could improve translation skills, language use and content creation, writing quality and quicker task completion.

These observations, in combination with the limited meta-analytic work on writing seems to indicate that there are potentially many positive effects for the improvement of writing when technology is used as an intervention.

We also believe there is a need to look closer at how technology use can improve writing in specific learning environments. While the majority of previous meta-analyses have focused on averaging effects out across EFL and ESL contexts, there are many valid reasons for focusing exclusively on the MENA context of Saudi Arabia. First, there is a plethora of literature to support the belief that the skill of writing is a constant problem for Saudi students in Higher Education. This is evident in their performance in international proficiency tests (e.g. IELTS) with Grami (2010) highlighting how Saudi students' IELTS writing scores are often their weakest scores and are noticeably lower than other L2 learners. Further to this, a number of exploratory Higher Education studies have not only pointed out this weakness but established a number of linguistic areas that students perform poorly in. These include the use of articles (e.g. Al-Mohanna, 2014), grammar, spelling, prepositions and vocabulary problems (e.g. Mohammad & Hazarika, 2016).

In line with these established difficulties, Alghizzi (2017) also comments that the use of technology as a general teaching and learning tool has only recently started to become established in Saudi Arabia because it has invested in the infrastructure to support its implementation. This is also clear from the increase in Higher Education projects across the country that promote the use of technology for teaching language and specifically writing. These projects have included E-learning initiatives, deanships and directives from multiple universities in the private and public sector (e.g. projects have appeared at King Saud, King Khalid and King Abdulaziz universities) (Weber, 2018). With these advances in mind, there is a clear need for an attempt to be made to synthesise understandings of how technology is being used to improve writing proficiency and provide an empirical measurement of its effectiveness. When we also consider the points raised by meta-analytic scholars about the influence of context and application, we believe such a meta-analytic study in Saudi Arabia at this time of innovation is a timely one.

2.4 Research Questions

The subsequent meta-analysis was guided by the following research questions:

RQ 1: To what extent do studies vary in their study quality when examined according to Plonsky's (2013) indicators of study quality?

RQ 2: To what extent are technological interventions effective in improving writing?

3 Methodology

The meta-analysis consisted of the following steps. First, setting the initial study domain: establishing search techniques and retrospectively adapting to the search results by updating terms to broaden or narrow the search accordingly; then coding the studies for study descriptor and study outcome variables; writing up a narrative synthesis of the research so as to capture the broad patterns of the data; and finally carrying out the meta-analyses of the data by calculating effect sizes that measure the importance of technology on writing.

3.1 Data Collection

The meta-analysis was carried out by following the steps outlined in Plonsky and Oswald (2014). We began by delimiting our domain, setting out our key search terms, developing and refining a coding scheme before and after data collection, and establishing a concise collection of studies. Upon collecting the studies that met our inclusion and exclusion criteria, we calculated and interpreted the effects of those findings by calculating each study's effect size as well as qualitatively looking at the claims researchers were making about the generalisability of their findings and the overall effect their technological intervention had on students' writing improvement.

In delimiting our domain, we focused on aspects of our aim including: Higher Education, Saudi Arabian students and writing improvement or writing gains. With respect to the wide-ranging use of terms and types of technology, we kept our inclusion criteria broad. We included both types of communication (asynchronous/synchronous) and devices classified as CALL and MALL devices. We kept our understanding of technology broad and inclusive of these divisions because we believed we stood the best chance of accurately tapping into learning about the use of technology by not excluding studies because of their theoretical orientations and differences in terminology.

With these points in mind, we generated appropriate key search terms. These search terms included: Saudi AND (writing performance* OR writing ability* OR writing gains* OR technology*). These search terms were used in the following databases: ERIC, LLBA, Psych INFO, Academic Search Premier, ProQuest Dissertations and Theses (for USA postgraduate dissertations/theses) and the British Library EThos library (for UK postgraduate dissertations/theses). We also independently searched a list of the 20 highest ranked journals in TESOL/Applied Linguistics from SCImago (2019) (e.g. *Annual Review of Applied Linguistics, Applied Linguistics* and the *Journal of Second Language Writing*) in addition to local journals (focusing on Saudi Arabian Higher Education and the GCC countries, e.g. [*Journal of King Saud University Language and Translation*]) and international journals that would contain articles on English language writing in Higher Education (e.g. *Foreign Language Annals, TESOL Journal, TESOL Quarterly, Written Communication*).

In our search for studies, we consciously acknowledged that some meta-analyses have excluded work in local less established or prestigious journals and postgraduate work with the rationale that this work would be less informed or reliable (see Li, Shintani, and Ellis [2012], for the discussion on study quality inclusion). However, we decided to include both types of work for two reasons. First, we wanted to present a comprehensive picture of work in this area and believed that the narrow domain we were focusing on would be more frequently represented in local publications/platforms. A second reason is the motivation to include these studies because of their potential ability to challenge or phase out any possible publication bias that may be present in international journals that favour reporting significant results, irrespective of their effect sizes.

For our last search activity, we compiled a list of our existing studies and carried out both an ancestry search of their reference lists and also used the 'cited by' feature of Google Scholar to locate later work that had been informed by this earlier work. Undertaking this last activity helped us recover several theoretical reviews of writing and assessment research in Saudi Arabia (e.g. Obeid, 2017) which contained previously undetected relevant studies.

We decided to exclude studies that focused on reporting writing gains from only a qualitative perspective or used self-reporting instruments (e.g. McMullen, 2009). We also excluded studies that were experimental/intervention based but contained little or no empirical information (e.g. Al-Jarf, 2002, 2005) and studies which measured supposed writing gains via a receptive test and not exclusively through productive extended writing tasks (e.g. Al-Subaie & Madini, 2018). We also excluded studies that did not appear to have a clear technology-oriented intervention (e.g. Al-Harbi, 2016; Al-Mansour & Al-Shorman, 2014; Fageeh, 2014; Jahin, 2012). These exclusions meant we based our meta-analysis on a final list of 27 studies. These studies are indicated in the final reference list with an asterisk (*).

3.2 Data Analysis

As part of our initial analysis, we began by developing a coding scheme which was divided into study descriptors and study outcomes to reflect the contextual and statistical information that we could record from the studies. The full coding Excel sheet is available via the IRIS database (Marsden, Mackey, & Plonsky, 2016) with a summary of the key variables presented in Table 1. Each study was coded for these variables by the first author and then the second author double coded the studies for the same variables. Coding reliability was calculated as a simple percentage. Agreement on this coding reached 92%. Disagreements and

Table 1 Coding variables for study descriptors (# = number)

Study descriptors	
ID	Year, Author; Reference Type; Journal; Article Title; Peer review turnaround; Fee payment; Published
Sample	Sample size; age; gender; proficiency level; level of education; major; year of study; past education; proficiency level judgements
Context	Teacher characteristics; researcher characteristics; course information; name of institution; institution type
Treatment/intervention	# groups; target features for improvement; method of instruction; intervention type; length of intervention; intensity of instruction/intervention; # instructors/researchers; writing type; task details of the intervention; test details

ambiguities were discussed and negotiated at the end of this second annotation process.

Study outcome variables included mean and standard deviation values (both if these were provided and what the actual values were), the effect size (if available), the p-value (both if this was reported and its actual value) and other statistical information related to the particular statistical tests being carried out (e.g. t-values). We also coded for reliability estimates. These related to reliability of rating the pre and post-tests (inter-rater reliability) as well as reliability and validity of designing the pre and post-tests (e.g. were the validity and reliability of the testing instruments checked before administration to students?).

These variables and the respective coding procedure allowed us to comprehensively establish the reporting practices and indicators of study quality thereby answering research question one.

To answer research question two, we carried out the following process. Since only four of the studies provided an effect size, we calculated effect sizes for each study. We used the effect size calculator from Lipsey and Wilson (2001) to do this. Where we could not calculate the effect size as a result of missing information, we have noted this separately in our results section. Where we calculated effect sizes by converting the original effect size given in the study into Cohen's d, we have also noted this separately. In line with general meta-analysis literature (e.g. Borenstein, Hedges, Higgins, & Rothstein, 2009) we also calculated a single effect size for all studies that included multiple effect sizes. After obtaining an effect size for each study, we then calculated a weighted effect size in a random-effects model using the '*metafor*' package in *R* (Viechtbauer, 2020).

4   Results and Discussion

4.1   Understanding Study Quality Across the Studies

In answering research question one, we begin by describing our study set in terms of reporting settings, sample sizes and other contextual variables following several indicators set out by Plonsky's (2013). Figure 1 indicates that the majority of the 27 studies occurred in the second decade (2010 onwards) of our search period. Figure 1 also highlights that most studies occurred in the years 2011 and 2014–2018 with a maximum

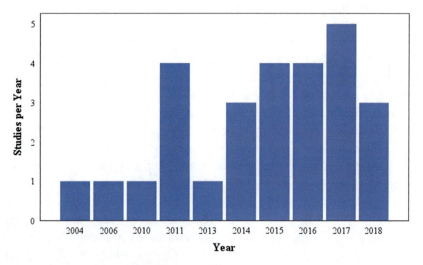

Fig. 1   Study breakdown per year

Table 2 Samples size in the meta-analysis (k = 27)

Total N	Modal N per study	Min–Max
1381	55	18–116

of 5 studies occurring in 2017. This trend appears to support observations that empirical technology-oriented studies have been increasing with time (Alghizzi, 2017).

Table 2 provides an overview of the number of students involved in each study. There is wide variation across the sample with a minimum of 18 students (which would be equal to approximately one undergraduate level writing class[1]) to a maximum of 116 students (which includes multiple classes). Table 3 brings together the many variables we coded to allow us to provide a description of the studies. Table 3 highlights how the vast majority of the 27 studies were published journal articles. However, one M.A. thesis (Al-Saleh, 2018) was coded as published because it appeared as part of the *Arab World English Journal*'s (AWEJ) theses repository publications. The majority of the studies were carried out in public government universities which is to be expected as they naturally outnumber private universities in Saudi Arabia.

Across the 27 studies, several observations were made regarding the recording of contextual information. Table 3 shows that when we coded for institution type, gender and age of participants, a number of these details were missing. In the case of gender, 8 studies did not report this. However, this may have been assumed as obvious to readers by the researchers because sex segregation in Saudi Arabia prevents instructors teaching the opposite sex. Therefore, readers may infer that male researchers conducted their studies on male students and vice versa for female researchers.

Age was another variable that was underreported with 15 studies not reporting students' age range. This oversight may have been because researchers reported the year of study or programme level instead, and in doing so assumed readers would infer an age range from this. For

---

[1] Coombe, Reinders, Littlejohn, and Tafazoli (2019) specify that in HE across the MENA region class size varies up to a maximum of 30 students per class.

Table 3 Study overview ($k = 27$)

Publication status		
Category	K	% of total studies
Published	22	81.48
Unpublished	5	18.52
Reference type		
Journal paper	21	77.78
Student M.A./Ph.D. thesis	6	22.22
Institution type		
Public	21	77.78
Unknown	4	14.81
Private	2	7.41
Gender		
Female	10	37.04
Male	8	29.63
Not given	8	29.63
Mixed	1	3.70
Age		
Not given	15	55.56
18–20	2	7.41
19–20	2	7.41
18–22	1	3.70
18–24	1	3.70
19–21	1	3.70
19–22	1	3.70
19–23	1	3.70
19–24	1	3.70
20–22	1	3.70
20–35	1	3.70
Proficiency levels		
Not given	10	37.04
Level 5	5	18.52
Level 2	4	14.82
Intermediate	3	11.11
Level 4	2	7.41
Low level	1	3.70
Levels 1 and 2	1	3.70
Levels 1–6	1	3.70
Proficiency level judgements		
Not given	21	77.78

(continued)

Table 3 (continued)

Publication status		
Category	K	% of total studies
Determined by GPA/module scores	3	11.12
Determined by college	1	3.70
Pre-test	1	3.70
STEP test	1	3.70

example, many studies specified study level as 'undergraduate', 'preparatory year' or 'freshman' perhaps inferring that students were at least 18 years old. However, in studies that did specify an age range and year of study and/or programme level, age range varied considerably with one study having a broad age range of 20–35 years old (e.g. Abdul Fattah, 2015) while others (e.g. Al-Shwiah, 2016) had narrower age ranges of 18–20. Therefore, in our analysis we did not infer age, where it was missing, from the year of study or programme level, when this was provided instead.

Further to these nuanced details, proficiency level was also underreported. Few studies made explicit to readers how their internal proficiency rating or scale related back to international scales (e.g. IELTS scores or CEFR bands). Few studies did (e.g. Al-Shumaimeri, 2011) help us relate learners' level to other contexts more globally while others did attempt to explain that a level equalled one term (e.g. Oraif, 2018) however since it is not made explicitly clear if all studies followed the same contextually specific level system equally, we felt our judgement of comparing the levels should be interpreted cautiously.

Table 4 also indicates that more studies were carried out across a range of different universities with few unknown ($k = 2$), a single study used a pseudonym to maximise university anonymity and King Saud University and King Khalid University were among the most frequent universities carrying out studies of this nature. This is because these institutions have active E-learning projects, departments and deanships (Weber, 2018).

Equally, Table 4 highlights several ambiguities related to the reporting of the year of study. Most studies specified an exact undergraduate year (Years 1–4) but other studies did not report any year ($k = 6$) or simply

Table 4 Context overview

Institution		
University	*K*	*% total studies*
Unknown	2	7.41
Pseudonym used	1	3.70
King Khalid University	5	18.52
King Saud University	5	18.52
King Abdulaziz University	2	7.41
King Abdulaziz University and Umm Al Qura University	1	3.70
Qassim University	2	7.41
University of Bisha	1	3.70
Al-Majmaah University	1	3.70
Prince Sattam bin Abdul Aziz University	1	3.70
Allman Mohammad Ibn Saud Islamic University	3	11.11
Qassim Private Colleges	1	3.70
Shaqra University	1	3.70
Taiba University	1	3.70
Year of study		
Year	*K*	*% total studies*
1	7	25.93
Specified as Undergraduate	7	25.93
unknown	6	22.22
2	4	14.82
3	1	3.70
4	2	7.41
Degree programme		
Major	*K*	*% total studies*
English Department	12	44.44
unknown	8	29.63
Business	2	7.41
Translation	1	3.70
Arabic	1	3.70
Mixed	1	3.70
Education	1	3.70

noted the year to be 'undergraduate' ($k = 7$). Similarly, Table 4 shows that programme of study was most commonly reported as English ($k = 12$) or unreported ($k = 8$), with other studies listing broad academic disciplines (Translation, Arabic, Business, Education or a mixture of different programmes).

Table 5 shows that from the published studies, the journals of *English*

Table 5 Journal information ($k = 22$)

Journal	K	% total studies
English Language Teaching	4	18.18
Arab World English Journal	3	13.64
Journal of Language and Literature	2	9.09
Journal of Computer Assisted Learning	1	4.54
European Journal of Research and Reflection in Educational Sciences	1	4.54
International Review of Social Sciences and Humanities	1	4.54
International Journal of Linguistics and Communication	1	4.54
Procedia Social and Behavioral Sciences	1	4.54
International Journal of Humanities and Social Sciences	1	4.54
Journal of Education and Practice	1	4.54
Journal of Education and Human Development	1	4.54
Sino-US English Teaching	1	4.54
Journal of Education and Practice	1	4.54
Foreign Language Annals	1	4.54
Journal of King Saud University	1	4.54
Asian EFL Journal	1	4.54

Language Teaching and the *Arab World English Journal* emerged as popular choices. This may be most likely because of their focus on MENA region interests compared to more wide-ranging international journals (e.g. *Foreign Language Annals*).

The publication standing of the journals was difficult to determine because such claims about ranking comprise of multiple indices (e.g. impact factor, readership number and databases where the journal is indexed (e.g. See Al-Hoorie & Vitta, 2019). However, it was observed that most studies were published in journals that served MENA region scholars and readers, of which 15 of these studies appeared in a journal that charged a publication or administration fee and had a minimum peer review turnaround time of one week and a maximum peer review time of 12 weeks. Among the international journals, we recovered studies in: *Foreign Language Annals* and the *Journal of Computer Assisted Language Learning* (CALL) these did not appear to charge a publication

Table 6 Design features associated with quality in experimental research ($k = 27$)

Variable	Category	K	% total studies
Allocation of groups	Random	13	48.15
	Unknown	7	25.93
	Non-random	4	14.82
	Partly random	1	3.70
	Deemed irrelevant	1	3.70
	Split according to GPA scores	1	3.70
Balance of students in groups	Equal numbers per group	12	44.44
	Unequal numbers per group	10	37.04
	Unreported division	1	3.70
Pre and post-test	Reported	26	96.30
	Not reported	1	3.70
Checking of statistical assumptions	Not reported	25	92.59
	Reported	2	7.41
Reporting of research questions	Reported	25	92.60
	Not reported	2	7.41
Reporting of hypotheses	Reported	17	62.96
	Not reported	10	37.04

or processing fee[2] and had a longer peer review time of a minimum of 8–12 weeks.

In answering research question one, several indicators that concerned research experimental design and the reporting of statistics were also coded and analysed. These focused on the design features associated with experimental research (Table 6), the statistical tests used (Table 7), how descriptive and inferential statistics were reported (Tables 8 and 9), and how the reliability and validity of the writing tests and their grading were reported (Table 10).

Table 6 shows that under half of the studies followed the expected or traditional stance for experimental research in that students were randomly allocated to a treatment or comparison/control group ($k = 13$), while 4 of the studies did not employ random allocation. It is perhaps surprising given the studies' reliance on experimental pre and

---

[2]Information was not provided on their websites at the time of publishing this chapter.

Table 7 Statistical analyses used ($k = 27$)

Type of analysis	K	% total studies
Independent or paired sample *t*-tests	14	51.85
ANCOVA	2	7.41
Wilcoxon rank test	2	7.41
Mann Whitney U and Wilcoxon rank test	2	7.41
t-tests and ANOVA	1	3.70
Paired *t*-tests and ANCOVA	1	3.70
Paired sample correlation	1	3.70
Repeated measures ANOVA	1	3.70
ANOVA and Scheffe post hoc test	1	3.70
Chi-squared test	1	3.70
No inferential statistical tests	1	3.70

Table 8 An overview of reporting practices (Descriptive statistics) ($k = 27$)

Mean and standard deviation values

Category	K	% total
Mean values reported	27	100
Standard deviation values reported	24	83.87
Range values reported	1	3.70
Minimum and Maximum values reported	2	7.41
Variance values reported	1	3.70

Table 9 An overview of reporting practices (Inferential statistics) ($k = 27$)

Effect sizes

Category	K	% of total studies
Not reported	23	85.18
Reported	4	14.82
P-values		
Reported exact measure	17	62.96
Reported (< or > 0.05; < or > 0.001)	9	33.33
Not reported	1	3.70
Other inferential statistics reported		
F values		
Reported	6	22.22
T-values		
Reported	14	51.85
Degrees of freedom		
Reported	11	40.74
Standard error of mean		
Reported	2	7.41

Table 10 An overview of other reporting practices ($k = 27$)

Reliability and validity checks

Category	K	% of total studies
Inter-rater reliability on test grading		
Not reported	18	66.67
Reported with measure and rate specified	4	14.82
Reported but no measure specified	2	7.41
Not reported but reliability of scoring reported from another study	1	3.70
Not reported but raters given sample papers to practice on	1	3.70
Reported but no measure or rate specified	1	3.70
Reliability of the tests (statistical reliability)		
Reported	15	55.56
Not reported	12	44.44
Validity of the tests (statistical validity)		
Not reported	24	88.89
Reported	3	11.11
Validity checks on the tests		
Reported	14	51.85
Not reported	13	48.15

post-tests that 7 of the studies did not report their group allocation procedure since this allocation is seen as a key hallmark of experimental research and for some is a key component of research reliability (Plonsky, 2013). Other studies indicated that random allocation was not particularly relevant ($k = 1$), or partly random ($k = 1$), and another study was split according to GPA scores.

In terms of the number of students per group, it should be noted that four studies did not appear to have a control group and so the observations concerning student numbers in each group shown in Table 6 relate to the 23 studies which clearly used a control/comparison group. Table 6 shows that under half of the studies had equal numbers of students in each group ($k = 12$). This may have been due to the fact original course numbers prevented this or that the course suffered from student attrition.

In line with findings in other SLA work (e.g. Plonsky, 2014), Table 7 indicates that null hypothesis testing analyses were most popular with fewer ANOVA or regression-based analyses. It is unsurprising to see such a reliance on *t*-tests given that these tests continue to be relied on by many in our fields (Plonsky, 2013, 2014). This reliance may also in part be due to the fact that recent research indicates that researcher training in statistical methods is not adequate for novice researchers and they experience only an introduction into these tests (e.g. Al-Hoorie & Vitta, 2019). However, a small number of studies *did* use follow up tests (e.g. Scheffe post hoc tests) to move beyond a simple exploration of differences and pinpoint where differences may in fact occur.

Table 8 shows that the reporting of descriptive mean and standard deviation statistics was fairly consistent with all of the studies reporting mean values and the vast majority ($k = 24$) also reporting standard deviations. Few studies reported other descriptive statistics with only a single study each reporting a range or variance value and only two studies reporting minimum and maximum values. The failure to report or make available individual raw scores and instead base the analysis solely on mean values had implications for trying to calculate an eventual effect size for the studies. For example, incomplete information in Ferheen-Bukhari (2016) made effect size calculation impossible. A failure to provide inferential statistics also limits the generalisability of the study itself because these claims are only based on potentially naturally occurring differences between the student writer groups.

Table 9 shows that the majority of the studies did not report an effect size ($k = 23$) however when reporting the significance of their results the majority of the studies that used *t*-tests or other null hypothesis based tests, did include exact *p*-value results ($k = 17$) as opposed to simply stating that the *p*-value obtained was < or > 0.05 or 0.001 ($k = 9$) or not reporting *p*-values at all ($k = 1$). The majority of these studies also included *t*-values ($k = 14$) but just under half ($k = 11$) reported degrees of freedom. With ANOVA or ANCOVA tests, 6 studies reported F values but only 3 reported standard error of means. None of the studies reported confidence intervals, power analysis, predetermined alpha or adjustments for multiple tests being conducted (where appropriate).

Table 10 indicates that the majority of the studies did not report any procedure for inter-rater reliability ($k = 18$) while a small number of studies ($k = 4$) reported both the measure of inter-rater reliability (e.g. Cronbach's alpha) and the rate of agreement (expressed as a percentage), with other studies reporting a rate of agreement but not how this was calculated ($k = 2$), or relying on reliability indicated in an earlier study in a different writing context ($k = 1$), or not reported but instead indicating that raters were given practice papers to try out the rating scale ($k = 1$), or it was claimed that inter-rater reliability was carried out but no measure or rate were specified ($k = 1$).

In examining the design of the pre and post-test writing instruments, a different pattern emerges. For reporting the statistical testing of reliability, just over half of the studies reported this ($k = 15$) while the statistical checking of validity was largely unreported[3] ($k = 24$) some studies did include human evaluations of the tests as validation checks ($k = 14$). These human evaluations involved 'jury' evaluation where panels of teachers and assessment experts evaluated the tests for clarity, length and content suitability.

Several differences related to the pre and post-test design practices that studies relied on. Although most studies focused on argumentative essay writing, there were other instances of descriptive paragraph writing (e.g. Idrees, 2017), writing a letter of complaint (e.g. Al-Shwiah, 2016), business reports, proposals and memos (e.g. Mohamed Kaseem, 2017).

The tests contained an array of different topics, test instructions and rating scales. Essay topics included those modified from international proficiency tests (e.g. IELTS and TOEFL): 'Use of genetically modified plants and health risks' (e.g. Al-Harbi, 2015), while other topics were created in house: '*My neighbourhood in Ramadan*' (Idrees, 2017). Similarly, a range of test instructions were used. These included instructions on time limit (ranging from 30 to 120 minutes), as well as word count guidance (no less than 120 words (e.g. Al-Saleh, 2018)—700 words in length (e.g. Fageeh, 2011) or in some studies the focus was on the number of sentences (no less than 5 sentences [e.g. Al-Shwiah, 2016], or 10–12 sentences [e.g. Al-Subaie & Alshuraidah, 2017]). Few studies provided explicit guidance on the content that was to be included in students' responses, but some did suggest areas of focus. For example, in

---

[3] Statistical validation included Pearson correlation coefficients.

asking students to describe their neighbourhood during Ramadan, Idrees (2017) provided a list of suggested content points (e.g. weather, visiting times, food).

A number of the rubrics used to measure improvements between pre and post-tests were taken from established assessment literature. These included studies that used Jacobs, Zinkgraf, Wormuth, Hartfiel, and Hughey's (1981) ESL Composition Scale (e.g. Fakhary-Tharwa, 2017) rubric while other studies used designed in-house rubrics (e.g. Mahmoud, 2014).

The meta-analysis also revealed several different intervention types. From the 27 studies, 7 studies did not give their intervention time in weeks. 6 of these 7 studies reported their time period in number of semesters or academic years (4 studies reported one semester, and 3 studies reported one academic year), and the remaining one study did not report an intervention time period. For the other studies, the intervention period ranged from 2 to 16 weeks with an average time of 8.90 weeks. One point of contention here that raises doubt in this reporting is whether or not the weeks stated take into account the weeks needed for pre and post-testing and whether or not the stated times include or exclude this. Readers of our chapter are therefore asked to bear this in mind when drawing any inferences about the intervention period.

There were several similar approaches to the types of technology used. Some of the studies used independent blogs ($k = 3$), wikis ($k = 4$), podcasts ($k = 1$) and Google Docs ($k = 1$) platforms as their interventions, while other studies used a context-related Learning Management System from their institution ($k = 3$) or a specially designed website with LMS-like tools (e.g. blogs/forums) ($k = 1$), or applications such as Showbie ($k = 1$) and Padlet ($k = 1$). A smaller number of studies used social media applications (e.g. Facebook, WhatsApp) ($k = 4$), mobile applications that acted as writing assistants to check language use ($k = 1$), mind mapping tools that appeared to be digital ($k = 1$), videos ($k = 2$), email ($k = 2$) or word processing software ($k = 1$) and a mixture of many of the above interventions ($k = 1$).

The tasks set with these interventions varied in their intensity and duration, difficulty and peer and teacher involvement. Many of the interventions were used actively to teach content (e.g. Idrees, 2017) while others were used to allow students to discuss aspects of writing (e.g. Fakhary-Tharwa, 2017). Many of the interventions were also used to carry out peer feedback (e.g. Sayed, 2010) or set up and write up pair and individual writing tasks (e.g. Al-Subaie & Alshuraidah, 2017).

The interventions were also set up to practice and elicit different features of writing proficiency. Table 11 highlights the broad range of features that the technological interventions sought to improve. Many of these features included nuanced areas of focus however Table 11 helps highlight multiple linguistic features and cognitive writing processes that appear to be shared across studies.

In listing these areas here, we attempted to group together constructs however this was intended to be deliberately broad so as not to distract from the number of different areas that the studies operationalised differently. The fine-grained differences that existed between studies is exemplified by examining how in some cases constructs such as mechanics

Table 11 Features of proficient writing

Features	Representative studies
Sentence structure/complexity	Abdul Fattah (2015)
Vocabulary/diction/word choice	Bamanger and Alhassan (2015)
Ideas/content/logic/reasoning/clarity of argument	Fakhary-Tharwa (2017)
Grammar (rules, form, errors/accuracy)	Oraif (2018)
Word count	Al-Jafen (2018)
Mechanics (punctuation, spelling, capitalisation)	Idrees (2017)
Organisation (rhetorical structure)	Sayed (2010)
Style	Algraini (2014)
Voice (tone)	Ahmed (2016)
Cohesion (and coherence)	AbuSeileek (2006)
Accuracy	Alghizzi (2017)
Paragraph length and structure	Ferheen-Bukhari (2016)
Word combinations	Grami and Alkazemi (2015)
Planning (making an outline)	Zaid (2011)

and spelling are pooled together (e.g. in Fakhary-Tharwa, 2017) while in others they are mentioned separately (e.g. AbuSeileek, 2006).

Examining the studies in the meta-analysis has highlighted a number of important study quality observations that warrant further comment. Although there a number of unreported points of information that introduce ambiguity into the studies, we especially note the reliance on null hypotheses testing statistical tests as well as a lack of statistical information in the studies.

A first comment we would like to make is that there is clear value in moving away from these monofactorial methods to allow researchers to acknowledge the influence of many of their design, reporting practices and contextual variables, and account for these variables in their analyses. It is noteworthy that there are few studies in our review that move towards such an appreciation. Many of the studies that use ANOVAs or ANCOVAs continue to treat their experimentally designed study in a linear manner with no control of intervening variables incorporated into their analyses (or indeed mentioned as limitations or points for future exploration). As Plonsky (2014) and Al-Hoorie and Vitta (2019) note, there are a number of alternative tests that allow researchers to study the multifactorial nature of their intended constructs. These include MANOVAs and mixed-effects regression models that allow more fine-grained analyses to take place. Such an analysis would allow Saudi researchers to move away from the often-simplistic picture they present and develop an understanding of the influence of technology on writing improvement that includes recognition for their specific experimental and contextual variables. As highlighted by our analysis, these variables may include: Proficiency levels, year of study, language tasks, gender and age. Regression analyses also avoids the need for multiple repeated tests because they can handle multiple variables in a single analysis. This is likely to mean these analyses can synthesise the interactions between variables such as time and treatment more conclusively rather than in the piecemeal fashion that repeated measure tests offer (e.g. Al-Jafen's [2018] use of repeated ANOVAs).

A second comment we make concerns the exclusion of information that is related to study quality. Across our studies, we noted the exclusion of variables relating to reporting practices (e.g. statistical tests, descriptive and inferential statistics), and while these influence study quality by presenting an incomplete picture of data analysis and results, they also hinder efforts to empirically synthesise the effect of technology on writing improvement across the body of literature. Failure to include a full set of statistics meant that providing an overall effect size that can empirically synthesise the literature was subject to many challenges. We elaborate on these challenges in the next section.

4.2 The Overall Effect of Technology on Improving Writing

We attempted to calculate a single weighted effect size to answer research question two and therefore establish an overall effect size for the effectiveness of technology in improving writing proficiency. However, as indicated in the previous section, a number of research design and reporting practices prevented us from including the complete set of 27 studies in this calculation. A total of 5 studies were excluded from this analysis. The studies were excluded for different reasons. Some studies were excluded because they did not report full statistics that allowed an effect size to be calculated (e.g. Al-Saleem, 2013; Ferheen-Bukhari, 2016) while other studies included paired up designs that did not allow us to compare them to studies that included single group members (e.g. Al-Subaie & Alshuraidah, 2017).

For the other studies, we calculated a single effect size by using the Lipsey and Wilson (2001) calculator or in some cases converted one effect size (e.g. partial eta squared) to Cohen's d to eventually provide an effect size that could be standardised across all of the studies.[4] Upon obtaining these effect sizes, we ran a random-effects model. The random model was created in R with the '*metafor*' package and produced an inverse-variance weighted effect size of Cohen's $d = 2.35$ ($p < .001$). Interpreting this effect size according

---

[4]We used the conversion calculator from https://www.psychometrica.de/effect_size.html (Effect Size Calculator 2020).

to Cohen's (1988) effect size benchmarks, we can interpret this as a large effect size (since it is greater than 0.8). When we also interpret this according to Plonsky and Oswald's (2014) alternative scale of effect sizes for second language research, the effect size is also considered large (since it is greater than their $d = 1.00$ threshold). This effect size tells us that, as an average estimation of effectiveness, those participants who received instruction via a form of technology scored 2.35 points more on their writing tests than the control group participants who were taught according to traditional instruction.

We then looked at the issue of publication bias. We created a simple publication bias funnel plot using the '*metafor*' R package with the effect sizes (on the x axis) and the standard errors (on the y axis). Looking at Fig. 2 and the number of studies that appear either side of the mean line, we can see some evidence of publication bias since the plot does not appear completely symmetrical with the number of studies either side of this line fairly uneven. There may be a number of other factors that account for this lack of symmetry outside publication bias. These include poor methodological design, inadequate reporting and the presence of moderators (Plonsky, 2011).

The effect size obtained aligns with those results found in holistic meta-analyses that provided an effect size specifically for writing. For example, Felix (2008), Li and Hegelheimer (2013) found moderate to

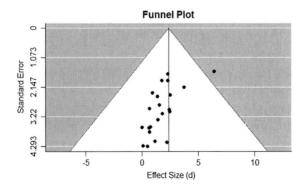

Fig. 2 Funnel plot of weighted effect size ($d = 2.35$; $k = 22$)

large effect sizes when they looked at L2 writing. However, it is worth bearing in mind that our study has focused on multiple aspects of writing proficiency as shown in Table 11 as opposed to a small number of aspects in these studies. We also looked at the effects of CALL and MALL types of interventions. CALL interventions had a weighted effect size of 2.38 ($p < .001$) and MALL interventions had a weighted effect size of 1.99 ($p = .147$).

5 Implications for the Context and Conclusion

A number of observations have been in this meta-analysis concerning the study quality of technology-oriented studies across the Saudi Arabian Higher Education domain. We believe these observations inform how we interpret study findings and how we carry out and report future experimental studies of this nature. First, we would like to propose that scholars in this area, more closely adhere to the experimental research practices that broadly underlie applied linguistics, TESOL and SLA research strands. Of immediate importance to these scholars should be the reporting of statistical information and making datasets publicly available on open science platforms such as the L2 research specific IRIS database (Marsden et al., 2016). Such transparent practices would result in more rigorous practice that would ultimately allow researchers to not only check the reliability and validity of study claims but would also allow meta-analysts the opportunity to access raw data and better establish more concrete effect sizes.

Our meta-analysis found that technology-interventions had a large positive effect on writing with an effect size of Cohen's $d = 2.35$. This seems to support that technological interventions have a positive effect on writing score gains when learners are subject to experimental treatment over traditional learning. However, researchers should be reminded that this effect size is in part subject to contextual variables (e.g. treatment length).

The meta-analysis also raised a number of pedagogically oriented questions. In summarising the task and writing trends, there are wide-ranging differences between tasks that learners are being assigned in terms of difficulty and what is considered appropriate for their level of study. It is also a concern to us as to the nature of this writing and how it relates to the writing the students experience later in their degree programmes. Taking some of the studies that focus on paragraph level (e.g. Idrees, 2017), it seems there is a gap between the reality of the students' writing ability (by asking them to write a personal descriptive paragraph) and what they are later expected to do on their degree programmes outside of the EAP/academic writing course programme (for example, complete reports and produce reader specific texts). It is difficult to see how these two realities are being brought together via the use of technology to help 'improve' student writing.

Another concern relates to the nature of the intervention tasks. In some cases, the intervention task seemed to have improved some aspects of language use (e.g. grammatical accuracy) however much like the point raised above, the use of such technology for general communication, seems to run the risk of countering improvement in actual academic writing since this communication differs widely from the genres students are expected to produce in their academic studies.

Indeed, while the findings seems to indicate there are improvements being made at a surface level for language (e.g. improving accuracy) and at the level of executing processing (e.g. developing organisation and cohesion), there is little in this meta-analysis that seems to focus on improving students' understanding of writing for audience or writing across different genres and considering the language needed to complete these tasks.

We encourage Saudi scholars to continue to consider the types of writing and tasks, and the connection these have with academic curriculum goals as they continue to strive for improving their students' writing. There is a need for these to be aligned with how technology is being used to seemingly support curriculum and the wider aims of academic writing instruction.

Further meta-analysis work on writing in the MENA region should be encouraged. As our chapter has shown, the research method of meta-analysis can be used to establish the effect of such technological interventions and in light of this, a fruitful future endeavour would be to compare the results found in Saudi Arabia with other MENA countries. Such an endeavour would help to synthesise the practice of using technology to achieve proficiency gains across the region.

References

*Abdul Fattah, S. (2015). The effectiveness of using WhatsApp messenger as one of mobile learning techniques to develop students' writing skills. *Journal of Education & Practice, 6*(32), 115–127.

*AbuSeileek, F. A. (2006). The use of the word processor for teaching writing to EFL learners in King Saud University. *Journal of King Saud University, 19*(2), 1–15.

*Ahmed, M. A. E. A. S. (2016). Using Facebook to develop grammar discussion and writing skills in EFL for university students. *Sino-US English Teaching, 13*(12), 932–952.

*Alghizzi, T. M. (2017). *Complexity, accuracy and fluency (CAF) development in L2 writing: The effects of proficiency level, learning environment, text type, and time among Saudi EFL learners*. Unpublished Ph.D. thesis. University College Cork.

*Algraini, F. N. A. (2014). *The effect of using Padlet on enhancing EFL writing performance*. Unpublished M.A. thesis. A-Iman Muhammad Ibn Saud Islamic University.

*Al-Harbi, M. (2015). Effects of Blackboard's discussion boards, blogs and wikis on effective integration and development of literacy skills in EFL students. *English Language Teaching, 8*(6), 111–131.

Al-Harbi, S. H. (2016). Effect of teachers' written corrective feedback on Saudi EFL university students' writing achievements. *International Journal of Linguistics, 8*(5), 15–29.

Al-Hoorie, A. H., & Vitta, J. P. (2019). The seven sins of L2 research: A review of 30 journals' statistical quality and their CiteScore, SJR, SNIP, JCR impact factors. *Language Teaching Research, 23,* 727–744.

*Al-Jafen, B. S. (2018). *Traditional vs. wiki: Saudi students' performance in and perceptions of collaborative writing in a wiki*. Unpublished Ph.D. thesis. University of Tennessee.

Al-Jarf, R. (2002, June 17–19). Effect of online learning on struggling ESL college writers. In *23rd National Educational Computing Conference Proceedings*. Texas.

*Al-Jarf, R. (2004). The effects of web-based learning on struggling EFL college writers. *Foreign Language Annals, 37*(1), 49–57.

Al-Jarf, R. (2005). The effects of online grammar instruction on low proficiency EFL college students' achievement. *The Asian EFL Journal Quarterly, 7*(4), 166–190.

Al-Mansour, N. S., & Al-Shorman, R. A. (2014). The effect of an extensive reading program on the writing performance of Saudi university students. *International Journal of Linguistics, 6*(2), 258–275.

*Al-Melhi, A. M. (2014). Effects of teaching argumentative reading and writing by integration in an E-learning environment on literacy development in EFL college students. *International Journal of Humanities and Social Science, 4*(5), 85–102.

Al-Mohanna, A. D. M. (2014). Errors in the usage of the English definite/indefinite articles among Saudi university-level students. *International Journal of Arts and Sciences, 7*(3), 79–95.

Al-Rashidi, O., & Phan, H. (2015). Education context and English teaching and learning in the Kingdom of Saudi Arabia: An overview. *English Language Teaching, 8*(5), 33–44.

*Al-Saleem, A. B. I. (2013). The effect of "WhatsApp" electronic dialogue journaling on improving writing vocabulary word choice and voice of EFL undergraduate Saudi students. *Arab World English Journal, 4*(3), 213–225.

*Al-Saleh, N. A. (2018). The impact of positive and corrective feedback via Showbie on Saudi students' English writing. *Arab World English Journal: Thesis Collection*. ID Number: 215, 1–121.

*Al-Shumaimeri, Y. (2011). The effects of wikis on foreign language students writing performance. *Procedia—Social and Behavioral Sciences, 28,* 755–763.

*Al-Shwiah, A. A. (2016). *The effect of applying Laurilland's conversational framework on the development of writing skills: Perceptions and engagement of students in a Middle East context*. Unpublished thesis. University of Leicester.

Al-Subaie, A., & Madini, A. A. (2018). The effect of using blogs to enhance the writing skill of English language learners at a Saudi university. *Global Journal of Educational Studies, 4*(1), 13–30.

*Al-Subaie, J., & Alshuraidah, A. (2017). Exploring writing individually and collaboratively using Google docs in EFL contexts. *English Language Teaching, 10*(10), 10–30.

*Al-Wasy, B. Q., & Mahdi, H. S. (2016). The effect of mobile phone applications on improving EFL learners' self-editing. *Journal of Education and Human Development, 5*(3), 149–157.

Aslan, E., & Ciftci, H. (2019). Synthesising research on learner perceptions of CMC use in EFL/ESL writing. *CALICO Journal, 36*(2), 100–118.

*Bamanger, E. M., & Alhassan, R. A. (2015). Exploring podcasting in English as a foreign language learners' writing performance. *Journal of Education and Practice, 6*(11), 63–74.

Borenstein, M., Hedges, L. V., Higgins, J. P. T., & Rothstein, H. R. (2009). *Introduction to meta-analysis*. Chichester: Wiley.

Burston, J. (2015). Twenty years of MALL project implementation: A meta-analysis of learning outcomes. *ReCALL, 27*(1), 4–20.

Chun, D. M. (2016). The role of technology in SLA research. *Language Learning and Technology, 20*(2), 98–115.

Cohen, J. (1988). *Statistical power analysis for the behavioral sciences* (2nd ed.). Hillsdale, NJ: Erlbaum.

Coombe, C., Reinders, H., Littlejohn, A., & Tafazoli, D. (2019). Innovation in language learning and teaching: The case of the MENA. In H. Reinders, C. Coombe, A. Littlejohn, & D. Tafazoli (Eds.), *Innovation in language learning and teaching: The case of the MENA* (pp. 1–19). London: Palgrave Macmillan.

Effect Size Calculator. (2020). Retrieved from https://www.psychometrica.de/effect_size.html. Last accessed 9 May 2020.

Elyas, T., & Picard, M. (2018). A brief history of English and English teaching in Saudi Arabia. In C. Moskovsky & M. Picard (Eds.), *English as a foreign language in Saudi Arabia: New insights into teaching and learning English* (1st ed., pp. 78–92). London: Routledge.

*Fageeh, A. I. (2011). EFL learners' use of blogging for developing writing skills and enhancing attitudes towards English learning: An exploratory study. *Journal of Language and Literature, 2*(1), 31–48.

Fageeh, A. I. (2014). The use of journal writing and reading comprehension texts during pre-writing in developing EFL students' academic writing. *Studies in Literature and Language, 9*(3), 1–18.

*Fakhary-Tharwa, F. F. (2017). Efficiency of using blog in developing some functional writing skills and reflective thinking for EFL majors at Al-Majmaah University. *European Journal of Research and Reflection in Educational Sciences, 5*(5), 13–45.

Felix, U. (2008). The unreasonable effectiveness of CALL: What have we learned in two decades of research? *ReCALL, 20*(2), 141–161.

*Ferheen-Bukhari, S. S. (2016). Mind mapping techniques to enhance EFL writing skills. *International Journal of Linguistics and Communications, 4*(1), 58–77.

Grami, G. M. A. (2010). *The effects of integrating peer feedback into university-level ESL writing curriculum: A comparative study in a Saudi context*. Unpublished Doctoral thesis. University of Newcastle.

*Grami, G. M. A., & Alkazemi, B. Y. (2015). Improving ESL writing using an online formulaic sequence word combination checker. *Journal of Computer Assisted Language Learning, 32*, 95–104.

*Idrees, M. W. K. (2017). *Effectiveness of the interactional approach to the teaching of writing compared with the traditional non-interaction-based approach of English language teaching used in Saudi Arabian university context*. Unpublished doctoral thesis. University of Exeter.

Jacobs, H. L., Zinkgraf, S. A., Wormuth, D. R., Hartfiel, V. F., & Hughey, J. B. (1981). *Testing ESL composition: A practical approach*. Rowley, MA: Newbury House.

Jahin, J. H. (2012). The effect of peer reviewing on writing apprehension and essay writing ability of prospective EFL teachers. *Australian Journal of Teacher Education, 37*(11), 60–84.

Li, S., Shintani, N., & Ellis, R. (2012). Doing meta-analysis in SLA: Practices, choices and standards. *Contemporary Foreign Language Studies, 384*(12), 1–17.

Li, Z., & Hegelheimer, V. (2013). Mobile-assisted grammar exercises: Effects on self-editing in L2 writing. *Language Learning & Technology, 17*(3), 135–156.

Lin, H. (2012, August 22–25). The effectiveness of computer-mediated communication on SLA: A meta-analysis and research synthesis. In L. Bradley & S. Thouësny (Eds.), *CALL: Using, learning, knowing, EURO-CALL Conference* (pp. 177–181). Gothenburg, Sweden, Proceedings.

Lin, H. (2014). Establishing an empirical link between CMC and SLA: A meta-analysis of the research. *Language Learning & Technology, 18*(3), 120–147.

Lipsey, M., & Wilson, D. (2001). *Practical meta-analysis*. Thousand Oaks, CA: Sage.

Liu, G.-Z., Lu, H.-C., & Lai, C.-T. (2016). Towards the construction of a field: The developments and implications of MALL. *Digital Scholarship in the Humanities, 31*(1), 164–180.

*Mahmoud, S. S. (2014). Email and Facebook to promote foundation year students' EFL writing at King Abdulaziz University. *International Review of Social Sciences and Humanities, 6*(2), 157–172.

Marsden, E., Mackey, A., & Plonsky, L. (2016). The IRIS repository: Advancing research practice and methodology. In A. Mackey & E. Marsden (Eds.), *Advancing methodology and practice: The IRIS repository of instruments for research into second languages* (pp. 1–21). New York: Routledge.

McMullen, M. G. (2009). Using language learning strategies to improve the writing skills of Saudi EFL students: Will it really work? *System, 37,* 418–433.

*Mekheimer-Gawad, M. A. A. (2011). The impact of using videos on whole language learning in EFL context. *Arab World English Journal, 2*(2), 5–39.

*Mohamed Kaseem, M. A. (2017). Developing business writing skills and reducing writing anxiety of EFL learners through wikis. *English Language Teaching, 10*(3), 151–163.

Mohammad, T., & Hazarika, Z. (2016). Difficulties of learning EFL in KSA: Writing skills in context. *International Journal of English Linguistics, 6*(3), 105–117.

Obeid, R. (2017). Second language writing and assessment: Voices within the Saudi EFL context. *English Language Teaching, 10*(6), 174–181.

*Oraif, K. I. M. (2018). *An investigation into the impact of the flipped classroom on intrinsic motivation (IM) and learning outcomes on an EFL writing course at a university in Saudi Arabia based on self-determination theory.* Unpublished thesis. University of Leicester.

Plonsky, L. (2011). The effectiveness of second language strategy instruction: A meta-analysis. *Language Learning, 61*(4), 993–1038.

Plonsky, L. (2013). An assessment of designs, analyses and reporting practices in quantitative L2 research. *Studies in Second Language Acquisition, 35,* 655–687.

Plonsky, L. (2014). Study quality in quantitative L2 research (1990–2010): A methodological synthesis and call for reform. *The Modern Language Journal, 98*(1), 450–470.

Plonsky, L., & Oswald, F. L. (2014). How big is "big"? Interpreting effect sizes in L2 research. *Language Learning, 64,* 878–891.

Plonsky, L., & Ziegler, N. (2016). The CALL–SLA interface: Insights from a second-order synthesis. *Language Learning & Technology, 20*(2), 17–37.

*Sayed, O. H. (2010). Developing business management students' persuasive writing through blog-based peer feedback. *English Language Teaching, 3*(3), 54–66.

SCImago. (2019). *Journals in Applied Linguistics*. Accessed at https://www.scimagojr.com/journalrank.php?category=3310. Last accessed 1 Mar 2020.

Sung, Y.-T., Chang, K.-E., & Yang, J.-M. (2015). How effective are mobile devices for language learning. *Educational Research Review, 16,* 68–84.

Taj, H. I., Sulan, B. N., Sipra, A. M., & Ahmad, W. (2016). Impact of Mobile-Assisted Language Learning (MALL) on EFL: A meta-analysis. *Advances in Language and Literary Studies, 7*(2), 76–83.

Viechtbauer, W. (2020). *Metafor*. Available at https://cran.r-project.org/web/packages/metafor/metafor.pdf. Last accessed 4 Apr 2020.

Weber, A. S. (2018). Saudi Arabia. In A. S. Weber & S. Hamlaoui (Eds.), *E-learning in the MENA region* (pp. 355–381). London: Springer.

Yang, J. (2013). MALL: Review of the recent applications of emerging mobile technologies. *English Language Teaching, 6*(7), 19–25.

*Zaid, M. (2011). Effectiveness of organised email exchanges and online reading/writing on college students' literacy development and their attitudes towards English: A study from Saudi Arabia. *Asian EFL Journal, 13*(1), 10–47.

Index

A

Accuracy 9, 20, 36, 49, 62, 69, 78, 94, 95, 97, 99–103, 105, 120, 123, 125, 126, 128, 129, 135, 153, 154, 157, 160–163, 177–179, 216, 279, 301, 327–329, 337, 340, 364, 416, 421

Alignment 16, 19, 21, 22, 29, 30, 64

Analytical 26, 31, 32, 34, 203, 235, 275, 277, 289

Analytical rubric 276

Analytic (marking scale) 75, 77

Arabic 4, 72, 80, 196, 227, 229, 276, 279–281, 360, 362, 363, 365, 367, 368, 373, 375–383, 386, 408

Argumentation 7, 226–229, 232–234, 260, 261

Argumentative essay 44, 51–53, 56, 64–66, 117, 149, 228, 229, 414

Assessment methodology 18

Assessment principles 21, 29, 32, 33

Assessment tasks 5, 14, 19–21, 23, 26, 29, 31–33, 176, 200

Attitudes 82, 212, 261–263, 269, 270, 273, 274, 276, 277, 279, 281, 283–287, 303, 316–318, 330, 333, 339, 344–348

Attributes 95, 102–104, 118, 176–178, 260

C

Cambridge *Write & Improve* 298, 302, 319

Case study 115, 273, 274, 287, 364, 381, 383

Cognitive Diagnostic Assessment (CDA) 6, 101–104
Complexity 5, 6, 78, 93–103, 114, 120, 123, 125, 128, 129, 209, 216, 229, 260, 364, 416
Computer feedback 7, 306, 317
Consistency 61, 71, 98, 103, 148, 149, 155, 158, 172, 173, 182, 185, 189, 200, 201, 215, 250, 373, 379
Construct 6, 7, 9, 14, 17, 18, 32, 36, 44–46, 49, 51–53, 60, 62, 77, 94–98, 100, 103, 114, 137, 171, 181, 183, 201, 204, 214, 215, 217, 227, 243, 245, 258, 263, 301, 416, 417
Construct-irrelevant variance 74, 144, 201
Corpus linguistics 7, 359–361, 369, 386
Creational Reverse Engineering (CRE) 44
Critical thinking 7, 44, 52, 65, 207, 225, 226, 228, 234, 282
Cultural background knowledge 74
Culture 70, 77, 227, 242, 261–263, 346, 381

D

Descriptive statistics 253, 397, 411, 413

E

English as a medium of instruction (EMI) 116–119, 197, 271
Error analysis 158, 363
Essay prompt 6, 46, 47

F

Feedback effect 333, 334, 345, 347
Feedback provision 7, 162, 163, 202, 298, 325–330, 332–335, 338, 341–343, 345–348
Feedback types 303, 306, 311, 327, 333, 334, 336, 340, 345–347
Feedback uptake 317
Fluency 36, 78, 94–97, 99, 100, 174, 301

G

Genre 22, 24, 25, 28–30, 36, 47, 54, 55, 63, 85, 93, 126, 129, 130, 147, 152, 156, 163, 172, 202, 207, 212, 228, 244–249, 251–264, 271, 369, 421

H

Halo effect 145
Holistic 75, 117, 153, 173, 203, 204, 211, 273, 397, 398, 419
Holistic (marking scale) 75, 77
Holistic rubric 173, 176, 204–207, 216

I

Inferential statistics 397, 410, 411, 413, 418
Instruction 15, 19, 20, 32, 45, 46, 52, 55, 56, 95, 103, 114, 118, 125, 132, 134, 147, 151, 164, 173, 176, 228, 229, 231, 234, 244, 248, 249, 258, 263, 270, 272, 275, 286, 300, 319, 326, 334, 338, 342, 346, 347, 383, 393, 403, 414, 419, 421

Index 431

Integrated tasks 242, 245, 248, 260, 261, 263
Inter-rater variability 144
Intervention 8, 270, 273, 274, 283, 285, 286, 329, 342, 348, 361, 394, 396–398, 400, 402, 403, 415, 416, 420, 421
Intra-rater variability 144
Iran 6, 94, 96, 98, 100, 175, 177, 180, 196, 246, 247, 260, 262, 298–300, 302, 303, 318–320, 332, 333, 347

K

Kurdistan Region of Iraq (KRI) 114–118, 123, 129, 131, 132, 138

L

Language Assessment Literacy (LAL) 5, 10, 14, 18, 29, 32, 33, 117
Language placement test 43
Language test design 18, 82
Learner corpus 359, 362, 363
Learner language 359
Learner profiles 101, 381
Lebanon 195, 269–271, 273, 274, 280, 285–287
Libya 195, 332, 333, 360, 366, 373, 381

M

Measurement 15, 18, 45, 52, 77, 86, 94, 96, 97, 102, 104, 144, 146, 172, 174, 182, 207, 214, 215, 399

MENA 3–8, 10, 19, 71, 83, 144, 164, 195–198, 204, 216, 217, 326, 330–333, 345, 347, 349, 359, 360, 363, 364, 386, 399, 405, 409, 421, 422
Meta-analysis 8, 394, 396–398, 400, 402, 404, 405, 415, 417, 420, 421

N

Native speakerism in writing assessment 82

P

Persuasive essay 75, 228
Placement test 6, 43, 45, 46, 51, 53, 54, 60, 63, 120, 304
Plagiarism 206, 241, 248, 254, 262–264, 341
Preliminary B1 372
Primary trait 211, 213
Primary trait (marking scale) 75
Process writing 7, 130, 160, 270, 271, 273, 398
Publication bias 402, 419

R

Rater behaviour 114, 117, 127
Rater severity 145
Rater training 98, 114, 117, 136, 137, 213, 214
Rater variability 113–115, 117, 118, 130, 143, 144, 146, 147
Read-to-write 44
Reporting practices 397, 403, 411, 412, 417, 418

Resume writing 6, 172, 175, 177, 181, 184, 186
Reverse engineering (RE) 44, 50–54
Rhetorical tradition 70, 73, 84, 227
Rubric 3, 6, 7, 9, 20, 52, 57, 59, 60, 66, 75, 117, 119–123, 126–128, 132, 134, 136, 137, 144, 145, 153, 158, 172–177, 180–187, 198–204, 207, 208, 211–217, 230, 233, 236, 275, 277, 308, 415
Rubric development 174–176, 186, 213

S

Saudi universities 5, 8, 14, 20, 21, 33
Scoping review 7, 331, 332
Scoring focus 146
Scoring validity 49, 144, 147
Security 44, 48, 51, 54, 57, 60–62
Sentence level 20, 298, 318, 320
Source-based writing 44, 47
Spelling 22, 24, 30, 34, 65, 78, 128, 153, 161, 178, 179, 189, 271, 276, 289, 308, 359, 363, 364, 369, 371–373, 375–378, 381–384, 399, 416, 417
Spelling error 7, 9, 128, 359, 360, 363, 364, 370–374, 375, 376, 378–381, 383, 384, 386
Spelling variation 371, 386
Student confidence 162, 181, 185, 284, 286
Student learning outcomes 14, 16, 19, 20, 27, 28
Study quality 394, 397, 400, 401, 403, 417, 418, 420

Subcorpora 359, 360, 363, 365, 368, 371–373, 376, 378, 380, 381
Summarising 420
Synthesising 5, 8–10, 19, 208, 286, 331, 397, 398, 400

T

Teacher feedback 7, 306, 315, 339
Test bank 6, 44, 47, 48, 51, 57, 60–62
Test pool 47
Test specification 19, 33, 44, 46, 50–54, 57, 62, 135
Textual borrowing 241–244, 246, 247, 249–256, 259–264
21st century skills 197, 299, 346

U

UAE 6, 7, 225–228, 234, 332, 333, 368

W

Washback 85, 263, 320
Washback effect 19, 86, 127, 183, 184, 242, 320
Writing assessment scales 73
Writing development 94, 95, 97, 102, 162
Writing difficulties 271
Writing improvement 7, 394, 400, 401, 417, 418
Writing proficiency 5–9, 55, 63, 69, 77, 82, 93, 95, 157, 161, 298, 317, 393, 399, 416, 418, 420
Writing prompt(s) 46, 47, 52, 55, 73–76, 84, 229